Creating Sustainable Work Systems

Since the first edition of this book was published, the subject of sustainability has risen to the forefront of thinking in almost every subject within business and management. Tackling the latest developments and integrating practical perspectives with rigorous research, this new edition sheds light on a vital aspect of working life.

Current trends reveal that increasing intensity at work has major consequences at individual, organizational and societal levels. Sustainability in work systems thus requires a multi-stakeholder approach, emphasizing a value-based choice to promote the concurrent development of various resources in the work system. This sustainability grows from intertwined individual and collective learning processes taking place within and between organizations in collaboration.

In exploring the development of sustainable work systems, this book analyzes these problems, and provides the basis for designing and implementing 'sustainable work systems' based on the idea of regeneration and the development of human and social resources. The authors, who are leading researchers and practitioners from around the world, consider the existing possibilities and emerging solutions and explore alternatives to intensive work systems.

Peter Docherty is a Faculty Member of the Institute for Management for Innovation and Technology, Sweden. He is also Senior Research Fellow at the Department of Quality Sciences at the Chalmers University of Technology, Gothenburg and a Senior Researcher at ATK Arbetsliv AB, Stockholm.

Mari Kira is an Academy Research Fellow at the Helsinki University of Technology, Finland.

A.B. (Rami) Shani is Professor and Chair of Management at California Polytechnic State University, San Luis Obispo, USA and Research Professor at the School of Management, Politechnico di Milano, Italy.

Creating Sustainable Work Systems

Developing social sustainability

Second edition

**Edited by Peter Docherty,
Mari Kira and A.B. (Rami) Shani**

Routledge
Taylor & Francis Group

LONDON AND NEW YORK

First published 2009
by Routledge

Second edition published 2009 by Routledge
2 Park Square, Milton Park, Abingdon, Oxon OX14 4RN

Simultaneously published in the USA and Canada
by Routledge
711 Third Avenue, New York, NY 10017

*Routledge is an imprint of the Taylor & Francis Group, an informa
business*

© 2009 Peter Docherty, Mari Kira and A.B. (Rami) Shani

Typeset in Times New Roman by Graphicraft Limited, Hong Kong

British Library Cataloguing in Publication Data
A catalogue record for this book is available from the British Library

Library of Congress Cataloguing in Publication Data
Creating sustainable work systems : developing social sustainability /
edited by Peter Docherty, Mari Kira and A.B. Rami Shani. —
2nd ed.p. cm.

Includes bibliographical references and index.

ISBN 978-0-415-77271-6 (cloth : alk. paper) — ISBN 978-0-415-77272-3
(pbk : alk. paper) — ISBN 978-0-203-99538-9 (ebook)   1. Quality of
work life.   2. Sustainable development.   I. Docherty, Peter.   II. Kira,
Mari, 1972–   III. Shani, Abraham B.

HD6955.C83 2008
331.12′042—dc22
2008009685

ISBN 13: 978-0-415-77271-6 (hbk)
ISBN 13: 978-0-415-77272-3 (pbk)
ISBN 13: 978-0-203-89002-8 (ebk)

ISBN 10: 0 415 77271 0 (hbk)
ISBN 10: 0 415 77272 9 (pbk)
ISBN 10: 0 203 89002 7 (ebk)

To Elisabeth, Mackillo, Elaine

Contents

Figures

Tables

Contributors

Mona A. Amodeo, Ph.D., believes the most innovative answers to the many questions facing today's world are found at the intersection of research and practice. As the founder and President of id*group*, a creative and consulting firm, she consults with clients in the areas of organization development and change, values-based branding, and corporate responsibility. She is also an active researcher, speaker, and writer.

Richard Boyatzis, Ph.D., is Professor, Departments of Organizational Behavior and Psychology, Case Western Reserve University, and Adjunct Professor at ESADE. He is the author of more than 150 articles and books, including: *The Competent Manager*; *Primal Leadership* with Daniel Goleman and Annie McKee, translated into in 28 languages; and *Resonant Leadership*, with McKee.

Hilary Bradbury, Ph.D., is Director of Sustainable Business Research at the University of Southern California's Center for Sustainable Cities. She is editor of the international, peer-reviewed journal *Action Research* and co-editor of the best-selling *Handbook of Action Research*. Hilary lives with her family in Los Angeles.

Peter Brödner was born in 1942 in Berlin, and was awarded a Dr.-Ing. from Technical University of Berlin. After seven years as researcher and 13 years as project manager for large industrial R&D projects, he became director of the production systems department at Institute for Work and Technology (Gelsenkirchen) focusing on design and implementation of skill-based computer-supported manufacturing systems and organizational change.

Markus Buch has a Diploma in Psychology (1996) and a Ph.D. in Work Science and Ergonomics (2001). Since 1997 he has been researcher at the Institute of Industrial Science and Ergonomics, University of Kassel, since 2005, researcher in the project Age-based Job Design in the Automotive Industry, and since 2006 assistant of the priority programme Age-differentiated Work Systems, funded by the German Research Foundation.

Doug Cerf is the Associate Dean of the Orfalea College of Business at California Polytechnic State University, San Luis Obispo. Doug's research interests include financial management and accounting tools that support sustainability. Doug has taught courses on environmental accounting and financial management for the Donald Bren Graduate School of Environmental Science and Management at University of California, Santa Barbara.

Keith Cox, Ph.D., is a seasoned facilitator of positive change with 18 years in the Organization Development (OD) field. He is President of Tirawa Consulting and in 2007 he co-founded the Branch Creek Collaborative, a consultancy-focused value creation within the context of social and environmental stewardship. He is also adjunct faculty at Bowling Green State University and DeVry University.

Peter Docherty, Ph.D., is Visiting Professor at the Department of Quality Sciences and the Centre for Healthcare Improvement at the Chalmers University of Technology, Gothenburg, Sweden and senior researcher at ATK Arbetsliv AB, Stockholm. He has researched and published on individual, collective, and organizational learning and the management and organization of sustainable organizations.

Marianne Döös, Ph.D., is Associate Professor in Educational Psychology within the field of organization pedagogics, affiliated to the Department of Education, Stockholm University, and the Swedish Agency for Innovation Systems. Her research deals with the processes of change and experiential learning in contemporary settings, on individual, collective, and organizational levels.

Frans M. van Eijnatten is an Associate Professor at the Institute for Business Engineering and Technology Application at Eindhoven University of Technology, the Netherlands. His main research interest is in Socio-Technical Systems Design, initiating and coordinating design-oriented action research projects in R&D, and information systems design. Currently, Dr. Van Eijnatten is studying the implications of Chaordic Systems Thinking for organizational renewal. He founded the European Chaos and Complexity Network ECCON.

Ekkehart Frieling, has a Diploma, Ph.D. and a post-doctoral degree in psychology. He is Professor and head of the Institute of Industrial Science and Ergonomics at the University of Kassel, Germany. He has been the coordinator of the priority programme Age-differentiated Work Systems funded by the German Research Foundation, since 2005.

Tony Huzzard, Ph.D., is currently an Associate Professor at the Department of Business Administration, Lund University and was formerly Visiting Research Fellow at the National Institute for Working Life in Malmö. He has researched and published widely on organizational development, work organization, industrial relations, and health care management.

Mari Kira is an Academy Research Fellow funded by Academy of Finland at Helsinki University of Technology (HUT), Finland. She has a Ph.D. degree (2003) from Royal Institute of Technology, Sweden. From 2004 to 2006, she was a Marie Curie Fellow at the University of Kassel, Germany, and in winter

2007/2008 she was a visiting faculty at the Leeds School of Business, University of Colorado at Boulder, USA. Her research interests focus on sustainability of individuals at work and of work organizations as a whole.

Svante Lifvergren, M.D., currently works as Development Director in the Strategic Management Committee at the Hospital Group of Skaraborg (SkaS), where he is also a resident consultant physician with 20 years clinical experience. He is a Ph.D. student in Quality Sciences at the Chalmers University of Technology in Gothenburg, Sweden.

Sharon Moore, Ph.D., is head of the APM College of Business and Communication, Sydney, that is a higher education faculty of the Think: Education Group. As an international leader in Triple Bottom Line and Sustainability, strategist, academic and researcher, with a 25-year career spanning Public Affairs and Business Development to Corporate Social Responsibility, in Chief Executive and Board Directorship roles.

Mikael Román is Senior Research Fellow at Stockholm Environment Institute (SEI), specializing in sustainability and climate change issues, with a particular focus on public and private competitive strategies. He holds a Ph.D. in political science from Uppsala University and was a Wallenberg Post-doc Fellow at the Center for International Studies, MIT, Cambridge, Massachusetts.

Arline Savage has a Doctorate of Commerce from the University of Port Elizabeth, South Africa, is Professor of Accounting at California Polytechnic State University, San Luis Obispo, and is additionally a Chartered Accountant. Her research interests include corporate social and environmental reporting, accounting education, and financial information systems.

Jim Sena has a Ph.D. in management information systems from the University of Kentucky. He is professor in management information systems at California Polytechnic State University's Orfalea College of Business in San Luis Obispo. His main research interests are the individual and organizational impacts of network technologies, computer-supported collaborative work, and decision-support systems.

A. B. (Rami) Shani, Ph.D., is Professor and Chair of Management at California Polytechnic State University, San Luis Obispo, and Research Professor at the School of Management, Politecnico di Milano, Milan. He has researched and published on organizational learning, learning mechanisms, collaborative research in organizations, change and the management of change, and sustainable organization.

Michael W. Stebbins, Ph.D., is Emeritus Professor of organizational design at California Polytechnic State University's Orfalea College of Business. His research and consulting interests include new product development, change processes and building sustainable work systems. In retirement his interests include travel with his wife Margaret, gardening, and visiting his new granddaughter, Stella Buckley.

Dirk Urban has a Diploma in Mechanical Engineering and since 2006 has been a researcher and Ph.D. student working on the project Age-based Job Design in the Automotive Industry at the Institute of Industrial Science and Ergonomics, University of Kassel, Germany.

Judy L. Valenzuela, Pharm. D., is pharmacy services director for Orange County in Kaiser Permanente's Southern California region. She has more than 25 years' experience in pharmacy management and is responsible for outpatient, inpatient, ambulatory care, and drug education/utilization services for a patient population of more than 350,000 health plan members.

Julia Weichel has a Diploma in Psychology (2005), and has been a researcher and Ph.D. student working on the project Age-based Job Design in the Automotive Industry at the Institute of Industrial Science and Ergonomics, University of Kassel, Germany, since 2005.

Lena Wilhelmson, Ph.D. and Reader in Educational Psychology, is a senior researcher at the University of Dalarna, Sweden. Her research deals with individual and collective learning in renewal processes in working life. Other areas of interest are adult education, dialogue, and learning processes in adult life.

Julie Jie Wen, Ph.D., is a Lecturer at the University of Western Sydney. She has worked as a lecturer in China, a hotel manager, and a marketing manager in Hong Kong. Her research interests include management, environmental economics, sustainability issues, modelling of regional economy, and China economic reform.

Acknowledgements

Our journey into and through the practical and scientific field of sustainability began about ten years ago. Over the past ten years, each of us has pursued various research projects, all connected in one way or another to sustainability, and we have maintained our collaboration and sought chances to join forces to work on work-system sustainability. Through the years, the issue of work-system sustainability has turned into more than just our academic niche; it has become a life's task – a commitment to contribute to the creation of better workplaces for the sake of people, society, economy, and ecology.

Our journey started when the National Institute for Working Life in Sweden together with the three central union organizations, the Swedish Trade Union Confederation (LO), the Swedish Confederation of Professional Employees (TCO) and the Swedish Confederation of Professional Associations (SACO) initiated the European collaborative research programme Work Life Development in Europe, known as SALTSA. The programme formed several projects in which researchers and practitioners from different countries worked on important and timely working-life issues. In each network, the members pursued research or practical work on the same specific issue in their own country, while the SALTSA activities gave the members an opportunity to exchange ideas and experiences and to carry out joint conceptual work in an international network. SALTSA financed the network and publication costs of the projects. One of the first projects in this programme was Creating Sustainable Work Systems; its main report was the first edition of this book. Twenty-two researchers from 13 countries and eight disciplines participated in the project. We wish to thank the members of the SALTSA Work Organization working group for the unforgettable first deep dive into the complex world of work-system sustainability, and we would like to thank SALTSA representatives P.O. Bergström, Monica Brejdensjö, Mats Essemyr and Charlotta Krafft for their support and interest in our work with sustainability. In particular, we wish to acknowledge Jan Forslin of the Institute for Industrial Management and Economics at the Royal Institute of Technology (KTH) for stimulating and fruitful collaboration, both in the initial SALTSA project (Jan was the leader of the initial SALTSA network on Sustainable Work Systems) and in our later work together.

Other colleagues with whom we have discussed through the years the issues of intensity and sustainability and the interrelationships among ecological, social, and economic sustainability are Frans van Eijnatten, Technical University of Eindhoven, Netherlands; Michel Gollac and Serge Volkoff, Centre d'Études de l'Emploi, Noisy-le-Grand, France; Armand Hatchuel, École des Mines, Paris, France; and Helge Hvid and Henrik Lambrecht Lund, Roskilde University, Denmark. The work of and discussions with Tomas Brytting, Ersta-Sköndal University College, Sweden and Barry Nyhan, CEDEFOP, Thessaloniki, Greece, have taught us much when it comes to the values and ethics regarding sustainability. The ongoing discussion with Mike Stebbins and Jim Sena at California Polytechnic State University, Bengt Stymne at the Stockholm School of Economics, and Flemming Norrgren and Bo Berggren at Chalmers University of Technology in Gothenburg, Sweden, have taught us much about the challenges of technology, design, change, and the management of change when sustainability is at the focus. Colleagues at ATK Arbetsliv in Stockholm, Eva Amundsdotter, Monica Bjerlöv, Per Tengblad, and John Ylander, have been sounding boards for ideas about tackling practical issues in sustainability development. Many thanks to you all for helping to develop our conceptions of sustainability and potential hindrances and difficulties in addressing it in practice. Other colleagues have generously shared their research insights and experiences, for example David Buchanan, Cranfield University, UK; Matti Vartiainen, Helsinki University of Technology, Finland; and Ekkehart Frieling, University of Kassel, Germany. We also had the opportunity to present our ideas in this book to a faculty research seminar of the Orfalea College of Business at California Polytechnic State University. Many thanks to you all for our lively, enlightening, and occasionally perturbing discussions.

The research and editorial work of Rami Shani has been supported by the Orfalea College of Business at the California Polytechnic State University and the MIP School of Management at the Politecnico di Milano. The research and editorial work of Mari Kira has been supported by the Academy of Finland, the Finnish Work Environment Fund, and the Laboratory of Work Psychology and Leadership at the Helsinki University of Technology. We wish to thank the Leeds School of Business at the University of Colorado at Boulder and especially David Balkin for hosting Mari Kira as visiting faculty during the winter of 2007/2008. In Peter Docherty's case, the support has come from the Institute for Management of Innovation and Technology at Chalmers University of Technology.

The idea for this edition of the book came from our separate experiences of the increasing importance of sustainability in work systems and in working life. Work is a central activity in people's lives, and it impacts all the areas where the lack of sustainability is experienced. Economic, ecological, human, and social resources are all either strengthened or threatened by what takes place in workplaces. We noticed that researchers, students, companies, and organizations of different sorts need more unified information and insights on how they can sustain work systems and work-systems resources, and how work systems can contribute to sustainability in their economic, social, and ecological environments. In collaboration with Routledge and especially with Jacquelin Curthoys, Francesca Heslop and Simon Alexander at Routledge, we embarked on the journey toward this second edition.

Conducting this book project has required much administrative and professional support. Here we wish to mention several people in particular: first, Halim Dunsky of QuodBonumSit, who was our language editor. Starting with 17 chapters written by 25 researchers from nine countries and six academic disciplines, he has won the full admiration of all the contributors in honing our manuscripts into easily accessible, excellent, and professionally and technically correct English. Anita Söderberg-Carlsson, who was our editorial assistant at the Stockholm School of Economics, has had the task of creating publishable manuscripts to given publisher standards from our highly individual compositions. Bengt Åkermalm from Stockholm University Library has checked the reference lists to ensure their accuracy and completeness. This trio's efforts are a schoolbook example of work as a value-creating process. Thank you for the significant increase in the book's value that you have provided. The computer support unit of the Orfalea College of Business at the California Polytechnic State University set up and administered a website that provided all authors with the basic background information for writing the book and for keeping track of the book's development through different drafts. We wish to thank the college and especially Joe Emenaker, our webmaster, for providing such excellent service.

While it may not come as a surprise to the reader that producing an international scientific anthology requires a virtual organization and specialist professional assistance, supporting such activities is a non-routine event for research funding agencies. We are very grateful therefore that the Swedish Council for Working Life and Social Research together with the Swedish Governmental Agency for Innovation Systems provided us with a grant for the special costs associated with this project. We also wish to thank the late National Institute for Working Life, the Stockholm School of Economics, and Dean Dave Christy of the Orfalea College of Business at the California Polytechnic State University for their generous hospitality in providing us with a roof over our heads for our editorial meetings.

Finally, deepest thanks to our families and especially our partners, Elisabeth, Mackillo, and Elaine for understanding, if perhaps not quite accepting, that our work situation was, as ever, "rather intensive just now."

Peter Docherty, Mari Kira, Rami Shani
Stockholm, December, 2007

Foreword: I

Ray Anderson

As I take pen in hand (literally) to write this Foreword, I am sitting on an airplane on the tarmac of LaGuardia, waiting in line to take off. The flight is an hour and a half late leaving. This is my life these days, and this is an experience to which I have grown accustomed – too accustomed. Since my company Interface, Inc., set its sights in 1994 on becoming the first name in industrial ecology and transforming our petroleum intensive carpet making business into a totally sustainable company, I get lots of invitations to tell the Interface story, thus lots of airplane rides (for which, incidentally, Interface has planted lots of trees).

What brought me from my home in Atlanta to New York City, ultimately to endure this particular all-too-common frustration, was yet another keynote speech. This one was to a conference that brought angel investors together with entrepreneurial CEOs of companies seeking venture capital investment in the field of green technologies. In this case the focus of the conference was narrowed still further to an area of mutual interest to investors and companies: the green building market.

The conference was a sign of the emerging times. The green building (building in an environmentally responsible way) marketplace is exploding, moving very rapidly toward mainstream. A few illustrative data points from my personal experiences: In August 1995, I delivered the opening keynote address for the United States Green Building Council (USGBC) annual conference in Big Sky, Montana. I counted heads in the audience. There were 135 people there. Ten years later, I spoke again to the USGBC annual conference, that time in Atlanta. There were 12,000 people present. Two years after that in Chicago, 40,000 people showed up! Now, in business, that is a growth curve to die for.

So, it's no wonder that entrepreneurs are entering the field with product innovations and service ideas and dreams of striking it rich. And it's no wonder that venture capital investors are appearing at such conferences as the one in New York today, looking for the most likely winners. This heightened activity is a very good thing for the earth and *all* its inhabitants, because what is happening here is defining the early days of a new industrial revolution.

Indeed, there are new fortunes to be made in making the earth a healthier place; and I can say early days, because only 46 years have gone by since Rachel Carson's *Silent Spring* launched this new industrial revolution in 1962. This is the successor to Thomas Newcomen's industrial revolution, the one with which we have grown up, taking for granted that this is the way things are and ought to be: that taking and taking from the earth to grow our economy and our civilization is the natural order of things. That dumping our poisonous waste into the biosphere is quite alright, too.

Oh, Thomas Newcomen? Well he invented the steam driven pump in 1712 to pump water out of the English coal mines, so the miners could dig for coal rather than haul buckets of water. His goal: more coal per man hour. From that invention, the industrial revolution unfolded, one invention after another, more or less with similar goals: more everything per man hour. This was natural enough in the 18th Century, when people were the scarce resource and Nature was abundant. Using abundant Nature to increase human productivity was good business, because the earth seemed so large! Surely, nothing could really hurt it.

But in Rachel Carson's on-going new industrial revolution, here in the 21st Century, it is now Nature that is scarce and diminishing, and we have learned that we *can* hurt the earth. Globally, the living systems of the earth are in decline. Biodiversity plummets. The planet warms. Environmental quality declines. People become more and more abundant. The human footprint on the planet grows and grows at Nature's expense.

Now, of necessity and out of enlightened self-interest, the focus must shift to resource productivity from labour productivity. Furthermore, following Rachel Carson's thoughtful lead, we must hasten to address the qualitative environmental issues as well, such as the toxicity of those resources we seek to use more efficiently, as well as the ones we send back to Nature via the landfill or incinerator.

Furthermore, with four billion very poor people on the earth, surely humankind's great ethical and moral challenge is to put people to work and lift the poorest among us out of grinding poverty without "breaking" the fragile Earth. That is a goal of this revolution. The challenges are immense; the rewards for those who devise a better way will be commensurately so.

I can say it is early days in the new industrial revolution, because 46 years into Thomas Newcomen's, the cotton gin had not yet been invented. But, alas, today we don't have the luxury of time Eli Whitney had in getting around to making the next landmark invention. The inventors and entrepreneurs in New York today know this, too. Time is short. Nature's distress grows; an abyss looms.

Meanwhile, Thomas Newcomen's disciples just won't yet let go of the old and destructive ways. The first industrial revolution goes on, still digging up and drilling up the earth, converting it to products and waste that very quickly end up in landfills and incinerators. Wastes, emissions, and effluents – of various degrees, poisonous—inexorably disperse throughout the biosphere and wreak untold havoc on the natural systems upon which all of life – including the polluters' own lives – utterly depends.

This weird dance between the past and the future, the first industrial revolution and the new, goes on. Massive old fortunes, tied to the first, continue to compound; even as the new struggles to gain traction, searching for and, one by one, finding that better way for the entrepreneur and the right deal for the investor.

Lurking on the edge of the dance floor, trying to determine its role in shaping the dance floor gyrations, is the educational system. The Academy.

The Academy. It changes so slowly, so ponderously, clinging to the opiate of the *status quo*. What can it do? How can it influence the contest of wills taking place on the dance floor? Thoughtful people everywhere, including academia, know that the new must, in time, supplant the old; that Rachel Carson must subdue Thomas Newcomen, and the sooner the better. For all that is at stake in the outcome is . . . well, everything. On a finite Earth, the linear, take-make-waste, abusive industrial system (Newcomen's) simply cannot go on and on and on.

But how can the Academy shake off its lethargy, get out of its comfortable chair on the edge of the dance floor, and give Rachel a hand? That is the question the authors seek to answer in this timely (as timely as that New York conference today) road map to an educational system that is equal to the challenge of shaping a sustainable workplace.

This is a scholarly work whose immediate aim is to reshape, to reformulate, the way we think about the workplace and its role in supporting Rachel Carson's sustainability revolution. Its means for doing so – its active agents – will be the young people who enter the workplace from colleges and universities, with a clear allegiance to new ways of this thinking. The authors' zeal, intelligence, and creativity, firmly grounded in their equally zealous regard for scholarship, each in his/her own chapter, represent the very qualities the new industrial revolution needs. Preparing graduates with a firm grounding in the new paradigm of sustainability is a critical ingredient in sweeping that old, destructive dancer right off the floor and out of the dancehall, into the dust bin of history.

A new, more responsible day dawns in education and the workplace. And that is a good thing.

Ray Anderson
Chairman
Interface Inc.,
Atlanta, Georgia

Foreword: II

Michael Beer

How might business organizations create a work system – the system of roles, responsibilities and relationships for getting work done – that achieves the proper balance between involvement and engagement on the one hand and life-work balance on the other? How might organization and work be designed to ensure both high performance and employee growth and development? Organizations that are able to do this are likely to be sustained over time. What mechanisms can organizations design to enable a conversation to take place between stakeholders about the many tradeoffs that are involved in ensuring that interests of various stakeholders are brought into decisions? These are some of the very important questions about which the authors in this volume have been thinking and doing action research. The impact of work system design on people's motivation and well-being are issues that have been of concern to academics and practitioners for approximately four decades.

In the mid 1960s, I received a request from an instrument manufacturing plant at Corning Glass Works (now Corning Inc.) where I was employed as an Organizational Psychologist, to help the factory implement the ideas of Douglas McGregor. What evolved was a five-year organization development effort that focused on redesign of the works system. Assembly lines were torn down and, following the ideas of Frederick Herzberg, whole jobs in which workers were given responsibility for assembling the total instrument and doing their own inspection followed. Communication practices were totally overhauled. Employees received information from physicians about how the product was used with patients and from management about the performance of the organization, its revenues, costs and profits. High levels of employee engagement and satisfaction as well as plant performance made this instrument factory a model, at the time, for other organizations inside and outside the company.

This plant level organization development effort reflected the major concern of the time. Work in most organizations, certainly for production employees but also for many white-collar employees, was narrow, boring, un-involving and de-motivating. Since the seminal book "Man on the Assembly Line" by Robert Guest, much research has confirmed that rationalizing work in the manner espoused by Frederick Taylor has negative consequences for the human condition at work and often many unintended consequences. Alienation and health problems have been found on the human side and resistance to change as well as low levels of innovation, quality, and commitment contribute to the underperformance of the business.

What if anything has changed in the past four decades? How sustainable were the change efforts in the instrument factory example and the other organization development efforts at the working and management level carried out at Corning by my associates and me as well as by colleagues in other corporations in the US and Europe?

As the authors in this volume point out, while rationalization of work is still a problem in many blue and white-collar jobs, an equally ominous force is creating new human problems at work. The rising power of capital markets, globalization of financial and product markets and rapid technological change are creating pressures for speed and high performance at the corporate and individual level. This in turn is causing what authors in this volume call "work intensity" – under-bounded jobs, pressure for results, long working hours and little time for reflection and personal development. These conditions are creating work-life balance problems of a different but equally difficult nature when compared to the narrow and boring work of the assembly line. In recent work I have been doing with a number of corporations, employees report that the organization and they are overloaded and out of capacity. There are too many initiatives coming from the top. Feeling the pressure for higher performance and a burgeoning business management literature, top managers are unleashing program after program in their effort to adapt their organizations to perceived competitive threats.

And what do we know about the sustainability of the many improvements in work systems made in the last four decades? Ten years after the Corning manufacturing experiment started few of the innovations made were still in place. Changes in business conditions, plant growth and rotation of managers had simply overwhelmed the innovative work system. Innovative work systems in other companies suffered the same fate. Changing the "what" of job and organization design does not seem to change the "how" of organizational adaptation. That is, improvements in work systems did not create an underlying capacity of organizations – managers and employees – to adapt to changing circumstances while remaining consistent with the values and principles that gave rise to the innovation in the first place. What organizations internalized was a new system of management. They did not internalize the skills, attitudes and behaviors needed to adapt work systems to new circumstances in a way that would preserve the inevitable balance that must be struck between all the stakeholders of a corporation – investors, customers, employees and community.

How organizations might create sustainable work systems is a practical matter worthy of organizational experimentation as well as conceptualization and theory development. In this volume practical scholars concerned with the human condition in organizations have come together to discuss their ideas about how work systems that meet the needs of multiple stakeholders can be sustained over time. In effect, they are searching for an understanding of how organizations might learn to adapt work systems to an ever-changing context while maintaining the delicate but necessary balance between economic goals and human development. This is not an easy problem. Nor is it one that can be solved by this volume alone. The contributors to this book have, however, made an important contribution to a much-needed debate.

Michael Beer
Professor Em.
Harvard School of Business
Cambridge, Massachusetts

1 What the world needs now is sustainable work systems

Peter Docherty, Mari Kira, and A.B. (Rami) Shani

Introduction

The working population in Europe is ageing. For example, in Germany people over 65 are projected to make up 30 percent of the population by 2035. One of the measures to guarantee the availability of workforce in this situation is to increase the retirement age – and this is what the German Parliament decided in March 2007. The retirement age was lifted from 65 to 67. There is an urgent need to support individual employees so that they will be able to continue to work to this age. It is an especially difficult challenge to ensure the sustainable work capacity of employees in shift work and in physically demanding manufacturing jobs. Two major German car manufacturers have initiated a research and development project with researchers from the University of Kassel. The project explores working conditions, organizational designs, technological solutions, and human resources management practices that can support the ageing workforce. The sustainability of human resources is dependent on the way work and organizations are designed. One day, there will be a 66-year-old worker assembling your next car (see Chapter 5).

The competitive nature of the software development industry led the top management team of a medium-sized software development company to search for mechanisms that would result in a sustainable new product development process. Following a study of alternative technologies and work design configurations, the study team recommended the utilization of a technology-based solution. Software Development Firm established a process for product development using a platform-based architecture. The technology utilized and the business/ organization design choices made, coupled with the integration of learning mechanisms, resulted in increased innovation, continuous improvement, and positive economic performance (see Chapter 6).

Sustainable Enterprise Executive Roundtable (SEER) is a project of the University of Southern California Center for Sustainable Cities. Twenty-four business leaders – from companies such as the Port of Los Angeles, Disney, Toyota, Mattel, CDM, Volvo, and Waste Management – agreed to participate with researchers from the centre in discussions on possible synergies with regard to the movement of products, materials, and services through the Alameda Corridor, a major distribution channel for imported goods in the Los Angeles area. They agreed that the collaboration would focus on making the transport system more sustainable in terms of increased efficiencies, savings, innovations, better environmental outcomes, and stakeholder satisfaction for the participating companies. The firms agreed to meet quarterly and to engage in at least one concrete project. Multiple projects were launched, such as a project that focused on creating strategies for optimizing the journey of a standard transport container unit and simplifying/greening supply chains (see Chapter 12).

The politicians in Lidköping, Sweden, feared that health care efficiency and efficacy did not realize their potential due to the separate organization of primary health care clinics, hospitals, and municipal after-care. In 2002, these three groups of health care providers formed a development coalition to improve their health care system as a whole. Their first move was to launch projects to develop patient pathways for different patient groups, such as the elderly (aged over 70), diabetes patients, and dementia patients. The projects involved personnel from the different care providers, patients, and their relatives. The resulting pathways became the formal infrastructure for the flow of information about and care to patients. The project resulted in a radical reduction in the number of steps taken in connection with patient care, the elimination of waiting times for reception at the hospital medical clinic (with the exception of heart ailments), reduced the number of referrals and visits to the medical clinic by 15–18 percent, improved communication and relations among staff in different clinics, increased awareness and learning of the staff regarding the patient pathways, and led to the continuation of the study of patient pathways for other patient groups. The three health-care providers decided to form a permanent sustainable development coalition of the health-care system as a whole in 2005 (see Chapter 11).

Each of these vignettes briefly describes a case that addresses different sustainability challenges. All attempted to help work systems become more innovative and more adaptable, to improve continuously and/or to attain some long-term complex system purpose. As we can see from the vignettes, different levels of work systems seem to attract the focus of sustainability efforts. Creating sustainable work systems can be examined by focusing on work design, by focusing on change, and/or by focusing on systems or networks. In this book, we will illustrate and examine the practice and theory that centres on creating sustainable work systems in different settings, organizations, sectors, and nations.

In this chapter, we present the concepts of sustainability and sustainable development. These are broad concepts covering such fields as ecology, sociology, social psychology, and economics. This book focuses on work systems, on organizations and groups of organizations – networks, coalitions, supply chains – and on social sustainability. Naturally, the different dimensions of sustainability are interdependent; these interdependencies are broached where they are of particular relevance in the examples presented. After a general presentation of the concept of sustainability in work systems, we relate this to several of what we regard as the main definitions of the concept. We then discuss some of the features of the concept that may give rise to problems in its application, especially the issue that the concept is distinctly value-loaded. Another related and possibly sensitive feature of sustainability is that its application involves learning, and that this learning is of a deep nature, namely second-order or double-loop learning. Finally, before presenting the organization of the book, we address why it is particularly timely to address work system sustainability at this point in history.

Sustainability in work systems

Sustainability is most often defined as a general worldview according to which people should strive to fulfil their needs in a manner such that the ability of future generations to fulfil their needs is not endangered (World Commission on Environment and Development 1987). Sustainability in this sense means protecting the richness of the world's resources in such a way that their utilization does not destroy them but rather leaves equal opportunity to future generations to benefit from them as well. The sustainability concept has thus a value dimension stating that no population has the right to devour the world's resources for the satisfaction of its needs – much less its wants and ambitions.

In this book, we discuss sustainability in the context of *work systems*: private and public, for-profit and nonprofit organizations of different sorts that have been formed for the purpose of work. In the systems we study, the defining and unifying activity of their members is working. We define work as an intentional value-creating process. This general definition gains meaning with the specification of the goals and rules, resources, and context for the work process. These parameters are related to the stakeholders in the process – workers, investors, suppliers, customers, and communities. The resources are financial, material, physical, intellectual, and technological. The context is cultural, ecological, economic, historical, and social. Addressing sustainability in a work system means, therefore, addressing all these elements that form it, influence it, and are influenced by it. This generally entails recognizing a broader circle of stakeholders than is commonly acknowledged: not only local communities (already a stretch for some), but the communities that customers and participants in the entire supply chain live in, and their ecologies.

Sustainability entails concurrent development in the economic, ecological, human, and social resources engaged in work processes. A sustainable work system is able to function in its environment and to achieve its economic or operational goals. This functioning also entails development in various human and social resources engaged in its operations. In a sustainable work system, employees' capacity to deal with the world's demands grows through work-based learning, development, and well-being. The growth of social resources is secured through equal and open interaction among the various stakeholders, leading to better mutual understanding and a greater capacity for collaboration. The diversity and regeneration potential of ecological resources are safeguarded as well. Central questions in the book are: How can we create and maintain economically viable work systems that also contribute to human, social, and ecological sustainability in a positive manner? How can we engage human and social resources in work systems without expending them, but rather by supporting their growth? How can we ensure the continued functioning of the processes that regenerate human and social resources?

A work system cannot simply satisfy certain needs of certain stakeholders. It has to be able to satisfy the needs of many stakeholders. Moreover, we cannot focus only on short-term, static efficiencies such as productivity and profitability; we must also focus on long-term, dynamic efficiencies such as learning and innovation. A sustainable work system does not merely make trade-offs between the short term and the long term or between different stakeholders, but aims to attain a just balance in development for them all. Past unsustainable decisions in work systems and in societies have something in common: they have all sub-optimized, focused too much on one or more stakeholders at the expense of others. Recent management rationalizing methodologies have achieved marked cost reductions but have given the workforce less employment security and more intense and stressful work, with radically increased losses of time through sickness (Rydh 2002; Kira 2003; Askenazy *et al.* 2006; Green 2006). For many companies, the "business of business" is only seen as "business," yet many of the new "economy-first remedies" for lagging competitiveness have exacerbated the unsustainable exploitation of human, social, and natural resources without having met the competitiveness requirements of even the immediate future (Docherty *et al.* 2002). These interventions, in effect, have failed even on their own terms; the still bigger problem is to align an understanding of the requirements of competitiveness with those that represent long-term sustainability.

We perceive the diversity and richness of work system resources as an important source for, and an important result of, sustainability. A work system formed by diverse kinds of people and diverse tangible and intangible resources is more sustainable than a uniform work system relying only on a limited set of resources, strategies, and responses. Work systems never stay the same. The diversity in such systems allows them to respond to environmental challenges and opportunities in a creative, changing manner. Therefore, the search for sustainability has to also be the search for ensuring diversity in a work system through work design, work-organization design, and technology development measures.

Thus, a sustainable work system is definitely not in a static or steady state – it changes continually as a social and technical system. During its life cycle, a sustainable work system strives toward a higher level of development – but, evolving along with natural cycles of change, it may also transform beyond recognition or even cease to exist. Sustainability simply means that the existence of a work system has created a platform for the future existence of new work systems and processes; its heritage is resource-regenerative rather than resource-consuming for future work processes.

To summarize, some of the principles for sustainable work systems are:

- The operation of a sustainable work system is aimed at the regeneration of the resources it utilizes – human, social, material, and natural resources.

- Moreover, the development of one type of resource does not exploit resources of other types. For instance, material gains are not achieved at the expense of human, social, or natural resources. Similarly, any actor in a sustainable work system does not seek to gain at the expense of other actors.
- A sustainable work system does not strive to secure its existence by exploiting resources external to it. A sustainable work system "gives back" to society rather than simply exploiting the resources made available to it by its social and natural environment. A sustainable work system takes some measure of responsibility for externalized costs and "free goods."
- Since a sustainable work system has to be able to regenerate resources of different types and take into account the legitimate needs of different stakeholders, we need more complex tools for understanding what a work system is and how it functions. Oversimplified models of work systems lead to oversimplified models of responsibility and regeneration.

Defining sustainability and sustainable development

The United Nations (UN) has played a key role in the development of sustainability concepts and the global sustainability movement. The issue of sustainability was initially broached in an international context at the UN conference on the Human Environment in 1972. A major step forward came when the UN formed the World Commission on Environment and Development, often referred to as the Brundtland Commission, after its chairperson. Its report, entitled *Our Common Future* (1987), provided the now classical definition of sustainable development as:

> development that meets the needs of the present without compromising the ability of future generations to meet their own needs. It contains within it two key concepts:
>
> - the concept of "needs," in particular the essential needs of the world's poor, to which overriding priority should be given; and
> - the idea of limitations imposed by the state of technology and social organization on the environment's ability to meet present and future needs.

We read several important meanings in this definition. First, it has *a principle dimension* stating that no single generation has the right to consume the world's resources for the satisfaction of its needs. Instead, every generation has the responsibility to safeguard the resources it uses and the processes through which these resources form or are regenerated. The definition thus emphasizes protecting the richness of the world's resources through their preservation, regeneration and development. Second, the definition emphasizes the satisfaction of needs, not wants. The sustainability concept has thus *a priority dimension* that sets the satisfaction of needs by all people now and in the future ahead of the satisfaction of the wants and ambitions of privileged people in the present. Third, the definition concludes that the developmental state of technology and social organizations has a strong impact on the environment. The concept thus also has *a progress dimension*, according to which ecological sustainability can be achieved through social and technological innovations. Even though ecological resources have been damaged and put at risk because of some technological and social innovations that have aimed to achieve economic goals, it will be possible to reverse the ecological damage and reduce the risks only through other social and technological innovations. For such innovations to emerge, a relative economic prosperity and sustainable economic development will naturally be needed.

Thus, the interconnectedness of ecological, social, and economic factors in sustainability was already recognized in the Brundtland Commission report. In 1997, economist John Elkington conceptualized this idea further and coined the term "Triple Bottom Line" or P^3: people, planet, and profit. The main idea here is that in a sustainable system, human and social resources along with ecological and economic resources should all be able to grow and develop. It is acknowledged that a company or any other work system is not only responsible for its shareholders; its operations also affect other *stakeholders* such as employees, customers, suppliers, the natural environment, and the surrounding economic system. "The business of business" cannot only be "business," but must include a positive contribution for all these different stakeholders. As a consequence, the single economic bottom line needs to be extended into a triple bottom line measuring the work system performance in terms of economic, ecological, and social outcomes. As Elkington puts it (1999): "At the heart of the emerging sustainable value creation concept is recognition that for a company to prosper over the long term it must continuously meet society's needs for goods and services without destroying natural and social capital."

Any human action can be seen to have various obvious and more obscure consequences, and often the more obscure consequences may also turn out to be unwanted consequences. During the past 200 years, it has become increasingly clear that economically driven industrial production has had profound ecological and social consequences, such as those associated with pollution or urbanization. Moreover, what happens today influences tomorrow. In economical, ecological, and human/social systems, the interdependent actors influence one another. At the core of the sustainability concept is the realization of the interconnectedness of the world in time and in space, and the realization of how human actions may – given this interconnectedness – have unexpected consequences. Sustainability is about being responsible to this interconnectedness, and making decisions such that the various interconnected consequences of those decisions are taken into account.

The concept of sustainability therefore can be understood as an overarching worldview recognizing the interconnectedness of ecological, social, and economic factors in human activities. They all have to be part of the same developmental equation to lead to true sustainability, reducing the risks of unintended side effects in other factors that are greater when only economic factors are consciously pursued. Pim Martens (2006) identified the following aspects as common in various definitions and interpretations of sustainability:

- Sustainability is an *intergenerational* phenomenon where the actions of the present generation create or delimit the opportunities of the coming generations.
- Sustainability is a *multiscale* phenomenon: local actions have regional and potentially global effects. Also, Gunderson and Holling (2002) describe how one should move between aggregation levels to understand truly the process of sustainability. For instance, to understand the sustainability of a work system, one has to understand what happens at the levels of people, groups, departments, organizations, branches, and economies.
- Sustainability focuses on *multiple domains*: ecological, social, and economic domains all have to be taken into account to create better living conditions for people and the planet.

The content analysis of Gladwin *et al.* (1995) on various conceptions of sustainability and sustainable development leads to a rather similar outcome. They (1995: 878) define sustainable development as:

> a process of achieving human development (widening or enlarging the range of people's choices . . .) in an inclusive, connected, equitable, prudent, and secure manner. Inclusiveness implies human development over time and space. Connectivity entails an embrace of ecological, social, and economic interdependence. Equity suggests intergenerational, intragenerational, and interspecies fairness. Prudence connotes duties of care and prevention: technologically, scientifically, and politically. Security demands safety from chronic threats and protection from harmful disruption.

The following basic assumptions connect the ecological, economic, human, and social aspects of sustainability and underlie the present book:

- The opportunity to develop as a person, a professional, and a member of a society through work experiences – or, in other words, to be sustained as a person by work – is a basic human right.
- In contemporary working life – characterized by rapid changes, knowledge-intensive work, global competition, and social values emphasizing equality and human dignity – the sustainability of human and social resources is one of the foundations of economic sustainability.
- The sustainability of human resources at work is one of the foundations for social development and the sustainability of whole societies.
- The sustainability of human and social resources is needed to secure ecological sustainability, because only people and groups who operate sustainably are able to grasp, prioritize, and work toward ecological sustainability.

We have used the concept of *sustainability*, while the Brundtland Commission wrote about *sustainable development*. Both of these concepts are misunderstood and sometimes contested. Sustainability is misunderstood as a search for a status quo, while sustainable development is perceived as an oxymoron: development toward the existing state. We wish to clarify how we see these two concepts. First: for us, sustainability means the dynamic state of becoming sustainable – a process founded on conscious efforts to create new opportunities for existence in multiple domains and at multiple levels, now and in the future. Second: by sustainable development, we mean the active efforts of people to support this dynamic state of sustainability. We agree with Carl Holling (2001: 390) who wrote:

> Sustainability is the capacity to create, test, and maintain adaptive capability. Development is the process of creating, testing, and maintaining opportunity. The phrase that combines the two, "sustainable development," thus refers to the goal of fostering adaptive capabilities and creating opportunities. It is therefore not an oxymoron but a term that describes a logical partnership.

Sustainability can be seen as the dynamic state of resource regeneration and growth while sustainable development means those actions taken to reach and maintain this state.

Another concept closely related to sustainability is corporate social responsibility (CSR). For instance, the World Business Council for Sustainable Development (WBCSD) defines CSR as follows:

> Corporate social responsibility is the continuing commitment by business to behave ethically and contribute to economic development while improving the quality of life of the workforce and their families as well as of the local community and society at large.
>
> (Holme and Watts 2000)

Social responsibility can be economic, achieving profitability; legal, obeying laws; ethical, doing what is expected and avoiding harm; and discretionary, going beyond expectations.

People's values and the sustainability of work systems

Sustainability is an essentially contestable subject in the sense that no authoritative, universally valid definition can be formulated – not even by the United Nations. The balancing of ecological, social, and economic values is inherently subject to opinion. Sustainable development may need to accommodate conflicting values, beliefs, and points of view as to what is a sensible, desirable, and feasible thing to do (Loeber *et al.* 2007). There is no way of determining what is "really sustainable" other than through collective and contextual deliberation and learning. Sustainability is also a concept that claims normatively to offer desirable directions for action. Thus, the learning entailed in this context is more than joint fact-finding and involves processes of value judgment.

Sustainable development needs to be elaborated in an action-oriented way, in which a balance is found between the desirable and the feasible in a given context. Again, the balancing of feasible and desirable proposals for action is particularly complex, given that sustainable development is radical, even revolutionary. It requires a critique of the existing less-sustainable or unsustainable present circumstances and processes, and entails reassessing and changing assumptions, values, rules, structures, and routines. It involves a critical review of what is taken for granted in the organization, namely reflection on assumptions, beliefs, and theories underlying "the way we do things here." Sustainability is about challenging our mental models, policies, and practices, not just about accommodating new considerations into current work or finding common ground between related programmes. It entails envisioning and accomplishing change rather than sustaining the status quo. All of these activities are value-based.

Pioneering studies of executive roles identified the creation of morals for others as a key management task. Barnard (1938: 272) stated that responsibility for the development of an organization's moral framework distinguishes managers from subordinates. In today's language, we might say that the executives are meant to influence and shape corporate ethics. A common feature of different ethical schools, such as those formulated by Aristotle, Bentham, Donaldson, and Kant, is their emphasis on concern for others over self-interest (Jones *et al.* 2007). These ethical schools differ in that some, e.g., the Kantian, relate ethics to the actions taken by actors, while others, e.g., the Aristotelian, to the qualities and virtues of the actor. New kinds of business structures such as project organizations, networks, alliances, and virtual organizations have based their success more on Aristotle's ideas of virtues, such as loyalty and trust, than on formal rules and agreements for behaviour (Hedberg *et al.* 1997). In this context, Nyhan (2006), a neo-Aristotelian, and De Geus (1997) distinguish between moral and instrumental value attitudes toward corporate social responsibility or sustainability: "genuine" decisions are morally motivated, whereas "instrumental" decisions appear morally motivated, but are actually made out of self-interest, usually in terms of economic gain. Although enlightened self-interest can be an important and legitimate motivator to bring an organization toward values of sustainability, self-interest narrowly conceived can lead to attempts to manipulate public opinion by taking on the appearance of concern for sustainability, but not the substance.

Argumentation for managerial moral responsibility challenges the presumption that shareholder wealth confers unilateral privilege. Stressing the commonality between business activity and other forms of human endeavour means recognizing that economic activity is subject to fundamental moral principles and responsibilities – an essential requirement for sustainable social action (Whetten *et al.* 2002). Lund-Thomsen (2007) also underlines the necessity of adopting a critical (or moral) perspective of illuminating issues that are more central to other stakeholders than to shareholders. However, sustainability does not have to be contradictory to shareholder values. Socially and ecologically responsible corporate strategies and actions can offer win–win opportunities to various stakeholders (see Hart 1997). This book will offer several examples on this point.

The stakeholder theory may be used to identify moral or philosophical guidelines for the operation and management of corporations (Donaldson and Preston 1995). This theory is fundamentally normative, as is the sustainability concept. A central tenet of stakeholder theory is that management's role is to satisfy a wider set of stakeholders than simply the shareholders. This theory is the implicit basis of much current practice, labour law, and joint agreements in many countries that confirm the stakeholders' legitimate interest in the organization. However, these practices, agreements, and legislations reflect the values of the parties involved, as well as other beliefs as to causal relationships and questions of fact – they are not purely the outcome of logic or empirical scientific evidence. Donaldson and Preston (1995) point out that there is as yet no compelling empirical evidence that the optimal strategy for maximizing a firm's conventional and market performance is stakeholder management.

Similarly, regarding sustainability itself, more than a third of the managements of the companies in the World Business Council for Sustainable Development do not have much faith in the business case for sustainability and do not actively support the concept internally (Blackburn 2007: 7). This reflects what Hart (2007) calls the "Great Trade-Off Illusion" – the belief that companies must sacrifice financial performance to meet social obligations.

Learning for sustainability

Progress in relation to sustainable development hinges on a social capacity that allows for different sectors and interests to be able to constructively engage with each other. Bawden *et al.* (2007: 135) point out that the quest for a more sustainable world hinges on development, while sustainability itself provides a moral and intellectual focus for social as well as cognitive development: we must "learn our way out" of our present situation toward a more sustainable world. This may be achieved in appropriate "learning situations" in which it is not merely a matter of participation, but of critical reflection, dialogue, and acts that challenge roles, power structures, beliefs, values, and assumptions and communicate in the broadest sense of the term. To quote a British government report, "rights will become real only as citizens are engaged in the decisions and processes which affect their lives" (Department for International Development 2000).

Sustainable development is a change, a learning process (Shani and Docherty 2003). Learning in sustainable development must take place at all levels in the organization: the individual, collective, and organizational levels, and indeed, beyond that – among organizations in networks, coalitions, and systems. At the individual level, it may involve acquiring new knowledge and skills, but definitely involves thinking through one's assumptions, attitudes, beliefs, and values. In this context, Schön (1983) sees learning as a process of reviewing theories-in-use in the light of unexpected events and unexpected discrepancies in the details of a problem situation. Loeber *et al.* (2007) maintain that it is especially useful in the context of sustainable development to regard learning as a social event, as changes implied in sustainable development require joint action by many actors. Double-loop or second-order learning questions the assumptions behind how things are or how they are done (Argyris 1982). Such learning is particularly relevant – even imperative – for sustainable development, which requires important shifts in values. Learning for sustainability focuses on encouraging people to think about why certain decisions are being taken and what the available real alternatives are.

Innovative projects may provide settings in which participants must explain and scrutinize their tacit theories, beliefs, and assumptions and thus be helped to radically change their behaviour. Thus learning in interaction is a central feature of the cases presented in this book: tacit knowledge is explicated and different practices may be aligned on the basis of congruency of meaning between different parties, strengthening the dynamics that contribute to sustainable development.

Loeber *et al.* (2007) underline the relevance for sustainable development of system learning in which actors challenge and redefine the very structures that hinder their efforts for more sustainable practices. The cases presented in this book illustrate improved feedback mechanisms and transformative workplace learning experiences. At the collective level, the cases provide examples of dealing with serious challenges in the workplace, in which efforts are made to provide an atmosphere of trust and mutual dependence (reciprocity). When tacit beliefs, assumptions, and values underlying present conditions become apparent, they become accessible to reflection and action.

Learning-based change for sustainability encourages collaborative learning environments that not only impart knowledge, but increase the capacity of the learner. Collaborative learning requires the development of learning mechanisms (Shani *et al.* 2008). Learning-based change for sustainability underpins organizational change for sustainability. This book includes examples of:

1) Visioning processes to align the entire organization with sustainability principles (Cox, Chapter 2, and Amodeo, Chapter 3 in this volume).
2) Participation in decision making as a way of motivating stakeholders to engage in changes in sustainability (Stebbins and Valenzuela, Chapter 9 in this volume).
3) Developing partnerships and coalitions to stimulate dialogue and assist with the implementation of strategies and action plans (Lifvergren *et al.*, Chapter 11 in this volume).
4) Developing networks for collective learning from pooling experiences, striving to attain a shared understanding of common problems (Bradbury, Chapter 12 in this volume).

The systemic approach offers a better way to understand and manage complex situations because it emphasizes the holistic and integrative perspectives that take into account the relationships among system components. Sustainable development often involves deep changes in the choices people make day-to-day in their work. This requires an extensive, emergent, and reflective process, in sharp contrast to the ever-present offer in the marketplace of the "quick fix." Participation in both the development process and the resulting organization offer the possibility for co-workers to build the skills to exercise discretion in decision-making and to shoulder responsibility for the outcomes.

Timeliness of social sustainability at the macro level

The concept of sustainability applies at all levels in the social sphere, from the entirety of humankind in a global perspective, down through geographical, market, or sectoral regions to organizations, work systems, and individuals – i.e., at macro, meso, and micro levels. The scope of this book is restricted to consideration of the micro and meso levels. The macro level was the subject of the United Nations' Brundtland Commission report referred to earlier. This focused the situation of the developing countries. Focusing on the essential needs of the world's poor, Hart (2007) emphasizes improving the lot of the 4 billion people who constitute the BoP, the base of the (world socioeconomic) pyramid. He calls investment in this group "the Great Leap Downwards." Hart underlines an urgent need to couple the sustainability agenda to value creation. Thus, he urges multinational corporations to become indigenous, developing both new local capabilities and fully contextualized solutions to real problems in ways that respect local culture and natural diversity. This will eventually lift billions out of poverty and desperation – and avert the social decay, political chaos, terrorism, and environmental meltdown that are certain to result if the gap between rich and poor continues to widen. Multinational companies have a special role to play in realizing the sustainability opportunities available in the developing economies. Hart provides detailed cases illustrating breakthrough projects of this kind, e.g., the sustainability assessment of a mobile phone service in 950 rural villages in Bangladesh.

Hart (1997) points out that few companies have yet realized that a) in meeting our needs we are destroying the ability of future generations to meet theirs, b) the root problems – explosive population growth and rapid economic development in the emerging economies – are political and social issues that exceed the mandate and the capabilities of any corporation, and c) environmental opportunities might actually become a major source of revenue and growth. The 1980s saw the crossing of the "chasm" between seeing social responsibility as a trade-off or *obligation* to seeing it as a possible win-win *opportunity*.

Timeliness of work system sustainability

In the industrialized nations, sustainability is a timely issue because of the changes taking place in working life. There are several developing trends that challenge the way we work and organize work in companies, i.e., at the micro and meso levels. In the Western industrial countries, the bureaucratic era of Tayloristic mass-production is seen to be giving way to postbureaucratic power structures in companies that operate with a primary basis in information and that provide services rather than concrete products. Even though there are clear indications that the bureaucratic approach is still alive and well in many workplaces today (Schumann *et al.* 1995; Huys *et al.* 1999; Landsbergis *et al.* 1999), it seems that some kind of transition is going on. Broad social, technological, legislative, and economic changes are giving birth to new kinds of work realities (Heckscher and Applegate 1994). That is why we need new ways to comprehend contemporary work organizations. Only when properly understood in their complexity can they be managed and developed in a sustainable manner, as citizens are engaged in the decisions and processes which affect their lives (Department for International Development 2000).

Workers' perceptions of their work are changing. Surveys carried out in Europe, Australia, and the United States show that workers have been experiencing an increase in work intensity throughout the 1990s, due mainly to technical change and work reorganizations (Green 2006). Computer and communication technologies enable the faster delivery of work to workers in many jobs with high degrees of autonomy and discretion. Modern technologies have the potential to breach the psychological and physical barriers between work and nonwork activities. Multiskilling and the integration of tasks in teams have led to simultaneous extra demands on workers – both for greater effort and for increased skill (e.g., Adams *et al.* 2000). The predominant form that technological change has taken in the 1990s has inclined to demand higher effort levels from workers.

The increase in perceived work intensity is matched by increases in sickness at work. For example, in Sweden, 14 percent of the population aged 25–65 are either on early retirement, sick pensions, or long-term sick leave (more than 365 days) (Rydh 2002). Furthermore, the number of people on sick leave in Sweden has increased remarkably in recent years. From 1997 to 2002, the number of people on sick leave exceeding 15 days increased 119 percent (from 135,000 to 296,300 persons), and sick leave exceeding one year increased 182 percent (from 44,800 to 126,100 persons). Early retirement pensions increased during the same period. The largest part of this increase is due to psychological issues, including stress-related diagnoses. A recent report confirms the relation between this increase and changes in the psychosocial working conditions experienced by large numbers of employees (Marklund *et al.* 2005).

In addition to changes in the nature of work and work organizations and in the attitudes of employees, we can also detect demographic and social changes that promote the urgency of human and social sustainability in work systems. When it comes to demographics, the old world of the industrialized countries is literally growing rapidly older. In the EU, for example, in the period from 2000 to 2035 the number of people under 15 years will decrease from c. 17 percent to 13 percent and the number over 65 will increase from c. 16 percent to over 30 percent. In order to secure the availability of labour, many European countries are raising or considering raising the retirement age. As a consequence, work systems of various types need to find way to create sustainable work – work that sustains the resources of employees and allows them to work productively into their sixties and seventies.

At the societal level, increased competitive pressure on employers has been responsible for work intensification (Burchell *et al.* 1999). Competitive pressure has led to a focus on productivity, which is more easily and immediately improved by cutting costs than by increasing revenues. New management regimes such as total quality management and lean production have led to the elimination of activities that do not explicitly contribute to added customer value. Organizational slack and the micro pauses in work that are so essential to personal learning and physical regeneration have been rationalized away. The bursting of the international real estate bubble at the beginning of the 1990s and of the dot-com bubble a few years later occasioned considerable downsizing. In the private sector, there has been a certain tendency to couple such drastic reductions in resources to more or less integrated programmes including the introduction of new technology, work redesign, and the introduction of teams, new competence profiles, and reward systems. These measures aim at ensuring that the immediate gains from rationalization will be followed by further gains in efficiency and effectiveness.

Unfortunately, though the public sector has been subject to the same cost-cutting policies, they have not been accompanied by programmes to ensure that the reduced staff are better prepared to deal with the growing demand for their services. This has been the case in several European countries in sectors such as the police, schools, and healthcare services. In healthcare in the UK, the commitment of nurses to their patients has been the rock upon which work intensification was built by management, by simply imposing higher service requirements through increased patient flows (Ackroyd and Bolton 1999). Similar pressure was experienced in Sweden in the 1990s, when 5,000 nurses simply moved to Norway. A similar crisis was played out in Finland in November 2007 when 16,000 nurses resigned their jobs to force through a radical improvement of their working conditions and compensation.

The strength of surveys is that their repeated use allows the study of changes in perceptions over time. Such studies show an increase in work intensification experienced throughout the 1990s (Askenazy *et al.* 2006). The strength of case studies is that they provide a more detailed picture of factors influencing the experience of intensity. Swedish case studies, mainly in the service sector, show that marked perceived intensity is related to:

- cultural issues such as differences in values and attitudes at work between management and staff;
- factors undermining people's understanding of their work situation, such as ambiguity, uncertainty, and diffuse boundaries regarding duties;
- poor management, with incomplete information, little communication, little influence or discretion, poor balance between the demands made and the resources available;
- poor dialogue, difficulty in being heard, little understanding, and insufficient feedback.

(Kira and Forslin 2008, Bjerlöv *et al.* 2006)

Sustainable work systems – the organization of the book

In the six years that have passed since the first edition of this book in 2002, there has been a marked increase in research and development conducted in organizations striving to attain and maintain sustainability. These efforts have often been organized as collaborations between management and staff, the organization and its stakeholders, and practitioners and researchers. Thus, the core of this edition is made up of practical, pioneering efforts to realize sustainability by committed organizations that in many cases have been working in the field for many years. Figure 1.1 shows the issues addressed in the book.

The overarching feature of an organization giving it its distinctive character is its value set: in our context, comprising values such as concern for others, i.e., different stakeholders; for ecological, social, and economic sustainability; for fairness and participation; for learning, development, and creativity; for stability and change. Values are the cornerstones for building sustainability and must permeate the culture of a sustainable organization. Establishing a company's values with clarity and emphasis is a key task for management. Values have been shown to be the key bearing or reference point for action in organizations in turbulent

National and business cultures influence the ways organizations come about to seek sustainability.

Personal and business purpose: A vision and values for sustainability.

National legislation, business trends and public opinion influence the ways organizations come about to seek sustainability.

Personal and company identity transformation for sustainability.

Work and work-system solutions for sustainability:
- Situation-based work design for, e.g., knowledge work or ageing workforce to promote sustainability.
- Organization design and reliance on emergent organizing for sustainability.
- Organization and work design balancing the needs of various stakeholders.
- Technology development to promote sustainability.
- Networking, development coalitions and stakeholder interactions for sustainability.
- Benefitting from regulations and making product/processes innovations for sustainability.

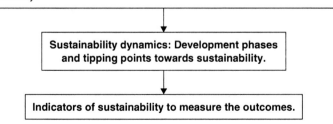

Sustainability dynamics: Development phases and tipping points towards sustainability.

Indicators of sustainability to measure the outcomes.

Figure 1.1 Key issues in sustainable work systems: a synopsis of issues addressed in the book

environments or experiencing very rapid growth. Thus, the role of values in sustainability efforts is a focus of this book.

The work organization is the basic structural element in the organization. The issue of the design and organization of work is of key importance to realize sustainability at the micro level, for individuals and groups. Our main concern here is people in working life, and the new challenges emerging through the changing nature of work, the changing pressures on organizations from the marketplace, and the changing characteristics of workforce demographics. Handling these issues involves addressing fields of operations at a higher system level than an individual organization. This entails looking at coalitions, supply or value chains, networks, and societies. Within the scope of this book, we can only give individual illustrations of these levels. Given our stakeholder perspective, we are not solely interested in employees, but in several examples illustrate how customers, suppliers, and even competitors are involved.

Meeting challenges involves change, development, learning, and innovation. These are key features of sustainable development; our illustrations deal with models, methods, and mechanisms for these change and learning processes, which are usually by their nature demanding and extended. Presenting and embedding sustainability values in an organization that sees itself and its positive history as bound up in economic goals and shareholder loyalty is clearly an enterprise that will take considerable time. The "star cases" presented here are (by our definition) ongoing sustainability efforts that have been in progress for years, if not decades. These continual change processes require management, monitoring, and decision making. We also present examples of methods and tools used to monitor and make decisions on sustainability investments and processes.

The following 16 chapters are grouped into four sections. The chapters in the first three sections are based on empirical studies of organizations, often extensive case studies. They describe organizations' efforts to attain and maintain sustainability.

The first part of the book, "Focusing value frameworks," consists of two chapters, which deal with establishing a clear and distinct value base regarding sustainability in the organization. In Chapter 2, Keith Cox presents a study of how CEOs (often founders) develop their company visions: their personal values form the basis of their business visions. This is accomplished by working closely in partnership with multiple stakeholders as their organization emerges. In Chapter 3, Mona Amodeo describes and analyzes how the sustainability vision of the founder and CEO of Interface Inc. transformed the culture and the identity of the company and its personnel. This is an ongoing process that started over ten years ago, involving personnel, organizational change, and technological development with a new and marked R&D profile.

The second part, "Focusing work and work systems," presents three chapters on the design and organization of sustainable work. In Chapter 4, Peter Brödner analyzes the contradictory work demands on system engineers in the German software industry. He offers developments in sociotechnical systems theory that entail increased management responsibilities for the engineers, enabling them to resolve the contradictions and exert more control over important aspects of their work. Chapter 5 deals with the urgent issue of adapting working conditions in assembly-line work in the manufacturing industry to changes in workers' capabilities as they grow older. Julia Weichel and her colleagues present findings from two German car manufacturers and, based on their study, make suggestions on age-differentiated work design. In Chapter 6, James Sena and Rami Shani present a study of a software firm producing advanced logistics systems. The company is using developments in information and communications technology to ensure leading business performance and the continual development of its personnel's capabilities. This is achieved by the joint optimization of social and technological factors, not only for the sake of personnel, but also for the various needs of other stakeholders.

Part III, "Focusing change in sustainable organizations," deals with organizational change and development for sustainability. In Chapter 7, Richard Boyatzis presents a model for the sustainable development of teams using intentional change and complexity theory, with the key concepts of "tipping points," unexpected elements of surprise, and resonant leadership. Examples of these concepts are given from the performance of professional sports teams in the United States. In Chapter 8, Lena Wilhelmson and Marianne Döös present and analyze an R&D company in a rapidly changing environment in which the company must allow individuals considerable room for exploring and exploiting their personal work situation. When an organizational unit is disbanded, the heritage of its former employees persists in its products that remain in the marketplace, which provide reference points for organizational and personal capability development. The case relates to the design and management of tipping points in change processes.

Michael Stebbins and Judy Valenzuela present in Chapter 9 a longitudinal case study of a health care provider. The study focuses on a development forum responsible for decisions on changes in therapies and drug formularies for an organization including over 10,000 physicians. The forum had responsibility for the information and training programmes required to ensure a smooth transition in treatment protocols throughout the organization. The forum is made up of a variety of professional participants, though pharmacists and physicians predominate. The authors focus on the various mechanisms used to promote and support the learning processes, both within the forum and as they are extended out into the organization. In Chapter 10, Doug Cerf and Arline Savage systematize and analyze the financial tools available to management for estimating economic results and risks for different types of ecological and social decisions. The three basic types are financial tools and techniques, such as socially responsible investing and emissions trading programmes, internal reporting tools and techniques, such as the sustainable balanced scorecard and eco-efficiency, and external reporting tools and techniques, such as sustainability reporting based on Global Reporting Initiative Guidelines.

Part IV, "Focusing systems," presents a systems perspective. It is made up of four chapters. The first two deal with organizations that work to attain sustainability by collaborating with other organizations with which they have a natural relationship. In Chapter 11, Svante Lifvergren, a resident consultant physician and hospital head of development, together with two external researchers, describes and analyzes an extensive project in which three health care providers, primary care clinics, a hospital, and six after-care authorities formed a development coalition together with university researchers. The purpose of the coalition was to improve the efficiency and efficacy of the health care system as a whole for patients in their geographical region. Their initial efforts and their positive results for the various stakeholders involved, not least the mutual trust and respect, led to the partners institutionalizing the coalition as an ongoing function with joint management, its own goals, a budget and a balanced scorecard system, and a development unit. In Chapter 12, Hilary Bradbury describes and analyzes the functioning of a company network formed on an initiative from researchers at the University of Southern California. The companies function as a collaborative learning system by integrating feedback processes, which enables more intelligent management of the shared work system, creating synergies in the movement of products, material, and services through the Alameda Corridor in the Los Angeles area.

The other two chapters in Part IV concern interactions between business organizations and NGOs or government bodies that have a responsibility for promoting and supporting sustainability. In Chapter 13, Mikael Román chooses the critical situation in the coffee market to illustrate the particular sustainability challenges facing developing countries where weak institutional structures and high dependency on external economic markets affect the social and environmental conditions for both societies and individuals. He discusses to what extent the creation of sustainability labels, with the ambition of boosting the global coffee market and simultaneously creating sustainable working conditions, has had the intended effects. In Chapter 14, Sharon Moore and Julie Jie Wen focus on the work–life balance of middle managers in China. Their experiences indicate an inherent conflict between traditional Chinese values and the requirements of contemporary Chinese capitalism, placing enormous pressures on Chinese society. The political commitment to the nation and its economic development seems to be unfolding at the expense of environmental and social sustainability.

Part V, "Future of sustainable work systems," is made up of three chapters that indicate directions forward in the development of research and practice regarding social sustainability and its coordination with ecological and economic sustainability. In Chapter 15, Mari Kira and Frans van Eijnatten present a new framework for analyzing and designing sustainable work, developed from sociotechnical systems, complexity thinking, and models on salutogenic or health-enhancing work. The authors suggest how focusing on the interplay between resource development in individuals and social systems, on their simultaneous interior and exterior development, and the emergent development of resources can offer keys for sustainable work.

In Chapter 16, Michael Stebbins and Rami Shani present the development of a sustainable design and change methodology that draws on the intersection between streams of thought in the design and development and change fields. The design perspectives considered are based on the information processing, sociotechnical systems and self-design schools, while the change and development perspectives draw on the schools of collaborative research, action research, and sociotechnical system planned change. They examine the IDEO Company case and propose a concurrent design model and an integrated, eclectic, planned, sustainable work system design change process. In Chapter 17, we draw lessons from the cases and ideas presented here and outline a number of issues that need to be studied more closely to develop more balanced knowledge about sustainable work systems.

Questions for reflection

Here are three questions for your further reflection on the issues broached in this chapter:

• How would you define a sustainable work system?
• How do the different aspects of sustainability (human, social, economic, and ecological) relate to each other and impact one another?
• Why is work-system sustainability a timely topic at this point in history?

References

Ackroyd, S. and Bolton, S. (1999) "It is not Taylorism: Mechanisms of work intensification in the provision of gynaecological services in a NHS hospital," *Work, Employment and Society*, 13, 2, 369–387.

Adams, A., Lugsden, E., Chase, J., Arber, S., and Bond, S. (2000) "Skill-mix changes and work intensification in the provision of gynaecological services in a NHS hospital," *Work, Employment and Society*, 14, 3, 541–555.

Argyris, C. (1992; 1982) "Why individuals have difficulty with double-loop learning," in C. Argyris, *On Organizational Learning*. Cambridge, MA: Blackwell, pp. 7–38.

Askenazy, P., Cartron, D., de Coninck, F., and Gollac, M. (eds) (2006) *Organisation et intensité du travail* [Organization and work intensity]. Toulouse: Octares Éditions.

Barnard, C.I. (1938) *The Function of the Chief Executive*. Cambridge, MA: Harvard University Press.

Bawden, R., Guijt, I., and Woodhill, J. (2007) "The critical role of the civil society in fostering societal learning for a sustainable world," in A.E.J. Wals (ed.), *Social Learning towards a Sustainable World: Principles, Perspectives and Praxis*, Wageningen: Wageningen Academic Publishers, pp. 133–147.

Bjerlöv, M., Söderberg, I., and Docherty, P. (2006) "Intensité, confiance et stratégies durables" [Intensity, trust and sustainable strategies], in P. Askenazy, D. Cartron, F. de Coninck, and M. Gollac (eds), *Organisation et intensité du travail*. Paris: Octares, pp. 303–312.

Blackburn, W.R. (2007) *The Sustainability Handbook*. Washington, DC: Environmental Law Institute.

Burchell, B.J., Day, D., Hudson, M., Lapido, P., Mankelow, R., Nolan, J., Reed, H., Wickert, J., and Wikinson, F. (1999) *Job Insecurity and Work Intensification: Flexibility and the Changing Boundaries of Work*. York: Joseph Rowntree Foundation Report.

De Geus, A. (1997) *The Living Company*. Boston, MA: Harvard Business School Press.

Department for International Development (DFID) (2000) *Realising Human Rights for Poor People: Strategies for Achieving International Development Targets.* London: DFID.

Docherty, P., Forslin, J., Shani, A.B. (Rami), and Kira, M. (2002) "Emerging work systems: From intensive to sustainable," in P. Docherty, J. Forslin, and A.B. (Rami) Shani (eds), *Creating Sustainable Work Systems: Emerging Perspectives and Practices.* London: Routledge, pp. 3–14.

Donaldson, T. and Preston, L.L. (1995) "The stakeholder theory of the organization: concepts, evidence and implications," *Academy of Management Review,* 20, 1, 65–91.

Elkington, J. (1999) "Triple bottom-line reporting: Looking for balance," *Australian CPA,* 69, 2, 18–22.

Fricke, W. and Totterdill, P. (eds) (2004) *Action Research in Workplace Innovation and Regional Development.* Amsterdam: John Benjamins.

Gladwin, T.N., Kennelly, J.J., and Krause, T.S. (1995) "Shifting paradigms for sustainable development: Implications for management theory and research," *Academy of Management Review,* 20, 4, 874–907.

Green, F. (2006) *Demanding Work: The Paradox of Job Quality in the Affluent Society.* Princeton, NJ: Princeton University Press.

Gunderson, L.H. and Holling, C.S. (eds) (2002) *Panarchy. Understanding Transformations in Human and Natural Systems.* Washington, DC: Island Press, pp. 25–62.

Hart, S.L. (1997) "Beyond greening: strategies for a sustainable world," *Harvard Business Review,* 75, Jan.–Feb., 66–67.

Hart, S.L. (2007) *Capitalism at the Crossroads.* Philadelphia, PA: Wharton School of Finance Press.

Heckscher, C. and Applegate, L.M. (1994) "Introduction," in C. Heckscher and A. Donnellon (eds), *The Post-Bureaucratic Organization: New Perspectives on Organizational Change,* Thousand Oaks, CA: Sage Publications, pp. 1–13.

Hedberg, B., Dahlgren, G., and Olve, N.-G. (1997) *Virtual Organizations and Beyond: Discover Imaginary Systems.* New York: J. Wiley & Sons.

Holling, C.S. (2001) "Understanding the complexity of economic, ecological, and social systems," *Ecosystems,* 4, 390–405.

Holme, R. and Watts, P. (2000) *Corporate Social Responsibility: Making Good Business Sense.* Geneva: World Business Council for Sustainable Development.

Huys, R., Sels, L., Hootegem, G., van Bundervoet, J., and Hendericks, E. (1999) "Towards less division of labor? New production concepts in automotive, chemical, clothing and machine tool industries," *Human Relations,* 52, 1, 67–93.

Jones, T.M., Felps, W., and Bigley, G.A. (2007) "Ethical theory and stakeholder-related decisions: The role of stakeholder culture," *Academy of Management Review,* 32, 1, 137–155.

Kira, M. (2003) "From Good Work to Sustainable Development – Human Resources Consumption and Regeneration in the Post-Bureaucratic Working Life," unpublished Ph.D. thesis. Stockholm: Royal Institute of Technology.

Kira, M. and Forslin, J. (2008) "Seeking regenerative work in the post-bureaucratic transition," accepted for *Journal of Organizational Change Management* (forthcoming), 21, 1, 76–91.

Landsbergis, P.A., Cahill, J., and Schnall, P. (1999) "The impact of lean production and related new systems of work organization on worker health," *Journal of Occupational Health Psychology,* 4, 2, 108–130.

Loeber, A., van Mierlo, J., Grin, J., and Leeuwis, C. (2007) "The practical value of theory: Conceptualising learning in the pursuit of sustainable development," in A.E.J. Wals (ed.), *Social Learning towards a Sustainable World: Principles, Perspectives and Praxis*. Wageningen: Wageningen Academic Publishers, pp. 83–97.

Lund-Thomsen, P. (2007) "Corporate social responsibility: Towards a new dialogue," in A.E.J. Wals (ed.), *Social Learning towards a Sustainable World: Principles, Perspectives and Praxis*. Wageningen: Wageningen Academic Publishers, pp. 297–311.

Marklund, S., Bjurvald, M., Hogstedt, C., Palmer, E., and Theorell, T. (eds) (2005) *Den höga sjukfrånvaron – problem och lösningar* [The high sick leave – problems and solutions]. Stockholm: National Institute for Working Life.

Martens, P. (2006) "Sustainability: Science or fiction?," *Sustainability: Science, Practice & Policy*, 2, 1, 36–41.

Nyhan, B. (2006) "Collective reflection for excellence in work organizations: An ethical 'community of practice' perspective on reflection," in D. Boud, P. Cressey, and P. Docherty (eds), *Productive Reflection at Work*. London: Routledge, pp. 133–145.

Rydh, J. (2002) *En Handlingsplan för Ökad Hälsa i Arbetslivet* [An action plan for improved health in working life]. Stockholm: Ministry of Health and Social Affairs, Swedish Government, SOU, p. 5.

Schön, D.A. (1983) *The Reflective Practitioner: How Professionals Think in Action*. New York: Basic Books.

Schumann, M., Baethge-Kinsky, V., Kuhlmann, M., Kurz, C., and Neumann, U. (1995) "New production concepts and the restructuring of work," in W. Littek and T. Charles (eds), *The New Division of Labor, Emerging Forms of Work Organization in International Perspective*. Berlin: Walter de Gruyter, pp. 95–133.

Shani, A.B. (Rami) and Docherty, P. (2003) *Learning by Design: Building Sustainable Organizations*. Oxford: Blackwell Publications.

Shani, A.B. (Rami), Mohrman, S., Pasmore, W.A., Stymne, B., and Adler, N. (eds) (2008) *Handbook of Collaborative Management Research*. Thousand Oaks, CA: Sage Publications.

Whetten, D.A., Rands, G., and Godfrey, P. (2002) "What are the responsibilities of business to society?," in A. Pettigrew, H. Thomas, and R. Whittington (eds), *Handbook of Strategy and Management*. London: Sage, pp. 373–408.

World Commission on Environment and Development (1987) *Our Common Future* (General Assembly Resolution 42/187). New York: United Nations.

Part I
Focusing value frameworks

2 Organizational visions of sustainability

Keith Cox

There are always flowers for those who want to see them.

Henri Matisse

Introduction

Along with a myriad of stakeholders, activists, and other voices throughout society, Docherty *et al.* (2002) have challenged business leaders to create more sustainable work systems. Indeed, one of the most pressing questions today in corporate boardrooms around the world is, "How can we as business leaders be a force for social change – while running companies that are financially healthy as well?" (Albion 2006: 3).

For many organizations, this bold call to action represents counterintuitive, unrealistic thinking that would require a drastic departure from "business as usual" into the uncharted waters of sustainability. Furthermore, for those progressive organizations and business pioneers considering transforming their current organizations into exemplars of "green," sustainable business, there are still the overriding questions, "What is sustainability? And how does a company take this elusive concept and bring it to fruition in everyday organizational life?"

In a broad sense, sustainability is about "stabilizing the currently disruptive relationship between earth's two most complex systems – human culture and the living world" (Hawken 2007), or, as the Brundtland Report phrased it, ensuring that humanity "meets the needs of the present without compromising the ability of future generations to meet their own needs" (United Nations 1987: 24). More specifically, for the purposes of our discussion in this chapter, sustainability can be seen as an integration of economic prosperity, social responsibility, and environmental stewardship.

Research (Amodeo 2005, Cox 2005) shows that there is no easy, one-size-fits-all sustainability blueprint applicable to all companies. As Quinn and Norton point out, each organization "must develop its own vision, explore opportunities and potential changes within its own operations and markets, and come up with its own action plan" (2004: 5). However, making sense of the multiple worldviews (e.g., rationalism, naturalism, humanism) underpinning the notion of sustainability

(Senge *et al*. 2007) and the existing sustainability creeds, codes, values, and principles (Edwards 2005) in order to develop a coherent, collaborative vision of the future – a conceptualization that clarifies, reinforces, and strengthens commitment to the core business purpose while simultaneously presenting the aspirations, changes, and progress to be attained in an envisioned future – can be a daunting task. It requires the ability to engage whole systems (Holman *et al*. 2007) in dialogue and synergistic relationships in such a way that mental models are surfaced and explored, spurring deep personal growth and development; new knowledge, structures, processes, practices, and stories are collaboratively created and shared; and diverse voices and perspectives are heard, leading to transformed relationships, all capable of bringing about a sustainable society (Robért 2002).

This chapter will address these challenges by introducing a nascent sustainability development framework. This framework explores the dynamic relational and dialogic processes associated with the discovery and corporate self-analysis undertaken in order to identify opportunities and improvements that will continually push the organization to act/operate in a more sustainable manner on multiple, simultaneous levels – to be responsible for their entire "footprint," both social and environmental. This chapter will also examine the implications of these new ideas and practices on the corporate world of work in the twenty-first century.

The research project

This qualitative research project (Cox 2005) examined the dynamic stories of organizational founders striving to bring to life the idea that a for-profit business can be both financially prosperous and a catalyst for global sustainability. The study intensely examined what the leaders and followers in these sustainability-leading organizations were doing and what they were saying as they collectively moved their firms to higher levels of economic prosperity, social responsibility, and environmental stewardship. The researcher's primary goal was to develop a grounded, generative theory (Gergen 1978, Strauss and Corbin 1998) that shed light on the leadership required to achieve such a new and exciting organizational vision.

The participants included in this study (see below) were, and still are, modern-day business pioneers who were "undisputable" in their desire, dedication, and passion for building and leading an organization to financial success while serving as a catalyst for positive change. In addition, a conscious effort was made to try to select a balance of individuals and organizations representing a diverse range of industries, company size, ownership structure, and gender. Each research participant also met a stringent set of criteria before being included in the study.

Data for this research were collected and analyzed over a two-year period. Eighteen in-depth interviews were conducted using traditional unstructured and semistructured interview processes (Rubin and Rubin 1995), combined with appreciative interview protocols consisting of 12 to 15 questions. Overall, these appreciative conversations lasted approximately two hours each, and were instrumental in encouraging deep reflection while giving voice to the individual's strengths, knowledge, wisdom, and visions of the future.

In the first phase of data collection 11 exploratory interviews were conducted with: 1) Ray Anderson, Interface, Inc. (see also Chapter 3); 2) Godric Bader, Scott Bader; 3) Joan Bavaria, Trillium Asset Management; 4) Ron Grzywinski, ShoreBank Corporation; 5) Jeffrey Hollender, Seventh Generation; 6) Mary Houghton, ShoreBank Corporation; 7) Laura Markham, Dragonfly Media; 8) Anita Roddick, The Body Shop; 9) Rory Stear, Freeplay Energy Plc; 10) Hal Tausigg, Idyll, Ltd; and 11) Judy Wicks, White Dog Café. These conversations revolved around the broad conception and practice of leadership at the intersection of business and society, or, in other words, how organizational visions of sustainability originated and were implemented.

The idea of theoretical sampling (Strauss and Corbin 1998) was invoked for the development of the "Round 2" interview guide, which focused the interviewee on the most prominent codes (topics) emerging from the collected and analyzed data. Round 2 interviewees included: 1) Mike Gilliland, Sunflower Markets; 2) Seth Goldman, Honest Tea; 3) Gary Hirshberg, Stoneyfield Farm; 4) Jim Kelly, Rejuvenation; 5) George Siemon, Organic Valley Farms; 6) D. Wayne Silby, Calvert Group, Ltd; and 7) Bob Stiller, Green Mountain Coffee Roasters.

It should also be noted that, when available, a number of secondary data sources (e.g., researcher memos, interviewee speeches, and social responsibility reports/audits) were collected and analyzed to supplement the primary in-depth interviews. All research data was converted to an electronic format for use with QSR's N6 qualitative data analysis software.

The data were analyzed and coded for emergent themes, using grounded theory coding conventions appropriate for exploratory research and theory generation (Strauss and Corbin 1998). Outside coders were employed in a code-checking process that produced an overall reliability rating of 97 percent, well above the 90 percent range that Miles and Huberman (1994) deem acceptable. Throughout this rigorous data analysis process, research memos were written, reread, and rewritten, and diagrams were constructed and redrawn until the properties, dimensions, categories, and subcategories all became clear and a nascent framework had emerged to represent the genesis of organizational visions for sustainability and how they come to fruition.

The findings: toward a collaborative sustainability development framework

The burgeoning Collaborative Sustainability Development Framework is grounded in five core commitments: 1) working from a deep sense of personal purpose; 2) redefining the purpose of business; 3) working with a broad range of stakeholders; 4) engaging in transformational interactions; and 5) embracing emergent organizing.

The first commitment, working from a deep sense of personal purpose, is a values-driven, emotionally intelligent approach to leadership and transformation

Table 2.1 Examples of working from a deep sense of personal purpose

The Body Shop	Seventh Generation
It [embracing sustainability] was the only way I knew how to behave. It was never, never something that was just clothes to wear. If I'm not going to do this in life, why am I going to do it for my business? To me, you've got to live every part of it. (Anita Roddick interview)	Jeffrey Hollender stated, "you need to be committed to the personal growth, the personal work and the personal change that will unquestionably be required of you to succeed in making these kinds of [sustainable] changes at your business." (CSRwire 2004)

that enables individuals to "be the change they want to see in the world" while calling forth commitment and creativity from others. Thus, the genesis for the sustainability journey rises from the values, formative experiences, and core life purpose of the organizational leader(s). It is these initial thoughts and ideas that spark the ongoing conversation and interaction of those inside and outside the organization, which ultimately inform the organizational purpose and subsequently the vision, mission, and strategic direction of the firm. Both Anita Roddick, founder of the cosmetics company The Body Shop, and Jeffrey Hollender, founder of household products company Seventh Generation, provide a visceral description of this first core commitment (see Table 2.1).

In discussing the second core commitment required to bring about increased sustainability, one research participant described the organization's business purpose as its "DNA," that which creates a strong sense of identity for the organization. For those driven to create a sustainable work system, there is a commitment to a different organizational path, an expanded business purpose that transcends shareholder value and regulatory compliance. Viewed as a creative, positive alternative to business as usual, this new business purpose revolves around profitability, and the equally important social goals, collective responsibility, sustainable development, and unwavering ethics that reflect a higher purpose and the moral duty of creating a better world. Again, Roddick and Hollender provide useful examples of this radical shift in conventional thinking (see Table 2.2).

This expanded, reconceptualized business purpose is a critical driver of sustainability. In addition to engaging others and projecting a positive image of business to the rest of the world, it perhaps most notably shapes and influences every aspect of the organization (e.g., values, culture, corporate brand, priorities). Table 2.3 illustrates The Body Shop's and Seventh Generation's organizational vision for sustainability, which grew from this redefined business purpose.

The third commitment made during the pursuit of increased levels of sustainability is proactively working with a broad range of stakeholders. While almost all modern-day organizations pay close attention to their core stakeholders (customers, suppliers, competitors, employees, government regulatory agencies, and shareholders) what is distinctive about the leaders in this study is that they

Table 2.2 Examples of redefining the purpose of business

The Body Shop	Seventh Generation
The New Corporate Responsibility is as complex as changing our basic notions of what motivates us as business people, of what our basic corporate goals should be. This shocks many people; they think it is a radical idea to consider anything other than financial profits. But remember, corporations are invented. They are human institutions, not species found in nature. We, as business leaders, can and must change our views and our values. Less than a century ago . . . depressions and world wars changed us; global poverty and environmental destruction must change us now. (Anita Roddick 1998 speech)	It [sustainability] is about linking our company's financial success with its ability to effect the kind of societal change we want to see. It's our acknowledgement that if we don't make money (in an ethical and responsible way, of course) we won't be in business very long. And if we lose our business, we lose our power to effect change. So this principle is about keeping everyone focused on economics in addition to ecology and continually emphasizing the crucial balance that must be maintained between the two. (Jeffrey Hollender interview)

Table 2.3 Examples of organizational visions for sustainability

The Body Shop	Seventh Generation
Our reason for being is to: • Dedicate our business to the pursuit of social and environmental change. • Creatively balance the financial and human needs of our stakeholders: employees, customers, franchisees, suppliers and shareholders. • Courageously ensure that our business is ecologically sustainable, meeting the needs of the present without compromising the future. • Meaningfully contribute to local, national and international communities in which we trade, by adopting a code of conduct which ensures care, honesty, fairness and respect. • Passionately campaign for the protection of the environment, human and civil rights, and against animal testing within the cosmetics and toiletries industry. • Tirelessly work to narrow the gap between principle and practice, whilst making fun, passion and care part of our daily lives. (The Body Shop 2007)	**Leadership, inspiration, and positive change** A company with the authority to lead, the creativity to inspire, and the will to foster positive social and environmental change. **Make the world a better place** A community in which individuals possess the resources, knowledge, courage, and commitment to make the world a better place. **Sustainability, justice, and compassion** A society whose guiding principles include: environmental sustainability, social justice, and compassion for all living creatures. **An earth restored** An earth that is restored, protected, and cherished for this generation and those to come. (Seventh Generation 2007)

Table 2.4 Examples of working with a broad range of stakeholders

The Body Shop	Seventh Generation
For us, socially responsible [sustainable] business is also about reaching out to other organizations and corporations. . . . [For example,] we carried out our first full social audit in 1995 and published the independently verified results for everyone to see – warts and all. But this was just the start of the most meaningful ongoing process of social auditing, which essentially is about creating dialogue between the Company and all our stakeholders. In order to put together our social audit, more than 5,000 individuals and organizations with a stake in TBS [The Body Shop] were consulted on issues of importance to them. And we found that quite often they told us exactly what we didn't want to hear. (Anita Roddick 1998 speech)	You know . . . a lot of businesses would say, well, that's wasting a lot of time trying to understand [discuss] the labor issues that are involved with one of your customers. No, that's what we have to do because that's the kind of business we want to be. Ultimately, as this circle widens you have to take these values into mind when you think about everybody you do business with. And again, it's not just buying the right product that meets the right health and environmental specifications; it's who's making them. What do you expect of them? (Jeffrey Hollender interview)

have extended their defined stakeholders to include groups and individuals that most companies either ignore or are not aware of, or what Hart and Sharma (2004) refer to as "fringe" stakeholders (e.g., local and global communities, NGOs, non-profit organizations, indigenous peoples). For example, Roddick and Hollender's comments (see Table 2.4) demonstrate an understanding of the importance of the role of stakeholder connections and relationships in cocreating, and ultimately achieving, the defined sustainability vision.

Engaging in transformational interactions is the fourth commitment on the path to sustainability. Transformational interactions are openly accessible practices grounded in relational and dialogic processes that are ubiquitous in the organization. The majority of the research participants talked about six vital categories of transformational interactions at the heart of creating and moving toward a sustainability vision: 1) dialogic competence – building a communication-rich, open environment, which is critical for information flow and dissemination; 2) raising the bar – experimenting, risk taking, and challenging the organization at every turn; 3) dynamic stakeholder engagement – initiating and facilitating a multitude of ongoing synergistic stakeholder connections (e.g., reaching out to educate customers); 4) building leadership capacity – a community of dedicated leaders, change agents, and activists all focused on achieving the sustainability vision; 5) modelling leadership; and 6) appreciative recognition – recognizing accomplishments and seeing the best in individuals and the situation at hand. While there numerous examples of each type of transformational interaction, the examples that follow (see Table 2.5) give a sense of the kind of collaborative

Table 2.5 Examples of engaging in transformational interactions

The Body Shop	Seventh Generation
Get out of the bloody office. Get out of the office and move. And move towards people, organizations, or to suppliers, and get an understanding of it. [It's] just the best thing I ever did, was get out of the office and I moved, and I've moved toward people that have a better vision than I have. (Anita Roddick interview)	I want an office where the real world, with all its joys and sorrows, doesn't get locked out from 9–5. I don't want any part of a company that thinks it's more important than the lives of the people it's composed of. And I want work to be more like play. I want it to be more like life and life, while there, to be less like work. In my experience, this is often the hardest part of the whole equation because there are so few roadmaps to follow. The only way to know if you're on the right path is to listen to your own heart and make sure that everyone at all levels of the company feels free to let you know whenever they think you're not. (Hollender 2002)

dialogue and relationships that are paramount to identifying new ways forward and accelerating progress toward the sustainability vision.

This belief in and need for interaction is imperative and intimately intertwined with the fifth and final commitment driving the Collaborative Sustainability Development Framework, the need to embrace emergent organizing. The majority of leaders in this study described their organizations as dynamic human systems, largely unpredictable environments, where tension, paradox, and chaos are accepted as the norm and where strategic outcomes can emerge as the result of ongoing actions and conversations that are happening at all levels, inside and outside the organization. Thus, in order to survive and excel, the capacity for self-organization, or, in other the words, the frequent coming together of individuals in unplanned ways to make things happen, is a necessity (see also Chapters 15 and 16 in this volume). It is understood that there are no "ten easy steps" to becoming a sustainable organization.

As a result, intuition is valued and tapped; the modus operandi is "think fast;" and experimentation and calculated risk taking are the norm. The final two examples from Roddick and Hollender (see Table 2.6) highlight the chaotic nature of blazing a trail through the ever-growing, shifting, and developing sustainability movement.

Reaching systemic sustainability

These five core commitments of the Collaborative Sustainability Development Framework, especially when interpreted through a chaos and complexity theory literature (Stacey 2001, Wheatley 2005), highlight the relational and dialogic processes leaders undertake to tap into the strengths and wisdom of the entire system. By doing so, they enable the collective cocreation of a more sustainable

Table 2.6 Examples of embracing emergent organizing

The Body Shop	Seventh Generation
We made our first steps to trade with communities in need in the late 1980s. We knew we were entering uncharted territory for a high street retailer. It's hard to believe, but ten years on, we're trading with over 25 communities in Africa, Asia, the Americas and Europe. There are no signposts when tackling community trade, we led the way, and so we encountered the incredible problems that come with this, like dealing with indigenous cultures. (Anita Roddick 1998 speech)	The link between our values and our behaviors is manifested mostly in small, day-to-day deliberations that you can't really see until the big picture, created by the culmination of individual deliberations, begins to emerge. (Hollender 2004b) On the whole, it's [sustainability] a messy process, and in many ways it's a relatively new one at that. It's also one plagued by poorly defined boundaries. . . . I think it's hugely important for everyone to remember that it's okay to make mistakes during the journey as long as we admit it honestly, openly, and with the best intentions. (Hollender 2004a)

work system that produces remarkable results at all levels, from financial success to the real goal: changing the world.

In the next section of this chapter, the focus shifts to relevance of the Collaborative Sustainability Development Framework for organizations struggling to develop and achieve a sustainability vision. Implications for practice management, personnel development, policy creation, and positive outcomes associated with the quest for sustainability will also be discussed.

Implications and practical next steps

The sustainability-seeking organization shows marked contrast with traditional organizations, which tend to be focused on more linear, planned change initiatives. The patterns and outcomes in the dynamic environment of the sustainability-seeking organization are largely unpredictable. Outcomes can range from new individual mental models to improved organizational structures, systems, processes, and business practices. Specific types of outcomes are highly contextual and the result of a number of individual and organizational variables. Yet even though no two organizations will have identical outcomes, most firms in this study did rely on traditional business levers such as compensation schemes, reporting relationships, and the like to enable transformation (see also Chapters 4 and 6 in this volume). However, the caveat typically stated was that there was a constant, conscious effort to look for novel ways to design those structures, systems, processes, and business practices so that they aligned with the sustainability-focused purpose, vision, principles, and values of the organization.

Any progress toward the sustainability vision, whether in the form of designing new corporate policies, sustainability programmes, or measurements and reports, stems from a reliance on new ways of thinking and acting. These may seem very foreign to organizations steeped in the mechanistic, analytic world of industrial-revolution thinking.

So what are the practical steps? How are leaders and organizations supposed to proceed? What is it they actually should do?

While there is no definitive step-by-step approach that this author can offer, what the research shows is that moving toward sustainability entails a time of energy, activity, intense questioning, soul-searching, and emergence, as countless generative, transformative interactions and conversations occur simultaneously inside and outside the organization while daily organizational life unfolds. As Wheatley and Frieze described it, the emergence of social innovations requires an emphasis on relationships, networks, communities of practice, and systems of influence (see also Chapters 11 and 12 in this volume).

> Rather than worry about critical mass, our work [to change the world] is to foster critical connections. We don't need to convince large numbers of people to change; instead, we need to connect with kindred spirits. Through these relationships, we will develop the new knowledge, practices, courage, and commitment that lead to broad-based change.
>
> (Wheatley and Frieze 2007: 1)

The Collaborative Sustainability Development Framework that has risen from this research helps one to better understand the leadership and transformation processes that Wheatley and Frieze are referring to – the ability to connect individuals, groups, and communities to a vision of what's possible – and then drive to economic prosperity, social responsibility, and environmental stewardship in the for-profit world. And even though this framework itself is not prescriptive, one can glean pragmatic guidelines for action regarding how individuals engage, relate, converse, reflect, self-organize, and become more self-aware; all critical dimensions of the five core commitments previously discussed.

Facilitating engagement

Success in moving to a more sustainable organization is considerably dependent on the coordination, cooperation, and combined thinking and dialogue of numerous stakeholders (see also chapters 9 and 11). Fortunately there are a bevy of rhetorical and relational practices that can be used to engage diverse stakeholders, including: large group meetings, facilitated discussions, informal dialogue, educational outreach, and storytelling, among others. When focusing on the quality of engagement, the key points to remember are to involve the system, give all stakeholders equal voice, maximize diversity, and connect with each other around meaningful issues.

Building relationships

Actions geared to increasing inclusion, participation, role clarity, and bringing a broad spectrum of voices together accelerate the building of shared meaning and strong bonds. To understand and strengthen the relationships that support and fundamentally drive the sustainability vision, it is important proactively to explore a wide range of individual, interpersonal, and organizational subjects (e.g., aspirations, accountability, morality, and power). Paying close attention to, and learning from, how organizational members and stakeholders relate opens the door for the creativity and innovation required to rethink, redesign, and restructure the organization (see also Chapters 7 and 16 in this volume).

Promoting conversation and dialogue

In order to improve the energy flowing throughout the conversational life of the organization, individuals should try to focus on facilitating a variety of ways of conversing (e.g., constant questioning) in order to keep participants engaged and enthusiastic. It is also important to be cognizant of the emergent themes that may be surfacing while looking for any barriers (e.g., physical structures) that might limit or block spontaneous, free-flowing communication and interaction. Finally, through constant attention to the conversational and political dynamics, for example identifying voices that are "silenced" by the current processes of conversing and relating, an individual can help modify nonproductive conversations, improve the nature of stakeholder interactions, and promote the diversity that keeps people in rich, deep dialogue.

Purposeful reflecting

In order to cope with the trials and tribulations in the midst of such complexity and continuous change, individuals need to find a way of making sense of their experience and begin to develop their own responses to it. Therefore, to make progress requires iterations of action and reflection. Individuals can monitor their own growth and development; collectively, it is important for the group to understand "who we are" and "what we are about" by examining its interactions, conversations, relationships, and outcomes (see also Chapter 7 in this volume). As a result, the exchange of ideas about organizational life and the sustainability journey can provide new perspectives that can lead to different thinking and action.

Nurturing self-organization

Living, being, and working in a sustainable organization require a shift to experimentation, trial and error, risk taking, learning from failure, developing creative alternatives, focusing on the "here and now," and a devotion to transparency, which ensures that information circulates freely. In addition, individuals need to put themselves in a state of ongoing inquiry in order to keep their fingers on the racing pulse of the self-organizing system. When we see that control is an illusion, that the little things count, and that every conversation matters, we are better able to see the myriad possibilities at hand, many of which will unfold through the ongoing conversations and interactions of organizational life. We open ourselves to the many paths toward equifinality that can serve our sustainability journey well.

Cultivating individual mindfulness

In terms of realizing the sustainability vision, paying attention to the quality of one's own experience may be one of the most important individual practices there is, because it can lead to a more sensitive, heightened consciousness, inner strength, self-knowledge, integration, wholeness, and an impassioned life. Consequently, by using any of numerous techniques (e.g., journaling, meditation, being in nature, etc.) one must reassess one's values, beliefs, and assumptions very frequently. It is particularly valuable to be aware of one's own thoughts, emotions, and feelings during times of excitement and stress.

Conclusion: understanding lessons of the collaborative sustainability development framework

In terms of developing and realizing an organizational vision of sustainability, it is clear that there are no "silver bullets" or quick fixes. Building a paragon of sustainable business in the twenty-first century through exploration and self-organization requires a long-term perspective, tremendous self-awareness (individually and organizationally), learning to surf the edge of chaos, and the inclusion and support of many. The Collaborative Sustainability Development Framework provides individuals and organizations with a schema to refocus their attention in both individual and organizational life. This fresh perspective provides the opportunity to think and subsequently act differently, which can further lead to novel changes in others' conversations and relationships. In the end, and perhaps most importantly, this framework helps one make sense of how a journey down the road to sustainability can unfold in the business world, something only a handful of others have addressed.

Questions for reflection

Here are three questions for your further reflection on the issues broached in this chapter:

- What is your personal passion and calling? How does it relate to your organization becoming a sustainable work system?
- How do you define key concepts such as sustainability and the purpose of business?

- What do you believe about leadership, control, predictability, managing change, and the like? How does this impact individual and organizational actions today and in the future?

References

Albion, M. (2006) *True to yourself: Leading a values-based business*, San Francisco: Berrett-Koehler.

Amodeo, R.A. (2005) "Becoming sustainable at Interface: A study of identity dynamics within transformational culture change," unpublished thesis, Benedictine University.

Body Shop (2007) *What We Believe*. Online. Available HTTP: <http://www.thebodyshop.com.au/infopage.cfm?pageID=53> (accessed 30 May 2007).

Cox, C.K. (2005) "Organic leadership: The co-creation of good business, global prosperity and a greener future," unpublished thesis, Benedictine University.

CSRwire (2004) "A question and answer session with Jeffrey Hollender about *What Matters Most*." Online. Available HTTP: <http://www.csrwire.com/article.cgi/2463.html> (accessed 3 February 2004).

Docherty, P., Forslin, J., and Shani, A.B. (Rami) (2002) "Sustainable work systems: Lessons and challenges," in P. Docherty, J. Forslin, and A.B. (Rami) Shani (eds), *Creating sustainable work systems: Emerging perspectives and practice*, London: Routledge, pp. 213–225.

Edwards, A.R. (2005) *The sustainability revolution: Portrait of a paradigm shift*, Gabriola Island, BC. New Society Publishers.

Gergen, K.J. (1978) "Toward generative theory," *Journal of Personality and Social Psychology*, 36, 1344–1360.

Hart, S.H. and Sharma, S. (2004) "Engaging fringe stakeholders for competitive imagination," *Academy of Management Executive*, 18, 7–17.

Hawken, P. (2007) *Blessed unrest: How the largest movement in the world came into being and why no one saw it coming*, New York: Viking-Penguin Publishing.

Hollender, J. (2002) *The non-toxic times newsletter*, 3, 11. Online. Available HTTP: <http://www.seventhgeneration.com/site/pp.asp?c=coIHKTMHF&b=84563> (accessed 13 January 2005).

Hollender, J. (2004a) *The non-toxic times newsletter*, 6, 1. Online. Available HTTP: <http://www.seventhgeneration.com/page.asp?id=1442> (accessed 13 January 2005).

Hollender, J. (2004b) *The non-toxic times newsletter*, 5, 4. Online. Available HTTP: <http://www.seventhgeneration.com/site/pp.asp?c=coIHKTMHF&b=84866> (accessed 12 February 2005).

Holman, P., Devane, T., and Cady, S.H. (2007) *The change handbook: The definitive resource on today's best methods for engaging whole systems*, San Francisco: Berrett-Koehler.

Miles, M.B. and Huberman, A.M. (1994) *Qualitative data analysis: An expanded sourcebook*, Thousand Oaks, CA: Sage Publications.

Quinn, L. and Norton, J. (2004) "Beyond the bottom line: Practicing leadership for sustainability," *Leadership in Action*, 24, 3.

Robért, K.-H. (2002) *The Natural Step story: Seeding a quiet revolution*, Gabriola Island, BC: New Society Publishers.

Rubin, H.J. and Rubin, I.J. (1995) *Qualitative interviewing: The art of hearing data*, Thousand Oaks, CA: Sage Publications.

Senge, P.M., Lichtenstein, B.B., Kaeufer, K., Bradbury, H., and Carroll, J. S. (2007) "Collaborating for systemic change," *MIT Sloan Management Review*, 48: 44.

Seventh Generation (2007) *About us: Operating principles*. Online. Available HTTP: <http://www.seventhgeneration.com/about_us/operating.php> (accessed 30 May 2007).

Stacey, R.D. (2001) *Complex responsive processes in organizations: Learning and knowledge creation*, London: Routledge.

Strauss, A.L. and Corbin, J. (1998) *Basics of qualitative research: Techniques and procedures for developing grounded theory*, Thousand Oaks, CA: Sage Publications.

United Nations (1987) *Report of the World Commission on Environment and Development: Our common future (No. General Assembly Resolution 42/187)*, New York: Brundtland Commission.

Wheatley, M. and Frieze, D. (2007) "Using emergence to take social innovations to scale," *Fieldnotes* (The Shambala Institute for Authentic Leadership), Winter: 5.

Wheatley, M.J. (2005) *Finding our way: Leadership for an uncertain time*, San Francisco: Berrett-Koehler.

3 The Interface journey to sustainability

Identity dynamics within cultural incrementalism

Mona A. Amodeo

Introduction

Many people around the globe enjoy a higher standard of living today because of the countless goods and services made available though the technological advances of the past century. However, in spite of the positive aspects of these advances, it has become painfully clear that this prolific and successful industrial system has brought unintended yet undeniable ecological degradation to the planet. Increasingly, corporations are being called upon to take responsibility for this collateral damage, ranging from global warming and ozone depletion to issues of social justice. The problems are so large and so complex that many believe the minds and the money behind the industrial complex that created many of the problems are best equipped to find the solutions (see also Chapter 12 in this volume). The premise is simple: "Corporations, because they are the dominant institution on the planet, must squarely address the social and environmental problems that afflict humankind" (Hawken 1993: xiiii).

The chorus for change continues to grow. People are looking to corporations to expand their definitions of value creation beyond-single-bottom-line measurements of profitability. The new business imperative is profitability within the bigger context of environmental and social responsibility. The challenge is to create products and services that serve the marketplace today, while ensuring that production does not negatively impact future generations. As this call to action increases in volume and intensity, business leaders are searching for ways to respond. These are big issues that will not be resolved by doing business as usual. Innovations driven by shifting paradigms about the purpose and responsibility of business are required. New ways of seeing, believing, and doing must emerge.

Today, sustainability-related issues capture headlines daily; however, questions about the role and responsibility of business and its relationship to the environment are not new. Over the past several decades, numerous authors have challenged the single-bottom-line measure of business success (profit at all costs) from both philosophical and practical perspectives (Makower 1994; Elkington 1997; Zadek 2001; Hawken, Lovins, and Lovins 1999; Hawken 1993). These thought leaders, together with others searching for answers, often point to pioneering companies such as The Body Shop, Tom's of Maine and Patagonia as sustainable business model exemplars (see also Chapter 2 in this volume). These companies are outstanding representatives of organizations with a deep commitment to the value of sustainability. However, because these companies were born with sustainability as an integral part of their culture, they tell us very little about how companies can incorporate this value into their culture.

This case study addresses this question by providing insight into one company's journey from being a self-proclaimed "plunderer of the earth" to becoming an internationally recognized leader in industrial sustainability. Interface Inc. (NASDAQ: IFSIA) is headquartered in Atlanta, Georgia. It is a global manufacturing company with locations on four continents. This analysis examines a ten-year period of deep change during which the value of sustainability became a central and defining factor in every decision made by the organization. This metamorphosis transformed the organization as it redefined itself in radically new ways. In the process, the company questioned many long-held assumptions about its purpose and its responsibility to the larger world. The Interface story is an example of change that reaches deep into the organizational values and assumptions (culture) and illustrates substantive changes in the organizational responses to the identity question, "who are we?" From the academic perspective, this case offered a rich opportunity to study the relationship between identity change and culture change. From a more practical perspective, the findings offer inspiration and instruction for leaders looking to respond to the new challenges facing business today by engaging organizational members in embracing the value of sustainability. While prescriptive, cookie-cutter change recipes seldom, if ever, prove successful, it is valuable for leaders to have a conceptual roadmap when embarking on a new journey (see also Chapter 2). The hope is that the Interface story will provide that guidance and inspiration for those who decide to travel the road to sustainability.

The Interface case

Background

In 1994, Interface was an internationally recognized carpet manufacturer – an industry leader. Its founder, Ray Anderson, was considered an innovator and an exemplar of entrepreneurial moxie. In 1973 Anderson had invested his life savings and wagered his future on a rather radical idea for the time. While working for another carpet manufacturer, he was introduced to a popular European product – carpet tiles. He believed so surely there was potential for the product in the United States that he decided to leave his secure employment to take an entrepreneurial leap. He and three business partners joined forces. With financial backing of friends, together with both financial and technical backing from a UK carpet manufacturer, the group struck out on their own. Interface was born.

By 1994, Anderson had bootstrapped his once-fledgling company to success. Overcoming economic and personal challenges, Anderson and Interface became, as he puts it, "successful beyond anyone's dreams." For most founders, this type of success would have been the defining lifetime achievement. And, until early in 1994, this self-described Bentley-driving, Georgia-Tech-educated testament to capitalism certainly thought it would be for him. However, a question, a book, and a speech changed the course of Ray Anderson's life and redefined the destiny of his company.

The inquiry approach

Grounded theory (Strauss and Corbin 1998) and learning history (Roth and Kleiner 1998; Mirvis *et al.* 2003) provided methodological guidance for this case study. Because this also appeared to be a very compelling story, a decision was made to incorporate the researcher's past experiences as a documentary film producer into the research methods. Each of 12 storytelling sessions held at Interface included only people who were employed at Interface during the ten years defined as the period of change (1994–2004). The sessions included a cross-section of people. Because of time and limited resources, the storytelling sessions focused on corporate employees and employees of Interface Flooring, the largest of the Interface divisions. Each session was videotaped, transcribed, and coded for emergent themes and concepts. This data was triangulated with secondary data sources, as well as formal and informal conversations with various internal and external stakeholders. In hopes of providing a less academic and perhaps more accessible version of the formal written research findings, a video documentary was produced, reflecting the research findings told in the words and emotions of those who were a part of this journey.

Findings

Foundational to the understanding the Interface change process is the acknowledgement of sustainability as an *organizational value* (see also Chapter 2 in this volume). When organizational members embrace sustainability as a foundational value, it defines and directs all decisions and behaviours (see also Chapter 11). Like other values, such as honesty or integrity, it is definitional. While simple first-order changes, such as recycling or carbon offsets, are important first steps on the journey to becoming sustainable, the real potential lies in an organization's willingness to grapple with questions about the purpose and responsibility of business. The Interface journey is a story of both the head and heart, involving both human and technical change.

   When organizational members fully embrace sustainability, they begin to see the world through a different lens. As a result, new questions arise, new answers emerge, and innovations are born. These innovations can translate into bottom-line potential through the development of new products and services that respond to what is referred to as the triple bottom line. This means that products and services meet three criteria: good for people; good for the environment; and will make money. Increasingly, the marketplace is looking to do business with companies that take this perspective. Consequently, an authentic commitment to sustainability offers the potential for increased marketplace differentiation and value while building good will, all of which can translate to real bottom-line advantages. This was the case at Interface. However, this does not happen by merely doing more of the same a little differently.

The Interface process can be described as a simultaneous, integrated process of identity change and culture change, defined in theoretical terms *as identity dynamics within cultural incrementalism.* Viewing the data through these two theoretical lenses helped us make sense of what happened at Interface and produced practical answers to how a new value such as sustainability can be introduced, embraced, and ultimately embedded into an organizational culture.

Theoretical framing

It has been postulated that deep culture change occurs when new values and beliefs are incorporated into the core assumptions of the organizational culture (Schein 1985). Cultural incrementalism as defined by Gagliardi (1986) speaks to the connection between culture change and incorporation of new values into the organization; however, he does not address the process whereby the new values are incorporated. Connecting Gagliardi's work with the theory of identity dynamics (Hatch and Schultz 2002) within the context of the Interface story offers insight into this unanswered question.

Hatch and Schulz propose a theoretical connection between the domains of identity, culture, and image, postulating that interactions between these domains account for both stability and change in organizational identity. Identity has also been conceptualized as providing essential linkages between observable manifestations of culture and its underlying meanings (Fiol *et al.* 1998). The findings of this study connect these theories by providing empirical support for the linkage between identity change and culture change within the context of one company's process of becoming sustainable. Establishing this connection responds to the question left unanswered by Gagliardi and provides leaders with a practical framework for introducing and embedding the value of sustainability as an integral part of an organization's culture.

Cultural incrementalism

Gagliardi's (1986) model of cultural incrementalism defines a four-phase framework outlining the stages of embedding organizational values into organizational culture. These phases show values moving from passive acceptance by the organization to a point where the values automatically orient the behaviour of the organization.

According to Gagliardi the first phase is driven by the vision of the leader. Organizational members may not share the entrepreneur's ideas, but because of the power position of the leader he is able to orient the behaviour of organizational members in the desired direction. The second phase of integrating the new values into the culture is driven by the success of the new value in creating the desired effect. This means success defines the new values as a reference criterion for action. As the values move into the third phase of integration, the organization has seen evidence of the validity of its belief and concentrates on identifying itself with the "cause". The value becomes something important in and of itself, rather than a means to an end. At this point, the organization is willing to fight for what it believes. In the fourth and final phase, the value automatically orients behaviour. At this point, the new values become a cultural assumption.

Viewing the stages of cultural incrementalism defined by Gagliardi in conjunction with identity dynamics provides greater insight into specific factors that facilitate movement through these phases.

Identity dynamics

Organizational identity is defined as the collective response to the question "who are we?" Identity dynamics offers theoretical insight into stability and change in identity. Through this lens, identity is a verb rather than a noun. It is an active process of expressing, reflecting, impressing, and mirroring. Through this process, the organization's answer to the question "who are we?" is constantly affecting and being affected by both internal and external audiences.

Identity dynamics facilitates sense making. As organizational members *express* cultural understanding through verbal and nonverbal behaviours, these behaviours leave *impressions* on others, and in turn, these impressions are *mirrored* back to the organization. The mirrored impressions are *reflected* upon and serve to reinforce and further embed this collective response to "who are we?" into the culture. Over time, this ongoing process serves to inform, direct, or adjust future behaviour. Values expressed through behaviours eventually become deeply engrained as taken-for-granted cultural assumptions about "how we do things."

Identity dynamics within cultural incrementalism at Interface

Viewing the Interface change process from a perspective of identity dynamics indicates that Interface was gradually able to close the vision–identity gap by creating new behaviours consistent with the value of sustainability as defined by the identity statement, "the first name in industrial sustainability – in deeds, not just words." Identity dynamics facilitated cultural incrementalism at Interface. These processes not only worked to create new answers to the question "who are we?" but simultaneously functioned as an active force in creating acceptance of the new value of sustainability. When Anderson first introduced his sustainability vision of who Interface would become, organizational members reluctantly experimented with new behaviours associated with the expanded organizational identity (expressing). As they began to experience small successes and reinforcement from the marketplace (mirroring), understanding and belief and eventually commitment to the value of sustainability replaced scepticism. The value of sustainability incrementally became a part of the cultural assumptions of the organization (reflecting). Key levers through each of the five stages of change propelled Interface forward. While the model presents a linear depiction of the change process, in reality it is more accurately visualized as hermeneutic spiral. Each evolution of understanding was built upon and informed by the preceding. With each new interpretation and new levels of understanding and acceptance, the process incrementally inched forward.

Discussion

The Interface change model

Vision–identity gap

The vision–identity gap defines the tension that initially drove the change process. This tension was created between Anderson's vision of Interface as a sustainable enterprise and the existing self-perceptions of organizational members about who they were. Organizations, like people, must find alignment between values and behaviours. This new vision represented a value that challenged the people of Interface. In order to relieve the dissonance, they began to experiment with new behaviours consistent with the underlying value of sustainability. Over the next several years, they worked to resolve this gap between the current identity and Anderson vision of what they would become. As a long-time Interface employee shared,

> At first there was a lot of talk that maybe Ray had gone "round the bend." We really just hoped it would go away, but after a while we realized Ray was serious and we just had to figure this out.

In 1994 during this first phase, defined in the model as Awakening, scepticism and high levels of resistance were present in the organization. Many of the employees questioned, why? Although Anderson was a revered leader, his vision of sustainability offered alien perspectives of the purpose of business. Anderson's unrelenting commitment to his vision and the organization's respect for him were important elements during this period.

The five-stage change process that follows depicts Interface closing the vision–identity gap by experimenting with behaviours and language that are consistent with the value of sustainability (see also Chapters 2, 7, 9, 11, 12, and 16 in this volume). Much like the chicken-and-egg dilemma, this is not a question of identity change versus culture change. Rather, it is a case of incremental, reciprocal, simultaneous change in both identity and cultural values. Identity dynamics defined the process that gradually moved the organization from scepticism about sustainability to intense commitment to the value. For some in the organization, it has taken on the characteristics of a cause. Anderson's definition of "who we are" and the way the organization defines itself have become one. Today, most at Interface would say: "We *are* the first name in industrial sustainability – in

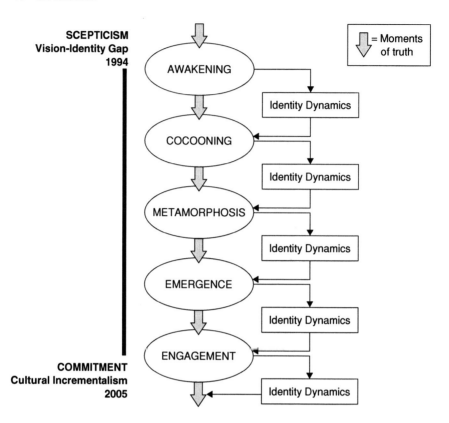

Figure 3.1 Identity dynamics within transformational culture change at Interface Inc.

deeds, not just words." This process has produced an organization that embodies the value of sustainability and a company whose behaviours are defined by that value. Today, Interface and sustainability are one.

Awakening

In the summer of 1994, a small group of customers asked some Interface sales people about Interface's environmental policy. When it become apparent that there were no real answers beyond compliance, frustration arose among some inside the company and a task force was formed to find better answers. As part of their work, the task force invited company founder Ray Anderson to give a speech about his views regarding Interface's environmental policy. This request led him first to frustration, since, as he readily admits, he did not have an environmental vision beyond compliance. However, the urgency he felt to find something meaningful to say in that speech, eventually led him to the threshold of what would become a ten-year journey. In his book, *Midcourse Correction*, Anderson describes the first step in his journey. While Anderson was struggling for what to say in his speech to the task force, someone sent him a copy of Paul Hawken's *Ecology of Commerce* (1993). Reading the book brought him face to face with a troubling conflict between his long-held, traditional view of the purpose and responsibility of business and the antithetical ideas presented by Hawken. The book had a powerful impact on Anderson. "As I closed the book, I wondered, who will do this?" referring to the environmental challenges presented by Hawken. He recalls thinking, "why not us?" This marked the beginning of a personal awakening – a new understanding about the relationship between industry and the environment (see also Chapter 2). A new vision for Interface was born from these revelations. Motivated by what he describes as a "spear in the chest," and a conviction that he was a "plunderer of the Earth," he charted a new direction for his company. On August 31, 1994, during the speech to the task force, Anderson challenged the 21-year-old carpet manufacturing company "to lead the way to the next industrial revolution by becoming the first truly sustainable industrial corporation and, eventually, a restorative enterprise." With this new vision, he launched the company on a new trajectory toward becoming a sustainable enterprise. Since that time, the company has emerged as the pioneer in industrial sustainability and is respected worldwide as a leader in the triple-bottom-line business paradigm. While Interface has made impressive strides toward "becoming sustainable," they are careful to define their journey as a continuous process.

> (This journey) is a momentous shift in how we see the world. How we operate within it, what systems will prevail and which will not. At Interface we are completely reimagining and redesigning everything we do, including the way we define our business. Our vision is to lead the way to the next industrial revolution by becoming the first sustainable corporation, and eventually a restorative enterprise. It is an extraordinarily ambitious endeavor; a mountain to climb that is higher than Everest.
>
> (http://www.interfacesustainability.com)

Cocooning: From scepticism to understanding

"We really had no idea how to get there," Anderson recalls. For the next several years, the company went into what he calls a "figuring-it-out mode." This period between 1994 and 1996 is identified in the change model as a period of Cocooning. This was a time of intense internal reflection, research, and translation. In 1994, there were no models of a manufacturing company doing what Interface was attempting to do. And while the vision was clear, how to get there was not. Beyond the jargon and philosophical pondering, sustainability had to be translated into behaviours meaningful to the people of Interface. Interface searched internally and externally for answers. Seeking the best minds to help them "get their map straight" led to the formation of what become known as the Dream Team. This group of sustainability thought leaders such as Paul Hawken, Amory Lovins, John Picard, Dr. Karl-Henrik Robert, Daniel Quinn, and Bill McDonough provided guidance, inspiration, and motivation during the early years. This group and others like them also provided new social referents – a new yardstick for measuring success and a mirrored image of how they wanted to see themselves.

What emerged from this time was a clear, albeit incomplete, roadmap for what would soon be known as the Interface Climb up the Seven Faces of Mt. Sustainability. Metrics and reporting methods (see also Chapter 10 in this volume) were assigned to measure the progress up each of the seven fronts: waste elimination, benign emissions, renewable energy, closing the loop, resource-efficient transportation, sensitizing stakeholders, and redesigning commerce. These were defined as the areas where the company would commit its energy and resources. The expressed goal was (and continues to be) to reach the summit of Mt. Sustainability by the year 2020. In this period of discovery and translation, the company was able to clearly define what sustainability meant to them and how they would achieve their goals. As one of the manufacturing managers shared,

> We understood what was being said on a high level, but we also knew we needed to help everyone on the floor understand. We weren't sure how to do it, but we found out that little by little we were able to explain Mt. Sustainability. It gave us a way to make everyone understand where we were going.

This use of metaphors, together with clear metrics, rewards and celebration, ongoing exposure to new information, and ongoing education about environmental issues, became foundational to the Interface journey. Together with the allocation of needed resources and Anderson's continued commitment, this moved the organization. Scepticism gradually gave way to understanding as Interface moved into a new phase of its journey to sustainability.

Metamorphosis: From understanding to belief

While scepticism reigned during the early days of the Interface journey, over time incremental successes emerged and the people at Interface gradually embraced this new definition of their purpose. New understandings about the interrelationships between the world, the company, and their actions gradually emerged. As more and more people "got it," new ways of thinking took hold.

> Each time we have a decision to make around here, we have to consider three questions: Is it good for the environment? is it good for people? and will it make us money? We are constantly juggling these three questions. As new processes emerged, and successes generated more success, understanding grew into belief.

This metamorphosis was driven by a growing belief in the values of sustainability. Innovative products born of new perspectives fuelled external validation and marketplace acceptance. The once-foreign values of sustainability were embraced and celebrated. Anderson and Interface seemed to be proving Anderson's theory that this was not only the ethically right approach to business, but also the smart approach. The business world was listening and watching as the business case for sustainability began to unfold. Anderson and Interface garnered international recognition as Interface was heralded on the world stage as the exemplar for industrial sustainability.

Emergence and engagement: From belief to commitment to cause

Between 1999 and 2002, Interface persevered through many trials and tribulations that would have turned a less committed company back. As one executive shared, "There were many times we wondered what we were doing, but we believed that we really had something here and we knew if we could just hold on to what we believed, we would be okay." Through huge market downturns of the Y2K period, emotionally charged leadership changes, and periods of economic challenge, Interface did not waver in their commitment to living the value of sustainability. This period was perhaps the ultimate test of whether the value had taken root in the Interface culture. The organization emerged from this period more committed and more determined than ever to reach the summit of Mt. Sustainability.

The Interface journey has been challenging and inspiring, but most importantly it is proving the business model and proving that sustainable business practice is not only the right thing to do, it is also a smart thing to do. Impressive strides have been made on the climb up the seven faces of Mt. Sustainability – although the people at Interface are the first to say they still have a long way to go, and often talk about this as perhaps the steepest part of the climb. According to data published in the 2006 EcoMetrics™ report available at http://www. interfacesustainability.com, measurable progress on the seven fronts of Mt. Sustainability indicates that the value of sustainability continues to define the organization's behaviour. For example, total waste elimination activities since 1995 have totaled over $336 million. An emphasis on initiatives that improve energy efficiency and conserve energy has reduced the total energy used at carpet manufacturing facilities per unit product, down 45 percent since 1996. On an absolute basis, Interface reduced its greenhouse gas emissions by 37 percent from its baseline, through improved efficiencies and direct renewable energy purchases. Water intake per square meter of carpet is down 80 percent in modular carpet facilities and down 62 percent in broadloom facilities from 1996, due to conservation efforts and process changes. The ReEntry program diverted 103 million pounds of material from landfill between 1995 and 2006. In 2006, 18 million pounds were diverted from landfill and used in recycling (84 percent), energy capture (14 percent), and repurposed applications (2 percent).

Today, the people at Interface feel their work represents something bigger than making carpet. Many times during the conversations, people connected their work with a cause. "Some people may think we make a commodity, something you walk on or wipe your feet on, but every day I come to work, I believe I am here for a higher purpose." Perhaps one of the conversations with a product engineer best sums up the depth of the connection to the values of sustainability:

When I am lying on my death bed, who cares if I made a million yards of carpet? but if I can tell my grandchildren that I, we, were a part of changing the business model, so industry works with the environment, not against it, that will be saying something.

Summary

The new business paradigm of sustainability positions business as an integral part of the ecosystem, yet just one part of the interdependent web. This new way of seeing removes the artificial barriers between the actions of business and the consequences of those actions. Value is redefined within the context of social and environmental responsibility, and profitability is seen as an integrated part of the whole. Simply stated, this is a dramatic shift in the purpose of business, requiring new ways of thinking, and consequently, a different kind of organizational culture. Embracing sustainability as a defining value requires companies to expand the definition of stakeholder value beyond quarterly earnings reports to the consideration of a larger responsibility to future generations but very importantly not at the expense of quarterly earnings. Deep changes are needed for organizations to move in this direction. Interface has demonstrated it is possible to bring about this level of change – synthesising ideas previously thought to be diametrically opposed. Interface is proving the viability of this new business model – doing well by doing good is not only the right thing to do, it is the smart thing to do.

The courage to ask new questions, combined with the freedom, support, and resources needed to explore new answers, and an unwavering commitment from the top were key elements in the Interface success story. The process was incremental and emergent, personal and organizational (see also Chapters 16 and 17 in this volume). Beginning with Anderson's vision, which challenged assumptions, followed by organizational members' willingness to grapple with the question, "what does this mean to us?" incremental action, small successes, and positive reinforcement from the marketplace were all factors of identity dynamics that ultimately moved the organization along a path from initial feelings of scepticism to high levels of commitment to the value of sustainability.

Values and identity are inextricably linked. These finding show identity dynamics (Hatch and Schulz 2002) facilitating cultural incrementalism (Gagliardi 1986) and support the position that one cannot create a truly sustainable organization without addressing issues of identity and cultural values. Further, being satisfied with simple, surface-level changes and failing to challenge traditional assumptions limit the upside potential of what sustainability can produce, as evidenced by Interface. Anderson challenged his organization with a big vision and then gave them room and resources to find answers – and as a result, product innovations emerged. This positioned Interface as innovators and translated directly to positive bottom-line results. As one of the product engineers summarized when asked about Interface innovations, "Had we not been challenged to think differently, we would have never come up with some of the ideas that we have. Ask different questions and you get new answers."

Rachel Carson's book *Silent Spring* (1962) tells us that "the history of life on earth has been a history of interaction between living things and their surroundings" (Carson 1962: 5). This work is considered by many to have been the first call to action regarding the role and responsibility of business to the environment. For many, it served as the stake in the ground that marked the beginning of the public struggle between economic and environmental passions. Even though the book was published in 1962, its message remains relevant today. The drama between humankind and the natural environment continues to unfold on the business stage today, as an increasing number of organizations struggle with the seemingly polar opposites of profitability and responsibility. At this time in our history, there is no more urgent or important quest than for us to effectively grapple with this dilemma. This passion, the recognition of the struggle, and the specific story of one company's journey toward becoming sustainable set the stage, the context, and the purpose for this study.

In the words of Robert Frost and the sentiments echoed by Rachel Carson in *Silent Spring*, the Interface story is of a company that has taken "the road less travelled." I believe the story can be inspirational, and its process instructive, for companies desiring to travel the road to sustainability and for scholars seeking to understand more about the process of identity change and its role in creating transformational organizational change. While each company's journey will be different in content and interpretation, the Interface model provides a framework and a starting point for helping leaders understand key factors and forces that moved Interface along its journey. My hope is that this will be helpful to leaders who want to move beyond surface level change to incorporation of the value of sustainability into the identity and cultural values of their organizations.

Questions for reflection

Here are three questions for your further reflection on the issues broached in this chapter:

- What role did organizational values play in the Interface transformation journey?
- Explore the dynamic relationship between identity and organization culture. Provide an illustration of the relationship from the Interface company case.
- Identify and describe the phases in the transformation process that Interface went through. What were some of the key issues in each phase?

References

Anderson, R.C. (1998) *Mid-course correction*. White River Junction, VT: Chelsea Publishing Company.

Carson, R. (2002) *Silent spring* (40th anniversary edition). New York: Houghton Mifflin Company.

Elkington, J. (1997) *Cannibals with forks: Triple bottom line of 21st century business*. Mankato, MN: Capstone Press.

Fiol, C.M., Hatch, M.J., and Golden-Biddle, K. (1998) "Organizational culture and identity: What's the difference anyway?", in D.A. Whetten and P.C. Godfrey (eds), *Identity in organizations: Developing theory through communications*, Thousand Oaks, CA: Sage, pp. 32–82.

Gagliardi, P. (1986) "The creation of change of organizational cultures: A conceptual framework," *Organizational Studies*, 7, 117–134.

Hatch, M.J., and Schultz, M. (2002) "Dynamics of organizational identity," *Human Relations*, 55, 8, 989–1018.

Hawken, P. (1993) *Ecology of commerce*. New York: Harper Business.

Hawken, P., Lovins, A., and Lovins, L.H. (1999) *Natural capitalism*. Boston, MA: Little, Brown, and Company.

Makower, J. (1994) *Beyond the bottom line*. New York: Simon & Schuster.

Mirvis, P., Ayas, K., and Roth, G. (2003) *To the desert and back*. San Francisco: Jossey-Bass.

Roth, G., and Kleiner, A. (1998) "Developing organizational memory through learning histories," *Organizational Dynamics*, 27, 2, 43–61.

Schein, E. (1985) *Organizational culture and leadership*. San Francisco: Jossey-Bass.

Strauss, A., and Corbin, J. (1998) *Basics of qualitative research* (2nd edn). Thousand Oaks, CA: Sage.

Zadek, S. (2001) *The civil corporation*. London: Earthscan Publications Ltd.

Part II
Focusing work and work systems

4 Sustainability in knowledge-based companies

Peter Brödner

The particularities of knowledge work

Knowledge-based companies are key actors in advanced economies. They can be characterized as sharing knowledge rather than dividing labour. Wealth increasingly depends on the knowledge and competence of human agents: on their creative dealing with knowledge (i.e., on what companies are *able to do*), rather than on the capital employed (i.e., on *what they own*). The way knowledge is created and used in complex interaction processes of dividing and sharing knowledge is becoming the most powerful productive force and is crucial for performance or competitiveness (see also Chapter 6 in this volume).

Explicit or codified knowledge is generated by observation, in processes of reflection and concept formation, and can be expressed in the form of linguistic terms or technical artefacts. Its meaningful application for problem solving, however, always requires, due to its abstract conceptual nature, some implicit practical knowledge, some specific skills or competences that enable experts to adopt and make sense of relevant codified knowledge, to recontextualize and enact it for specific purposes and situations. This implicit, practical, and actionable knowledge itself grows through experience and by appropriating explicit knowledge for effective acting; it is embodied and cannot be expropriated from the knowledgeable actors owning it. Based on this dialectic of partially explicating experience in knowledge and of expanding experience through adopting knowledge, the use of knowledge creates new knowledge, in contrast to material products that wear out in use. "Intellectual capital is not a stock of knowledge, but a capacity to innovate" (Stewart 1997). Knowledge grows, like a tree, through branching, by differentiation, specialization, and segmentation into specific knowledge domains, disciplines, and areas of expertise. Hence, its use for problem solving, as most problems are complex and cross borders of specialization, requires that relevant knowledge from different domains is identified and integrated or synthesized through sharing expertise and collaboration (Brödner *et al.* 1999; Helmstädter 2003; Nonaka and Takeuchi 1995).

These basic characteristics of dealing with knowledge have a number of far-reaching consequences with respect to the work of "knowledge workers" (Drucker 1993) or "symbol analysts" (Reich 1991). First, as knowledge grows through use, innovation – i.e., the successful creation of new products, new processes, or new institutional settings – becomes the dominant form of competition. Hence, companies as well as workers have to permanently cope with new situations, surprise, and uncertainty. Second, this requires continuous problem-solving activities, which in turn call for the implicit embodied sense-making skills of human actors, in particular expert knowledge workers. Hence, in knowledge-based companies human competences are the most important and indispensable resources to be continuously developed in quality and quantity. Third, innovative and problem-solving activities require knowledge sharing and collaboration among experts from different domains. That is why project work in multidisciplinary teams to accomplish a unique and common task is becoming a widespread form of work organization in knowledge-based companies. Fourth, due to the fact that knowledge work is always subject to uncertainty and surprise, the course and outcome of projects is context-dependent and unforeseeable and can, therefore, neither be planned in advance nor governed by command and control. In this sense, knowledge work is "deconfined" (Hatchuel 2002) with respect to course, outcome, and effort, and therefore requires new forms of indirect or contextual control.

Deconfinement of knowledge work proves to be the root of its intensity indicated by long working hours and persistent stress reactions. Due to challenging tasks, wide action scope, and ample opportunity to learn, knowledge workers on the one hand typically are highly motivated to do a good job. They always face, however, due to the context-dependent and unforeseeable course of events, a high risk of lacking resources to accomplish their task, on the other. As compared to Tayloristic forms of work organization, their work appears to be privileged (see Chapter 5), while actually it is likely to be intensive and subject to high risk of excessive demands that may even lead to stress disorders if lasting for a long time. These health risks tend to wear out the human resources on which knowledge-based companies are so dependent. According to the resource-centred perspective presented here, sustainable work is being achieved, in contrast, if necessary resources are maintained or developed rather than consumed (see also Chapters 8 and 15 in this volume). This chapter focuses on personal and social resources in an organizational context that are generative in nature and may grow in use, if appropriate working conditions are provided (Docherty *et al.* 2002). From this perspective, knowledge work frequently turns out in practice not to be socially sustainable.

In fact, the incidence of work-related stress disorders has increased with the total workforce's share of knowledge workers. They are becoming epidemic: In Germany, for instance, cases of early retirement due to work-related stress disorders have over the past 20 years surpassed those due to cardiovascular diseases and reached a level of 14 percent of all cases for men and 32 percent for women (Brödner 2002). A study by the International Labour Organization (ILO) states that 5.9 percent of all sick days in Germany are caused by mental strain and that in the EU the cost of these sickness leaves adds up to 3–4 percent of GDP (Gabriel and Liimatainen 2000). In the UK, stress disorders account for

38 percent of all incapacity benefit recipients, amounting to 12 billion GBP in annual expenses (LSE 2006). These figures indicate that management is not treating knowledge workers with adequate care, contrary to its mantra that the knowledge workforce is its "most important capital."

Although stress disorders such as sleep disturbance, depression, burnout, or drug abuse, indicating intensive and unsustainable work processes, are rapidly spreading among knowledge workers, their work-related causes as well as possible remedies have been insufficiently investigated so far. The present chapter intends to fill this gap. The case-based scrutiny it presents focuses on highly qualified, computer-supported knowledge work in software development and consulting projects in the German software and telecommunication industries. The type of project work investigated can be regarded as a typical manifestation of high-skill knowledge work and thus represents work processes in the vast majority of other knowledge-based companies.

The chapter starts with an outline of the conceptual framework for the resource-based perspective used to explain the causes of specific stress reactions and health risks inherent in highly skilled knowledge work. This theoretical perspective serves as background for the empirical investigation, the data basis, procedure, and selected findings of which are then presented. The chapter concludes with design-oriented considerations including some guidelines for designing more sustainable work systems in knowledge-based companies.

Conceptual framework: a resource-centred perspective

Paramount characteristics of industrial work have been a high degree of horizontal division of labour and the vertical separation of work conception from implementation, thus creating "simple tasks in complex organizations" (Sitter *et al.* 1997) that could be performed on a rather low skill level. Although intended to allow for being performed over long periods of time without health impairment on the basis of scientifically determined harmless work demands, this type of industrial work actually produced a number of other detrimental effects such as health impairments through one-sided repetitive work loads or atrophied skills and demotivation restricting personal development (Brödner and Forslin 2002).

In order to reduce these motivational and health risks, enlarging and enriching work tasks, widening the action scope, and creating more opportunities to learn have been predominant measures of the socio-technical work design perspective striving for better and healthier jobs. This perspective basically assumed that creating complete and meaningful tasks with more discretion over work processes in terms of means, methods, and procedures would enhance variation of work, reduce strain by providing an opportunity to balance the workload, and foster personal development (Emery and Trist 1960; Trist 1981; Ulich 1994). Accordingly, from this perspective, knowledge work – and in particular team-based project work – with its complex tasks and high degree of discretion has long been regarded as privileged, since it scores high in all these dimensions. In contrast to what can be expected from this perspective, however, knowledge work, often appears to be subject to high workload and severe stress reactions (Gerlmaier 2004). This socio-technical design paradox indicates that there must be something wrong with underlying assumptions.

Similarly, the so-called "demand-control model" (Karasek 1998; Karasek and Theorell 1990), widely accepted in stress research, emphasizes the important function of autonomy for fostering the workers' well-being and personal development. According to this model, the strain and stress relationship in work may be influenced by two factors: work demands such as challenging work tasks or time pressure on the one hand and the extent to which work processes can be controlled on the other. Autonomy in this model has a primarily moderating effect on stress reactions: Increased work demands may cause less stress if a working person has control over the working process, i.e., the means, methods, and procedures to achieve the task. Moreover, a high degree of control in connection with high job demands may lead to well-being and personal development insofar as they initiate or foster learning processes.

By further developing the idea of balancing demand and control, Maslach and Leiter (1997) emphasize that stress is caused by a variety of imbalances or "mismatches" between work demands and available resources that, if they persist, may lead to burnout, characterized by physical and emotional exhaustion and reserved indifference. In particular, they pay attention to mismatches between workload and resources, to lack of control, to insufficient rewards, to unfair treatment, to the loss of supporting social relations at work, and to conflicting individual and organizational values. They thus not only focus on workers' needs and resources, but also recognize conditions of the working environment (Maslach and Leiter 1997; cf. Kira 2002, 2003). Their approach is closest to the stress-generation model presented here, although it still lacks sufficient awareness of the relational nature of resources.

The problem with these approaches is that they consider resources, in particular the degree of the worker's control or autonomy, as resources *per se* without paying attention to contextual or situational circumstances. Knowledge work differs, however, in several respects from industrial manual work: It demands complex problem-solving capability operating with mostly unknown solutions that require changing collaboration with other experts and even customers. Hence, it strongly depends on the knowledge worker's individual working capacity. And as deconfined work, it further requires new forms of contextual control. Consequently, an appropriate conceptual approach needs to put a relational perspective on work demands and resources at its centre. Resources can no longer be determined as such, but in relation to the context conditions only, under which workers attempt to make them effective.

The conception of "contradictory work demands" (Moldaschl 2005) is a theoretical perspective based on this relational view of resources that has been adopted for the research presented here. According to this approach, work-related strain is an effect of contradictions or mismatches between actual work requirements, established rules, and available resources. Stress reactions are generated if workers have to cope with contradicting demands, rules, and resources that constrain efforts to achieve their work objectives and lead to negative consequences for health and motivation. Based on this perspective, this study focuses on organizational aspects of knowledge-based project work – i.e., on work design and framing conditions rather than personal traits or individual prerequisites such as qualification.

In this relational view, resources are defined as effective means that can be activated and used by workers for attaining their goals. Whether something can serve as a resource or not depends on context and the framing conditions under which the work is performed. Resources can only be determined in use: some means may be applied as resources to resolve contradictory work demands; the same means may instead turn out to generate stress under different circumstances. As an example, social support can be a resource for achieving a task, if talking with colleagues helps, for instance, to solve a design problem; but this talk may be very disturbing and stressful for the workers involved, if they have to act under time pressure. Similarly, autonomy may be a resource for optimizing work procedures; it will be ineffective, though, if frame conditions do not allow for using it. To take a final example, an IT system may serve as a resource for performing operations more efficiently; it may, however, also be a hindrance, if it lacks task conformity.

Most human resources are generative in nature, i.e., they develop and grow in use due to experience. They comprise, for instance, personal capabilities and competences or social relationships such as trust or commitment. They will, however, be destroyed over time, if opportunities to recover from stress or to further develop competences are restricted. The resource-centred perspective thus is consistent with the concept of "sustainable work systems" (Docherty *et al.* 2002), according to which these systems generate and regenerate at least as much resources as they consume, while "intensive work systems" reduce or erode the resources in use (Kira 2003; Moldaschl 2005).

In a more operational view, mental strain is indicated by the additional work and self-regulation needed to cope with mismatches between demands and resources, by extensive time pressure, and by work interruptions that further contribute to the time pressure experienced. When adopting the concept of "contradictory work demands" for this investigation in a heuristic model of strain generation, stress reactions are assumed to emerge if the knowledge workers can neither resolve nor compensate or "buffer" contradictions or mismatches they are exposed to (e.g., by mobilizing social support). Negotiating about constraining factors with management or with the customer (e.g., with respect to delivery dates or additional product functions) can be another way of coping in order to resolve such contradictions. If the knowledge workers' activities are restricted in a way that none of these solutions is possible, stress reactions are likely (Gerlmaier 2006; Latniak and Gerlmaier 2005; see Figure 4.1).

The model distinguishes five different types of mismatches or contradictions (marked with flashes in Figure 4.1) that can lead to mental strain in circumstances where there is no chance to negotiate work constraints and conditions or

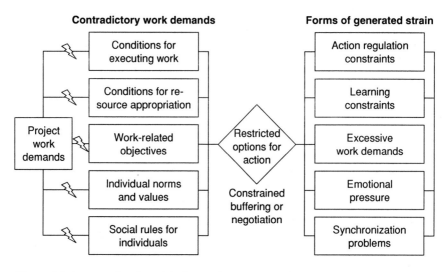

Contradictory work demands   **Forms of generated strain**

Figure 4.1 An operational model of mental stress generation

to generate time or capacity buffers. Examples below are taken from the cases investigated.

(1) Contradictions between tasks and work execution conditions: These are action regulation constraints due to inadequate tools that require additional effort (e.g., a software development framework that is unable to generate software functions as intended, or a server computer at a customer site that is not available as needed for testing).

(2) Mismatches between tasks and learning conditions: These hinder the ability of workers to appropriate necessary knowledge or technical artefacts (e.g., insufficient experience of a customer's IT system environment in which software is applied, so that workers do not exactly know how it is used).

(3) Contradictory project objectives: These put workers in double-bind conflicts between inconsistent but equally important expectations – for instance, to obey company rules by keeping the budget and timeframe while being "loyal" to the customer by meeting his demands (e.g., the obligation to fulfil additional software functionality for a customer while, at the same time, core functionality has to be finished within existing time and budget constraints).

(4) Contradictions between work-related and individual objectives or values: These put workers in conflict between project objectives and professional behaviour or standards (this happens, for example, if, due to time pressure, the documentation of the software source code is neglected in order to keep the milestones and delivery time for the software).

(5) Contradictions between work demands and rules or needs of the social context: These put workers in conflict between meeting project objectives and

maintaining social relationships (e.g., in the final stage of a software development project, workers may have difficulty integrating family roles with work demands that lead to extended working hours).

The model is based on a dynamic understanding of strain generation and specifically allows the analysis of main impacts and rules of the work situation and context, on the one hand, together with internal values and goals of the employees (e.g., values of professional behaviour) on the other. While contradictory work demands can be clearly identified, the forms of strain generation (indicated on the right-hand side of Figure 4.1) normally result in combination, and cannot be separated. Moreover, the model emphasizes an active role for employees in resolving strain and stressful situations. By finding a "workaround" for emerging problems, by mobilizing social support or other substantial resources, employees can take an active part in changing the mismatch situation. This is even more important, as coping with difficulties is a specific kind of success experience that provides motivation, self-esteem, and "fun" at work (see also Chapter 8 in this volume).

Finally, the model provides categories to classify strain and stressful situations such that causes are precisely described and starting points for work design become visible. By reducing work constraints, work can, as a guiding principle, simultaneously be made more efficient and more healthy or sustainable for the workers. The range of possible remedies covered by the model stretches from individual competences and values (training), to organizational measures and rules (strategic agreements, process definitions), up to the work environment at large (working-time regulations).

Empirical investigation: methodology and major findings

Data and methodology

Due to the novelty of the underlying conceptual model, the study was designed as an explorative, longitudinal investigation based on in-depth case studies of seven software development and IT consulting project teams (N = 34 employees) in four different German companies. The intention was to observe each project team from the beginning to the end in order to capture the dynamics of knowledge-based project work and identify the impact of contradictory demands and mismatches at work. In one case the customer cancelled the project before completion.

The IT projects ranged from consulting and implementation of standardized IT products up to custom software development and programming. Five projects were located in large IT service companies with more than 3,000 employees; two projects were done in a small multimedia startup company. Projects T1 and T2 were subprojects within large composite projects for the telecom industry providing integration tests for customers: respectively, the development and implementation of a software application for coordinating customer-related data on different servers. Projects E1 and E2 were located in an IT service company primarily offering outsourcing services. Both teams closely cooperated with their customers in public administration, for whom they developed software applications. Ti1 and Ti2 were projects in a small "new economy" startup with 14 employees focusing on the development and hosting of interactive web design applications (Ti1) and the development of a mobile online booking system (Ti2). Project H in a large company with *c*.3,000 employees for consulting and implementing IT services focused on implementing an adapted solution for a car supplier based on a SAP R/3 system.

The study was based on a mix of different methods: In order to identify the background of the project work, semistandardized interviews with management and project managers focused on the competitive situation, on the company structure, on work organization and working time, and on HR strategies (N = 15). Additionally, group interviews were used to investigate project related work constraints, asking all team members to describe their specific work demands, encumbering situations, and the ways they were coping with them. They were further asked to specify favourable and supportive conditions for doing their work. Finally, the encumbering situations were categorized according to the five different forms of contradictory demands (see Figure 4.1).

According to their significance for affecting strain generation, the forms of project regulation and control were analyzed by questionnaire (a modified version of the so-called "self regulation pattern," cf. Ulich 1994): Two members of each project team were asked who is responsible for certain decisions and who else in the team is taking part (concerning, e.g., working times, planning of HR allocation, project acquisition; N = 14). Moreover, in order to identify changes in strain during project duration, a monthly diary about well-being and critical incidents was applied, based on an adapted screening questionnaire sent to all team members every month for about one year (with a recall after one week if no answer arrived). One month after each project's end, a standardized questionnaire was sent to all team members for a final evaluation of project outcomes, asking for economic success, waste or generation of resources, and personal development issues, e.g., vocational training opportunities, recreation opportunities, development of social relations and support at work. The research findings are presented below (Gerlmaier 2006; Latniak and Gerlmaier 2005).

Mismatches and contradictions: encumbering situations and strain

Based on data collected in the group interviews, 92 different strain situations in seven projects were identified and 83 of them (90 percent) could be assigned clearly to one of the five different categories of contradictions or mismatches.

Contradictions between tasks and their execution conditions (*type 1*) were an everyday problem in the projects investigated. Five of seven teams were regularly struggling, due to management's restrictive budgeting, with functionally inadequate software and hardware that hindered and restricted their ability to accomplish tasks; this caused additional work and reduced performance. Also, missing or delayed management or customer decisions led to stress reactions: they affected project schedules (or could even stop a project), while the workers, although not responsible, had to compensate for the delays and work overtime as delivery dates remained unchanged.

Mismatches between tasks and learning conditions (*type 2*) were identified in T1 and T2 and in the multimedia projects Ti1 and Ti2, while the customer-driven projects E2, E2, and H hardly exhibited this type of mismatch. Difficulties arose from the fact that workers lacked sufficient experience with the customer's system environment and had no time for adequate training. Resolving the dilemma caused extra work and strain at the workers' expense in order to get their work right.

Contradictory objectives were the most common mismatches (*type 3*) leading to intensified work and increased workload. Typically, the definition of the intended software functionality remained relatively vague during project specification. In the course of development, customers often generated additional ideas and wishes to be integrated in the software, causing additional workload, as schedules were not modified ("planning dilemma"). Most of the teams passively accepted that kind of extra burden associated with extended working time ("close your eyes and pass through it"). Only in two projects were efforts taken to avoid this by providing "checks and balances" in the contracts. Four of the projects reported that they received instructions from customers conflicting with defined work packages in the project plans. The teams tried to fulfil most of these extra wishes, while, at the same time, they tried to keep the schedule by increasing work pace or by extending working times. With this strategy, they tried to avoid lengthy negotiations between management and customers. An active coping strategy was found, in contrast, in only one project, where the team asked the project manager to negotiate with the customer.

Similarly, increasing quality demands from central departments were reported by three teams, raising the dilemma that higher quality standards should be applied, while necessary time buffers for performing the tests were reduced in order to cut costs. Moreover, during project acquisition, project managers often had to calculate time and cost budgets under high time pressure, causing miscalculations for which workers later had to compensate. Three teams additionally had problems with increasing documentation needs while no additional time was given. This aggravated a more general problem: Managers tended to deploy the same individuals on multiple projects at the same time, in order to achieve, as they thought, maximum efficiency. As a consequence, team members had to coordinate different project time schedules and priorities individually and they had to rapidly and repeatedly shift their attention and focus among a set of projects. This led to an increasing number of mistakes, especially when phases of intensive work in different projects overlapped. Team members tried to cope with the overload by mobilizing the social support of colleagues, no matter how limited it proved to be.

Contradictions between work-related and individual objectives and values (*type 4*) showed up when management did not show team members adequate appreciation of their work and performance, while a high degree of commitment and personal flexibility were simply presumed. A further dilemma was the mismatch between individual and project-related quality standards: Many knowledge workers saw their professional ethics violated by having to deliver software that was incompletely tested, as testing was reduced in order to keep the delivery dates.

Finally, due to the emphasis on work-related aspects, contradictions between work demand and values or rules of the social context (*type 5*) tended to be underestimated by management. The teams mentioned difficulties of coordinating work on weekends with family commitments. Furthermore, the need to travel to (remote) customers and the extended travelling times often reduced the chance to spend time with the family. Concerning solutions, workers were quite passive in this respect – these difficulties being regarded as an unchangeable part of work.

Looking at resources available to the teams, cooperation within the teams, opportunities to individually plan working times, and intellectual challenges of development tasks were primarily mentioned as resources to cope with contradictions. However, the projects' contextual conditions, first of all time pressure and underestimated budgets, often impaired the success of these coping strategies, particularly in the case of social relationships. Self-determined working times and the chance to recover at weekends, therefore, need to be defended against management and customer demands.

In sum, the study reveals that the underlying conceptual model and the different types of contradictions can well explain strain generation in project work. The most common stress situations mentioned were those caused by simultaneous work in several projects and by additional work due to inadequate equipment and delayed management or customer decisions. In order to overcome these problems, a majority of knowledge workers tend to extend their working times – which causes other difficulties and mismatches, however, for instance with family roles; consequently, it can be seen that solutions of one strain aspect often lead to new contradictions on a different level. These rather passive modes of coping were predominant, while more active attempts to negotiate on the project context conditions were less common. From a work design perspective, it is decisive that knowledge workers get influence on the definition of the overall working conditions as they affect strain generation.

Autonomy: self-control versus management control of project work

The influence of project teams on work organization, on planning and scheduling, and on work design was a prevailing research aspect. This was surveyed by a self-regulation pattern questionnaire to find out which tasks and decisions were self-regulated by the teams or individuals and which aspects were controlled and coordinated by management. Figure 4.2 shows that these decisions exhibit no consistent pattern.

Coordination of projects T1 and T2 – as sub-projects of large composite projects – was comparatively hierarchical: In both teams, project managers were

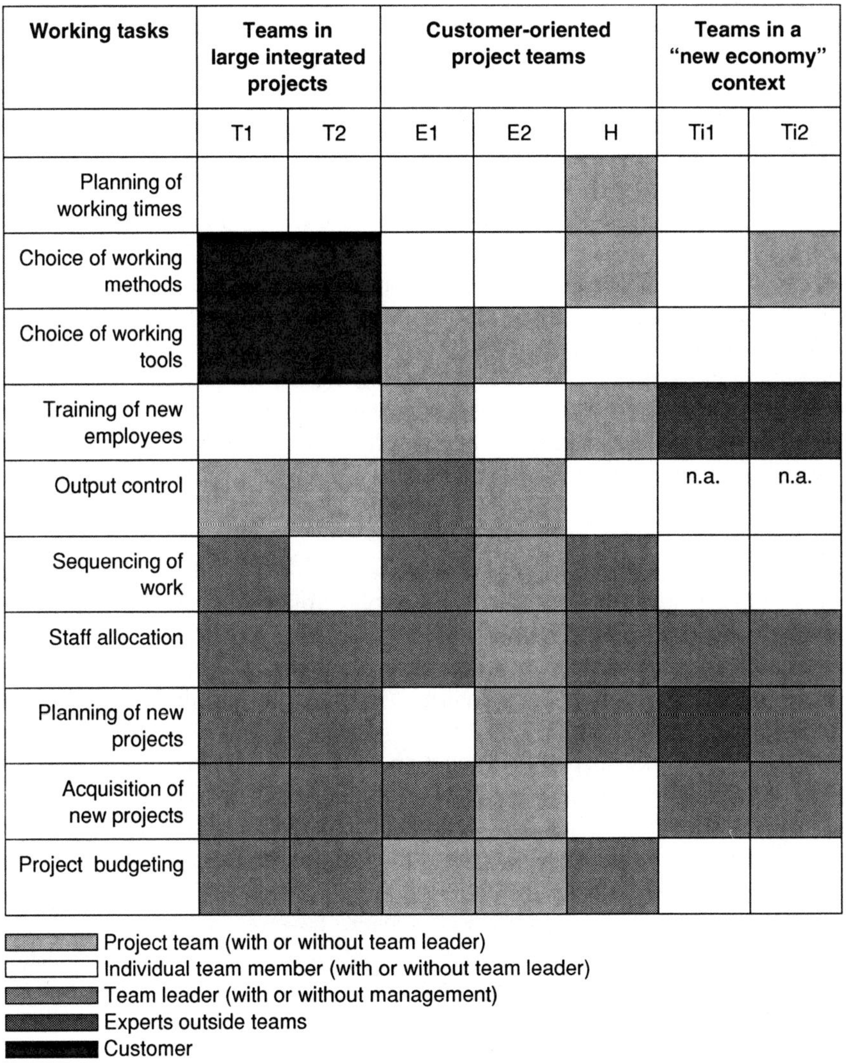

Working tasks	Teams in large integrated projects		Customer-oriented project teams			Teams in a "new economy" context	
	T1	T2	E1	E2	H	Ti1	Ti2
Planning of working times							
Choice of working methods							
Choice of working tools							
Training of new employees							
Output control						n.a.	n.a.
Sequencing of work							
Staff allocation							
Planning of new projects							
Acquisition of new projects							
Project budgeting							

Project team (with or without team leader)
Individual team member (with or without team leader)
Team leader (with or without management)
Experts outside teams
Customer

Figure 4.2 Findings: operational autonomy under management control of projects

responsible for the acquisition of new projects, project planning and budgeting, definition of tasks, and staff allocation, while equipment, tools, and methods applied were determined by the customer. After fixing the contract, further interaction between customers and project team was not intended. The responsibilities of the project teams were limited to working-time regulations and to the control of working progress.

Teams in projects E1, E2, and H, in contrast, had considerably more space for self-regulation. Work planning and design were accomplished in close cooperation with the team members. Furthermore, all teams had a comparatively high scope for team-based regulation: The individual workers decided on working times and holidays, while the team was in charge of selecting tools, methods, and equipment as well as the training of new staff. Except for one team, however, the team members were excluded from budgeting and staff allocation. In two of these teams, team members with specific knowledge were also involved in the acquisition of new projects.

Similarly, there was a close and rather informal cooperation between project teams and customers in both multimedia projects. The chief manager, alone charged with planning, budgeting, and acquisition, partially involved technical experts in discussing these aspects. Similarly to all other teams, workers decided on their working times. The project manager discussed work-related decisions on equipment or tools with team members individually in a rather informal way as compared to a formalized project management found in the other companies. This "short way" communication reduced coordination efforts, but clearly also led to a lack of structure and clear responsibilities.

The study thus reveals a broad range of self-regulation and autonomy among the IT projects investigated. But except for one project, the influence on project planning and decision-making was evidently restricted to working-time regulation, to the selection of equipment and methods, and to vocational adjustment of new staff – i.e., *job control*. The majority of project staff remains excluded from *management control*, i.e., the design of contextual framing conditions for their work, and from influencing the negotiation of substantial resource commitment. There is a remarkable impact of the team members on operational aspects of work, while the influence on the work environment is very limited in most projects investigated; teams or team members are not allowed to influence the basic and most significant strain-generating factors.

The contrasting case of project E2 indicates, however, that an option exists to act differently in two respects: First, the individual management style of the project manager in E2 is very participatory, and he involves the team in most decisions. Second, he is not avoiding conflicts with upper management or making risky decisions (i.e., acting against the company internal regulations) to keep his projects going.

Mental stress and increasing burnout risks

Findings on the degree of stress experienced in the projects' contradictory working situations reveal that approximately 41 percent of the workers complain about difficulties to "come to an end with work" and to relax at the end of the day, while 50 percent report feeling worn out or exhausted. About one-third of the employees agreed to the question that they would not be able to bear the workload continuously. With respect to the risk of work-related stress disorders, the results of the monthly diaries on well-being and critical incidents show

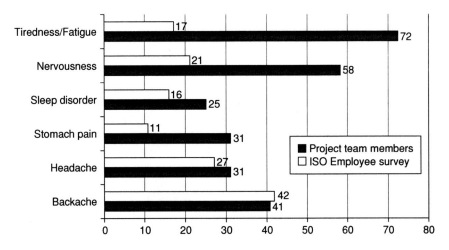

Figure 4.3 Stress reactions of project team members as compared to sample of all workers

significant differences as compared to those of a recent representative employee survey in Germany (Bauer *et al.* 2004). In our sample, many more employees suffer from tiredness or fatigue, nervousness, and sleep disorders (see Figure 4.3).

The analysis of the monthly diaries provided further insight into the course of individual stress generation. By comparing the mean values of mental exhaustion scores between different groups of employees, it was observed that project team members who reported high degrees of stress for more than eight weeks suffer significantly more often from mental exhaustion (burnout) than comparable groups with lower degrees of stress or with the ability to relax sooner. There was no similar effect for employees with high values of stress for less than two months. This indicates that a period of stress lasting longer than two months drastically increases the risk of burnout – a relevant finding for work design.

Conclusion: lessons learned for sustainable work design

The expanding incidence of stress disorders due to intensive work, especially knowledge-based project work; the distress effects on knowledge workers' health; and the high costs and economic damage caused for companies and societies call for immediate and effective action. To this end, the research findings deliver a number of promising approaches for designing sustainable work systems. First of all, it is obviously not sufficient, and frequently even not possible, to constrain or reduce single strain factors. Rather, as this type of work is essentially deconfined, it requires efforts of process design instead of structural design (as in industrial work), i.e., efforts to create working conditions and rules under which given work demands and available resources can continuously and dynamically be balanced for the sake of mental health and business performance alike. As deconfined work is characterized both by process-dependent work demands that are not determinable *ex ante* and by context-dependent resources that are only relationally effective, methods of *reflexive work design* (Moldaschl and Brödner 2002) are required for maintaining this balance.

Effective approaches for creating sustainable work systems need to attack work intensity and contradicting work demands at two levels: at the level of the externally given objective working situation as well as at the level of internally developed personal coping capabilities. On the company level, this requires the establishment of new strategic regulations and rules for the appropriate management of process-dependent workloads and, on the individual level, the creation of favourable conditions for workers to (re)generate sufficient resources for coping (see also Chapters 6 and 9 in this volume). In particular, insofar as management control excludes employees from influencing the framework underlying their work and this turns out to be a significant cause of stress, sustainability can be enhanced by letting employees participate in the design of the framing conditions under which they do their work. Moreover, reflexivity in work design can be realized by a cyclic and evolutionary procedure of continuous reflection and work redesign during which improvements are regularly explored, reflected upon, and evaluated. In this respect, the lessons learned from the research, using the resource-centred perspective with its contradictory work-demands approach, go considerably beyond the socio-technical design tradition. The first step for achievements would be to raise management's awareness of the new challenges and risks to mental health as a significant resource and to direct employees' awareness toward their responsibility for developing both coping capabilities and work-design capacities for controlling framing conditions.

Specifically, with respect to management's responsibility for sustainable work design, new specific *regulations and procedural rules* on the project contract level should be introduced by which frequent *ad hoc* or "quick fix" reactions to customer requests can be avoided. This would help to harmonize workloads and to alleviate time pressure, and thus help to considerably reduce strain and increase product quality alike.

Further improvements can be achieved by organizational measures for restricting workload in cases where project team members are working on different projects in parallel and where they are compelled to coordinate their activities individually. In order to avoid additional demands from this stressful situation, the *role of a co-coordinator* ("assignment manager") *for multi-project work* can be defined, whose task is to continuously check for staffing demands of the projects on the one hand and for actual individual capacities and workloads on the other.

Moreover, existing *schemes of continuous improvement* should be expanded to include aspects of developing and using personal, organizational, and social resources for coping with work demands (see also Chapter 17 in this volume). Similarly, the practices of *health circles* could be refocused on the reflection of work demands and coping capabilities, thus connecting working with learning activities, with particular focus on reflecting possible mismatches between workloads and available resources. Such practices might be further supplemented by specific *coaching* for highly demanded workers, helping them to better understand causes and symptoms of stress reactions and to effectively develop coping capabilities. Finally, rules for *systematic allowance of time for recreation* for highly in-demand workers should be developed. According to the findings, it is important to provide recovery periods close to stressful and intensive working periods, while it appears not to be helpful to foster sabbaticals or long recovery times for this purpose; no matter how useful for other objectives they might be, they do not help to avoid burnout or reduce burnout risks.

This research was designed as an exploratory study to test the significance of the resource-centred perspective on work. Although its usefulness for better comprehending the causes and effects of mental strain in highly skilled project work has been demonstrated, its scope is still limited. More methodological and empirical research is needed for extending design-oriented knowledge by answering questions such as: How widely spread is mental strain in different industries and professions? What are practical conditions and modalities to create and maintain sustainable work systems? What effects do they produce with respect to workers' health and economic benefits?

Questions for reflection

Here are three questions for your further reflection on the issues broached in this chapter:

- How would you describe the distinctive characteristics of so-called "knowledge-based" work?
- What types of contradictory work demands can arise in knowledge-based work?
- What kinds of measures can management take to eliminate such demands and create positive conditions for the development and regeneration of knowledge-based workers?

References

Bauer, F., Groß, H., Lehmann, K., and Munz, E. (2004) *Arbeitszeit 2003. Arbeitszeitgestaltung, Arbeitsorganisation und Tätigkeitsprofile* [Working time 2003. Design of working time, work organization and activity profiles], Cologne: ISO.

Brödner, P. (2002) "Flexibilität, Arbeitsbelastung und nachhaltige Arbeitsgestaltung" [Flexibility, work demands and design of sustainable work systems], in P. Brödner and M. Knuth (eds), *Nachhaltige Arbeitsgestaltung. Trendreports zur Entwicklung und Nutzung von Humanressourcen* [Design of sustainable work systems. Trend reports on development and use of human resources], Munich: Hampp, pp. 489–541.

Brödner, P. and Forslin, J. (2002) "O tempora, o mores! Work Intensity – Why Again an Issue?," in P. Docherty, M. Kira and A.B. Shani (eds), Creating Sustainable Work Systems: Emerging Perspectives and Practices, London: Routledge, pp. 15–26.

Brödner, P., Helmstädter, E., and Widmaier, B. (ed.) (1999) *Wissensteilung. Zur Dynamik von Innovation und kollektivem Lernen* [Dividing and sharing knowledge. On the dynamics of innovation and collective learning], Munich: Hampp.

Docherty, P., Forslin, J., and Shani, A.B. (Rami) (eds) (2002) *Creating Sustainable Work Systems. Emerging Perspectives and Practice*, London: Routledge.

Drucker, P.F. (1993) *Post-Capitalist Society*, New York: Harper Collins.

Emery, F.E., and Trist, E.L. (1960) "Sociotechnical Systems," in C.W. Churchman and M. Verhulst (eds), *Management Science: Models and Techniques*, Vol. II, Oxford: Pergamon Press, pp. 83–97.

Gabriel, P., and Liimatainen, M.-R. (eds) (2000) *Mental Health in the Workplace*, Geneva: ILO.

Gerlmaier, A. (2006) "Nachhaltige Gestaltung in der Wissensökonomie? Zum Verhältnis von Belastungen und Autonomie in neuen Arbeitsformen" [Design of sustainable work systems in knowledge-based economies? On the relationship of work demands and autonomy in new forms of work], in S. Lehndorff (ed.), *Das Politische in der Arbeitspolitik. Ansatzpunkte für eine nachhaltige Arbeits- und Arbeitszeitgestaltung* [The political in the politics of work. Approaches to design of sustainable work and working time systems], Berlin: edition sigma, pp. 71–98.

Gerlmaier, A. (2004) "Projektarbeit in der Wissensökonomie und ihre Auswirkungen auf die Work Life Balance" [Project work in knowledge-based economies and its effects on work life balance], in M. Kastner (ed.), *Die Zukunft der Work Life Balance: wie lassen sich Beruf und Familie, Arbeit und Freizeit miteinander vereinbaren?* [The future of work life balance: How can professional and familiy life, work and leisure time be reconciled?], Kröning: Asanger, pp. 282–304.

Hatchuel, A. (2002) "Sources of Intensity in Work Organizations," in P. Docherty, M. Kira and A.B. Shani (eds), Creating Sustainable Work Systems: Emerging Perspectives and Practices, London: Routledge, pp. 40–51.

Helmstädter, E. (ed.) (2003) *The Economics of Knowledge Sharing. A New Institutional Approach*, Cheltenham: Edward Elgar.

Karasek, R. (1998) "Demand/Control Model: A Social, Emotional, and Psychological Approach to Stress Risk and Active Behavior Development," in J.M. Stellman (ed.), *Encyclopaedia of Occupational Health and Safety*, 4th edn, Geneva: ILO, pp. 34.6–34.14.

Karasek, R., and Theorell, T. (1990) *Healthy Work. Stress, Productivity, and the Reconstruction of Working Life*, New York: Basic Books.

Kira, M. (2003) *From Good Work to Sustainable Development – Human Resource Consumption and Regeneration in the Post-Bureaucratic Working Life*, Stockholm: KTH.

Kira, M. (2002) "Moving from Consuming to Regenerative Work," in P. Docherty, M. Kira and A.B. Shani (eds), Creating Sustainable Work Systems: Emerging Perspectives and Practices, London: Routledge, pp. 29–39.

Latniak, E., and Gerlmaier, A. (2005) "Working in IT Projects – Options and Limits of Work Design," paper presented at the 9th International Workshop on Teamworking (IWOT 9), Monte de Caparica, Lisbon/Portugal, September.

LSE (2006) *The Depression Report. A New Deal for Depression and Anxiety Disorders*, London: LSE.

Maslach, C., and Leiter, M.P. (1997) *The Truth about Burnout. How Organizations Cause Personal Stress and What to Do about It*, San Francisco: Jossey-Bass.

Moldaschl, M. (ed.) (2005) *Immaterielle Ressourcen. Nachhaltigkeit von Unternehmensführung und Arbeit I* [Immaterial resources. Sustainability of management and work I], Munich: Hampp.

Moldaschl, M. and Brödner, P. (2002) "A Reflexive Methodology of Intervention," in P. Docherty, M. Kira and A.B. Shani (eds), Creating Sustainable Work Systems: Emerging Perspectives and Practices, London: Routledge, pp. 179–189.

Nonaka, I., and Takeuchi, H. (1995) *The Knowledge Creating Company. How Japanese Companies Create the Dynamics of Innovation*, Oxford: Oxford University Press.

Reich, R.B. (1991) *The Work of Nations*, New York: Knopf.

Sitter, L.U. de, Hertog, J.F. den, and Dankbaar, B. (1997) "From Complex Organizations with Simple Jobs to Simple Organizations with Complex Jobs," *Human Relations* 50, 5, 497–533.

Stewart, T.A. (1997) *Intellectual Capital. The New Wealth of Organizations*, New York: Doubleday.

Trist, E. (1981) *The Evolution of Socio-Technical Systems*, Ontario: Ministry of Labour.

Ulich, E. (1994) *Arbeitspsychologie* [Work psychology] (3rd edn), Stuttgart: Schäffer Poeschel and Zürich: vdf.

5 Sustainability and the ageing workforce

Considerations with regard to the German car manufacturing industry

Julia Weichel, Markus Buch, Dirk Urban, and Ekkehart Frieling

What is sustainability?

In this chapter, the concept of sustainability is approached in the context of the ageing workforce in the German car manufacturing industry. We explore how work systems can sustain employees and, especially, we take into account the increasing number of ageing employees. As a theoretical framework, we use an extension of the sociotechnical approach in order to address various subsystems and dimensions of sustainable work systems. Empirical illustrations are provided based on the project "Age-based job design in the car manufacturing industry," and on related projects. Finally, we present practical recommendations as to how work systems can support healthy ageing in the context of work and, therefore, ensure the sustainability of people engaged in work processes.

The aim of this chapter is to present ideas about how a sustainable work system supporting healthy ageing in the process of work can be designed with the help of the sociotechnical approach. First, we define sustainability in the context of the sociotechnical approach (see also Chapters 4, 6, and 15 in this volume). Next, we describe and discuss the demographic change in the workforce and its problems, and the working conditions in the car industry. Then we describe our own research project, which analyzes the work of the ageing workforce in the car industry. Finally, we discuss our results in the context of the sustainable sociotechnical approach.

As shown in this book, the concept of sustainability is multifaceted and the various definitions have different foci. The definition provided by the Brundtland Commission (1987; see Chapter 1 in this volume) stresses meeting present needs without putting the needs of future generations at risk. This definition has highly influenced both scientific and political discourse in Europe. However, we can find some historical forerunners for the popular concept – for instance, in the area of forestry. In the early eighteenth century, a Saxon mining inspector, Hans Carl von Carlowitz, expressed a concern about the practice of deforestation without replanting. At that time, wood was an important raw material and energy source in many sectors, not only in mining. Wood shortages entailed poverty. In his work "*Sylvicultura Oeconomica – Directions for the Growth of Wild Forests*", published in 1713, Carlowitz called for the sustainable use of forests to ensure the long-term supply of wood. His proposition was that those who cut trees should also plant new ones.

On a more abstract level, sustainability integrates different needs: not only present and future, but also individual and societal, as well as national and international (Hargroves and Smith 2005). In the following, we connect sociotechnical system theory (Emery 1978; Emery & Trist 1997) with the concept of sustainability. This approach will provide a foundation for efficient and humane jobs in organizations. According to sociotechnical system theory, equal attention should be given to the different subsystems as well as the system as a whole. The work system contains the technical, organizational, and personnel subsystems, and these should be analyzed and designed by taking into account and understanding the interactions among them. Figure 5.1 shows a sociotechnical system model of organizations.

The sociotechnical system as a whole also influences its subsystems, and that is why we deal with complex reciprocal cause–effect relationships (see also Chapters 4, 6, 8, and 9 in this volume.)

Technical subsystem: The technical subsystem includes the working equipment, tools, and machines of the production systems. To a great extent, it defines work execution and chemical and physical working conditions.

Organizational subsystem: Conditions of employment and work hours are important issues for the organizational subsystem, as are considerations such as outsourcing versus insourcing, and centralization versus decentralization.

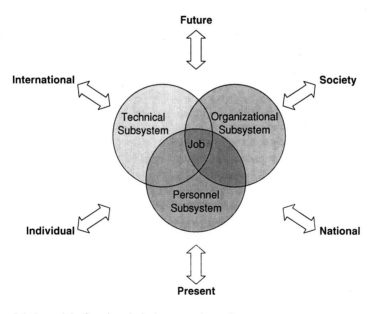

Figure 5.1 A model of sociotechnical system dynamics

Personnel subsystem: Skills, knowledge, abilities, formal education, including training and competence development, and informal qualifications such as experience, as well as demographic characteristics such as age and gender, are included here.

These subsystems of the sociotechnical system interact with each other and with the dimensions of sustainability shown in Figure 5.1, such as individual–society and present–future, as illustrated in the following examples. It is now customary solely to recruit young employees for physically demanding work. However, as the average age of the workforce increases rapidly (see below), organizations will be confronted with an older workforce. Organizations will have to figure out new ways for carrying out physically demanding work. Pre-retirement programmes in sociotechnical systems address the individual–society dimension. On the individual level, early retirement can promote health and stimulate psychological growth, while on the level of society these practices put social security systems under pressure. The national–international dimension is typically addressed by protectionism or offshoring. National economies may profit from protectionist interventions, but fast-developing nations lose development potential. When considering the three dimensions present–future, individual–societal, and national–international, there is not a single, fixed parameter value that can be applied to attain and maintain sustainable solutions in all situations. A system's positioning along the dimensions has to be altered continuously to attain balance. The model of Sustainable Sociotechnical Systems represents these efforts to attain balance in the search for sustainable development. Moreover, the three need dimensions influence the technical and social subsystems of the production system. This will be true whether we focus on need satisfaction in the present or in the future, on the national or international level, or of the individual or of society.

Age-based work systems are work systems that enable employees to age in good health in efficient and competitive jobs. Sustainability enlarges the concept of age-based work systems by taking into account the balance of individual and societal, national and international, as well as present and future needs. In other words, the implementation of age-based work systems is a social and historical challenge in an international context. The concept of Sustainable Sociotechnical Systems, as discussed above, provides conceptual leverage to address this challenge in practice.

The ageing work force in the car manufacturing industry

The demographic change

In Germany and other European countries, the proportion of employees aged 50 and over is continuously increasing in the labour force, and the number of young people entering the labour market is decreasing. At the same time, there is a tendency for people to leave the labour force before the legislated retirement age.

One can rarely find employees older than 50 in the heavy manufacturing industry because they are not able, or are not seen to be able, to cope with the requirements of the workplace. Until now, companies have made use of part-time work schemes for older employees – an opportunity that will exist in Germany only until the end of 2009. After 2009, companies must keep workers fully employed until they are 65 or 67 years old. This creates a need to establish job and work-organizational solutions that make it possible for older workers to remain in full employment and in good health to these ages. This is an especially difficult challenge for jobs that are physically demanding.

According to Vetter (2003), absenteeism due to musculoskeletal disorders begins at the age of 20, and increases dramatically in terms of workdays lost when people reach the age of 50. The comparison of young and old employees with regard to this kind of absenteeism showed that there was no difference in the frequency of absenteeism. However, older employees, once they are actually sick, are absent for a longer period of time.

The profile of an ageing worker

Stereotypes about the strengths and weaknesses of older employees are widespread. When it comes to the relation between age and performance, for example, the relevant literature shows some studies in which older workers performed better than younger workers, but there are also studies in which older workers' performance was poorer, while most studies found no relationship between age and performance at all (e.g., McEvoy and Cascio 1989; Warr 2000). The correlations range from $r = -0,44$ to $r = 0,60$. It seems certain, however, that the *variance* of performance increases with increasing age due to many factors that affect performance and health. Differences in lifestyle, education, and experience in various jobs may contribute to this increasing variance of performance in the ageing population.

The Selection, Optimization, and Compensation Model – or the SOC model – seeks to explain the increasing variance in job performance with age (Riediger *et al.* 2006; Baltes and Baltes 1990). The model assumes that older people develop various *strategies* to cope with deficits of old age. A popular example used to illustrate the model is the pianist Artur Rubinstein. As Rubinstein recognized that his age was causing his speed of playing to slow down, he chose to play only a reduced subset of his established repertoire, and he practised these pieces more than in the past, to optimize his performance. In addition, he incorporated more changes of speed while playing, to make fast passages appear faster and slow passages slower than they really are; he compensated for his generally slower playing speed by relying on more dramatic speed changes. The model thus provides one possible explanation for the diversity in job performance within the ageing workforce.

Working conditions in the car manufacturing industry

Profound changes in working life have heightened the competitive pressures facing the German car industry. Perhaps one of the greatest challenges in global competition comes from the lower production costs in competing countries. The German car industry also faces pressure to adapt new technologies (automation, robots, electronic devices, new materials). Various factors may contribute to maintained competitiveness. Especially, we note internal factors such as work organization and work design as important elements in promoting the performance of employees and the competitiveness of a company (see also, e.g., chapters 4, 6, 8, 9, and 11).

We now describe some special features of work organization in the car industry and connect these features to the challenges for ageing employees. In this section, we will refer (in addition to our ongoing study) to the results from the Future Working Structures (FWS) project, which analyzed 15 different production plants in the car industry (Frieling 1997).

Much of the production work in the car industry is organized by using assembly line systems (Frieling *et al.* 1997a, 1997b). There are also work stations outside the line system, e.g., stations for assembling components or stations for routine quality checks during the production process. Most of the jobs on assembly lines are characterized by short cycle times, high standardization, low degrees of decision latitude, high physical demands, shift work, and low qualification requirements.

Length of work phases, standardization, and decision latitude: The cycle times in assembly work are becoming shorter and shorter. Today, cycle times of 30 to 70 seconds are not uncommon. Some work stations outside the line system have cycles of longer duration. Detailed instructions for work steps lead to high standardization, and in consequence to low degrees of decision latitude and little opportunity for self-directed action. Standards do help in improving quality and in promoting the idea of the one best way of doing a task. They also lead to the possibility of training on the job and to a reduction in training times. However, standards also can entail the risk of reducing decision latitude and task variety in the workplace (see Schmid 2005). They can result in poor flexibility in finding solutions when disruptions occur in the production process.

High physical demands: Many work stations have also demanding physical requirements. Imagine a station where the worker installs a wiring system in a car. The worker has to work in a stooped posture, while leaning inside the car. Alternatively, he has to work inside the car with little space for body movements. Some work stations also include the lifting of heavy workloads – for example, unhinging the doors of a car, with or without a carrier. Unbalanced physical load is therefore a high risk in jobs with short cycle times and high physical demands without space for alternative actions.

Shift work: In the car manufacturing industry, working times are often scheduled with a shift-work plan. Studies analyzing the relationship between shift work and somatic complaints found more complaints among shift workers when compared to nonshift workers. Shift work, especially night work, can lead to a number of problems like a disturbed biological circadian rhythm, increased risk for insomnia, intestinal diseases, heart disease, and disruption of social life (Knauth 2007).

Low qualification requirements: Many jobs on the assembly line have low qualification requirements, while many workers are fully qualified. The workers cannot make use of their skills and cannot expand their knowledge or qualifications.

The combination of these intense features of work in the car industry leads to an extreme workload that becomes more demanding the longer one works under these conditions.

Age-differentiated work systems

The priority programme "Age-differentiated work systems"

The project "Age-based job design in the car manufacturing industry" is part of the priority programme "Age-differentiated work systems" funded by the German Research Foundation (Deutsche Forschungsgemeinschaft, or DFG). The priority programme consists of different projects that address the following issues:

1 *Age-specific distribution of tasks*: Which kinds of tasks are appropriate for younger employees, and which kinds for older employees?
2 *Age-specific design of work and work equipment*: Which organizational, technical, and social conditions can support the work ability and health of younger and older employees?
3 *Age-specific personnel development*: Which age-dependent variations of methods for personnel development can efficiently promote maintenance of health and occupational performance?
4 *Influences of working life*: Which characteristics of work and working conditions influence the ageing process and work ability in a cumulative way?

The project "Age-based job design in the car manufacturing industry"

The project "Age-based job design in the car manufacturing industry" is based on case studies of two car manufacturers. The project has three phases. The first is an initial analysis of current work systems and their deficiencies. Several indices are used to describe the features of the current work systems and to measure employees' health and performance status in order to analyze age-critical working conditions and age differences in a cross-sectional design. The second phase is the development of a conceptual framework for the improvement of the work design and its actual implementation. The third will be devoted to evaluation of the effects of the implemented concepts within the work systems. In the second and third phases, we make the same measurements as in phase one, in order to enable a longitudinal analysis of the ageing processes. Phase one of the project started in October 2005, and was completed in October 2007. In order to create an age-based work system that is also adaptable to new technical and economic developments, researchers from different disciplines such as industrial science, ergonomics, and psychology are involved in the project.

The departments of the two car manufacturers taking part are the semiautomated assembly of automatic gearboxes (company A, sample size: 160 workers) and the final assembly of cable harnesses in the car body (company B, sample size: 249). In phase one of our project, lifting and carrying of workloads as well as working postures were assessed by standardized observation methods (Ovako Working Postures Analysing System, or OWAS, and National Institute for Occupational Safety and Health, or NIOSH: Schaub *et al.* 2004; Bongwald *et al.* 1995). Questionnaires were used to measure personal performance, stress and somatic complaints, workability and health status (i.e., Work Ability Index, or WAI, Tuomi *et al.* 2001; Ilmarinen and Tempel 2002; Occupational Stress and Coping Inventory, or AVEM, Schaarschmidt and Fischer 1996). Another questionnaire was used to obtain workers' subjective assessment of their working conditions (Udris and Rimann 1999).

In the following sections, we review the first results from phase one (i.e., the analyses of the work systems and the subjective assessments of performance, well-being, stress, and somatic complaints). We focus especially on the age-dependent relationships and age differences regarding the tasks assigned to older employees in the work systems.

Technical subsystem

Both companies use assembly lines in production. In company A, the workers start the material flow of the work objects at the assembly line. In company B, the cars are placed on moving platforms. The workers do their work on the platforms and go back to the beginning of their work station. In company B many working steps are also carried out inside the car. The lengths of the work cycle times in company A and B range from 72 to 85 seconds per phase. That means that the employees repeat the same task every 72 to 85 seconds.

We used the Ovako Working Postures Analysing System (OWAS, Schaub *et al.* 2004) to measure the working postures needed to work at the work stations. This allowed us to classify the working postures into four categories (green, yellow, orange, and red) from "green" (working posture is not demanding, no need for action) to "red" (working posture is highly demanding, immediate action is needed). The results show that, on average, older employees are assigned less demanding working postures than their younger colleagues (company B). However, analysis of the strain due to maximally demanding working postures showed clearly that a high percentage of older employees have to work on one or more work stations with "yellow" or "orange" working postures. In company B, more work stations are categorized as yellow than in company A.

Organizational subsystem

A questionnaire was used to study employees' perceptions of both the strains and requirements, and the organizational and social resources at their workplace.

Each question was a statement rated on a five-point scale, from "totally disagree" to "totally agree." The assessment showed medium-to-low values for the scales of task variety, job autonomy, participation, and the possibility for competence development at the workplace (mean values from 2.7–2.1). These results indicate that the work does not provide many possibilities for the use of advanced qualifications or participation in decision making. The tasks are quite similar and the workers cannot decide and organize much on their own. This finding is consistent with our documentation of the high level of formal standardization within the work systems. In addition, the workers feel that jobs do not challenge them enough and that they are not overtaxed by work. Social conditions such as the presence of social support from superiors or colleagues at the workplaces were assessed slightly above 3.

Employees rotate between work stations in the work systems. Our analysis of age differences shows that older employees work on fewer work stations than younger ones in company B, and thus, they rotate between fewer work stations. Thirty-six percent of employees older than 45 years work on only one to five work stations.

Personnel subsystem

The sample consists of different age groups. In both companies, employees between the ages of 36 and 45 years represent the biggest age group. Employees older than 50 are a minority, making up less than 5 percent of those studied – a result that could be interpreted in terms of the "healthy worker effect": Only employees who are able to cope with the working conditions and requirements still remain at work.

More than 80 percent of the employees studied have a post-school vocational education. This implies that the majority of the employees are probably over-qualified for the jobs on an assembly line. The employees have held their present position for 9–12 years on average. This in turn implies that they have been exposed to the working conditions described above for very long periods of time.

Skills and abilities important for the promotion of health and well-being were also assessed by standardized questionnaires. Employees' capacity to work was measured with the Work Ability Index (WAI) (Ilmarinen and Tempel 2002). The WAI measures the ability of workers to do their work; both the work demands and the health as well as the psychological and physical resources of employees are taken into account. The WAI score is classified into four categories: poor, moderate, good, and excellent work ability.

Most of the workers in company B have moderate work ability, and in company A, good work ability. We find that older employees report a lower work ability than younger employees ($r = -0,28$ (A), $r = -0,31$ (B)). In addition, we used the Occupational Stress and Coping Inventory (AVEM) to measure work-related behaviour and coping styles (Schaarschmidt and Fischer 1996). For instance, the AVEM problem-solving index describes the ability to manage problems at the workplace and to learn how to cope with unexpected failures and challenges in the work system. These are important skills to maintain flexibility and company productivity. We found that older workers assess their ability to cope with challenges and problems lower than younger workers do.

Scores on the AVEM inner balance scale (i.e., "I don't let myself get worked up") were found to decrease with increasing age. Older employees describe themselves as having a lower inner stability. There are no age differences in other scales of coping styles such as the tendency to resign or the ability to dissociate from work.

In order to take account of leisure activities compensating for work challenges, we assessed the frequency of sports activities. Most of the employees do no sports at all (company B) and older employees do less exercise than the younger employees.

Recommendations based on the sustainable sociotechnical model

The aim of this chapter is to understand how sustainable work systems can be designed with the help of our extended sociotechnical approach. Sustainability in this context means healthy ageing in the process of work in productive work systems. On the basis of our results and of the reported literature, we discuss some sustainable ways to realize age-based work systems within the organizations involved. Obviously, there is no one best way to design and implement an age-based work system. We therefore introduce technical, organizational, and personnel-related interventions that are able to promote age-based work systems and that simultaneously balance the different needs contained in our model.

Technical subsystem

The technical subsystem must be designed to ensure the age-based functioning of the work system. Many experts underline that technical systems designed according to general ergonomic know-how are helpful for both young and old employees. They correctly assume that ergonomically designed workplaces are less age-differentiated because they already emphasize reducing musculoskeletal strains. We hope that, as the workforce gets older, ergonomic principles become even more pronouncedly integrated in work-systems design. We see ergonomics as a way to balance the needs of the individual with the needs of society, as ergonomic improvements can support the health of the individual and keep workers in employment for a longer time.

Based on our analysis, we recommend the following measures when redesigning the studied work stations:

- Use of carriers to lift gearboxes.
- Facilitation of material provision (e.g., electrical lifting carts).
- Elastic floor covering to reduce musculoskeletal complaints.
- Systematic changes of working postures: More work stations where sedentary work is possible and one-sided and unbalanced working postures can be avoided.

- Adaptation of screens and signs to improve legibility.
- Changed product design to reduce the parts of the assembly jobs inside the cars.
- The documentation of these measures in the specification books for future assembly systems.

Within the organizations studied, we have established project groups composed of members from research and development as well as from production planning. The aim is, with the help of these groups, to facilitate the implementation of the recommendations described above in the conceptual structure of future assembly lines and to stimulate the design of production-oriented products (cf. Sundin *et al.* 2004). Within a cross-sectional project group, it is also easier to consider and balance the various needs in the different subsystems and dimensions of our model.

Organizational subsystem

Considering the organizational subsystem, a crucial issue in many manufacturing organizations is that core competences are too narrowly defined. In order to allow for healthy ageing at work and therefore to balance present and individual needs with future needs, people should be able to carry out a broader range of tasks – not only the production work. Manufacturing jobs should be enriched with preassembly work, and with controlling and quality management tasks along with participation in error management. When many tasks are outsourced and fewer tasks remain within an organization, older employees have fewer opportunities for such enriched and versatile work. When outsourcing sends work to other countries, a further conflict is generated between national and international needs.

Older workers, in many cases, have greater expertise and knowledge about operational processes than their younger colleagues and are therefore capable of carrying out work that requires more highly-qualified personnel. We recommend expanding their areas of responsibility to include managerial tasks such as leading of group processes, quality management, controlling of the production process, or logistical tasks (see also Nyhuis *et al.* 2004). These or similar interventions will help in reducing the physical workload for older employees. Appropriate training for the additional tasks will be needed. A major obstacle to be overcome in this matter is that the creation of enriched jobs will naturally lead older workers to expect higher wages. As a result, many organizations consider these changes too expensive at present, disregarding future needs and benefits.

A possibility to support healthy ageing processes by including diverse tasks is to rotate jobs among the employees within a company. Our analysis shows that older employees work on fewer work stations and therefore have fewer opportunities to maintain or enhance their flexibility to cope with varying requirements. We also find that older employees' perceptions of their work ability and ability to cope with problems are lower than those of their younger co-workers. The longer an older employee has worked without the requirement to adapt to new elements of the work system, the more difficult it is to develop the ability to find ways to cope with challenges. As a consequence, employees need to gain experience with job rotation all through their career and learn that it is something they can do. When a positive job rotation attitude is learned early on, it is also natural later. But if job rotation is imposed on older employees late in their career, they naturally feel anxious about it. In this sense, the complaints of managers that people do not want to rotate may well relate to earlier bad job design choices. This is a systemic problem, not a personnel problem. It demonstrates clearly the challenge to companies to remember future needs while facing the daily pressure of present needs (e.g., higher production rates).

Sustainable job rotation can be implemented by including the following elements:

- Job rotation should be applied to young and old employees preventing work-related complaints for young employees.
- Job rotation has to become a part of the organizational culture.
- Comprehensive job rotation should take place in and between departments.
- Systematic job rotation with different degrees of decision latitude and varying working postures should be introduced.

To develop sustainable ways of working, workers' continuous and extended engagement in monotonous tasks with demanding physical requirements, as found in our sample, should be avoided. Opportunities for horizontal (specialist) and vertical (classical) careers are useful to keep employees in good health and enhance flexibility over their working lifespan. Continuous and attractive changes of requirements, as well as workplaces that contain learning opportunities, participation in error management, and more complex tasks also help to retain initial qualifications, to learn new skills, and to cope with challenging problems. Without using their initial qualifications, workers cannot keep or expand their knowledge and will gradually lose their qualifications.

The question of whether temporary employment contracts are suitable for age-based assembly-line systems is a matter of some contention in the present discussions between the social partners. We believe that such contract conditions conceal the necessity of improving working conditions in general (Frieling 2003).

Teamwork is another important tool for the design of age-based work systems. The respective strengths of younger and older employees can truly be realized in teams. We have therefore sought to establish age-mixed teams in our case organizations. We try to implement teams in which jobs rotate and younger and older employees have different tasks that vary in degree of physical and cognitive requirements. The aim is to create a balanced workload for every employee.

As described earlier, shift work is one of the demanding characteristics of work on assembly lines. Knauth and Härma (2003) give recommendations for how to adapt shift-work schedules to the individual needs of older employees. They recommend overall reduction in working hours or enhancement in the flexibility of working hours; this supports adjusting physical and mental work demands to an individual's working capacity. Participation of employees in the planning process of the shift schedules is of great importance. Ageing workers should also be offered the chance to take micro pauses, which can help them avoid faults and accidents due to increasing fatigue, among other causes.

Personnel subsystem

In the personnel subsystem, the assessments and interventions focus on health, competences, and motivation of ageing personnel. The concept of work ability (Tuomi *et al.* 2001) integrates these aspects. Current and future needs of employees and work systems can be addressed by interventions within the personnel subsystem. For instance, the promotion of employees' health at the workplace can support individual health-conscious behaviour and simultaneously keep employees in employment for a longer time. In our sample, many employees do no sports and older employees get less physical exercise than younger ones. Additionally, older employees' perceptions of their work ability are lower. Starting points for the improvement of health are interventions in the areas of sport activities (e.g., regular health checks, fitness areas) and nutrition. Age-based work systems should also offer the possibility of competence development regardless of the age of the employee. The aim is to maintain the workers' qualifications and to promote the development of new skills. Therefore, lifelong learning should be a self-evident feature of the company. To ensure the motivation of older employees to remain at work, incentives such as early retirement should be avoided.

Summary

The interventions within the technical, organizational, and personnel subsystems affect each other, and the integrated design of all these subsystems can create new and better jobs. In order to ensure the continuous operation of our production systems, we need to respond to the challenges presented by the ageing population and workforce. To ensure the sustainability of age-based work systems, they have to be continually adjusted on the three need dimensions of the Sustainable Sociotechnical Model: present needs have to be balanced with future needs, individual with societal, and national with international. Our chapter has indicated some ways for the successful management of demographic change and the satisfaction of these various need dimensions. Our research project and the present chapter thus make a contribution to the analysis of important factors for sustainability and to the process of the development of work systems sustaining an ageing workforce.

Questions for reflection

Here are three questions for your further reflection on the issues broached in this chapter:

82   *J. Weichel* et al.

- How would you describe sustainability in the context of the sociotechnical systems model?
- What kinds of problems would you expect with the assignment of job duties to older employees?
- What would you do to promote healthy ageing in the work setting?

References

Baltes, P.B., and Baltes, M.M. (1990) "Psychological perspectives on successful aging: The model of selective optimization with compensation," in P.B. Baltes and M.M. Baltes (eds), *Successful aging: Perspectives from the behavioral sciences*, New York: Cambridge University Press, pp. 1–34.

Bongwald, O., Luttmann, A., and Laurig, W. (1995) *Leitfaden für die Beurteilung von Hebe- und Tragetätigkeiten* [Handbook for the assessment of lifting tasks]. Sankt Augustin, Germany: Hauptverband der gewerblichen Berufsgenossenschaften (HVBG).

Brundtland, G.H. (ed.) (1987) *Our common future: The World Commission on Environment and Development*. Oxford: Oxford University Press.

Emery, F. (1978) "Analytical model for socio-technical systems," in F. Emery (ed.), *The emergence of a new paradigm of work*. Canberra: Australian National University, pp. 95–106.

Emery, F., and Trist, E. (1997) "The causal texture of organizational environments," in E. Trist, F. Emery, and H. Murray (eds), *The social engagement of social science: A Tavistock anthology*, Vol. 3, *The socio-ecological perspective*, Baltimore, MD: University of Pennsylvania Press, pp. 53–65.

Frieling, E. (ed.) (1997) *Automobilmontage in Europa* [Assembly work in the European automotive industry]. Frankfurt: Campus.

Frieling, E. (2003) "Altersgerechte Arbeitsgestaltung [Age-based job design]," in B. Badura, H. Schellschmidt, and C. Vetter (eds), *Fehlzeiten-Report 2003. Zahlen, Daten, Analysen aus allen Branchen der Wirtschaft. Demographischer Wandel – Herausforderung für die betriebliche Personal- und Gesundheitspolitik*, Heidelberg: Springer, pp. 101–114.

Frieling, E., Freiboth, M., Henniges, D., and Saager, C. (1997a) "Comparison of different organisations of assembly work in the European automotive industry," *International Journal of Industrial Ergonomics*, 20, 357–370.

Frieling, E., Freiboth, M., Henniges, D., and Saager, C. (1997b) "Effects of teamwork on the working conditions of short cycled track work: A case study from the European automobile industry," *International Journal of Industrial Ergonomics*, 20, 371–388.

Hargroves, K.C., and Smith, M.H. (eds) (2005) *The natural advantage of nations: Business opportunities, innovation and governance in the 21st century*, London: Earthscan.

Ilmarinen, J., and Tempel, J. (2002) *Arbeitsfähigkeit 2010 – Was können wir tun, damit Sie gesund bleiben?* [Work ability 2010 – What can we do to remain healthy?], Hamburg: VSA.

Knauth, P. (2007) "Schicht- und Nachtarbeit. [Shift and night work]" in K. Landau (ed.), *Arbeitsgestaltung – Best Practice im Arbeitsprozess*, Stuttgart: Universum Verlag, pp. 1105–1112.

Knauth, P., and Härma, M. (2003) "Working time," in A. Görn and M. Rentzsch (eds), *Solutions for effective design of work life within the demographical changes*, Berlin: IAS Stiftung, pp. 17–19.

McEvoy, G.M., and Cascio, W.F. (1989) "Cumulative evidence of the relationship between employee age and job performance," *Journal of Applied Psychology*, 74, 11–17.

Nyhuis, P., Mühlenbruch, H., and Heins, M. (2004) "Altersgerechte Qualifizierung für die Montage – Lebendige Qualifizierung mit dem Production Trainer" [Age-based qualification for assembly work – qualification with the production trainer], *wt Werkstatttechnik online*, 94, 426–432.

Riediger, M., Li, S.-C., and Lindenberger, U. (2006) "Selection, optimization, and compensation as developmental mechanisms of adaptive resource allocation: Review and preview," in J.E. Birren and K.W. Schaie (eds), *Handbook of the psychology of aging*, Amsterdam: Elsevier (6th edn), pp. 289–313.

Schaarschmidt, U., and Fischer, A.W. (1996) *AVEM – Arbeitsbezogenes Verhaltens- und Erlebensmuster* (Manual) [Occupational stress and coping inventory], Frankfurt am Main: Swets Testservices.

Schaub, K., Spelten, V., and Landau, K. (2004) IAD-Toolbox "Körperliche Arbeit" [Toolbox "Physical work"] (Version 2.1), Software des Instituts für Arbeitswissenschaft Darmstadt (IAD), Darmstadt.

Schmid, M.M. (2005) "Standards in der manuellen Automobilmontage – Akzeptanz und Reaktanz gegenüber Arbeitsvorschriften – eine empirische Feldstudie," [Standards in the automotive assembly work – commitment and reactance: an empirical field study]. Düsseldorf: VDI-Verlag.

Sundin, A., Christmansson, M., and Larsson, M. (2004) "A different perspective in participatory ergonomics in production development improves assembly work in the automotive industry," *International Journal of Industrial Ergonomics*, 33, 1–14.

Tuomi, K., Huuhtanen, P., Nykyri, E., and Ilmarinen, J. (2001) "Promotion of work ability, the quality of work and retirement," *Ocupational Medicine*, 51, 318–324.

Udris, I., and Rimann, M. (1999) "SAA und SALSA: Zwei Fragebögen zur subjektiven Arbeitsanalyse" [SAA and SALSA: Two questionnaires for the subjective analysis of jobs], in H. Dunkel (ed.), *Handbuch Psychologischer Arbeitsanalyseverfahren*. Zürich: vdf, pp. 397–419.

Vetter, C. (2003) "Einfluss der Altersstruktur auf die krankheitsbedingten Fehlzeiten" [The influence of age diversity on absenteeism], in B. Badura, H. Schellschmidt, and C. Vetter (eds), *Fehlzeiten-Report 2002. Zahlen, Daten, Analysen aus allen Branchen der Wirtschaft. Demographischer Wandel – Herausforderung für die betriebliche Personal- und Gesundheitspolitik*, Heidelberg: Springer, pp. 249–263.

Warr, P. (2000) "Job performance and the ageing workforce," in N. Chmiel (ed.), *Introduction to work and organizational psychology – an European perspective*, Malden: Blackwell Publishing, pp. 407–423.

6 Utilizing technology to support sustainability

James A. Sena and Abraham B. (Rami) Shani

Introduction

Sustainability entails the preservation, regeneration, and development of the ecological, economic, and social resources of a system. There is a clear movement afoot to change the generally unsustainable situation in the software development industry. Systems are regularly delivered late or over budget, if they are delivered at all. Systems often don't meet the needs of their customers and often have to be developed again and again. The difficulty stems from a lack of understanding and trust on the part of the customer. In an effort to succeed, software developers frequently work long hours and often become burned out (see also Chapter 4 in this volume). This chapter addresses the social and economic sustainability of a software development firm (referred to here as SDF) at the organizational, managerial, and individual levels. For SDF, sustainability means continuous strong technical leadership, continuous innovation, and ongoing development of its technical staff. These factors are reflected in a software industry manifesto (the "Manifesto for Agile Software Development") expressing four value preferences: individuals and interactions over processes and tools; working software over comprehensive documentation; customer collaboration over contract negotiation; and responding to change over following a plan (Ambler 2002).

For many businesses and industries, new product development has been the most important factor driving success or failure. Their strategic focus is directed at factors that will increase the likelihood of success of their new product development processes (Schilling and Hill 1998). Ensuring the firm's success requires addressing the firm's capability to continuously improve the sustainability of the new product development (NPD) processes. At SDF, this capability relies on keeping abreast of technological developments, working "smarter, not harder," and focusing on core technologies.

This chapter examines the use of a modular-based architecture framework and tools to sustain new product development projects, with special emphasis on individual and business sustainability (Krishnan and Gupta 2001; Muffatto 1999; Olin and Shani 2001). We address these relationships through a description of the steps and processes that a software firm uses to create new products. The chapter is organized in four parts. Following this introduction, we present a framework that synthesizes sociotechnical systems and strategic thinking (see also Chapters 4, 5, and 15 in this volume). Next, we briefly describe our methodology, followed by an overview of the SDF company and its product development processes. The analysis of the company, its NPD process, and sustainability then provide the basis for discussion and conclusion.

An alternative framework for NPD

Given the complex nature of new technology, standard approaches to the NPD process (Drucker 1985; Belliveau *et al*. 2002, 2004) may not suffice to explain or appreciate the potential of alternative work forms. By this we mean the use of a product-wide or project-wide slate of activities performed over time by various groups or teams. The teams enter into the product development at various stages. As such they provide services in the form of internal consultants or service providers. In this chapter, we recognize and integrate the strategic and sociotechnical character of a software product development process and apply the principles of sociotechnical systems to decisions that are made during the product development stages.

The sociotechnical systems (STS) perspective, as an analytical framework, considers every organization to be composed of a *social subsystem* (the people) using a *technical subsystem* (tools, techniques, and knowledge) to produce a product or a service valued by the *environmental subsystem* (e.g., Kolodny and Halpern 2008; Pasmore 1994; Taylor and Felton 1993; Trist 1982). The degree to which the designs of the technical, social, and the environmental subsystems are integrated can determine the success and competitiveness of the organization (Adler and Docherty 1998; Eijnatten *et al*. 2008; Pava 1986; Shani *et al*. 1992; see also Chapters 4 and 5 in this volume).

In order to link new product development and sociotechnical systems with sustainability, we propose an analytical framework that identifies six clusters of elements that affect performance and sustainability. These clusters are: the business environment; the social subsystem; the technical subsystem; the management system; NPD processes and the modular-based architecture; and system sustainability.

The *business environment cluster* consists of elements and forces in the firm's competitive marketplace. For software development firms, the industry is highly competitive, dynamic, and unstable, with rapid changes in technology. For SDF, the customer base has been primarily military and government agencies. Competition for software development in that sector is characterized by several large competitors.

The *social subsystem cluster* refers to the persons who work in the organization. Individual attitudes and beliefs, competences and skills, relationships between group members, relationships between supervisors and subordinates, relationships between groups, cultures, traditions, past experiences, assumptions, values, rites, rituals, work habits and practices, and emergent role systems all are integral parts of the social system cluster. SDF has a high level of informal communications, a casual environment that easily addresses conflict management, and a social atmosphere that supports self-direction and team building.

The *technical subsystem cluster* refers to the tools, techniques, devices, artefacts, methods, configurations, procedures, and knowledge used by organizational members to acquire inputs, transform inputs into outputs, and provide outputs or services to clients or customers. This is the key cluster that enables SDF's sustainability. The primary contribution to sustainability for SDF, as will be demonstrated, is the protection of SDF's intellectual capital in terms of personnel development and support, contracts that control and clearly define the code that is delivered such that it cannot be used by other competitors, and technical leadership. Methods include the set of reusable code, proprietary database mapping techniques, and task control tools.

The *management system cluster* refers to the systems that link the environmental, technical, and social subsystems. Business strategy, business design, business capabilities, business processes, and change management processes are key elements in this cluster. SDF initially employed a focused proof-of-concept strategy that later evolved to a differentiation strategy as their product base matured.

Methodology

The research reported in this chapter addresses the dynamics of a software development firm that has flourished and grown over its 15 years of existence. In the first study of SDF, the focus was on product development (see Shani and Sena 2002). This study revisits the company's approach to product development. The firm's focus has changed from one of producing the product within set specifications to one of client satisfaction as evidenced by consistent contract renewal and new business. A key aspect of sustainability at SDF is their transition from new product development to the continued, long-term development of ongoing products. At the time of the first study, most of the product work was focused on developing experimental proof-of-concept and prototype systems for the military. A number of these initial systems later formed the foundation for mainstream, working products. There is now less new product development work and more enhancement and refinement of major systems. The approach taken in this chapter is a retrospective, systematic reflection on what worked and what has changed. The data collections involved ethnographic observations of activities and decisions in the firm, the periodic sharing of data, and ongoing semistructured interviews with staff regarding their views of the firm, their working experiences, and the firm's success.

AN overview of the SDF company

SDF is in the business of building, implementing, and supporting agent-based "Cooperative Decision Making" tools for distributed problem solving. Application areas include: facilities management; transportation planning; military logistics and control; and engineering design. SDF had its origins in a university-based research facility. SDF's differentiating factor is their development of an agent-based methodology designed to address spatial problems for engineering design with respect to space management, space constraints, and storage priorities using an architectural perspective. Spatial agents provide the ability to place and arrange objects, such as military supplies, in some constrained area. They use a series of agents (an agent being a piece of software with specialized artificial intelligence and directed expert system components – knowledge rules and procedures for specialized problems in areas such as ordinance or logistics) to complement human decision making. There is much that is unique in SDF's approach to these technologies, which is based on the architecture training and discipline of the company founders, both of whom were architecture professors and computer scientists.

Agent technologies are self-contained, intelligent, adaptive software capsules used as building blocks to construct complex software products. Collaborating expert agents provide the flexibility and range needed for product design sustainability. In effect, these expert agents work together and "collaborate" – each complementing the skill set inherent in the system. As an example, one of SDF's projects involves the cargo loading of military ships – a specific agent would determine the optimal location for each cargo item based on its content, size, and other parameters (e.g., the heat sensitivity of explosives). A second agent would examine the other cargo to be loaded or already placed, tempering the assignment. Through the use of interoperability standards and methods, information can flow seamlessly through an application across heterogeneous machines, computing platforms, programming languages, and data and process representations (Lander 1997).

The organization of SDF

At SDF, departmental units function with a minimum of supervision, behaving in a manner that resembles an internal form of outsourcing. Some of the product work is conducted by cooperative supporting groups that provide functions such as documentation and quality control, separate from the department structure. The main organizational unit is the product team. In the first study, leadership of the product team was divided between a product lead and a technical lead. This had changed by the time of the second study; under the new arrangement, solely the technical lead directs the project development and coordinates with the product lead. The product team previously was divided into software development specialists and information technology specialists (individuals with particular expertise in software and hardware architecture, tools, operating environments, and design). By the time of the second study, the team members were all termed developers – all were capable of performing any and all tasks related to the software development product. The team members are cross-trained specialists who span the core disciplines. They provide the elements needed to create the software system: the Graphical User Interface (GUI); database modelling; and the selection/designation and inclusion of a specific set of agents from the software tool kit. In support of these product teams are service groups including system testing, customer support and equipment, and network software/hardware support.

In the first study, the dual leadership for new product development was intended to address problems associated with external and internal direction, and as a check-and-balance control mechanism. By the time of the second study, control resided with the technical lead – the reason mainly being the technical nature and complexity of the products. Under the new arrangement, the product lead controls the financial aspects and monitors the overall development progress. It was not uncommon for the development team (a subset of the product team consisting of actual developers, independent of leads and other participants) to be involved during the bid process. After the contract was awarded, the technical and product leads (managers) discuss the ingredients in the product deliverable with the development team. Once all team members and leads have a common understanding of the product goals, the team develops the project plan together. The work is divided into tasks, which are sized such that each spans no more than a month's time. One month is considered to be the period of work, referred to as an iteration. The technical and product leads together provide feedback to the team and contribute to the task definitions.

It is important to note that the development team may be simultaneously participating in several product development projects. The development team is a cohesive group that potentially could work under various leads – or at times be pulled into a product development to "rescue" it. The task definitions need to take into account what percentage of time the various members can allocate to the product development in the period of consideration. The team members provide the number of hours that they are available. The available hours and the task requirements are matched under the direction of the two leads.

Priorities are set for the tasks. During each iteration, the specifications and tasks are reviewed with the customer. Given the customer feedback, the tasks may change and the product content may be further clarified. There is no fixed, detailed design for the product set at the beginning. The team employs an incremental or "iterative" approach to progressive refinement of the design. The major element for gathering information is the customer dialogue.

Disputes or differences have to be resolved through discussion or are brought to senior management for resolution. This is not currently a significant problem at SDF because the teams are now very experienced and familiar with the product and with working together. New products evolve from existing products and involve technology transfer and adherence to well-established technologies that utilize the spatial agent approach.

The product development process

SDF has a well-defined process for product development (see Figure 6.1). Preceding the modular architecture process is the product initiation phase, in which

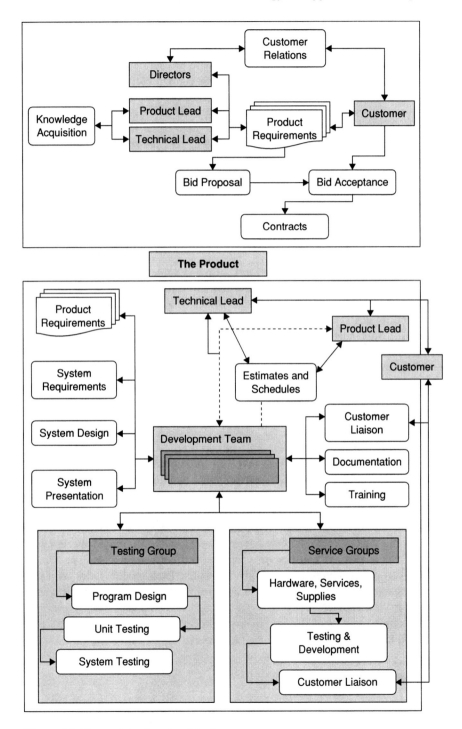

Figure 6.1 The modular-based architecture

responses to customer RFPs (Requests for Proposals) are prepared. This involves customer liaison and knowledge acquisition. As in most organizations of this nature, the goal of such an interactive process is the awarding of a contract.

The technical lead is responsible for specific product development elements, in concert with their development team and the support groups. The central focus of the product development organization is the development team. On one side of the lower panel in Figure 6.1 the technical work products are depicted – these include the product requirements that were defined in the product proposal; the system requirements; system design; and system presentation. On the other side of the panel are the external interface elements such as the estimates and schedule; the documentation and training; and the customer liaison. The design and development phase depicts the system requirement activities as being jointly shared by the development team and the technical lead. The technical lead must rely on the development team members – the majority of whom are full-time, experienced programmers (a significant change from the first study, as noted above).

The technical lead oversees the work of the development team, reviews task assignments, collaborates with the development team to review the work of the software developers, and coordinates and schedules testing and quality control. The product lead interfaces with the technical lead but is not involved in the actual software development. Instead, he handles the external interfaces with the customer and management. Hardware, services and supplies, management and customer liaison, training, and documentation are the responsibility of the entire development team in coordination with the service groups. Everyone contributes in an ongoing manner to the documentation and training materials to be delivered with the software product.

Over the time periods of the two studies, SDF has worked primarily in a military environment – most of their contracts were spread over a series of years or periods. SDF has frequently been involved in demonstration and experimental products. The military used SDF to experiment by creating prototype, proof-of-concept systems. These products evolved by adding features and capabilities to become full-fledged, industry-standard products under long-term contracts. In an effort to diversify and limit their dependence on government sector contracts, SDF made some ventures into the commercial market, but with limited success.

SDF's core product consists of a basic set of software agents. The typical system can be retrofitted to a particular customer. Each product takes on a particular character by adding agents that are specifically developed to meet unique needs for the customer.

The various phases of the development process are discussed in more detail in the following sections.

Product initiation

The directors of the firm operate as the initial and primary contacts with the military and private firms. Once an opportunity is identified, dialogue is initiated with the agency or the firm. As the work scope takes form, product leads and technical leads are introduced into the dialogue. In some cases, area experts or consultants are brought in to assist in the knowledge collection from the customer. This phase supports a key aspect of SDF's modular approach – a more stable, certain product goal and scope definition.

Product design

The product design phase consists of identifying system requirements, deciding on a format for system presentation, and specifying the system design. Throughout the product development, there is an internal customer champion who maintains consistent, ongoing contact with the product developers. The spatial agent technology employed relies on the acquisition of data by artificial intelligence techniques in the form of data definition and rule specification. SDF created an integrated mapping tool [IMT] to facilitate the incorporation of heterogeneous data elements from a variety of sources and storage sources into a homogeneous database. The IMT instrument provides a methodology for clear, concise, and consistent data definition for all products and a basis for common understanding by the development team and its customers.

The customer reviews and approves the front-end (Graphical User Interface) before delivery of the to-be-completed functionality. A set of reusable software and hardware formulations is used to construct a collaborative data management product, called the Interactive Collaborative Data Management (ICDM) Tool Kit. The tool kit is one of SDF's primary competitive advantages because it insulates, insures, and protects their intellectual property. Products developed in most government and military work are usually available to any company for use. The wording in all SDF contracts explicitly protect the source code contained in their Tool Kit.

The product manager and the technical lead together compile the estimates and schedules for the product construction with input from the development team. Arrangements are made with the testing groups and service groups, and preparations are made for documentation and training. A key element of SDF's sustainability is the deployment of the support teams as an overlay on the modular product development structure – another kind of reusable feature. Since SDF currently has major ongoing products with the military which have been fully implemented and are now in a support and maintenance mode, these business units provide a supporting function.

One change that occurred between the two studies is the method of product design and implementation. In the present situation, the product work is divided into tasks. Each task is designed to be completed within a period of up to one month. The tasks are defined initially by the technical lead, and refined by the development team members working on the task. At the end of the period, there are concrete deliverables tied to the task work. The term *task work* is key, because the task focus helps to ground the product development in terms of work completed or in progress.

The iterative, task-based approach used at SDF exemplifies an emerging software industry practice known as "Agile" development, which is employed with the intent to provide more predictable and successful software delivery at a sustainable pace for the people involved. This allows companies like SDF to eliminate the frequent *death marches* (high-pressure endgame races to complete a project, involving long hours of overtime) that are often experienced in the computer industry when using older, more traditional project management methods (cf. Chapter 4 in this volume). Agile development focuses on team empowerment and self-direction. Agility is supported by the selection and acculturation of team members to assume responsibility and to self-monitor their work. "Extreme programming," employed at the time of the first study, focused on short, iterative development cycles with overarching long-term project goals. The agile approach takes the project a step at a time. For agile development, all of the elements related to the tasks are contained in SDF's Task Tool Kit. The kit allows the leads to be more effective managers by empowering their teams (Simons 2007). The kit is more intangible than the earlier SDF tools discussed in the chapter. It comprises a set of guidelines and a roadmap for the development team to use in defining their deliverables, the distribution of work, and the associated timeframes for the forthcoming period. In support of this process, the kit has a variety of diagnostic controls – plans, budgets, goals, objectives, and ultimately performance (achievements compared to expectations).

Product construction and delivery

The product construction consists of parallel operations. The technical lead and the product manager work somewhat independently. The computer programs are written by the development team. *Reusable modules* are deployed – taking advantage of existing technology/expertise and work already tried and tested. This is another ingredient in sustainability; teams do not have to create a new product from scratch. The product definition and design and the team skill sets and cross-training are such that all development team members are somewhat interchangeable.

Each module goes through a variety of tests – unit testing of each module and system testing of the modules together. Before any product is presented to the customer, it is tested for internal reliability and adherence to specifications. As the testing and programming proceeds, documentation is updated. An independent group produces professional quality manuals, online and web-based materials. When the production of the software reaches a stage where the user needs to be involved (and because the documentation is to be presented to the customer) the documentation staff accompanies the product lead, technical leads, and key members of the development team to the customer site. While the programs are being developed, tested, and documented, the service group arranges for the purchase and configuration of the network and workstations or for the installation of the system on the customer's hardware and network.

After the equipment becomes operational, the new software is installed by the technical lead and area specialists with support from the service groups. Here the user testing and development are supported by the service group and the technical lead. Training is conducted simultaneously and documentation needs are noted.

Product development and sustainability

Table 6.1 summarizes the mechanisms and requisite capabilities for sustainability in effect at time 1 and time 2, corresponding to the two studies. There are several factors that set SDF apart with respect to supporting and enhancing business sustainability. First, there is a clear and understood path for product development. Second, the team is supported by permanent or "persistent" teams and support staff throughout all product development activities. In the software development industry, the typical project life cycle ends upon the delivery of the product, and teams are often disbanded at that point and then reassembled again later when and if needed. At SDF, because teams are persistent, there is not the project ramp up process of team assembly (with associated costs) that often occurs in software development. In a ramp-up development environment, team members are assembled and scheduled as needed, often using contingent staff (contractors), and transition in and out of the development team based on the applicability of their skill set. In contrast, at SDF, the persistent teams and the team clusters (e.g., development team, testing, and service) provide a sense of identity, stability, and long-term balance (see also Chapter 8).

Before a contract is negotiated and formalized, time is set aside to develop shared understanding of the purpose and scope. The customer has a clear picture of the product scope. Constraints and deliverables are clearly specified. This is an important aspect in sustainability – developing toward a moving target can be counterproductive. In many software product development efforts, especially those related to government and military work, considerable time is spent on rework and renegotiation to accommodate changes in the product scope over the product life cycle.

On the other hand, even though scope and purpose do receive careful definition at the beginning of the project, clarification and refinement of details are viewed as an important ongoing process. Information-sharing and decision-making mechanisms are facilitated through deliberation. The driving force for the ongoing deliberation is the shared fundamental norm that says that "It is better to develop the product correctly the first time rather than having to do expensive remakes." We observed that there was very little rework in any of the SDF products. In the software groups, we observed that face-to-face dialogues and mediated help sessions seem to be an important aspect – almost as much as using formal help desks and online retrieval from technical libraries. One change observed in the later study was the mode of interaction within the development team – instead of extended discussions online, more face-to-face messaging and dialoguing took place.

In the product construction phase, using the task tool to assist the product development team is critical. The task emphasis makes the work more manageable, rather than placing the work to be done exclusively in a long-term perspective. The

Table 6.1 Mechanisms and capabilities for sustainability

	Time 1	Time 2
	Technical features (mechanisms)	
Design strategy	Focused – prototype, demonstration systems for military and government agencies	Differentiated – fully functional, rich-featured systems for military and government agencies
	Internal development – build staff expertise and core software pieces	Diversified – some inroads in commercial market for agent-based systems
Design platform	Modular-based architecture – dual leadership	Modular-based architecture – technical leadership
Knowledge database management	Database specialists used to create database structures – requirement to incorporate into adaptive knowledge database structure	Created and deployed Integrated Mapping Tool (IMT) to create homogeneous data structures from heterogeneous data sources
	Agent-based spatial management orientation	Agent-based spatial management orientation
Software development aids	ICDM Tool Kit – set of reusable code deploying object-oriented agent-based systems and data elements	ICDM Tool Kit – set of reusable code deploying object-oriented agent-based systems and data elements – expanded to contain object repository to enhance new and differing versions of code sets
	Iterative-based process for product development – initiation, design, construction, and delivery – use of traditional project management software to define entire project path at inception	Task Tool Set – end-product goal is specified at inception but steps to attain goal are not defined. Instead, a monthly set of tasks are self-selected by team members together with technical lead. Specific, concrete deliverables in the form of code, screen designs, documentation, and other product elements are designated by the development team. Each task month builds on the previous deliverables leading to the attainment of the product goal

		Social capability features
Programming approach	Extreme programming employed – focused on short iterative development cycles. Direction from product and technical leads	Agile development is used – this focuses team empowerment and self-direction. Minimal direction from technical or product leads
Team orientation	Team-based organization with technical and product leads jointly directing team work (extensive hands-on involvement)	Self-directed teams under hands-off direction of technical lead. Product lead serves as liaison and facilitator. Both leads support, mentor, and coach development team
	Promotes teamwork – all team members actively participate and contribute regardless of experience level	Team members are cross-trained software specialists – they focus on software issues rather than domain specifics (complementary skill sets)
	Team comprising mix of part-time and full-time developers with wide variation in skill set	Team composed of experienced cadre of senior developers with complementary skill sets and few part-time developers
Social aspects	Emphasis on customer involvement at beginning and end of product development	Regard customer to be partner in product specification and development – continuous involvement through and after product completion
Software development approach	Dual product team leadership – responsibilities shared between product and technical leads	Technical lead is sole team leader and assumes responsibility as domain specialist. Product lead handles liaison with customer and support groups
	– Iteration planning meetings – Release plan-driven – Test and acceptance plan	– Fewer meetings, more ongoing communication – People over process – Flexible, people-driven

software coding and testing are confined to specific tasks and integrated as needed. The product is run past the customer for review as it passes through the stages of development. Equipment and network infrastructure installation, training, and documentation, which must interface with the software product as it reaches completion, are integrated and phased, as well.

Individual development

The SDF culture emphasizes the need for individuals to maintain and develop their technological expertise. The firm invests continuously in its human capital, using a variety of mechanisms. All employees are expected to spend at least 10 percent of their work time in continuing education by taking outside training, in-house training, attending workshops and conferences, and through self-study. Formal seminars and forums are held weekly to share expertise and to provide the big picture – the firm's plans, current and proposed projects, and technological developments. During the growth of the firm, care has been taken to insure that new employees are fully integrated. During that time, the constituency of the individual members has changed with respect to their work habits – there is less time spent at work and more time devoted to work-life balance. At the time of the first study, the typical developer would spend ten or more hours per day – perhaps a six-day week. That has changed to a more normal eight-hour, five-day week. The developers are now more experienced and have a greater degree of expertise. On the personal side, many of them have been with SDF for over ten years – during which time they have transitioned from being recent graduates to having families, with all the associated challenges of work–life balancing.

Specific efforts have been made to develop and retain permanent staff. The majority of the development team members have been with SDF for over ten years. All members of all of the development teams have identical training and education – everyone graduated from the same university and majored in computer science. In contrast to other firms in the software industry, SDF has a very low turnover rate. The challenge that SDF has successfully addressed is how to manage people who don't want to be led – people who value self-discovery and learning by doing, who have a desire not to be told how to do specific tasks (Goffee and Jones 2007). The employees realize that they cannot function without the resources and leadership that SDF provides. Management recognizes that their development teams and leads are sources of great ideas but that some measure of discipline needs to be in place. The challenge has been to make the development team feel that they are independent and special while simultaneously recognizing their interdependence.

Discussion

The study of new product development in the SDF case provides initial support to the argument that sustainability can be designed and managed in the NPD environment in various ways. These can be described as a set of dimensions that fit neatly into SDF's architecture schema, each of which fulfils a necessary requirement for achieving sustainability. The set of necessary (but not sufficient) requirements for achieving sustainability can be referred to as design requirements. Looking at the case, the following are a few of the design requirements that seem to have been utilized: legitimate formal and informal arenas for the exchange of ideas were created; continuity of support and improvement efforts for the products were maintained over a long period of time; the composition of the team reflected the totality of the business functional areas of expertise; goals, scope, and purpose for the teams were defined and refined on an ongoing basis; and there were effective processes for implementing continuous improvements during the NPD process. The deployment of modular-based components at various phases of the product development cycle mirrors SDF's architecture.

Modular-based work design provides the foundation for sustainability at both the team and organizational levels. This approach allows for simultaneous autonomy and scope definition for work at different levels and phases. The various tool kits and intellectual properties enhanced ongoing knowledge acquisition, the flow of information, and continuous improvement of the NPD process. The strain of adding unbudgeted additional features during software development, as well as the software development death march, were virtually eliminated by deploying task tools to create working modules, building blocks, and defined boundaries. The time-to-market for the product was insured through the use of the agent structure and the task tool kit deployment.

One of the key findings from the case is that SDF established a legitimate forum for the exchange of ideas and actions. From an organization design perspective, the forum is seen as a mechanism with a structural configuration and processes that are devoted to improvements and learning (Shani and Docherty 2003, 2008). The agile programming approach, coupled with the deliberation mechanisms for information-sharing and viewing echoed by SDF's modular software design, provides an ongoing opportunity to improve and sustain business results and a way to foster learning at all levels and across all levels of the firm. We conjecture that SDF's product development process suggests that not only are learning mechanisms (such as mentoring and face-to-face and online dialogues) an integral part of sustainability, but that the type of learning mechanism is a clear managerial choice that has a significant influence on the organization's ability to develop and nurture sustainability. The very way that the firm chooses to lay out the work environment and the support patterns facilitates and establishes the ongoing learning environment.

The findings and differences at SDF in terms of the utilization of technology over the two time periods were presented in Table 6.1. SDF started with a focused strategy, but modified this to a differentiation strategy as the product base evolved from prototype to fully functioning systems. This is perhaps the main key to SDF's sustainability in terms of growth and retention of staff and revenues. Most software firms continually face the problems of obtaining new and continuing business.

The team orientation changed slightly over time in terms of leadership. The joint technical and product lead arrangement was not workable and evolved to a greater emphasis on technical direction. Some changes in team composition took place to make the development team more workable, cohesive, and complementary in terms of skill sets, division of responsibility, and natural understanding of task requirements – each team member having their specific skill and role, as well as a certain amount of cross-training.

There were some subtle differences as the development team moved from extreme programming to agile programming. The idea was not to force the project into a set of iterative plans and milestones, but instead to take the work by period – to divide the work into manageable timeframes and regularly reassess status and direction in a joint, collegial fashion.

Conclusion

Sustainability in new product development environment in the software industry emerged as a set of major challenges in the "new" economy. Sustainable work systems are characterized by opportunities for individuals to continuously regenerate resources, skills, and knowledge. This chapter advanced an integrative framework to explore the interplay between modular-based NPD work and sustainability.

The study of new product development in the SDF company illustrated that the proposed integrative framework can be a useful analytical tool to examine the dynamics of work intensity and sustainability in the new economy. Furthermore, it provides initial support to the argument that sustainability can be designed and managed in the NPD environment in various ways. Design is viewed as a clear set of choices among alternatives. It was further argued that the various ways can be described as a set of dimensions which fit neatly into the modular-based architecture schema, each of which fulfils a necessary requirement for achieving sustainability.

Learning mechanisms seem to have played a critical part in sustainability at SDF. Managers at SDF made choices about the design and deployment of specific learning mechanisms. The modular-based architecture for NPD work provided a context that has the potential to foster work environments that increase the organization's ability to develop and nurture sustainability.

Questions for reflection

Here are three questions for your further reflection on the issues broached in this chapter:

- Identify and describe the role that learning mechanisms played in the development of a sustainable work system at SDF.
- Discuss how the platform-based architecture framework and tools facilitated and sustained new product development projects.

- The argument that sustainability can be designed and managed in various ways in a new product development environment was advanced in this chapter. What are some of the design dimensions and requirements that were utilized at SDF?

References

Adler, N., and Docherty, P. (1998) "Bringing business into sociotechnical theory and practice," *Human Relations*, 51, 3, 319–345.

Ambler, S. (2002) *Agile Modeling*, New York: John Wiley and Sons.

Belliveau, P., Griffin, A., and Somermeyer, S. (2002) *PDMA ToolBook 1 for New Product Development*, New York: John Wiley.

Belliveau, P., Griffin, A., and Somermeyer, S. (2004) *PDMA ToolBook 2 for New Product Development*, New York: John Wiley.

Drucker, P.F. (1985) "The discipline of innovation," *Harvard Business Review*, 63, May–June, 67–72.

Eijnatten, F., Shani, A.B. (Rami), and Leary, M. (2008) "Socio-technical systems: designing and managing sustainable organizations," in T. Cumming (ed.), *Handbook of Organization Development and Change*, Thousand Oaks, CA: Sage (in press).

Goffee, R., and Jones, G. (2007) "How to manage the most talented," *Harvard Business Review*, March, 72–79.

Kolodny, H.F., and Halpern, N. (2008) "From collaborative design to collaborative research: A sociotechnical journey," in A.B. (Rami) Shani, S.A. Mohrman, W.A. Pasmore, B. Stymne, and N. Adler (eds), *Handbook of Collaborative Management Research*, Los Angeles: Sage, pp. 263–276.

Krishnan, V., and Gupta, S. (2001) "Appropriateness and impact of platform-based product development," *Management Science*, 47, 1, 52–68.

Lander, S. (1997) "Issues in multiagent design systems," *IEEE Expert*, March/April.

Muffatto, M. (1999) "Introducing a platform strategy in product development," *International Journal of Production Economics*, 60–61, 145–163.

Olin, T., and Shani, A.B. (Rami) (2001) "New product development and sustainability: Learning from Ericsson," paper presented at the 8th International Product Development Conference, EIASM, Enschede, The Netherlands, June.

Pasmore, W.A. (1994) *Creating Strategic Change*, New York: John Wiley.

Pava, C. (1986) "Redesigning sociotechnical systems design: Concepts and methods for the 1990s," *Journal of Applied Behavioral Science*, 22, 3, 201–222.

Schilling, M.A., and Hill, C.W.L. (1998) "Managing the new product development process," *The Academy of Management Executive*, 12, 3, 67–81.

Shani, A.B. (Rami), and Docherty, P. (2003) *Learning by Design: Building Sustainable Organizations*, Oxford: Blackwell Publications.

Shani, A.B., and Docherty, P. (2008) "Learning by design: A fundamental foundation for organization development change programs," in T. Cumming (ed.), *Handbook of Organization Development and Change*, Thousand Oaks, CA: Sage (in press).

Shani, A.B. (Rami), and Sena, J.A. (2002) "Integrating product and personal development," in P. Docherty, J. Forslin, and A.B. (Rami) Shani (eds), *Creating Sustainable Work Systems: Emerging Perspectives and Practice*, London: Routledge, pp. 89–100.

Shani, A.B., Grant, R., and Krishnan, R. (1992) "Advanced manufacturing systems and organizational choice: A sociotechnical system approach," *California Management Review*, 34, 4, 91–111.

Simons, R. (2007) "Control in the age of empowerment: The creative company," *Harvard Business Review On Point: Executive Edition*, Spring, 106–114.

Taylor, J.C., and Felton, D.F. (1993) *Performance by Design: Sociotechnical Systems in North America*, Englewood Cliffs, NJ: Prentice Hall.

Trist, E.L. (1982) "The evolution of sociotechnical systems," in A.H. Van de Ven and W.F. Joyce (eds), *Perspectives on Organization Design and Behavior*, New York: John Wiley, pp. 19–75.

Part III

Focusing change in sustainable organizations

7 Creating sustainable, desired change in teams through application of intentional change and complexity theories

Richard E. Boyatzis[1]

Introduction

Before we can help others guide desired change, we must understand how change occurs. For all the time and energy devoted to change, there are surprisingly few theories about it. In this chapter, we present Intentional Change Theory (ICT). Briefly, ICT postulates that sustainable, desired change occurs as a discontinuous, nonlinear process through a series of emergent discoveries. In teams, the first discovery must be a shared vision, which engages the motivational pull of the Positive Emotional Attractor. It will be shown how this invokes neuro-endocrine processes within the team members that allow (Boyatzis and McKee 2005) creative, open, and complex thought. This arousal allows team members to adapt, innovate, and be resilient. But unless team members are pulled to alternate between two *emotional attractors* (the *Positive Emotional Attractor* and the *Negative Emotional Attractor*), no change occurs.

It is also evident that sustainable, desired change is a multileveled phenomenon. It requires comparable change to occur contemporaneously at the individual, team, organizational, and larger social systems levels. It will be shown that resonant leadership relationships are a connective factor in the emergence of sustained, desired change in teams across the levels.

While there is a large literature on small groups and teams, there is dramatically less on team development (Akrivou *et al.* 2006). Most of the work on team development occurs in practice, by consultants. The result is that there are few theories of team development. The major theories are Bennis and Shepard (1956), Freud (1959), Bion (1961), and Bales (1970). From a complexity perspective, little has been written about team or small group development.

A complex system is a multilevel combination of systems that may behave in a way independent of any one of the component systems.[2] A complex system is more than a simple system (which exists at a single level) or a complicated system (such as a simple system with nonlinear dynamics).

Specifically, to be considered complex, a system must have three properties. One is *scale* (Eric Baer articulated this concept in the Complexity Forum). Scale refers to the existence of dynamics that are parallel at multiple levels of a system (Casti 1994). For example, change within individuals appears to follow the same dynamics as change within groups, teams or families, organizations, communities, and countries. Nested systems with this property are sometimes inaccurately called "fractals," but that is a technical term that refers only to one type of scaled system. For example, to obtain sustained development in a team, change must occur in the behaviour of individual team members, as well as within the organization that manages or owns the team (see also Chapter 15 in this volume). A second property is *interaction*. That is, identification of the factors that provide inter-action among the levels – and description of how they do it. For example, some-thing has to provide bidirectionality of information between each of the pairs of levels in a complex system. The third property is *function* – a description of how the components of the system function or affect each other. This is often referred to as the input–output transformation that occurs within a system. For example, you chew food, which is then reduced to its constituent chemicals and nutrients by stomach acids and moved into the cellular system of the body through the lining of the stomach, small intestines, or large intestine.

Team development as intentional change

Sustained, desired change can be described by Intentional Change Theory (ICT) (Boyatzis 2006a). *Desired change* is something that a person would like to occur. It is not accidental or the result of acts of nature, such as earthquakes. It is not inevitable, as is the effect of aging on the loss of elasticity of muscle tissue.

The change is *sustainable* if it endures over time. It has a characteristic of self-perpetuation, repeated reinvention, or replication. Sustainable, in this definition, means that the components do not atrophy or become exhausted during the change process. Intentionality is required to achieve a desired, sustainable change or to maintain a current desired state, relationship, or habit. Knowing that things can atrophy or drift into a less desired state, the desire to maintain the current state requires deliberate investment of energy in this maintenance.

Desired sustainable changes in a team's norms, shared beliefs, purpose, roles, and identity are most often discontinuous. That is, they tend to appear as emergent or catastrophic changes, which is a property of complex systems (Casti 1994). The experience of these changes is one of surprise or discovery (Boyatzis 2006a). The degree of surprise is often inversely proportionate to the degree of self-awareness or mindfulness (of self and context, both social and natural). If a team member is mindful of the group's dynamics, changes may be expected and, therefore, may appear more as a set of smooth transitions. For example, a mindful or observant team member may notice a particularly close, personal rela-tionship developing among three team players. When these three people begin to act toward team issues as a coalition (with the same perspective on issues), it is not surprising. But to another team member, the appearance of a coalition within the team may seem puzzling and sudden. But as a complex system, team develop-ment has moments of surprise even for the most observant members or coaches.

The dynamics of emergence often result in the changes being nonlinear. For example, a linear relationship between team practice and team performance would mean that with each practice session comes a noticeable and predictable improvement in performance. Any team member knows that you may see no improvement over three sessions and then, in the fourth, it all comes together and the team executes a new play perfectly. Gersick (1991) called this discontinuity pattern *punctuated equilibrium* – moments of discontinuous, revolutionary change interspersed with periods of equilibrium-seeking behaviour. Therefore, *the team development process is often a nonlinear and discontinuous emergent phenomenon appearing or being experienced as a set of discoveries*. ICT attempts to isolate not merely *when* these differences emerge, but *why* they occur.

Tipping points and emergence

The discontinuities occur at tipping points (Holland 1995), like the emergence of a leader in a team. Malcolm Gladwell popularized this idea with his book *The Tipping Point*, but McClelland (1998) and Boyatzis (2006b) showed that up to a certain point, the relationship between a person's abilities and their performance as a leader may not appear to exist. Once a specific point is reached, the effect of a small incremental increase in certain behaviours produces a dramatic increase in the individual's leadership.

Effective use of a tipping point in sports teams is often expected when hiring a star player. Two stories illustrate how this may or may not work. In one case, the Cleveland Browns American football team hired star quarterback Tim Couch. A few years later, the Cleveland Cavaliers basketball team hired the top draft pick, LeBron James. The Cavaliers' record improved dramatically, while the Browns' record did not. James is a catalyst within the team. He provides emotional glue and embodies a commitment to team play – not merely to his own image or record. A sports reporter commented:

> The Cleveland Cavaliers are in the National Basketball Association finals for the first time in their 37-year history, and James – their preternaturally polished, selfless star forward – is the reason. Although he can dominate as a scorer . . . James is just as likely to defer to teammates and control a game with his passes. . . . And his emergence comes at a time when the NBA in general is criticized for being a league of too many one-on-one players, and the United States national team, with numerous NBA stars, has been embarrassed more than once on the world stage.[3]

The 1980 US Olympic Hockey Team won the Gold Metal. In contrast, repeated losses by the US Olympic Men's Basketball teams in 2000 and 2004 showed that having a team of superstars does not produce the magic that makes a team. Real Madrid, in the period from 2000 to 2007 was a World Association Football (known as soccer in the United States) team that was composed of extremely highly paid superstars, and performed poorly. It requires something else to hit the tipping point, something in addition to talent. The US Women's World Cup football (in the US, soccer) team showed this in 1999 and repeatedly thereafter. In interviews with the team, players all talk about the relationships they built and how key players like Brandy Chastain and Mia Hamm were an emotional glue that brought the team together (Bernstein and Greenburg 2005). Chastain and Hamm were team leaders and created the tipping point in the team's performance. The importance of sudden emergence of leaders was also linked to effective performance in self-managing work teams in an industrial manufacturing setting (Wolff *et al.* 2002).

The five discoveries of intentional change theory

Team development involves a sequence of discontinuities or discoveries, which function in an iterative cycle in producing sustainable change (see also Chapters 2, 3, 9, 11, 12, and 16 in this volume). These are: (1) *a shared vision* (i.e., shared image of the Ideal Team); (2) *the norms and practices of the team that constitute its Real Self*, and comparison to the Ideal that results in an assessment of team strengths and weaknesses – in a sense a Team Balance Sheet; (3) *a Learning Agenda and Plan*; (4) *Experimentation and practice* with the new behaviour, thoughts, feelings, or perceptions of effective teams; and (5) *Trusting, or Resonant Relationships* that enable all members of a team to experience and process each discovery in the cycle. The process of intentional change is graphically shown in Figure 7.1 (Boyatzis 2006a).

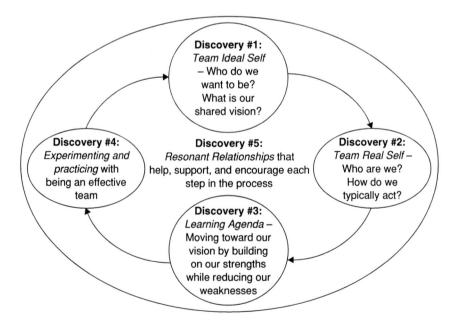

Figure 7.1 Team intentional change theory

The first discontinuity and potential starting point for the process of team development is the discovery of who the group wants to be. The team's Ideal Self is an image of what the team wants to be. It appears to have three major components that drive the development of a shared image of the Ideal Self: (1) an image of a desired future; (2) hope that they can attain it; and (3) aspects of their core identity, which includes enduring strengths, on which they build for their desired future (Boyatzis and Akrivou 2006). As the team's Ideal Self becomes conscious and explicit, it forms the focal point for the team's desire, or intention.

This team dream engages the power of positive imaging or visioning, well documented in sports psychology, meditation, biofeedback, and other psychophysiological research (Goleman *et al.* 2002). The purpose of a team was the heart of Bennis and Shepard's (1956) classic theory of group development. Meanwhile, in most work or educational groups, we skip over discussion of shared purpose and assume it is understood by all present. In doing so, we anesthetize ourselves against the possibilities of a vibrant, shared vision. Each component of Boyatzis' model of the Ideal Self (Boyatzis and Akrivou 2006) contributes to the emergence of the team's shared vision. For example, experiencing hope and a collective sense of efficacy directly helps improve teamwork and team performance (Tasa *et al.* 2007).

It is also clear from this framework that "strengths-based" approaches to development will probably work better than current methods but will fall short of what individuals and teams can achieve. In focusing on the team's established strengths, such approaches develop the Core Identity component of the Ideal Self as a driver of change, but fail to capture the energy inherent in dreams of the future and new possibilities, and fail to capture the emotional driver of hope.

The self-awareness of the current team – the team's understanding of their own norms and values and of how others see them – is elusive. For normal reasons, our ego defence mechanisms protect the human psyche, but they also conspire to delude us. At the team level, this has been labelled as "groupthink."

The greatest challenge to an accurate current self-image as a team is an open flow of evaluative information within the team, as well as between the team and the external environment. One of the group norms that predicts lower learning in teams is the practice of not openly confronting internal conflicts (such as unequal contributions to the group's work) (Druskat and Kayes 2000).

For teams to truly consider changing a part of themselves, they must have a sense of what they value and want to keep. These areas in which their Real Self and Ideal Self are consistent or congruent can be considered strengths. Likewise, to consider what they want to preserve about themselves involves admitting aspects that they wish to change or adapt in some manner. Areas where the Real Self and Ideal Self are not consistent can be considered gaps, or weaknesses.

All too often, teams explore growth or development by focusing on the "gaps" or deficiencies, especially in performance teams where scores are public and openly debated in the press. Many team training programs, periodic reviews, and even coaching often make the same mistake. There is an assumption that we can "leave well enough alone" and get to the areas that need work. It is no wonder that many of these programs, intended to help a team develop, result instead in the team feeling battered, beleaguered, and bruised, not helped or encouraged.

The third discontinuity is development of an agenda and focusing on the desired future. While increased performance or team morale may be the long-term intended consequence of the change effort, a learning agenda focuses on development, exploration, and novelty. A learning orientation arouses a positive belief in one's capability and the hope of improvement. It results in people setting personal standards of performance, rather than accepting normative standards that merely mimic what others have done. Meanwhile, a performance orientation evokes anxiety and doubts about whether or not we can change (Seijts *et al.* 2004).

The pull of two attractors

Team development produces sustainable, desirable changes as an iterative, cyclical process. ICT explains the five emergent discoveries of the process. In addition, an essential aspect of sustaining the desired change and continuing to improve or evolve involves iterations or repeated cycling through the discoveries. Because of the awareness from earlier cycles, subsequent discoveries are less surprising. Two strange or Lorenz attractors, the *Positive Emotional Attractor* (PEA) and *Negative Emotional Attractor* (NEA), determine the self-organizing process of change.

The human organism and our teams are not closed systems. Among other things, we need social interaction to allow our "open loop" emotional system to function (Goleman *et al.* 2002). Even more dramatic in its destabilizing effect is the continuing course of one's life and career cycles. There is a team level counterpart to individual life cycles (Bennis and Shepard 1956; Bion 1961; Bales 1970; Gersick 1991).

The Positive Emotional Attractor (PEA) can become a destabilizing force. It can pull the team toward their shared Ideal. In the process of drawing individuals to focus on future possibilities and filling them with hope, it arouses the Parasympathetic Nervous System (PSNS) (Boyatzis *et al.* 2006) in team members. Once the PSNS is aroused, each person has access to more of their neural circuits, finding themselves in a calmer, if not elated, state in which their immune system is functioning well and their body is sustained. They are able, in this state, to experience neurogenesis (i.e., the conversion of hippocampal stem cells into new neurons) as new learning becomes possible. It is even suggested that formation of learning goals or learning-oriented goals invokes this attractor and results in more successful change (Howard 2006). This works in teams in the same way. Having a sense of shared identity and aspirations reduces stress that others may experience in the same setting and propels a team into the PEA, with all of the benefits of sustainability (Haslam and Reicher 2006).

But another attractor is also at play in the system – the Negative Emotional Attractor (NEA). In an analogous manner, it arouses the Sympathetic Nervous

System (SNS), which helps the human to deal with stress and threat and protect itself. Within a threatening environment and threatened state, the NEA pulls a person toward defensive protection. In this arousal, the body shunts blood to the large muscle groups, closes down non-essential neural circuits, suspends the immune system, and produces cortisol – important for protection under threat (Sapolsky 2004). But cortisol inhibits or even stops neurogenesis and overexcites older neurons, rendering them useless (Boyatzis *et al.* 2006).

Each arousal of the PEA can provoke the system into a new level of activation. If the team's adaptation is self-organizing, then desired change not already part of this system is only possible when it is intentional. In addition, sustaining any change effort and repeated use of the emotional self-control that is required are difficult. Desired change, to be achieved and sustained, must be driven by a powerful force. This is where the shared Ideal activates the energy of the PEA (see Chapters 2 and 3 in this volume). This also helps us to understand why there is a need for more positivity than negativity in change efforts, as Fredrickson and Losada (2005) have shown the need for a 3:1 ratio for effective versus ineffective teams. Gottman *et al.* (2002) showed a 5:1 ratio for healthy, loving, stable marriages. But there are upper limits to the effectiveness of positivity as well, which has been mathematically suggested to be about 11:1 (Fredrickson and Losada 2005). By seeking out an appropriate balance of PEA to NEA, whether 3:1 or 5:1 or whatever it should be for a particular team at a point in time, each player is activated to be open to new learning and to be in a state of PSNS arousal. This results in the individual being sustainable, because of the renewing effect of the PSNS.

In addition to the pull of the PEA, the process of desired, sustainable change requires behavioural freedom and "permission" to try something new and see what happens. This permission comes from interaction with others, as we will see in the fourth and fifth discoveries in the process.

Metamorphosis and relationships

The fourth discovery is to experiment and practice desired changes. Acting on the learning plan and toward the goals involves numerous activities. Typically, following a period of experimentation, any member of the team may start to practice new behaviour in the team. At times, the team may experiment with new norms and practices. During this part of the process, intentional change looks like a "continuous improvement" process because it is actually cycling through the ICT with increasing speed.

This part of the process requires finding and using opportunities to learn and change. Team members may not even think they have changed until they have tried new behaviour in a performance setting.

Dreyfus (2008) studied managers of scientists and engineers who were considered superior performers. Once she documented that they used considerably more of certain competencies than their less effective counterparts, she pursued how they developed some of those competencies. One of the distinguishing competencies was group management, also called team building. She found that many of these middle-aged managers had first experimented with team-building skills in high school and college, in sports, clubs, and living groups. Later, when they became bench scientists and engineers working on problems in relative isolation, they still pursued the use and practice of this ability in activities outside of work. They practiced team building and group management in social and community organizations, such as 4-H Clubs, and in professional associations when planning conferences and such.

Our relationships are an essential part of our environment. The most crucial relationships are often within groups that have particular importance to us. These relationships give us a sense of identity, guide us as to what is appropriate and good behaviour, and provide feedback on our behaviour. In sociology, these are called reference groups. These relationships create a context within which we interpret our progress on desired changes and the utility of new learning, and even contribute significant input to formulation of the Ideal.

In this sense, our relationships are mediators, moderators, interpreters, sources of feedback, and sources of support and permission for change and learning. They may also be the most important source of protection from relapses or returning to our earlier forms of behaviour. Wheeler (2008) analyzed the extent to which MBA graduates worked on their goals in multiple "life spheres" (e.g., work, family, recreational groups). In a two-year follow-up study of two of the graduating classes of part-time MBA students, she found those who worked on their goals and plans in multiple sets of relationships improved the most, and more than those working on goals in only one setting such as work or within one relationship.

In a study of the impact of the year-long executive development program for doctors, lawyers, professors, engineers, and other professionals, Ballou *et al.* (1999) found that participants gained self-confidence during the program. Even at the beginning of the program, others would say these participants were very high in self-confidence. It was a curious finding. The graduates of the program explained the increase in self-confidence as an increase in the confidence to change. Their existing reference groups (i.e., family, groups at work, professional groups, community groups) all had an investment in them staying the same, but nevertheless the person wanted to change. The Professional Fellows Program allowed them to develop a new reference group that encouraged change.

Team development only appears possible with the emergence of a new reference or social identity group or the incorporation of elements of a new identity in the existing team. There was a poignant moment in the emergence of the 1980 US Olympic Gold Medal-winning hockey team when individual members began to introduce themselves to others, not as players from their home town or college team, but as members of Team USA. This was a signal to Herb Brooks, the coach, which he was waiting for, that they had begun to see themselves as a team – and a group to which they wanted to belong (O'Connor 2004). This was the emergence of a new reference or social identity group.

Scale and interaction among the levels

Now we come to an aspect of team development through ICT that makes it a complex system – its multileveledness. According to the theory, sustainable change occurs at any level of human and social organization through ICT. Thus far, we have discussed how desired, sustainable change within a team occurs through the group level definitions of the five discoveries of ICT (Akrivou *et al.* 2006). Similarly, desired, sustainable change occurs through ICT's five discoveries at the individual and organizational levels, and at the community, country, and global levels. The levels, listed in order of increasing social size, are:

- individual
- dyad or couple
- team, group, family, coalition
- organization
- community
- country/culture
- global

As a complex system, ICT predicts that team development is only sustainable when levels above and below it are also engaged in a change process (see also Chapter 12). Bidirectionality of information is necessary across levels of a complex system (Hartwell *et al.* 1999). There must be an agent that carries the "contagion" of emotional and other messages back and forth among the levels. ICT predicts that it is leadership, and resonant leadership in particular, that does this among the individual, dyad, team, organization, and community levels (Boyatzis 2006a). Resonant leaders have the trusting, engaged relationships with others around them that were described as the fifth discovery. These are relationships that invoke the PEA more than the NEA, and are energizing (Boyatzis and McKee 2005). For interaction among larger levels (such as community, country and global) to create sustained, desired change, resonant leadership *and* reference or social identity groups (often in the form of coalitions) are also needed.

ICT would claim that any sports team cannot succeed in sustainable performance improvement without a resonant leader within the team. The team captain is often the emotional glue that keeps people working together. The captain is the link between the individual and the team change. Meanwhile, the coach is the person who links the team and organization levels, often represented by the team management and ownership. The team owner or general manager has to move between the organization and the community, managing public relations, fans, and the political community.

The impact of these relationships on winning Super Bowls in professional football in the United States has seldom been clearer than in the comparative stories of the New England Patriots and Cleveland Browns. These teams both had the same coach during two respective periods. The Patriots established a winning team with three Super Bowl victories and an amazing record with Bill Belichick as head coach. In contrast, in the preceding several years the Cleveland Browns were a major disappointment to everyone with Bill Belichick as head coach. One major difference was the set of relationships among the players, coach, owner, and community. In Cleveland, Belichick removed the quarterback whom the community loved, Bernie Kosar, and earned the repeated enmity of the owner. This was often portrayed in the press. Art Modell, owner of the Cleveland Browns, said:

> He was the most difficult man I've ever known in a PR sense. Impossible. If I would have put up with some of his nonsense and other crap off the field that led to his parting company, I think he'd still be my coach. He was a tough guy to deal with. I brought him into my office several times and did the Pygmalion effect – "Sit up straight." I did the "My Fair Lady." He just got pissed off. But I have a high regard for him.[4]

Later, Robert Kraft, the owner of Belichick's new team, the Patriots, said:

> One of the reasons I like him as a coach and human being is that he is never boastful and self-important. He's not a phony, and to me, at this stage of my life, that's important. I think Bill's main focus after football matters are his children, and I have a great deal of respect for that.[5]

In another interview, Kraft added:

> He's not about ego and the sidebar privileges that come with being the head coach. He represents the face of our team and family with values that we feel are important. . . . When the tough times come in this business, the arrows start flying, and you have to stick together. We have the utmost trust in Bill Belichick.[6] . . . . Bill, we gave up the No. 1 pick to Parcells, and people thought I was insane. . . . Bill is cool, calm and analytical and develops a sense of team of people who bond together and make it happen.[7]

A resonant relationship between the head coach and the owner helps the intentional change process at the community and organization levels. In this multilevel context in which a football team plays, one owner, Robert Kraft, enjoyed the media and worked with the press. A result was that the community was behind the team (Halberstam 2005). The other, Art Modell, ran into conflicts and eventually the hatred of the community when he decided to move the team to Baltimore. Many say it was a decision based, in part, on Modell's lack of connection to the community.

At the same time, resonant relationships between the Head Coach and players, in particular the captain or quarterback, can produce desired changes within the team and organization levels. Resonant relationships among the captain or key players and the rest of the team provide the context for desired changes to spread at the individual player and team levels. While Belichick let the community star Bernie Kosar go, at the Patriots he also made tough decisions, like picking Tom

Brady as quarterback instead of playing the existing quarterback, Drew Bledsoe. But the team felt he understood them and the game and cared about them (Levin 2005). As David Patten, one of the players on the Patriots said:

> I have seen a more nurturing side of him. He'd pull me aside and say, "Look, man, we really hate that you're not out there with us. We miss you." Just letting me know how much he appreciated me. Once a coach establishes how much he cares about you, there's nothing a player wouldn't do for him on the field.
>
> (David Patten 2004; for more about this story, see the website www.Allthingsbelichick.com)

We observe a chain of resonant relationships that link desired change from the individual player level to the community level. If any one of those is missing, the team performance suffers and their ability to improve performance or sustain current performance is dramatically reduced.

The same dynamic applies in other teams. Boyatzis *et al.* (1992) reported a program to reduce development time in drug development teams at a major pharmaceutical company. By working on desired change at the individual level and fostering resonant leadership relationships within the team, between the team and other corporate functions, with the FDA, and with other drug development teams, the length of time the company was able to keep drugs under patent protection was almost doubled.

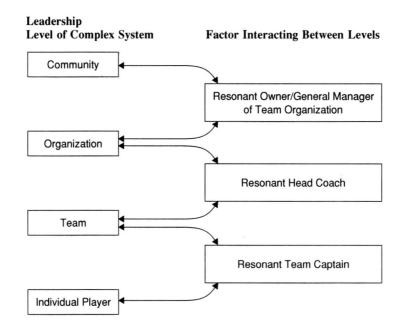

Figure 7.2 Multilevel model of team development and the other roles of leadership

Without this resonant leadership across and within the various levels, there does not seem to be the emergence of desired, sustainable change. Many of the organizational or small group conditions may have been present for a long time, but when a capable or effective leader appears, magic happens – or more accurately, ICT happens (see the August, 2006 issue of the *Journal of Management Development*, devoted to ICT at many levels).

Concluding thought

Sustainability of desired change is the key to effective change. Without intentionally maintaining desired changes, atrophy, entropy, and dissonance will dissolve the progress and may even return the team or other human system to a less desired condition than the one at which they started the change process. Intentional change can be explained through intentional change theory (ICT), but it requires concepts from complexity theory to comprehend what is occurring and when and why it occurs. Concepts like tipping points, emergence of leaders, the pull of attractors, and the multiple levels involved shine a light on the path to sustainability within the human body as well as for our collective systems such as teams and organizations. We cannot avoid stress or its ravaging effects on humans and human systems. But we can invoke alternative processes like the PEA that help to rebuild or build a new mental and emotional state, capacity to learn and adapt, and create desired change.

Questions for reflection

Here are three questions for your further reflection on the issues broached in this chapter:

- What interventions or processes can stimulate the Positive Emotional Attractor in teams and, therefore, help to sustain team effectiveness and improvement?
- How and when do you instigate or foster the emergence of resonant leaders in teams?
- If team development requires a multilevel, intentional change process, how do you involve the various levels, invite resonant leaders to help the process reach across levels, and address these issues at the most useful times?

Notes

1 The author would like to thank Michael Garred, Emure Yegen, and Joshus Sens from his MBA course, and Michael Bowling, Byron Clayton, Mark Engle, Ganesh Kumar, Kathy Overbeke, and Dinesh Shah from his Executive Doctorate in Management course, for insights developed during their class projects that helped in the development of the ideas presented in this paper.
2 Many of these advances in definitions and understanding of complex systems came from a three-year faculty seminar called the Complexity Forum (2001–2003) at Case Western

Reserve University. It was chaired by Professor Mihajlo Mesarovic, with Professors Alexander, Aron, Baer, Barmish, Beer, Boyatzis, Carlsson, Greenspan, Hutton, Kahana, Koonce, Loparo, McHale, Satry, Singer, Solow, Sreenath, Strange, Tabib-Asar, Taylor, and Voltz.

3 Beck, H. (2007) "Ready for the NBA throne, but not like Mike," *New York Times,* Wednesday, June 6, 2007, A1, C19.

4 *New York Daily News,* January, 2007, cited in www.Allthingsbelichick.com.

5 *Boston Globe,* March, 2007, cited in www.Allthingsbelichick.com.

6 *Boston Globe,* January, 2006, cited in www.Allthingsbelichick.com.

7 *New York Times,* November, 2003, cited in www.Allthingsbelichick.com.

References

Akrivou, K., Boyatzis, R.E., and McLeod, P.L. (2006) "The evolving group: Towards a prescriptive theory of intentional group development," *Journal of Management Development,* 25, 7, 689–709.

Bales, R.F. (1970) *Personality and Interpersonal Behaviour,* New York: Holt, Rinehardt and Winston.

Ballou, R., Bowers, D., Boyatzis, R.E., and Kolb, D.A. (1999) "Fellowship in lifelong learning: An executive development program for advanced professionals," *Journal of Management Education,* 23, 4, 338–354.

Bennis, W.G. and Shepard, H.A. (1956) "A theory of group development," *Human Relations,* 9, 415–437.

Bernstein, R. and Greenburg, R. (executive producers) (2005) *Dare to Dream: The Story of the US Women's Soccer Team* (HBO Sports Special; originally aired 11 December).

Bion, W.R. (1961) *Experiences in Groups,* New York: Basic Books.

Boyatzis, R.E. (2006a) "Intentional change theory from a complexity perspective," *Journal of Management Development,* 25, 7, 607–623.

Boyatzis, R.E. (2006b) "Using tipping points of emotional intelligence and cognitive competencies to predict financial performance of leaders," *Psicothema,* 18, 124–131.

Boyatzis, R.E. and Akrivou, K. (2006) "The ideal self as a driver of change," *Journal of Management Development,* 25, 7, 624–642.

Boyatzis, R.E. and McKee, A. (2005) *Resonant Leadership: Renewing yourself and connecting with others through mindfulness, hope, and compassion,* Boston. MA: Harvard Business School Press.

Boyatzis, R.E., Esteves, M.B., and Spencer, L.M. (1992) "Entrepreneurial innovation in pharmaceutical development," *Human Resource Planning,* 15, 4, 15–30.

Boyatzis, R.E., Smith, M., and Blaize, N. (2006) "Developing sustainable leaders through coaching and compassion," *Academy of Management Journal on Learning and Education,* 5, 1, 8–24.

Casti, J.L. (1994) *Complexification: Explaining a paradoxical world through the science of surprise,* New York: Harper Collins.

Dreyfus, C. (2008) "Identifying competencies that predict effectiveness of R&D managers," *Journal of Management Development,* 27, 1, 76–91.

Druskat, V.U. and Kayes, D.C. (2000) "Learning versus performance in short-term project teams," *Small Group Research,* 31, 3, 328–353.

Fredrickson, B. and Losada, M. (2005) "Positive affect and the complex dynamics of human flourishing," *American Psychologist,* 60, 7, 678–686.

Freud, S. (1959) *Group Psychology and the Analysis of the Ego*, trans. J. Strachey, New York: Liveright (original publisher, London: International Psychoanalytic Press, 1922).

Gersick, C.J. (1991) "Revolutionary change theories: A multilevel exploration of the punctuated equilibrium paradigm," *Academy of Management Review*, 16, 274–309.

Goleman, D., Boyatzis, R.E., and McKee, A. (2002) *Primal Leadership: Realizing the power of emotional intelligence*, Boston, MA: Harvard Business School Press.

Gottman, J.M., Murray, J.D., Swanson, C.C., Tyson, R., and Swanson, K.R. (2002) *The Mathematics of Marriage: Dynamic nonlinear models*, Cambridge, MA: MIT Press.

Halberstam, D. (2005) *The Education of a Coach*, New York: Hyperion Books.

Hartwell, L.H., Hopfield, J.J., Leibler, S., and Murray, A.W. (1999) "From molecular to modular cell biology," *Nature, 402* (supplement), December, 47–52.

Haslam, S.A. and Reicher, S. (2006) "Stressing the group: Social identity and the unfolding dynamics of response to stress," *Journal of Applied Psychology*, 9, 5, 1037–1052.

Holland, J. (1995) *Hidden Order: How adaptation builds complexity*. Reading, MA: Helix Books.

Howard, A. (2006) "Positive and negative emotional attractors and intentional change," *Journal of Management Development*, 25, 7, 657–670.

Levin, James (2005) *Management Secrets of the New England Patriots*, Stamford, CT: Pointer Press.

McClelland, D.C. (1998) "Identifying competencies with behavioral event interviews," *Psychological Science*, 9, 331–339.

O'Connor, G. (2004) *Miracle: The DVD (with the supplementary interview with Coach Herb Brooks)*, Disney Entertainment.

Sapolsky, R.M. (2004) *Why Zebras Don't Get Ulcers* (3rd edn), New York: HarperCollins.

Seijts, G.H., Latham, G.P.O., Tasa, K., and Latham, B.W. (2004) "Goal setting and goal orientation: An integration of two different yet related literatures," *Academy of Management Journal*, 47, 2, 227–239.

Tasa, K., Taggar, S., and Seijts, G.H. (2007) "The development of collective efficacy in teams: A multilevel and longitudinal perspective," *Journal of Applied Psychology*, 92, 1, 17–27.

Wheeler, J.V. (2008) "The impact of social environments on emotional, social, and cognitive competency development," *Journal of Management Development*, 27, 1, 129–145.

Wolff, S.B., Pescosolido, A.T., and Druskat, V.U. (2002) "Emotional intelligence as the basis of leadership emergence in self-managing teams," *Leadership Quarterly*, 13, 5, 505–522.

8 Sustainable heritage in a rapidly changing environment

Lena Wilhelmson and Marianne Döös

Introduction

Learning, development, and sustainability all have positive connotations. The processes they denote are easily thought of as being as harmonious and unproblematic as the outcome. Such processes, however, require change and new thinking that expands earlier understanding, leaving old paradigms and entering new ones. This implies fluctuations in the various aspects of sustainability, and is painful and laborious for individuals and organizations alike. This disharmonious duality, between process and outcome, is an assumption behind the present chapter, which illuminates the complex dynamics of sustainability.

A sustainable work system is seen as a system in which management and employees consciously strive for the personal growth of employees as a means of developing competitiveness. We agree with the idea of the resource-centred perspective (Moldaschl 2002; see also Chapter 4 in this volume), in which sustainability is defined in relation to organizational solutions and strategies, which are seen as "sustainable in a social sense if they maintain and reproduce the given social and human resources or even extend them" (*ibid.* 59).

Here we discuss sustainability as a process that includes periods of comfort, growth, and equilibrium, as well as phases of pain, fractures, and labour (see also Chapter 7). The aim is to use a case study for critical reflection and thus elaborate the sustainability concept by highlighting its complex dynamics and discussing some possible lasting effects.

The case offers an opportunity to reflect upon the issue of sustainability over time, in a rapidly changing environment (see also Wilhelmson and Döös 2002a, 2002b, and Chapter 6 in this volume). As a result sustainability is viewed in relation to phases of development over time in four different aspects of the ongoing business: *in products, in organization structure, in principles of how to organize work, and in individuals*. Within those aspects, phases of ups and downs were traced and related to the issue of sustainability. Concerning individuals, consequences of development work were seen as a heritage after the organization, the unit itself, had ceased to exist – a heritage closely connected to the products that were developed.

The case

A unit within a large global Swedish telecom company, Ericsson, provides the empirical background.[1] In 1995, the unit was a local design centre (LDC) with 200 employees. Most of the employees were graduate engineers (approximately 60 percent) with the main task of developing software for telecom products. The unit acted in an environment characterized by thorough-going and rapid changes in several areas. The telecom business in Sweden had recently been deregulated and the company now operated on a global market. Technology in itself had undergone rapid development; hardware had become smaller, faster, and more diversified, and software tools were easier to use. Technical progress had also brought on an ongoing merger between, and also a shift from, telecom to datacom. This created opportunities for new product development and new telephony services, and took place in a highly competitive market. Companies were competing through innovative product development and were totally dependent on human competence, which resulted in challenging demands on knowledge creation (Döös *et al.* 2005).

The environment of the organization can be compared to "turbulent fields" as described by Emery and Trist: "The turbulence results from the complexity and multiple character of the causal interconnections" (1963: 31). In such an environment the organization is dependent on commonly held values to be able to respond to the overall uncertainties in the field, thus the visions and ideas are crucial to be able to act in this kind of environment.

The unit that was investigated underwent a thorough renewal during the 1995–1999 period. New leadership took form; it changed its field of activity and also entirely changed its ways of organizing work in order to adapt to changing market demands (Döös and Wilhelmson 2003; Wilhelmson 2006). The unit strove for autonomy within the larger whole of the parent company and its tradition of hierarchy and strict rules, which had resulted in bureaucratic rigidity, according to managers in the unit. It was autonomous in certain respects (e.g., being a free zone relative to some rules), but was clearly dependent in other respects (e.g., being subordinate to the product area and business unit it belonged to). An important part of the renewal work concerned achieving a situation where employees would be able to act as knowledgeable individuals, making decisions based on their own interpretations of the current realities. There was a need for individuals to be responsible and able to handle change. Organizational structures and ways of working were thus required that would cohere with and lead to such understanding and acting among the organizational members.

Visions and ideas

Visions and ideas were the basis for the renewal (cf. Chapters 2 and 3 in this volume). The visions of the managers, as well as other dedicated and driving key actors, were explicit and important as guiding stars for coordinating all the changes. The visions were clearly in line with sustainability on several levels: for the nation, the company, the unit and the individual. An important and unusual part of the vision was that "added value for the individual" was regarded as of *equal* importance as "profitability for the company" in striving for a less hierarchical organization. Reciprocity in responsibility for fulfilling shared assignments, keeping promises of delivery dates and quality, meant a new and wider involvement of the employees in the complete product development process. Organizing work in teams and small "virtual companies" was important means of achieving the goals. All this was part of a vision of the empowered engineer, held by the managers and the key actors.

Important events

A rough overview of important events in the unit during the five years it existed is presented below.

The first merger and the first vision

The unit was formed in 1995, when two newly appointed managers (a man and a woman) agreed to merge their units and to lead the new unit together. A joint leadership (Wilhelmson 2006) took shape, and all of this was accepted by the level above in the organization. At this time the unit ranked[2] as number 19 out of 23 local design centres (LDCs). It was "one of the most expensive LDCs, never delivering on time, never within budget, with its products varying in quality and with a large employee turnover . . . there was a thick layer of problems on top of everything" (Manager). One way to deal with this was to emphasize the importance of "keeping promises and delivering on time with quality". This was the first vision, clearly articulated and quite down-to-earth.

Improvement work

Some 400 ideas for new product development and improvement activities were carried out in order to reduce the gap between current reality and the vision. Large meetings were held with all personnel, external speakers were invited and workshops arranged. This was aimed at making everyone conscious of the vision and its implications. The unit also moved into a new open-space building – a decision that was forced on the employees by the two managers – making communication easier. Teamwork was implemented, initially against the will of several middle managers and other employees.

After a year the improvement activities were paying off: now the unit was ranked as number 3 out of 34 LDCs. Did this give rise to complacency? No, the two managers raised new issues: "Where is the market heading? Now when we do things right, are we doing the right things?"

Renewal work and a second vision

In 1997 the answer to the second question was – No! Leaders on different levels of the unit had identified the need for change. The unit management decided to leave telecoms, eliminate cash-cow products and move into the internet tele-phony business. Together with many of the personnel they undertook a thorough restructuring of the unit to make this change of products and technology possible. To "embrace the whole chain," i.e., emphasizing the importance of engineers taking responsibility for a wider task and being acquainted with all the steps in a product development project, was now formulated as a second vision. A new organizational infrastructure was built on the basic principles behind the vision to support creativity and learning, to make new product development possible and to create the right and competitive competence quickly. The amount of changes caused worry and insecurity at all levels of the unit. Employees had to alter old habits as well as ways of thinking and acting in work. The renewal work was considered necessary due to the competitive pressure from the outer world. At the same time it had created a strong feeling of uniqueness and pride among many employees, not least among the key actors. By now the unit had achieved the position of a free zone, granted by the level above in the organization, which to some extent made them independent in relation to ordinary rules within the enter-prise, as a kind of incubator for new organization principles and structures.

The critical second merger and third vision

Early in 1998 the unit was merged with another Ericsson unit, a management deci-sion initiated within the unit. The two merging parts will be referred to as Tele-part (the original unit described above) and Data-part (the new part included through the merger). The main empirical base of the study comes from Tele-part.

The aim of the merger was to strengthen skills and competences needed for the new types of products. Data-part engineers were experts on software for internet telephony applications, possessing necessary datacom knowledge. Tele-part's skills concerned the performance issues reached through the improvement and renewal work. Out of the merger evolved the third vision: "to make Ericsson the lead-ing supplier of IP (Internet Protocol) telephony services."

However, the merger soon resulted in a severe cultural clash that was never resolved. The Tele-part management did not realize the full importance of get-ting the new organizational members "onboard the team train." Data-part was supposed to bring in new competence, but it turned out that this competence was heavily burdened with a culture of "gurus, cowboys, and experts." According to managers and key actors in Tele-part, the Data-part culture was both rather elitist and hierarchical and still "without sufficient order," e.g., concerning delivery time and the documentation of the software development process. The two fundamental principles for managing work in Tele-part – working in teams and having autonomous product companies – came into conflict at this time. Since the two parts did not share work tasks, the ideas and the culture of teamwork and shared responsibilities were never really transacted. Keeping the level of "telecom quality" in the project process that was achieved back in 1996 turned out to be problematic and this period was hard on several individuals – at both engineering and management levels.

The split

In the beginning of the summer of 1999 the unit was divided. Data-part remained a unit in its own right, while Tele-part was divided into other parts of the enterprise, depending on where their new products fitted in. This decision was taken on the level above the unit, by new management, since the unit now belonged to a new business unit. The decision was essentially based on the idea of organizing around similar products that belonged together. In Tele-part the spirit was still there, still relying on the renewal principles and on coming products, but after the split, organizational principles were abandoned for the time being, since products and people had been divided into other units. In Data-part, their product had been developed successfully and was reaching the market, which in turn created new demands. Further organizational improvement work was discussed, teamwork was at last wanted here also, as a way to handle problems of quality, economic control, and delivery on time.

Some years later, visions and organizing principles were coming about again in different ways in several organizations within and outside Ericsson, carried by managers and members with experience from this journey of change.

Fluctuations over time

The amount of change inside and outside the unit certainly did not mean linear development over time. We now present an account of fluctuations in the four aspects mentioned earlier, with phases of positive development and strength as well as of struggle and weakness. Strength and weakness, in different aspects of the life of the organization, are thus seen as inevitable ingredients of the sustainability-creating process.

Fluctuations in products

The products are the solid ground for the unit's existence. The history shows definite ups and downs in this respect. In the beginning the unit was poor on production, as the ranking showed. But after a year of improvement activities the unit was already at its peak, delivering upgraded software for the AXE telephony system. From this strong position, management decided to change the field of activity from mature cash-cow products in traditional telecom technology to an entirely new area of internet telephony, with emphasis on datacom technology. In moving from the well-established ground, production once again became shaky. It took time before new products were conceived, developed and sold. Learning the logic of datacom was time-consuming and work tasks therefore took more time. But the decision to shift products proved to be positive in the long run. When the unit was split, new products were about to be launched.

Several new products gained high market share. Approximately 160 ideas were generated and evaluated. These products often lived on with the managers, project leaders, and engineers who initially developed them. A living product creates a sustainable environment for its developers, as it goes into more indus-trialized phases from being an invention. Within the shelter of a successful prod-uct, project leaders and engineers can make use of developed competences and skill; they can rely on important experiences. Even if the product over time belongs to various units in the enterprise, a core group of people seems to follow the product on its way to maturity.

Fluctuations in organization structure

Being part of a large company and dealing with fast-moving product develop-ment also meant acting in an environment that was rapidly moving and chang-ing its structure. The general organizational principle was that every product should belong to the correct product area and business unit, which implied recurring merger and splitting adjustments and restructuring activities all over the global company as new products were moving along.

The organizational structure thus fluctuated a great deal over time. The two unit merger decisions referred to in this case were made on the initiative of the unit management itself, but the decision to split was made at a higher level in the enterprise. The unit was initially unstable after the first merger, but it soon regained stability as the two managers took firm hold of the development. The unit stood strong when looking for a partner to strengthen competence and cred-ibility as they entered a new technology area. The second merger proved not to be a very healthy one in terms of its effects on participants. The datacom unit, Data-part, had a strong identity of its own. It could not be integrated speedily or easily. Data-part retained its strong identity, guarding its boundaries as a com-pany within the company, working with its own product, which was very close to market launch. Tele-part was at the same time weakened by the strategy of transferring old products, which sometimes also meant transferring of staff, while its new products still were immature.

At the time of the split, Data-part was less robust. It had difficulties entering a more industrialized phase and difficulties in delivering on time with quality, and it was about to start new improvement work. Tele-part did not survive as an entity; its employees and managers went in different directions, mostly to other parts of the enterprise.

Fluctuations in organizational principles

On the overall level, ideas and principles guiding organizational development seemed to grow continually stronger in the minds of managers and key actors during the whole 1995–2000 period. The infrastructural means to realize the visions were mainly teamwork, small virtual product companies and a structured project process. Responsibility for products and competence was divided. Competence coaches were appointed to benefit the individual engineer, and were given the task of staffing projects and product companies. Teamwork, development of organ-izational competence, and learning in the work tasks were seen as the main road to new knowledge. According to the managers and other key actors, teamwork was considered fundamental for bringing the guiding ideas and visions into operation. Teams were created and trained at all levels in the unit: joint leadership, competence coaches as a team of their own, engineers working in project teams of three to four individuals and seen as self-responsible and self-managing. Also, cross-functional teams were created for special tasks in the projects.

Individual engineers say that their experience of working in teams gives them the opportunity to learn more efficiently from work tasks. Participation in planning processes and co-responsibility in work tasks means shared creation of meaning. Close cooperation and mutual responsibility give opportunities for collective learning. Working together in genuine teams makes dialogue an important working ingredient when the task is to develop new products, because this task is dependent on continuous learning. The team model for project planning supports working in iterations and making decisions en route based on earlier experiences, difficulties and possibilities encountered, and changes in demands and goals. Working in teams seems better suited to handling the recurrent uncertainties involved in the new-product-development type of work. At the same time it diminishes the need for management. A group can take on a larger task. The risk of misunderstandings is diminished when people need to talk to each other and develop ways of communicating that make it possible to carry out a joint task.

The teamwork principle stood strong during the first years. But employees came and went, and new teams were established without getting team training. In practice, the organizational principles were meeting resistance, especially in the merger between Tele-part and Data-part. The two units found themselves in a cultural clash concerning organizational principles. Tele-part had strong guiding visions realized in practice. Data-part had a way of doing things that in many ways was contradictory to the visions – e.g., teamwork was looked upon with suspicion. This part was the carrier of a totally different set of organizing principles, even if those principles were informal and never explicitly formulated, a state that Tele-part had left behind during their first improvement work. The clash was never handled openly. The organizational principles from Tele-part lived on until the split, when they finally collapsed, for the time being.

After the split, Data-part changed its attitude. After some time it discovered the need for a structured project process and teamwork. Their quality department carried on with establishing genuine teamwork and characterized this as the "heart of our challenge."

Fluctuation in individual development

On the individual level, sustainability fluctuates not only due to intensity in work tasks, but also in connection with organizational principles, products, and product development. How the individual can profit from experiences and go on in a sustainable way seems to be connected to work role and work tasks. Managers and other key actors talk about their experiences in quite a different way from engineers. Leading renewal work gives managers a comprehensive perspective through their learning about organizational principles and strategic matters. Concentrating on technical development in a product gives the engineer fresh factual knowledge along with competence to cooperate to reach a goal.

Managers and key actors

Managers and key actors get stronger when they create visions and transform them into organizational principles that are used to build organization structures. This strength comes to a large degree from being a group of devoted people, discussing these matters, learning from reinforcing new ideas. When the common frame falls apart, people go in different directions, truly disappointed, as their organization principles were not strong enough to keep the unit together. They are weakened for some time, but find new grounds where they start over again. The well-developed relations between these key actors are to some extent sustained over time, as individuals keep in touch and help each other to reuse the organizational learning gained in Tele-part in new workplaces. With values, visions, and goals built out of common experiences, relations live on. One year after the split, one of the managers started to gather some of the key actors in his new unit to reuse the experiences they had gained together.

The managers point to several lessons learned in order to be more sustainable in renewal work. They emphasize the importance of joint leadership; together they could create the strength needed to keep on struggling when problems appeared. It is not easy to lead renewal work alone in a sustainable manner. The struggle to put new ideas and visions into practice may lead to their being cherished as sacred cows. It is important to be aware of the risk of being trapped in the visions, not allowing continuous improvements when a goal is reached, the managers state. However, in retrospect the key actors also claimed that they should have kept up the team principle continually, and not just in the beginning during the improvement work.

Engineers and developers – the employees

The broadening of work tasks was intended to make people act consciously and be well-attuned to each other and to the overall task: to get the product out to market on time. This meant being involved in new product development in such a way that the individual engineer would come closer to the customer and to the product as a whole, rather than only working with some detail on their own. For this, the individual needs information and knowledge about the project as well as about the customer, the competitors, and the product, apart from the specific knowledge of the task of their own team. Knowledge of this kind is strengthening and is the foundation for shared responsibility.

Working in a business where change is ever-present means that the engineers become skilled at rethinking and restarting. To handle a changeable reality, people seemed to develop strategies to find something settled and solid that remained steady along with what was changing. Formulating personal goals, such as developing one's competence, provided a factor that survived temporary changes in work tasks and projects. Knowing that problems were always around to be solved contributed to the feeling of stability. Problems were part of the work and belonged there, just as uncertainty and vagueness were commonplace. In one way or another, each person formed their task and used it as a handle to hold on to. To change tasks had become a habit, you left the old task behind and grabbed the new one: "If only you know how it is supposed to be, what it looks like, you get hold of the task and you get acquainted with the new. So it works out well" (Engineer).

Many engineers strongly identify with the work task, as they enjoy being on the leading edge of technology. To acquire new knowledge is for most engineers of great sustaining importance in their career development. Competence is hard currency if one wants to be valuable on the labour market. In the follow-up inquiry the engineers mentioned new technical knowledge as the most important result of all the changes that took place in the unit. The painful technological shift of starting to develop internet telephony applications made heavy demands on learning for individuals, and this strengthened their standing in the long run. Engineers and developers also mentioned experiences of how to work in projects and teams as important learning acquired in the unit. Through this they built new contact networks. They appreciated the competence they got from working collectively, and having learned the importance of how to develop good project processes, how to keep a project in good order. This was the sustainable heritage that came into use in the start of their new working life in new surroundings. When the unit was divided and the organizational principles were no longer in use, the engineers were nevertheless strengthened by the new knowledge they had gained.

Fluctuations and the sustainable heritage

This case points to the importance of time and phases for sustainability. Looking back over a period of six years, it becomes evident that the occasion chosen for identifying sustainability in an organization makes a big difference, since we are dealing with processes that are not synchronized. Over time, products, organization, organizational principles, and individuals go through phases of change that are very often out of tune with each other.

When the unit splits, products stand strong but the bearing vision of small company structure falls apart. Organizational principles disappear as the key actors in Tele-part are scattered. Individual engineers stand strong with their products – going on to new units. Managers move on to new leading positions. People find new tasks, being the richer for experience. These ongoing processes can be illustrated as in Figure 8.1.

The ups and downs of sustainability illustrated in Figure 8.1 can be summarized in the following way. In the very beginning, production was poor, organization structure was weak, managers were struggling for improvements in organizational principles, employees were not used to shouldering responsibility. The improvement

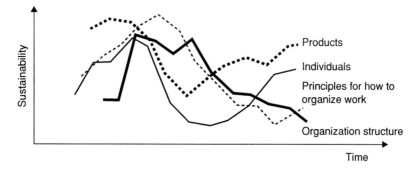

Figure 8.1 A schematic picture visualizing the ups and downs of sustainability over time and in the four different aspects of the ongoing business

and renewal work caused many painful and threatening changes for both middle managers and engineers. It was not possible to continue with old habits. Before the merger with the datacom unit, this laborious work had paid off: production was highly rated, organizational principles were highly regarded, and the unit was no longer under threat. Teamwork along with good planning processes for projects had been established as organizational principles. Employees were able to make decisions for themselves – e.g., choosing which competence coach to belong to, which project to work in, and which new skills to develop. This was sometimes hard on the individuals: "It was like applying for a new job," one engineer said. The joint leadership was strong, especially together with other key actors. People in the unit had become proud of themselves; self-esteem was once again high, according to managers.

Soon after the second merger, the picture becomes more blurred. New products are developing, but take time to reach the market. Organization structure is once again weakened. The two units remain apart and do not integrate into a single whole, which to some degree is due to differences in core values concerning organizational principles. Data-part is not interested in teamwork or detailed process planning. The principles are weakened, being no longer seen as the obvious way to organize work, even if Tele-part still works in that way. Competence coaches encounter difficulties in staffing the product companies now that they all need more people than are available. Individual engineers are not so disturbed by all this; they are fully occupied with the interesting work tasks and with learning new skills. In Data-part, engineers also struggle with intensity problems, as they are too few and have to depend on consultants to a large degree. Being three top managers instead of two does not work out well.

Although the unit and the specific small company organization ceased to exist, and although the change processes caused individuals pain and suffering, it would be an oversimplification to say that this is not an example of sustainability. Visions, ideas, and ambitions live on, as do products that successfully reach their customers. Organizational principles are reinvented after some time. Individuals acquire new competence, maybe with a larger capability of managing change. Contact networks and relations are built upon in new environments. The struggle for and the creation of new ideas and experiences can be reused in new settings. Sustainability for individuals and products seems to go on within and outside the unit – at least in this kind of business with the task of new product development, living under the conditions of short product life cycles and sharp competition.

Thus, the laborious development work leads to a sustainable heritage for managers and engineers when they go on in new directions in their working life. New resources have been generated, for the company in creation of new competitive products and for individuals in gaining new competences. The acquisition of new knowledge and new experience, such as being trained in how to create a collective mind and how to interrelate heedfully (Weick and Roberts 2001), produces a competence that individuals can carry with them onto the next mission. In other words, regenerative experiences (Moldaschl 2002), at individual and collective levels, are part of the sustainable heritage that derives from the ups and downs in the different aspects of the life of the organization and is carried on by the individual members in their ongoing lives. Though the organization as such was not sustainable, the organizational development work was sustainable, since individuals went on, strengthened in various ways.

Discussion

The concept of sustainability covers a complex phenomenon when seen over time and within different aspects of organizational life. This case shows some of the dynamic to be handled when managing nonsynchronized processes. Periods of weakness and struggle were the cradle for thinking and action, leading to transformation and change that opened the way to continuation, within and outside the specific unit.

Sustainability involves a capacity for change, on the part of both organization and individuals, and it is not the same thing as a harmonious life. To handle this kind of change invariably also includes pain; it has the character of transformative learning (Mezirow 1991). When surrounding conditions put pressure upon people to alter their cognitive structures, their ways of thinking, this has some very painful aspects to it. It can be seen as a process of accommodation (Piaget 1970) also on the level of an organization. To ask the question: "Are we doing the right thing?" was crucial. It contributed to competitiveness in high-tech development within the enterprise, new products were invented, employees developed new skills, and managers developed new organizational thinking.

In this work environment, sustainability for individuals is mainly realized by gaining good experiences and self-esteem that enhance the possibilities to go on to new tasks in new similar environments. Individuals find sustainability in their own competence development, making use of changes, seeing them as opportunities to work with new products and regarding work processes as learning.

The most important thing, then, is not whether a specific project, product or unit survives. There is always a new task to define and go on with. As changes are struggled through, the individual gains experiences that are useful for future work. This is the heritage that matters in the long run.

Knowledge can be developed in a team that works closely together, both in doing the work task and when it comes to interpreting information (see Chapters 4 and 6 in this volume). Jointly it is easier to make sense of information and develop new, transformed knowledge out of each and everyone's own experiences. Knowledge that is jointly produced has a more stable character than knowledge that is individually produced (Berger and Luckmann 1966). In this respect, collectively created knowledge can be an important part of sustainability for organizations as well as for individuals, as it brings together several persons' knowledge and experience. The knowledge thus created will in turn probably support speed and efficiency, since employees are able to handle extended work tasks in a more qualified manner.

The vision of the empowered engineer developed by managers and key actors can be seen as an example of how prevailing emancipatory concepts concerning people and knowledge are of importance for the possibility of creating work conditions that can contribute to sustainable heritage for the individual employee.

Implications

To see individuals as the builders of an organization might help us see the importance of giving individuals the opportunity to grow strong. That the engineers have the power to make decisions both as individuals and as members of a team was of importance to the two original unit co-leaders. They were influenced by contemporary ideas[3] about teamwork and organizational development, and together with other key actors made their own mix, adapted to their present reality. They developed a skill both in creating and communicating ideas and visions. New accessible meaning structures (Dixon 1994) were established; new organizational forms were created.

In conclusion, sustainability can be understood as the ability to interpret and deal with complexity, alterations, and dynamics. To develop new products and adjust the organization to cope – through creating a new organization structure, developing new organizational principles, and supporting competence development, all at the same time – we see as an example of a serious effort to reach sustainability. Learning, leading to competence, is a key feature in such a developmental process; it is the sustainable heritage in this kind of rapidly changing environment. Lasting effects were interpreted as sustainable heritage and found situated in interacting individual engineers and the products they developed.

Discussing sustainability requires both an awareness of which aspects to include and consider, and a time perspective long enough to experience (as participants) or observe (as researchers) the experiences of the phases of ups and downs. Longitudinal studies are needed to be able to catch those phases of ups and downs in future research. The results of our analysis point to the importance of focusing on several aspects and processes, when aiming at understanding sustainability in practice as well as a theoretical concept. This certainly poses problems for the possibilities of interpreting sustainability empirically at a specific workplace at a specific time. It is also important to stress that what can be learned from this rapidly changing environment might not be of immediate relevance for more stable and mature activities.

Questions for reflection

Here are three questions for your further reflection on the issues broached in this chapter:

- Why and when is it important to be aware of nonsynchronized aspects of sustainability?
- How is learning connected to sustainability, for individuals as well as for organizations?
- How can organizations create possibilities for their employees to develop sustainability for themselves in their working lives?

Notes

1 Data cover the 1995–2001 period. The main data collection took place in 1999, mainly through 23 semistructured interviews with managers, project leaders, quality assurance personnel, and product development engineers. Later, some contacts took place with representatives for the unit, two managers were interviewed in 2000, and a brief follow-up inquiry was made. Qualitative research methods were used with the purpose of understanding processes of learning in working life.
2 Index measuring software quality, delivery on time, price performance, productivity and service.
3 E.g., Dixon (1994, 1997), Drucker (1994), Edvinsson and Malone (1997), Hammer (1996), Katzenbach and Smith (1993), Senge (1990), and Morgan (1998).

References

Berger, P. and Luckmann, T. (1966) *The Social Construction of Reality: A treatise in the sociology of knowledge*. Harmondsworth: Penguin Books.
Dixon, N. (1994) *The Organizational Learning Cycle: How we can learn collectively*. London: McGraw-Hill.
—— (1997) "The hallways of learning," *Organizational Dynamics*, 25(4), 23–34.
Döös, M. and Wilhelmson, L. (2003) "Work processes of shared leadership," paper presented at the British Academy of Management Annual Conference, Harrogate, UK, Sept. 15–17.
Döös, M. , Wilhelmson, L., Backlund, T., and Dixon, N. (2005) "Functioning at the edge of knowledge: a study of learning processes in new product development," *Journal of Workplace Learning*, 17(8), 481–492.
Drucker, P. (1994) *Managing in a Time of Great Change*. Oxford: Butterworth/Heinemann.

Edvinsson, L. and Malone, M.S. (1997) *Intellectual Capital: Realizing your company's true value by finding its hidden brainpower*. New York: Harper Business.

Emery, F.E. and Trist, E.L. (1963) "The causal texture of organizational environments," paper presented at the XVII International Congress of Psychology, Washington, DC, Aug. 20–26.

Hammer, M. (1996) *Beyond Reengineering: How the process-centred organization is changing our work and our lives*. London: HarperCollins.

Katzenbach, J. and Smith, D. (1993) *The Wisdom of Teams.* Boston, MA: Harvard Business School Press.

Mezirow, J. (1991) *Transformative Dimensions of Adult Learning.* San Francisco: Jossey-Bass.

Moldaschl, M. (2002) "A resource-centred perspective," in P. Docherty, J. Forslin, and A.B. (Rami) Shani (eds), *Creating Sustainable Work Systems.* London and New York: Routledge, pp. 52–64.

Morgan, G. (1998) "From bureaucracies to networks: the emergence of new organizational forms," in G. Robinson Hickman (ed.), *Leading Organizations: Perspectives for a new era*, Thousand Oaks, CA: Sage, pp. 283–286.

Piaget, J. (1970) *The Principles of Genetic Epistemology.* London: Routledge & Kegan Paul.

Senge, P. (1990) *The Fifth Discipline: The art and practice of the learning organization.* New York: Doubleday/Currency.

Weick, K. and Roberts, K. (2001) "Collective mind in organizations: heedful interrelating on flight decks," in K. Weick (ed.), *Making Sense of the Organization.* Oxford: Blackwell Business.

Wilhelmson, L. (2006) "Transformative learning in joint leadership," *Journal of Workplace Learning*, 18, 7–8, 495–507.

Wilhelmson, L. and Döös, M. (2002a) "Sustainability in a rapidly changing environment," in P. Docherty, J. Forslin, and A.B. (Rami) Shani (eds) *Creating Sustainable Work Systems.* London and New York: Routledge.

Wilhelmson, L. and Döös, M. (2002b) *Sustainability and Innovative Organisational Change.* Solna, Sweden: National Institute for Working Life.

9 Learning mechanisms in sustainable work systems design

Michael W. Stebbins and
Judy L. Valenzuela

Introduction

The purpose of this chapter is to explore change processes in Sustainable Work Systems (SWS) design, with an emphasis on learning mechanisms created within one of the world's most successful health maintenance organizations, the Kaiser Permanente Medical Care Program (KPMCP) in Southern California. We will use the KPMCP case to demonstrate SWS values and principles and to show how learning mechanisms are used within SWS design programs. We will also pursue the implications for SWS design theory and the SWS redesign process.

During 1997–2007, the pharmacy division of KPMCP forged a strong partnership between pharmacists and physicians via a change initiative called Clinical Management of Pharmaceuticals (CMOP). This ongoing change program features continuous planned action at different levels of KPMCP, providing dynamic capability to adjust drug formularies and prescriptions for KPMCP health plan members. Within the US health care context, drug formularies are lists of approved medicines and guidelines for the selection, prescribing, dispensing, and administration of drugs. For most health plans, drug formularies are considered to be critical in setting quality and cost standards for physician providers.

Drug use management is a critical sustainability issue within health care organizations and countries worldwide. Organizations cannot effectively compete in the marketplace or advance the health condition of health plan members without careful attention to drug formularies. Drug use management requires attention to economic, social network, and ecological matters and receives scrutiny from a variety of stakeholders. Drug suppliers, drug providers, government bodies, and patients have different views about drugs that should be provided to patients, and drug costs are only one consideration. Drug efficacy, standards of health care, and benefits to society also come into play.

In this chapter, we reveal what has previously been unknown to companies outside Kaiser Permanente: How KPMCP manages to lead the industry on controlling drug costs and driving positive health outcomes through Clinical Management of Pharmaceuticals and related change programs.

.We begin the chapter with a brief theory section on large-scale organization change through consultative and educational interventions. Emphasis for this section is on guiding the intervention from within rather than from outside the organization. Throughout the chapter we will follow three types of change activities and processes: Those that relate to management of the overall program or intervention; those that relate to the particular learning mechanisms used; and those that concern dynamics within the operations part of the organization as the players implement specific initiatives. Regarding overall program management, we are interested in emerging theory about sustainable work systems (SWS) design activities that result in the creation of new organizational capabilities.

Following the section on change theory, sustainability, and learning mechanisms, we provide a brief section on our research methodology and then move to the KPMCP case study. The case discussion centres on a matrix that presents the CMOP structural learning mechanism, change process, learning dynamics at operating levels, and major outcomes. We conclude with reflection on the CMOP case study and implications for SWS design theory and practice.

Change theory and the field of organization design

During the past four decades, there has been growing attention to strategies for large-system change. Increasingly, change interventions are orchestrated and guided by internal change agents, including managers. Change interventions are defined as "behavior which affects the ongoing social processes of a system" (Beckhard 1969). These social processes include strategies and policies guiding the system, processes related to division of labour, and procedures intended to integrate activities through information gathering and dissemination, planning, goal setting, joint decision making, and shaping of attitudes and social values. In brief, consultants and managers interested in changing these social processes are involved in the field of organization development, and in particular, organization design (Cummings and Worley 2001).

While a review of leading organization design approaches and redesign change processes is beyond the scope of this chapter (for an overview, see, for example, Stebbins and Shani 1989), we will briefly discuss concepts underpinning the emerging design approach called Sustainable Work Systems. Organization design has evolved both as a field of academic study and as an applied organization development technology. Relatively few theories provide comprehensive frameworks that can shed light on the often chaotic process of redesign (Beer 2001). Design is thought to be a blend of theory, knowledge embedded in the particular industry/sector and work situation, and the contributions of those who participate in the redesign process (Mackenzie 1986). The process is both technical and political, and involves purposeful effort to design the organization as an integrated system (Stebbins *et al.* 2006a). All of these concepts apply to traditional and newer approaches to design that focus on sustainability.

Sustainability and SWS design

Sustainability entails the preservation, regeneration, and development of the economic, social, and ecological resources of a system (see also Chapters 4, 5, 6, 8, and 15 in this volume). Within health care systems, sustainability includes design of dynamic organizational capabilities that will improve services to patients. This is increasingly a complex task, in that there are so many competing treatment methods and drugs available in the marketplace to cope with different ailments. People have more information about their medical conditions, are more aware of technology advances and new treatment modalities, and seek the best care available. Accordingly, health care organizations must have strategies and mechanisms to sort through the various options. Health care companies must rely on both strategy and organization design. The Sustainable Work Systems (SWS) design approach seems particularly suited to the health care sector (see also Chapter 11).

SWS design values relate to the context for initiating change, the change process, and the desired outcomes (Stebbins *et al.* 2006a). For example, a strong value is dual emphasis on quality of work life and competitive organizational performance. Both are emphasized in front-end thinking about creation of the redesign change initiative, in the crafting of learning mechanisms to guide the change process, and in attitudes and behaviour during implementation (see also Chapter 16). Other values include consideration of redesign impacts at multiple levels and for different stakeholders: individuals, teams, larger work units, customers, the community, and the larger society (see also Chapter 7). The aim is to build capabilities so that organizations are able to cope with rapid change. This is our special interest as applied to health care organizations.

An organization striving toward sustainability needs to be a learning organization. Design is conceived as a reflexive methodology of intervention – a type of enlightened, self-critical process that accepts differences in science and practice. Reflection during the change initiative is critical. Collective reflection is the ability to uncover and make explicit what is planned, observed, and achieved in practice. Therefore SWS design is concerned with the reconstruction of meaning and results in work-based learning (Raelin 2000; also Chapter 8). As we will shortly see, these values and principles are emphasized in the CMOP case that is the heart of this chapter.

While there is no set, recommended redesign process in SWS redesign, certain principles have emerged related to management of the change process. SWS is an open process model with cyclical evaluation loops, rather than a linear phase model (see also Chapter 7). Within SWS design, strategic and operational aspects of redesign are not viewed as separate; the process is at the same time top-down and bottom-up. The process is iterative (invent, try, reflect, assess, adjust) and heavily relies on participants to self-apply new work concepts and methods. In the course of redesign, participants come together to address dilemmas – for example, that group autonomy can generate both solutions and problems for all concerned. Organizational arrangements are subject to continuous modification and improvement. In terms of theory, the SWS redesign process builds on prior self-design theories (see, for example, Mohrman and Cummings 1989). (For a more complete summary of SWS design theory and the SWS design process, please see Eclectic Design for Sustainable Development Processes, Chapter 16 in this volume.) Throughout the present chapter, we will argue that learning mechanisms are central to the successful completion of SWS redesign interventions and for organizations striving toward sustainability. Accordingly, we will now define and discuss the role of learning mechanisms during redesign.

Learning mechanisms

In order to understand learning mechanisms, one must consider the context, the actors, the type of collaboration, and the learning and knowledge produced during a change intervention. Learning mechanisms are planned proactive features that enable and encourage organizational learning (Popper and Lipshitz 1998; Shani and Docherty 2003). An assumption is that the capability to learn can be designed rather than left to evolve through the normal activities of the organization. Literature on learning mechanisms identifies three foci: cognitive, structural, and procedural (Shani and Docherty 2003).

Cognitive learning mechanisms

Cognitive mechanisms are the bearers of language, concepts, symbols, theories, frameworks, and values for thinking, reasoning, and understanding developed in creating new organizational capabilities. Cognitive mechanisms are management's main means for creating an understanding among employees on the character, need, and priority of new organizational capabilities, and the learning and changes needed to realize them. In complex systems, they enable various units of the system to operate with shared meaning. Cognitive learning mechanisms are fundamental, in that they support work-based learning.

Structural learning mechanisms

Structural learning mechanisms are organizational, physical, technical, and work-system infrastructures that encourage work-based learning (Shani and Docherty 2003). These mechanisms support discourse and the sense making entailed as individuals and groups learn from experience (Weick 1995). Structural mechanisms include creation of new communication channels, the establishment of lateral structures to enable learning of new practices across various core organizational units, changes in roles and teams, formal and informal forums for joint exploration and debate, and networks for mutual learning.

Procedural mechanisms

Procedural mechanisms concern the rules, routines, methods, and tools that can be institutionalized in the organization to promote and support learning

(Pavlovsky *et al.* 2001). These may include assessment tools and methods, new operating procedures, and methods for specific types of collective learning such as action learning and debriefing routines. In summary, the case below will show how cognitive, structural, and procedural learning mechanisms combine with change intervention processes to generate widespread improvements in drug utilization.

Methodology

The goal of the present research at KPMCP was to understand the origins and evolution of the CMOP program to improve drug utilization. The research methodology emphasized archive data and interviews with individuals who were associated with the program during 1997–2007. The company maintained excellent records of meeting notes and formal reports on the CMOP change program, processes, and outcomes. In the case of archives, the authors reviewed booklets prepared for initial day-long off-site meetings along with meeting notes provided by the managers who were guiding the overall interventions. The authors also relied on quarterly and monthly reports on success with annual drug change initiatives to gauge both the rate of change and level of change achieved. Interviews were conducted with managers associated with the CMOP intervention since its beginning in 1997, as well as with managers and drug education coordinators playing key roles at different levels of the pharmacy organization. All interviews occurred during 2006. Validation of factual information occurred when interviewees commented on drafts of this chapter and provided commentary on discussion and conclusion sections. All of the interviewees as well as the authors of this chapter have been associated with KPMCP and the CMOP program since its beginning.

The US health care context

For readers unfamiliar with the US health care sector, a basic description, although oversimplified, may be helpful. The health care sector is mainly private rather than public, but government plays a strong role for people who are older, for those who do not have health insurance coverage, and for military families and military veterans. The government also heavily influences the sector by setting policies on benefit coverage and reimbursement practices for Medicare and other federal programs. Independent health care providers, independent provider organizations such as hospitals, and networks of providers treat patients who are enrolled in various private and government-sponsored health plans. In most cases, the private health plans are financial intermediaries (insurers). The health plan organizations sell different benefit plans, negotiate fee schedules and drug formularies with providers, and reimburse both patients and providers according to specific covered benefits. The situation is further complicated in that people may gain health plan coverage through their individual employers, through employer networks, unions, government entities, and/or individual application to the health plans.

Kaiser Permanente – context and actors

The Kaiser Permanente Medical Care Program (KPMCP) is one of the oldest and largest health maintenance organizations in the United States. The nonprofit health plan component of KPMCP has a national population of about 8 million members. Through its various legal entities, it owns and operates hospital, medical office, and support facilities and contracts out only limited services where there is greater knowledge or expertise, such as in a university teaching-hospital setting. The health plan relies on a prepaid system, and therefore faces far fewer issues concerning reimbursement than other health care organizations experience. Within Southern California, the health plan is structured as a group-model health maintenance organization. It contracts with the Southern California Permanente Medical Group ("the medical group") to provide health care services to 3 million members.

The focus in this case is on the health plan's pharmacy operations unit in Southern California and its relationships with physicians in setting drug use management policies and practices. The pharmacy organization in Southern California is composed of strategy and operations central offices, a major central refill facility, a mail order pharmacy, warehouse facilities, staff services units, and diverse medical centre inpatient and outpatient pharmacies. The pharmacy organization dispenses over 20 million outpatient prescriptions a year, and the inpatient pharmacies perform wide ranging functions that support hospitalized patients. The pharmacy organization's facilities mirror KPMCP medical facilities; there are big inpatient and outpatient pharmacies at all major medical centres as well as eight to ten smaller pharmacies within area medical centres and satellite out-patient medical offices.

Pharmacy/medical group relationships

The organization's name – Kaiser Permanente Medical Care Program – reflects the partnership and cooperation between the health plan and the medical group. At the policy level, physician leaders work with pharmacy leaders and drug information experts to set the agenda for continuous innovation in drug management, including cost containment. The intervention described in this chapter, Clinical Management of Pharmaceuticals (CMOP) has a formal structural learning mechanism composed of representative managers and staff from the pharmacy and medical group organizations. At the Southern California region and at the medical centre levels, groups such as the regional pharmacy and therapeutics committee and local pharmacy and therapeutics committees work with medical chiefs of services, the CMOP representatives, and drug education coordinators to design and carry out various change initiatives and educational campaigns. Drug education coordinators are specially trained pharmacists who focus on education and drug utilization issues. The nature of the collaboration among the parties will be explored in detail below.

Background: setting the context for the CMOP change initiative

The CMOP change initiative was partly born from the fires of crisis, but mainly from success with a variety of loosely coordinated activities to improve drug utilization. In the 1970s and 1980s, plan administrators encouraged the use of generic drugs rather than name brand drugs where possible, and this clearly led to cost savings. In the early 1990s, the pharmacy organization worked with the medical group to increase therapeutic substitutions as well. These prior efforts were largely informal, relying on goodwill and voluntary cooperation among physicians, pharmacists, and managers to bring about changes.

During 1997, Kaiser began to experience severe competitive pressures, as other health care organizations began to reshape their benefit plans and to reduce Kaiser's market share. At the same time, costs in the industry and for KPMCP were escalating, and KPMCP began to experience overall losses. On advice from management consultants McKinsey, Inc., the health plan consolidated its northern and southern California regions and began to downsize. Special attention was given to pharmacy operations because drug utilization by patients was on the rise, pushing up drug costs for the entire Kaiser program.

The McKinsey consultants pressed the new California division toward reengineering of outpatient pharmacy processes through a system-wide change program called the Performance Improvement Program. A brief snapshot of the Performance Improvement Program and other important interventions that occurred during 1997–2007 within the pharmacy organization is provided in Table 9.1 below. In this chapter we focus only on CMOP.

At the beginning of our case (1997), KPMCP was in economic crisis and the organization was under pressure to reverse two years of company losses. A call to action was needed if KPMCP was to maintain costs below competitors and regain market share. The need to address drug utilization issues and raise the visibility of this topic within the organization was clear, and KPMCP leaders mounted a campaign to convince different stakeholders that dramatic change was needed.

In 1997, a few pharmacy executives and drug information staff members attended a "summit meeting" to share concerns about escalating drug costs within the context of continuing company losses. In terms of cognitive learning mechanisms, there was an attempt to highlight and define the change problem, to investigate the extent to which needs were apparent in different parts of the pharmacy system, and to set overall program goals. Initial CMOP goals included maintaining drug costs below competitor levels, reducing diversity in local drug education policies and procedures, and holding market share. The focus included reducing costs and improving quality. At this point, management was less concerned about building a new organizational capability, and more concerned with relying on existing players to engage drug utilization problems. Specifically, problems were framed primarily in terms of the pharmacy division within KPMCP and what the drug education coordinators and other pharmacy staff members could

Table 9.1 Summary of change interventions within pharmacy operations, 1997–2007

Change intervention name	Essence of change
Consolidation	Downsizing, restructuring of pharmacy organization in line with formation of KPMCP California Division.
Performance Improvement Program	Discovery and implementation of best practices within pharmacy outpatient operations.
Clinical Management of Pharmaceuticals (CMOP)	Pharmacy-led effort to reduce drug costs and improve quality.
Drug Utilization Action Team (DUAT)	Physician-led effort to improve drug therapies and reduce costs.
Central Refill Pharmacy	Creation of an automated refill facility to reduce drug volume pressures on local pharmacies and to reduce refill costs.
Over-the-Counter (OTC) Drug Sales	The clinic pharmacies began to stock and sell over-the-counter drugs as a new form of revenue.
Integrated Clinical and Administrative Record System	The pharmacy organization began to participate in KPMCP's new automated clinical record system.
Central Mail Order Pharmacy	The pharmacy organization established a separate mail order facility with cutover to the new Central Refill Pharmacy II facility.

do to facilitate change through the normal pharmacy hierarchy. There was little attention to physician participation in the program. However, pharmacy leaders soon learned that operating through the regular pharmacy hierarchy was inadequate (cf. Chapter 11).

In late 1997, pharmacy executives created the first CMOP structural learning mechanism (SLM). It was a parallel learning mechanism (Zand 1974; Bushe and Shani 1991) composed of representative pharmacy leaders, drug information experts, purchasing experts, and staff pharmacists brought together from throughout California. Parallel learning mechanisms coexist with the normal organizational hierarchy. The SLM was temporary, formed to launch the first drug utilization initiatives. As with most parallel learning structures, the CMOP SLM members had other jobs and worked at this part-time. The members solicited ideas broadly within pharmacy locations for both cost and quality interventions focusing on drug conversions. The SLM as a body then pursued the implications of change in detail, documenting potential impacts and obstacles to implementation. In broadly considering drug substitution options, the group also developed strategies for new drugs entering the market, especially those having high costs or drug management difficulties. After drafting recommendations, the SLM group members met with selected stakeholder groups (pharmacy leaders, physician leaders, local and regional pharmacy and therapeutics groups) to press toward action. The process was quite sequential. Reflecting on efforts in the first few years, SLM members felt that the pharmacy organization drove the entire process, and that while the overall goals and targets were sound, the dialogue and deliberation with physician providers were inadequate for the task at hand. They also observed that the lack of dialogue and coordination across different pharmacy and medical group department boundaries led to some poor decisions. For example, in a few cases physicians were asked to make a change, and then were asked to shift back to drugs used earlier, confusing both patients and physicians.

Despite the problems, the initial CMOP effort was impressive, as it resulted in the first-ever California-wide plan for drug conversions with specific pilot initiatives to convert specific drugs (for example, switching from brand to generic, or from one brand to another), a structural learning mechanism to coordinate the work, and new procedural learning mechanisms such as changed protocols, new metrics, methods of monitoring progress, and processes for following up on patient results. More importantly, SLM members learned from successes and mistakes and were now aware of the need to reexamine the way the overall CMOP intervention was conducted. The ability to regularly critique processes and results was established early in the history of the change program, creating built-in reflection and adjustments.

Over the next few years, the CMOP SLM operated as a loose federation of departments within pharmacy operations, coordinated by a newly appointed drug use management director. At the implementation level, most annual initiatives involved simple conversions that the local drug education coordinators could implement with physicians and pharmacists in their own ways.

The current Clinical Management of Pharmaceuticals program

By 2007, The CMOP program and change process had changed dramatically. The program had been expanded to include: uniform goals and targets for all pharmacies, guidelines for better prescribing and for improved patient compliance, reliable performance tracking at each medical centre, prescription to over-the-counter drug conversions, prescription-to-prescription drug conversions, aggressive attention to use of generic drugs in the KPMCP drug formulary, coordination with medical group providers at all levels, and reduced variability in prescribing patterns across medical centre and medical office facilities. Table 9.2 provides an abstract of the current program.

Today, the CMOP SLM is a broad-based learning mechanism composed of representative drug information, drug purchasing information, drug education coordinators, chiefs of medical services, and regional pharmacy and therapeutics committee members. The biggest change was inclusion of physicians in the SLM and at all stages of the annual CMOP change cycle. The new SLM now sets the change initiative targets and works with the drug use manager to tightly orchestrate annual change initiatives. The drug use manager acts as "quarterback" or team leader on the administration of changes throughout KPMCP.

As noted in Table 9.2, the CMOP SLM cycle begins with an annual brainstorming event that sets the agenda for drug substitution initiatives. It ends

Table 9.2 The learning mechanism and change process in 2007

Learning mechanism	The current CMOP SLM includes drug information, drug purchasing information, drug education coordinators, medical services chiefs, pharmacy and therapeutics committee members, and other representatives across KPMCP organizational boundaries.
	The drug use management department provides overall direction and coordination of the annual CMOP process.
Change initiative phases	The drug use manager sets the annual cycle of events.
	The CMOP SLM brainstorms possible initiatives.
	The drug information department and relevant physician groups review alternative drugs for efficacy, safety, and cost.
	The drug purchasing department secures bids on alternatives.
	Physician groups select the most cost-effective drugs.
	Approvals are secured from medical group committees and leaders.
	Dynamic, organization-wide implementation occurs.
Learning dynamics	The CMOP SLM has adopted a longer time horizon, so that the selection of initiatives is well thought through, and so that rework or the need to shift back to drugs used earlier does not occur.
	The early identification of candidate drugs allows for long-term deliberation/dialogue, careful investigation of therapeutic goals, examination of inside and outside studies of drug efficacy, and attention to the annual CMOP cycles.
	The CMOP SLM drives and coordinates the CMOP agenda, CMOP process, and decisions on timing and implementation. CMOP conversions occur throughout the year.
	At the local level, drug education coordinators guide CMOP initiatives and provide support materials needed by physicians, pharmacists, and patients.
Major outcomes	Variable cost savings of roughly 5 percent per year in the face of rising drug costs from manufacturers.
	Performance scorecards for each pharmacy within KPMCP track performance against goals for generic drug substitutions, dosage conversions, within-class substitutions, and cross-class substitutions.
	Most pharmacies achieve 90 percent conversions on specific drug initiatives within a six-month timeframe.
	Therapeutic benefits and cost savings from CMOP are widely communicated to MDs and pharmacists to reinforce the value of CMOP initiatives and to motivate further change.

Table 9.3 The CMOP SLM annual change process – a GI example

1	The CMOP SLM met for a day to brainstorm a list of potential drug conversion topics including alternatives in the gastrointestinal (GI) practice area.
2	The drug information department at the request of the drug use manager prepared a monograph that focused on comparison of brand and generic proton pump inhibitor drugs. The intent was to consider external and internal literature on drug efficacy in an unbiased way.
3	The monograph was then reviewed with a committee of GI physicians to gain decisions on drugs deemed comparable and the preferred choices. Clear alternatives surfaced.
4	The drug purchasing department contacted drug manufacturers to secure bids to supply the preferred drugs.
5	Based on the new bids and information provided by drug purchasing, a GI committee within the medical group then reviewed the most cost-effective drugs and recommended a change in the formulary – a conversion to a generic proton pump inhibitor.
6	A brand-to-generic conversion was prepared for medical group physician leaders.
7	Physician leaders granted approval to shift from brand drugs A and B to proton pump inhibitor generic C, and this was formally proposed to the Regional Pharmacy and Therapeutics Committee. Quick approval was given.
8	The CMOP SLM, coordinating with drug education coordinators, then set the timing for the drug conversion.
9	The individual drug education coordinators met with local GI chiefs and selected physicians to discuss the rationale for change and implementation issues. At some locations, forums involving GI physicians and other affected primary care physicians were convened.
10	The individual drug education coordinators then took the proton pump inhibitor conversion to the local pharmacy and therapeutics committees. Since this had already been discussed with the affected physicians, few issues were raised at the local level.
11	Drug education coordinators as a body determined the tool kit needed for the conversion (descriptive memos for physicians and pharmacists, patient information flyers, letters to patients in advance of changes, and other support documents).
12	The pharmacy organization searched databases to identify patients who currently had proton pump inhibitors A and B and to identify their physicians. These physicians were contacted and asked to review therapeutic approval forms, allowing the conversion from A or B to C (physicians would say "yes" or "no" to the conversion, reflecting the particular needs of each patient). In 85 percent of the patient cases, physicians approved conversions.
13	Local drug education coordinators worked with local pharmacy and therapeutics committees, pharmacists, and patients on transition to the new drug.

with drug education coordinator and provider work on behalf of patients at the local levels. Table 9.3 provides a glimpse of the SLM-orchestrated change initiative process, with special focus on a recent example of gastro-intestinal (GI) proton pump inhibitor conversions.

The learning dynamics depicted in Tables 9.2 and 9.3 are an oversimplification of what occurs, as the process is not always linear. At times, certain steps are skipped, and earlier steps are sometimes repeated. The proton pump inhibitor conversion is a dramatic example of what can possibly occur, and it was only one of nine drug substitutions orchestrated in 2000. Evidence-based discussions occur before initiatives are selected. As noted in Table 9.2, drug conversion campaigns typically last three to four months, achieving 90 percent of the established goals. The dynamics of the CMOP Structural learning mechanisms and learning processes at the local medical centre and patient level will be discussed below.

Clinical management of pharmaceuticals' dynamics

Both the CMOP SLM and the network of drug education coordinators play important roles in the change initiative process. The CMOP cycle starts with a look at utilization trends, the clinical evidence, and research literature on drugs in the marketplace. The CMOP members spend a day filling a board with possible conversion initiatives. This brainstorming occurs prior to any attempts to take specific initiatives to other formal groups such as the peer body of drug education coordinators or medical group chiefs of services. This process results in longer time horizons and additional checks and balances in that the CMOP SLM can postpone decisions on drug conversions until the evidence for change is clear and until needed resources are available.

The drug education perspective on the annual CMOP SLM process and eventual action is important, since coordinators provide key linkages at operating levels. Coordinators interviewed for this case study report that there is now very little wiggle room in implementation at the local level, in contrast to the situation that existed in 1995. In other words, once the CMOP change cycle has been completed and approvals have been secured, there is little autonomy in terms of what will be done and how it will be done. The point is that a great deal of discussion occurs at the front end, and drug education coordinators must be in close touch with their physician contacts at all stages. After decisions are made, the coordinators group develops the drug conversion tool kits, and a publications subgroup of this body prepares the common materials. Following approval by the local pharmacy and therapeutics committees, the coordinators prepare blanket or individual patient authorization forms for each physician. Physicians identify patients who should not make the change due to drug intolerances or other personal issues. For approved cases, letters go out to patients before they appear in the pharmacies, so that there are few surprises for either pharmacists or patients. Since new drugs are involved, pharmacists by law must counsel every patient when the new prescriptions are filled. At the medical centres, the individual drug education coordinators meet monthly with pharmacy and therapeutic committees to monitor progress on specific initiatives under way and to make course corrections where progress is not achieved. Since scorecards are developed for each initiative, it is easy to track which physicians and pharmacists are helping with a particular conversion. According to the coordinators, 90 percent of drug conversions are now done in the same way. The combination of cognitive, structural, and procedural learning mechanisms within CMOP has created a dynamic capability for renewal within the KPMCP organization.

CMOP and KPMCP-wide results

The combination of CMOP and DUAT (see Table 9.1) programs brings stability instead of the familiar pattern of increased drug utilization and increased drug costs. The multiple pharmacy change initiatives have resulted in the lowest per-member-per-month prescription costs of all health plans enrolled in the NCQA Quality Compass of 2006 (KPMCP is best in the United States). The health plan's generic utilization rate is about 80 percent, compared to 45 percent to 55 percent for most other health plans. The health plan reports that it is able to achieve variable cost savings of roughly 5 percent per year in the face of rising manufacturer drug prices (see Table 9.2). Widespread communication of successful performance serves to reinforce motivation and commitment to new achievements in drug utilization management. The CMOP and DUAT programs allow KPMCP to reduce annual pharmacy budget allocations in predictable ways.

Discussion – the clinical management of pharmaceuticals' case and sustainable work systems design

Perhaps the most striking aspect of the CMOP case is that it demonstrates sustainable work systems design values, principles, and processes. Regarding values cited earlier in this chapter, KPMCP has developed built-in capability to design work systems that will be innovative and cope with rapid change. As a provider organization, KPMCP can do little about the pace of new drug development or discover medical advances through basic research. But it can provide essential new information about new products in the marketplace, evaluate existing and new products, and apply them in efficient and effective ways. The case demonstrates that the pharmacy organization has found multiple ways to foster this type of innovation (see Table 9.1).

SWS design is a reflexive methodology of intervention that is self-critical. Collective reflection is the ability to uncover and make explicit what is planned, observed, and achieved in practice. The CMOP program has built-in ability to critique and reflect on plans, work in process, and outcomes. The CMOP SLM, through its structural representation, meetings, and activities that span multiple organizational boundaries, is now able to take a long-term perspective on drug utilization challenges. Two key points in the case are that the SLM promotes interprofessional dialogue between pharmacists and physicians, as well as formal learning activities designed to increase understanding about drug substitutions and implementation issues.

The CMOP program relies upon learning mechanisms and processes created by managers, who offer some insights about the change initiative. First, the program has followed the principle that strategic and operational aspects of redesign are not separate. Actors contributing to CMOP program development have had a real appreciation of environmental, strategic design matters, and operational realities in creating the new organizational capability. Second, both the construction of the CMOP SLM and the CMOP annual drug substitution process are iterative (invent, try, reflect, assess, adjust) and heavily rely on participants to self-apply new concepts and methods. Finally, the CMOP SLM members are able to come together regularly to address dilemmas; for example, that the pace of drug conversions benefits patients but creates new demands for training activities and coordination. Drug conversions require continual learning and unlearning on the part of pharmacy and physician providers. The former provide essential new information on different medicines and their expected performance, while the latter provide information on actual performance and attributes of medicines currently in use.

The economic issue of cost containment in health care is self-evident, but the difficulty of achieving any savings that will benefit patients in the face of cost increases from drug manufacturers along with rising labour costs is not well understood. The CMOP program addresses social and economic issues through a change process that relies on learning mechanisms. The mechanisms simultaneously support providers, employees, and patients, and the KPMCP organization. The notion of stakeholder parity is imperfectly followed in that health plan members and patients do not contribute to the change process, but the benefits to patients in the form of reduced health plan premiums and state-of-the-art drugs are evident.

Sustainability theory suggests that designers must be alert to the duality of stability and change. That is, the organization must be capable of both efficient production of services and dynamic development (see also Chapters 4, 6, and 8). The CMOP case shows that KPMCP has the ability to give development a prominent and integrated role in the work of the organization. There are numerous examples in the "CMOP Dynamics" section of this chapter, showing capacity to learn and innovate during normal operations through structural and procedural learning mechanisms.

Implications for theory and practice

The collective implications for SWS design theory from the CMOP case and this chapter rest mainly with the use of learning mechanisms. Cognitive, structural, and procedural mechanisms are needed to create the sustainable organization, and they will likely play prominent roles in SWS redesign programs and in guiding the change process (see also Chapter 16). Specifically, cognitive learning mechanisms provide the goals, priorities, and sense of urgency for the overall effort. Structural learning bodies provide dynamic capability to represent different stakeholder interests, plan specific change initiatives, and adjust to the inevitable problems that arise, while continually promoting individual and organizational learning. Participants in the structural learning mechanism have potential to be creative in crafting procedural learning mechanisms needed at various program stages, and continuously improving them if the organization is to develop a new capability in the targeted change area.

The implications for extension of SWS design theory, processes, and learning for other organizations within the US health care context are easy to see for direct

KPMCP competitors. Other health maintenance organizations have similar opportunities to manage care tightly and to take the lead on drug utilization matters. However, few competitors have organizational arrangements that promote strong evidence-based deliberations and decisions, intense communications and education around the need for drug conversions, and other capabilities to post significant results on drug quality and drug costs. Creation of information systems and learning mechanisms that cross organizational boundaries can be the answer to what otherwise might be a fragmented approach to drug utilization decisions in other settings. There would seem to be few barriers to adopting SWS design philosophy and learning mechanisms in other health care settings and on other change topics. Indeed, the SWS approach has been used in traditional health plan organizations to orchestrate complete company turnaround (Stebbins *et al.* 2006b) and to enable people to learn change management skills.

Applications of SWS design theory in industries outside the health care setting have already occurred in banking, aerospace, university, government service agency, and other knowledge-worker settings (see also Chapters 4, 5, 6, and 8). Companies are drawn to this approach because it focuses on development of human resources and capabilities at all levels (Stebbins and Shani 2002). The belief is that involvement and dialogue with a purpose will raise human needs above the technical and economic pressures that consume organizations in post-industrial society. As shown in this chapter, even where economic pressures are dominant, SWS design provides learning mechanisms that promote parity in weighing needs of diverse stakeholders. The challenge would seem to be centred on understanding how applications in diverse settings can contribute to an already strong theoretical foundation for eclectic SWS design. Eclectic self-design change processes have been used in diverse settings (Stebbins and Shani 1995; Stebbins and Shani 2002) and provide clear guidelines for managers hoping to create new organizational capabilities. Chapter 16 in this book provides additional insights regarding this growing field of study and practice.

Questions for reflection

Here are three questions for your further reflection on the issues broached in this chapter:

- Kaiser Permanente continues to thrive in the US health care context. How does Kaiser Permanente promote sustainable growth and development?
- What can we conclude about the change intervention regarding the clinical management of pharmaceuticals (CMOP) in terms of creating new organizational capabilities?
- Could the annual CMOP change process be used to orchestrate operations changes in your own organization, and if so, what kinds of learning mechanisms would be needed?

References

Beckhard, R. (1969) *Organizational Development: Strategies and Models*, Reading, MA: Addison Wesley.

Beer, M. (2001) "How to Develop an Organization Capable of Sustained High Performance," in *Organizational Dynamics*, 29, 4, 233–247.

Bushe, G.R. and Shani, A.B. (Rami) (1991) *Parallel Learning Structures: Increasing Innovations in Bureaucracies*, Reading, MA: Addison-Wesley.

Cummings, T.G. and Worley, C.G. (2001) *Organization Development and Change*, Cincinnati, OH: Thomson South-Western.

Mackenzie, K.D. (1986) *Organization Design: The Organizational Audit and Analysis Technology*, New York: Ablex.

Mohrman, S.A. and Cummings, T.G. (1989) *Self-Designing Organizations: Learning How to Create High Performance*, Boston, MA: Addison Wesley.

Pavlovsky, P., Forslin, J. and Reinhardt, R. (2001) "Practices and Tools in Organizational Learning," in M. Dierkes, J. Berthoin, J. Child, and I. Nonaka (eds), *Handbook of Organizational Learning and Knowledge*, Oxford: Oxford University Press, pp. 775–793.

Popper, M. and Lipshitz, R. (1998) "Organizational Learning Mechanisms: A Structural and Cultural Approach to Organizational Learning," *Journal of Applied Behavioral Science*, 34, 2, 161–179.

Raelin, J.A. (2000) *Work-Based Learning: The New Frontier of Management Development*, Englewood Cliff, NJ: Prentice-Hall.

Shani, A.B. (Rami) and Docherty, P. (2003) *Learning by Design*, London: Blackwell.

Stebbins, M.W. and Shani, A.B. (Rami) (1989) "Organization Design: Beyond the Mafia Model," *Organizational Dynamics*, Winter, 18–30.

Stebbins, M.W. and Shani, A.B. (Rami) (1995) "Organization Design and the Knowledge Worker," *Leadership and Organization Development Journal*, 16, 1, 23–30.

Stebbins, M.W. and Shani, A.B. (Rami) (1998) "Business Process Reengineering at Blue Shield of California: The Integration of Multiple Change Initiatives," *The Journal of Organizational Change Management*, 11, 3, 216–232.

Stebbins, M.W. and Shani, A.B. (Rami) (2002) "Eclectic Design for Change," in P. Docherty, J. Forslin, and A.B. (Rami) Shani, *Creating Sustainable Work Systems: Emerging Perspectives and Practice*, London: Routledge, pp. 201–212.

Stebbins, M.W., Freed, T., Shani, A.B. (Rami), and Doerr, K. (2006a) "The Limits of Reflexive Design in a Secrecy-Based Organization," in D. Boud, P. Cressey, and P. Docherty (eds), *Productive Reflection at Work*, London: Routledge, pp. 80–92.

Stebbins, M.W., Shani, A.B. (Rami), and Docherty, P. (2006b) "Reflection During a Crisis Turnaround: Management Use of Learning Mechanisms," in D. Boud, P. Cressey, and P. Docherty, *Productive Reflection at Work*, London: Routledge, pp. 106–119.

Weick, K.E. (1995) *Sensemaking in Organizations*, Thousand Oaks, CA: Sage.

Zand, D. (1974) "Collateral Organization: A New Change Strategy," *Journal of Applied Behavioral Science*, 10, 1, 63–89.

10 Financial management to support sustainability

Doug Cerf and Arline Savage

Introduction

Sustainability provides an important focus for financial managers. This chapter presents state-of-the-art financial tools and techniques that support sustainability goals. The primary purpose is to introduce markets, investments, reporting techniques, and analytical methods that can be used by firms to support sustainability.

We present the tools and techniques in three financial management categories: finance, internal reporting, and external reporting. The finance category relates to resource allocation, management, acquisition, and investment. The internal reporting category is accounting-related and is concerned with providing information to management for internal decision making. The external reporting category is also accounting-related and is directed toward providing information to outsiders, such as shareholders, financial analysts, creditors, prospective investors and employees, social activists, and the public in general.

Firms that implement accounting and finance tools to support sustainability are in one of two general categories. The first category consists of firms for which sustainable development is a strategic objective. The second category consists of firms that have separate environmental and occupational health departments, an arrangement that generally indicates or leads to weak integration of sustainability objectives into the firm's strategy.

The challenge for firms in the first category is to implement the sustainability tools throughout the organization. The goals of incorporating sustainability in the strategic plan of the firm are: (1) to create long-term economic sustainability; (2) to generate value through a system of corporate social responsibility; and (3) to generate value through environmental management (e.g., Kaplan and De Pinho 2007: 5). Issues that firms face in this category include implementation across divisions of the firm. Divisions may need to modify a specific sustainability tool to be consistent with the characteristics of the business. In an international environment, implementation is complicated by local management tradition. To encourage management buy-in, firms may consider linking outcomes from use of the finance and accounting sustainability tools to a compensation incentive system.

Firms have developed environmental and occupational health departments as they have evolved in their efforts to address sustainability issues. In some cases environmental and occupational health departments have operated in isolation from the main management of the firm. The challenge for the environmental and occupational health departments in these firms is to attract the attention of upper management to incorporate sustainability initiatives into the strategic plan. Reporting by the head of the environmental and occupational health department to top management increases the likelihood that these issues will be incorporated in the strategic plan. Once implementation into the strategic plan is achieved, success of the sustainability initiatives by the environmental and occupational health departments is more likely.

Once sustainability is embedded in a firm's strategic plan, financial managers have a critical role in addressing and reporting on the economic impact of sustainable business activities. In the next section we will discuss the prominent finance tools and techniques that financial managers can use to support sustainability.

Finance tools and techniques

Table 10.1 summarizes finance tools and techniques by presenting disciplinary roots, key contributors, a short description, stakeholders, and the outcomes that result from using the tool or technique.

Table 10.1 Summary of finance tools and techniques

	Socially responsible investing	*Social return on investment*	*Emissions trading programs*
Disciplinary roots	Finance and investments in debt and equity	Finance and financial return metrics	Finance and stock markets
Key contributors	Social investment forums	Lingane and Olsen (2004)	United States Environmental Protection Agency and European Union
Description of tool or technique	Investment strategy that allows firms to invest their capital in investments that are consistent with sustainability goals	Return metric that includes social return in currency units compared to currency units invested	Trading market where participants buy and sell the right to emit pollutants (e.g., greenhouse gases)
Stakeholders	Society, shareholders, employees, fund managers	Investors, management, fund managers, venture capitalists	Society, future generations, government entities
Outcomes	Provides an investment outlet for investors who support sustainability. Provides an additional source of capital for firms with a sustainable mission	Provides stakeholders with a tool that allows them to evaluate the social return for the amount of investment	Reduction in pollutants in the air; healthier humans and animals

Next, we provide a more detailed explanation of each tool and we explain how it supports sustainability.

Socially Responsible Investing

Socially Responsible Investing (SRI) allows firms to invest their short- and long-term capital into investments that are consistent with sustainability goals. The goal of SRI is to achieve competitive financial returns while fostering better social and environmental performance. Firms may use the following strategies to achieve SRI objectives: (1) investing in companies that meet certain social and/or environmental performance criteria; (2) using their rights as shareowners to encourage companies to be better corporate citizens; and/or (3) allocating some of the fund's assets for investment in disadvantaged urban and rural communities.

SRI mutual funds are an increasingly popular SRI vehicle. For example, in the United States socially responsible investment assets under professional management grew 4 percent faster than the entire universe of managed assets over the period 1995 to 2005. During this period, SRI mutual fund assets increased by 258 percent, from $639 billion in 1995 to $2.29 trillion in 2005. In 2005, nearly $1 out of every $10 under professional management was in socially responsible investing, or 9.4 percent of the $24.4 trillion under professional management (Social Investment Forum 2006).

SRI supports sustainability by allowing firms to invest their short- and long-term capital into investments that are consistent with sustainability goals. It allows firms to support other firms that have a sustainable mission (e.g., renewable energy), and may also support firms that do not have a sustainable mission, but operate in a sustainable manner.

Social Return on Investment

Social Return on Investment (SROI) allows firms to evaluate projects based on social return as well as financial returns. SROI provides investors and managers with a tool to support sustainability in their investment decisions. SROI is a complement to financial return on investment. SROI assists managers to optimize the impact of their operation on the environment and human well-being while achieving the shareholder returns that stockholders expect. By being able to measure SROI, managers and investors (e.g., venture capitalists) can help entrepreneurs as they plan their business to identify business model modifications or alternatives as well as market opportunities that could result in increased social benefit. Familiarity with SROI assists management with ongoing operational management and capital allocation decisions by helping them maximize both the social and financial bottom line. It also helps facilitate assessment of investment opportunities and their performance with respect to investors' specific social and financial goals. Lingane and Olsen (2004) provide steps and an example of a SROI calculation.

SROI is calculated in a manner similar to the common financial metric Internal Rate of Return (IRR). First, an estimate of the social cash flows is made for the life of the project. Social cash flows are cash flows generated by a project over and above the cash flows that would normally be generated. Environmental cash flows are part of social cash flows. For example, if a business venture generated greenhouse gas emissions permits that can be sold on an emissions trading market similar to the Emission Trading Scheme in the European Union, the resultant cash inflows are estimated. The discount rate at which the present value of these cash inflows equals the capital investment is the SROI. The SROI is equivalent to an IRR calculated using social cash flows.

SROI supports sustainability by providing investors and managers with a metric that allows for analysis of the social return for a given amount of investment. Investors who are interested in supporting sustainability can use SROI to differentiate between firms based on their social return.

Emissions trading programs

Emissions trading programs are cap-and-trade programs that respond to the climate change problem through the trading of emissions allowances. The cap-and-trade approach to controlling emissions originated in the sulphur dioxide (SO_2) market. SO_2 is a precursor to acid rain. A central authority, usually a government agency, sets an aggregate limit or cap on the amount of a pollutant that a set of entities (e.g., the utilities industry) can emit over a defined period. There have also been cases where an individual firm sets an aggregate limit for the total emissions of its companies or divisions (e.g., BP, formerly British Petroleum). Emission allowances are allocated to the individual firms based on historical emissions by the individual firms. The allowances represent the right to emit a specified amount of pollutant. The total amount of credits equals the aggregate cap, thus limiting total emissions. Firms that pollute beyond their allowances must buy credits from those who pollute less than their allowances. This transfer is called a trade, which may be made on a climate exchange, directly with other participants, or through a broker.

The overall goal of emissions trading is to reduce air pollution. The effect of emissions trading is that the buyer must pay to pollute, while the seller is rewarded for reducing emissions. Consistent with the law of supply and demand, the more entities there are that need to buy credits, the higher the price of the credits becomes. Reducing emissions becomes cost-effective in comparison. In some systems, the aggregate cap is lowered over time. In others, a portion of all traded credits must be retired, resulting in a net reduction in emissions each time a trade occurs. In many cap-and-trade systems, organizations that do not pollute may also buy credits. This allows environmental groups to purchase and retire pollution credits to reduce emissions and raise the price of the remaining credits. While the cap is usually set by a political process, individual firms freely choose how or if they will reduce their emissions. Moreover, the government does not need to regulate how much each individual firm emits, making cap-and-trade a very cost-effective method for controlling pollution on a large scale.

Emissions trading supports sustainability by controlling air pollution. It uses free markets to provide economic incentives for reducing emissions of pollutants and economic penalties for exceeding pre-specified emission limits.

Internal reporting tools and techniques

In this section we will discuss the prominent internal reporting tools that firms use to support sustainability. In Table 10.2 we summarize these tools by presenting disciplinary roots, key contributors, a short description, stakeholders, and the outcomes resulting from using these tools.

Sustainable balanced scorecard

The sustainable balanced scorecard links sustainability management to business strategy to achieve recognition of sustainability issues in a company's strategic plan. The balanced scorecard is an internal assessment, improvement, and reporting system. It supplies key indicators for management to perform its function. The key to the scorecard's success is the link to the firm's strategic plan. The successful implementation of this management system turns strategy into action.

The conventional scorecard measures performance by combining financial measures with non-financial measures, from the following perspectives: (1) financial; (2) customer; (3) internal business processes; and (4) learning-and-growth. The balancing is done by including nonfinancial measures (customer, internal business processes, and learning-and-growth) with conventional financial accounting measures. Learning-and-growth opportunities facilitate improvements to business processes, and also provide incentives for employees to increase their intellectual capital. For example, a learning-and-growth metric is the number of hours of continuing education training by management. Other examples are provided by Kaplan and De Pinho (2007: 19–20) in their exhibits. They refer to the learning-and-growth perspective as the human resource perspective.

The original balanced scorecard has been expanded to manage sustainability (Epstein and Wisner 2001; Figge *et al.* 2002; Idalina and Reijnders 2005; Idalina *et al.* 2002). There are two methods of incorporating sustainability into the balanced scorecard. Sustainability can be incorporated as part of any or all of the four standard perspectives. For example, in the internal process perspective, the objectives "Energy, Water and Material Efficiency" and "Elimination of Animal Testing on Products" would incorporate sustainability. In the customer perspective the objectives "Toxin-Free Product" and "Products Free of Animal Testing" would incorporate sustainability. An alternative method is the creation of an additional perspective that focuses on sustainability. The advantage of the first method is that sustainability is better integrated into the measurement system and becomes embedded in the corporate culture. If a company has a separate scorecard specifically for sustainability without also integrating sustainability into the main balanced scorecard, then sustainability does not get the appropriate emphasis by top decision makers in the firm.

Table 10.2 Summary of internal reporting tools and techniques

	Sustainable balanced scorecard	*Eco-efficiency*	*Environmental costs and product pricing*	*Environmental sustainability indexes*
Disciplinary roots	Strategic management and accounting	Finance, accounting, environmental science, and engineering	Management, accounting, manufacturing, and engineering	Sociology, economics, environmental science
Key contributors	Kaplan and Norton (1992, 1993, 1996a, 1996b, 1996c); Epstein and Wisner (2001); Figge et al. (2002); Idalina and Reijnders (2005); Idalina et al. (2002)	Schaltegger and Sturm (1989)	Kaplan and Bruns (1987)	Center for Environmental Law and Policy at Yale; Center for International Earth Science Information Network at Columbia; World Economic Forum
Description of tool or technique	An internal assessment, improvement, and reporting system that includes sustainability in the strategic plan	Ratio between two elements: environmental impact (to be reduced) and value of production (to be increased)	Activity-based system that is the basis for allocating environmental costs to products and processes	Indices that provide a methodology to understand how firms' actions impact aggregate sustainability in a specific country
Stakeholders	Management, employees, customers, stockholders, and creditors	Management, stockholders, and society	Management and consumers	Management, economists, researchers, government agencies, environmental protection agencies, society
Outcomes	Integrates sustainable management into mainstream business management	Reduces the damage caused to the environment while increasing, or at least not decreasing, shareholder value	Promotes management awareness of environmental and social impact of products/processes in order to realize cost savings and select products/processes that are more sustainable	Provides management with environmental indicators and statistics for internal decision making about doing business in a particular country

A balanced scorecard management system that incorporates sustainability gives management a tool to implement a strategic plan that includes sustainability goals. It offers a promising starting point for incorporating environmental and social aspects into the main management system. Sustainability management using a balanced scorecard helps to overcome the shortcomings of conventional approaches to environmental and social management systems by integrating the three pillars of sustainability (social, environmental, and economic perspectives) into a single and overarching strategic management tool (Figge *et al.* 2002). A balanced scorecard management system supports sustainability by integrating sustainability management into mainstream business management.

Eco-efficiency

Eco-efficiency describes a set of methods that provide information on environmental performance vis-à-vis financial performance. The concept was first defined by Schaltegger and Sturm in 1989 as a ratio between two elements: environmental impact (to be reduced) and value of production (to be increased). Eco-efficiency is based on the concept of creating more goods and services by using fewer resources and creating less waste and pollution. Eco-efficiency became widely accepted when the World Business Council for Sustainable Development (WBCSD) promoted it in its publication *Changing Course* (Schmidheiny 1992). The WBCSD (1996) includes a clear target level: An eco-efficient state is reached when economic activities are at a level at least in line with the earth's estimated carrying capacity. The United Nations Conference on Environment and Development in 1992, commonly known as the Earth Summit, also endorsed eco-efficiency in the adoption of Agenda 21, a universal blueprint for sustainable development in business.

The term eco-efficiency has since become associated with a management philosophy supportive of sustainability. DeSimone and Popoff (1997: 24–39) offer a comprehensive discussion of the financial benefits of eco-efficiency. These include: (1) reduced current costs of poor environmental performance; (2) reduced future costs of poor environmental performance; (3) reduced costs of capital; (4) benefits from increased market share and improved or protected market opportunities; and (5) benefits from enhanced image.

Eco-efficiency indicators are based on the *Manual for the Preparers and Users of Eco-efficiency Indicators*, developed by the United Nations Conference on Trade and Development (UNCTAD 2004). Eco-efficiency guideline areas are: (1) water use; (2) energy use; (3) global warming contribution; (4) ozone depleting substances; and (5) waste. The guideline also includes case examples. Eco-efficiency indicators provide information in a systematic and consistent manner over periods of time to enhance comparability. The manual therefore covers the technical issues of recognition, measurement, and disclosure of environmental transactions and variables.

Schaltegger (1998: 284–285) describes a structured management decision-making process, the Eco-rational Path Method (EPM), to guide a firm to eco-efficiency by integrating traditional accounting information (e.g., revenues, costs, expenses, income) – the "economic dimension" – with environmental accounting information (e.g., emissions, resource use) – the "ecological dimension." First, the firm gathers traditional financial results, including environmental compliance costs and earnings. Second, the firm uses environmental accounting to evaluate the ecological harm caused by the firm in units of environmental impact. Third, the firm uses regular accounting measures of economic efficiency (e.g., contribution margin per product). Fourth, the firm computes ecological efficiency (e.g., environmental impact added per product). Finally, eco-efficiency is calculated (e.g., the monetary contribution margin created per environmental impact added for a product). Ciba Specialty Chemicals Inc. (2006), a Swiss public company, provides an easily accessible example of eco-efficiency metrics in all five guideline areas for the 2002–2006 period.

Eco-efficient strategies, measured by eco-efficiency indicators, support sustainability by providing sustainability metrics that allow management to reduce the damage caused to the environment while increasing, or at least not decreasing, shareholder value (Schaltegger and Sturm 1989).

Impact of environmental costs on product pricing

The impact of environmental costs on product pricing considers whether environmental costs are appropriately included in the product price. Because of the costs related to compliance with environmental laws and regulations, firms include environmental costs related to past damage, as well as preventative costs, in product pricing. Past unrecognized costs – for example, costs related to the products whose production resulted in the creation of an environmental hazard – would have resulted in under-costing of these products at the time of production.

Current environmental costs should be assigned to the correct product(s). If these costs are instead included in a general overhead rate, products that cause the environmental costs will have costs understated and profit overstated. Accurate cost allocation will help a firm make appropriate product retention/elimination decisions. Activity-based costing (Kaplan and Bruns 1987) is one way of assigning costs appropriately.

Stakeholders expect firms to be responsible for the environmental and social costs of their products throughout the product's life cycle (see also Chapters 5, 8, 11, and 12 in this volume). For example, two recent European Union directives, the Restriction of Hazardous Substances Directive, effective in 2006, and the Waste Electrical and Electronic Equipment Directive, effective in 2003, require firms to eliminate certain hazardous materials in the design/production phase and to be responsible for the end-of-life disposal/recycling costs of their products.

Firms report on their efforts to better understand environmental costs. For example, Ford's 2005–2006 Sustainability Report provides a good example of the analysis of environmental and social costs incurred along its value chain. In addition, Toyota's approach to understanding the environmental and social costs of producing a product demonstrate the impact this topic can have on making sustainable decisions. The basis of Toyota's model, with its emphasis on Philosophy, Processes, People and Partners, and Problem Solving, is to "base management decisions on a long-term philosophy, even at the expense of short-term financial goals" (Liker 2004: 13).

Recognizing that product costs include environmental costs can help management decide what products to offer. As managers become aware of the environmental impact of their products and processes, they will select products that are more sustainable.

Environmental sustainability indexes

Environmental sustainability indexes track the environmental and social performance of countries. The Environmental Performance Project includes two country-level indices, namely the Environmental Sustainability Index and the Environmental Performance Index. The purpose of the project is to shift environmental decision making to firmer analytic foundations by using environmental indicators and statistics. This is a joint project between the Yale Center for Environmental Law and Policy at Yale University, the Center for International Earth Science Information Network at Columbia University, and the World Economic Forum. The project produces a periodically updated Environmental Sustainability Index, which is a composite index tracking a diverse set of socioeconomic, environmental, and institutional indicators that characterize and influence environmental sustainability and are aggregated at the country level. The second index is the Environmental Performance Index, which focuses on assessing key environmental policy outcomes using trend analysis and performance targets (Yale University 2006).

The Environmental Sustainability Index benchmarks the ability of nations to protect the environment. It does so by integrating 76 data sets into 21 indicators of environmental sustainability, tracking natural resource endowments, past and present pollution levels, environmental management efforts, and the capacity of a society to improve its environmental performance. The 2005 Environmental Sustainability Index provides indicators that permit comparison across a range of issues that fall into five broad categories: Environmental Systems; Reducing Environmental Stresses; Reducing Human Vulnerability to Environmental Stresses; Societal and Institutional Capacity to Respond to Environmental Challenges; and Global Stewardship (Yale University 2006).

The Environmental Performance Index provides a tool for improving policymaking and shifting environmental decision making onto firmer analytic foundations. It provides benchmarks for current national pollution control and natural resource management results. It also identifies specific targets for environmental performance and measures how close each country comes to these established goals. Issue-by-issue and aggregate rankings facilitate cross-country comparisons both globally and within relevant peer groups. The 2006 Environmental Performance Index centres on two broad environmental protection objectives: (1) reducing environmental stresses on human health; and (2) protecting ecosystem vitality.

It is derived from a review of the environmental literature and mirrors the priorities expressed by policy makers, most notably the environmental dimension of the United Nations' Millennium Development Goals. In the 2006 Environmental Performance Index, environmental health and ecosystem vitality are gauged using 16 indicators tracked in six established policy categories: Environmental Health; Air Quality; Water Resources; Biodiversity and Habitat; Productive Natural Resources; and Sustainable Energy. It also provides "Environmental Performance Indicator Rankings by Country," based on the six policy categories (Yale University 2006).

The indices support sustainability by providing management with environmental indicators and statistics for internal decision making regarding doing business in a particular country. This is particularly important with the extent of globalization in business, because the components of the indices can help managers understand a country's business and regulatory environment.

External reporting tools and techniques

In this section we will discuss the external reporting tools and techniques that firms use to support sustainability. In Table 10.3 we summarize these tools by presenting disciplinary roots, key contributors, a short description, stakeholders, and the outcomes resulting from using the tool.

Environmental liabilities

Environmental liabilities are reported by firms in their annual reports to disclose the current cost of environmental obligations related to past or current operations. Liabilities are defined as economic obligations that arise from benefits received in the past, and for which the probability, amount, and timing of payment are known with reasonable certainty. Generally accepted accounting principles require that environmental liabilities be disclosed in the balance sheet, along with the firm's other liabilities. The Environmental Protection Agency (EPA) definition of an environmental liability is a legal obligation to make a future expenditure due to the past or ongoing manufacture, use, release, or threatened release of a particular substance, or other activities that adversely affect the environment.

The term liability has accounting and legal dimensions (Rogers 2005: 19–30). The accounting dimension is that a liability is a present obligation to make a future expenditure. Significant challenges arise with regard to environmental liabilities. Even if there is acknowledgement that an obligation has been incurred, there may be ambiguity about whether the obligation is measurable. When there is ambiguity with regard to liabilities, management has inherent bias and incentive to understate liabilities to show a healthier financial position because excessive liabilities have a detrimental effect on the financial well-being of a firm. This leads to the legal dimension, where a liability is a legally enforceable obligation. If management does decide to record an environmental liability in the financial statements or even as a note to the financial statements, this may be

Table 10.3 Summary of external reporting tools and techniques

	Environmental liabilities	Financial reporting of emission credits	Sustainability reporting based on Global Reporting Initiative Guidelines	Greenhouse Gas Accounting and Reporting Standard and Guidance
Disciplinary roots	Accounting, law	Accounting	Accounting, operations management	Accounting, environmental science
Key contributors	International Accounting Standards Board; Rogers (2005)	International Financial Reporting Interpretations Committee; Rogers (2005)	Global Reporting Initiative	World Resources Institute, World Council on Sustainable Development
Description of tool or technique	Recognizing, measuring, and reporting environmental liabilities in financial statements	Recognizing, measuring, and reporting of emission credit assets and liabilities	Recognizing, measuring, and reporting of environmental and social strategies and metrics	Recognizing, measuring, setting reduction targets, and reporting of greenhouse gas emissions
Stakeholders	Shareholders, environmental groups, environmental protection agencies, attorneys	Shareholders, environmental groups, government agencies, emissions trading programs	Shareholders, environmental groups, employees, management, and insurers	Shareholders, environmental groups, management, government agencies
Outcomes	Discloses firms' financial responsibility for environmental remediation. The requirement to report liabilities discourages management from engaging in damaging economic activities	Firms' emission credits may be reported as an intangible asset or liability	The exercise of achieving GRI compliance can focus the efforts of the firm on measurable environmental and social actions	Reduction of greenhouse gases by firms to affect climate change

used as evidence of acknowledgement of guilt in legal proceedings and may, from management's perspective, put the company at greater risk of losing in court. Research shows that there is significant variation in the quality of financial statement disclosures on estimated environmental cleanup liabilities. The factors influencing these disclosures include regulatory enforcement, litigation and negotiation concerns, and capital market concerns (Barth *et al.* 1997).

The valuation of environmental liabilities can be problematic. The three issues are timing, amount, and likelihood. Payments of compliance and remediation obligations, for example, may be many years away and may stretch out over a long period of time. Compensation and natural resource damage liabilities, on the other hand, can arise in the near term but also have long timeframes. Different environmental liabilities may occur with different likelihoods. One way to consider the expected cost of environmental liabilities is to multiply the forecasted magnitude of the expense by its likelihood. This likelihood should account for factual and legal questions, and thus requires scientific and legal analysis. A more complete way to account for an uncertain liability is to calculate its expected cost based on a probability distribution of expense magnitudes. Estimates of future costs also have unavoidable uncertainties about magnitude of costs. The recommendation is to apply the standard uncertainty assessment methods of sensitivity and scenario analysis.

The disclosure of environmental liabilities makes company environmental performance more transparent. This transparency discourages management from engaging in economic activities that damage the environment. For existing environmental damage, mandatory disclosure forces firms to recognize the need to mitigate the damage.

Financial reporting of emission credits

Financial reporting of emission credits is related to emissions trading programs. This type of financial reporting recognizes whether a firm is holding excess emission credits or whether it has an obligation to purchase credits. The International Financial Reporting Interpretations Committee (IFRIC) issued an interpretation, IFRIC 3, on emission rights. Emission credits are recognized as intangible assets, but the interpretation also requires the recognition of the corresponding liability. Under IFRIC 3, emission credits are initially valued at fair value (i.e., as bought or sold in a current transaction between willing parties). The asset and liability are shown separately and are not offset against one another (Rogers 2005: 198–199). Although this accounting treatment remains conceptually sound and represents the economic reality of cap-and-trade transactions, IFRIC 3 has now been withdrawn after intense pressure from European politicians and business leaders who objected to the financial consequences of these disclosures.

Sustainability reporting based on Global Reporting Initiative Guidelines

Sustainability reporting based on Global Reporting Initiative Guidelines promotes the development and dissemination of globally applicable sustainability reporting that discloses economic, environmental, and social dimensions of the organization's activities, products, and services. Founded in 1997 by the Coalition for Environmentally Responsible Economies and the United Nations Environmental Program, the GRI employs a long-term, multi-stakeholder process to develop and disseminate globally applicable sustainability reporting guidelines (Global Reporting Initiative 2006; White 2003). These guidelines are currently in voluntary use by over 1,000 organizations for reporting on the economic, environmental, and social dimensions of their activities, products, and services.

A number of countries in Europe require some sustainability reporting (Waddock 2004). EU countries have shown a particularly strong interest in Sustainable Development Reporting. For instance in France, Germany, Denmark, Sweden, the United Kingdom, and Norway, it is already mandatory for corporations to disclose some form of environmental and/or social metrics. Other countries such as the Netherlands, and South Africa also have disclosure requirements. In the United States, sustainability disclosure is not yet required.

The GRI continues to work with the International Federation of Accountants' International Auditing and Assurance Standards Board to enhance the credibility of the GRI criteria. In their report on the future of sustainability assurance, Zadek and Raynard (2004) suggest the need to develop Generally Accepted Accounting Principles and Assurance Standards for Sustainability.

Some firms integrate sustainability reporting into their annual report. The sustainability disclosure is integrated in the report as opposed to reporting in separate sections of the report or in a separate report. For example, Novo Nordisk's annual report includes their sustainability reporting.

GRI supports sustainability by providing an established framework for an organization to report on its environmental and social performance. The framework facilitates the evaluation of a company's environmental and social performance. A firm's performance can be assessed over a number of years or compared to other firms in the same industry.

Greenhouse Gas Accounting and Reporting Standard and Guidance

Greenhouse Gas Accounting and Reporting Standard and Guidance assists firms in understanding and reporting their impact on global warming. Generally, greenhouse gas measurement and reporting is a section of a firm's sustainability report that is prepared based on Global Reporting Initiative (GRI) guidelines. Some firms prepare an annual report that includes their sustainability report (e.g., Novo Nordisk 2005 annual report). Because the greenhouse gas area of reporting is significant for many firms, the GRI guidelines refer to the Greenhouse Gas Corporate Accounting and Reporting Standard protocol for guidance. The Greenhouse Gas Corporate Accounting and Reporting Standard is a document that was prepared and is continuously improved through a joint venture of the World Resources Institute and the World Council on Sustainable Development. The mission of the Greenhouse Gas Corporate Accounting and Reporting Standard is to develop internationally accepted greenhouse gas (GHG) accounting and reporting standards for business and to promote broad adoption of the standard. The standard provides a step-by-step guide for companies to use in quantifying and reporting their GHG emissions.

The Greenhouse Gas Accounting and Reporting Standard has three key steps: (1) prepare an inventory of greenhouse gases emitted as a result of the firm's existence; (2) set a greenhouse gas target; and (3) develop a plan to reduce greenhouse gases over time. A common approach is to set a target to reduce greenhouse gases by a future date to a level that existed for the entity at a previous time. For example, BP set a goal to reduce annual emissions to 90 percent of 1990 levels by 2010.[1]

Possible future programs related to greenhouse gases include emissions trading programs such as the European Union Greenhouse Gas Emissions Allowance Trading Scheme that became effective at the beginning of 2005. This topic was discussed in the section above entitled "Emissions Trading Programs."

The Greenhouse Gas Accounting and Reporting Standard is designed to be program- and policy-neutral so a variety of GHG programs can use the Standard as their accounting and reporting protocol. The Standard does not include a verification process. However, if the GHG Standard is used as part of the GRI reporting guidelines it will include the GRI verification process. Cross-sector and sector-specific calculation tools are part of the GHG Standard. In a manner similar to financial statements prepared based on generally accepted accounting principles, the Greenhouse Gas Accounting and Reporting Standard is guided by principles rather than rules. The principles of the standard are relevance, completeness, consistency, transparency, and accuracy.

Because of growing international concern about causes of climate change that include greenhouse gases emitted by firms, the measurement, reporting, and planned reduction of these gases by firms helps support sustainability.

Conclusion

Financial managers in today's business environment must employ tools and techniques that support sustainability. In this chapter we presented these tools and techniques in three categories, namely finance, internal reporting, and external reporting. In the finance category we discussed topics with disciplinary roots in finance, debt and equity investing, and stock exchanges. Key contributors include the Social Investment Forum, the United States Environmental Protection Agency, the European Union and Lingane and Olsen (2004). These tools and techniques impact the following stakeholders: shareholders; employees; fund managers; investors; management; venture capitalists; government entities; and future generations. The outcomes from the use of these tools provide an investment outlet for investors who support sustainability, provide an additional source of capital for firms with a sustainable mission, and allow investors and management to evaluate the social return on their investment. Emissions trading programs reduce the total amount of pollutants in the air.

In the internal reporting category we discussed topics with disciplinary roots in strategic management, accounting, finance, manufacturing, environmental science, engineering, sociology, and economics. Key contributors include Kaplan and Norton (1992, 1993, 1996a, 1996b, 1996c), Schaltegger and Sturm (1989), Kaplan and Bruns (1987), Center for Environmental Law and Policy at Yale University, Center for International Earth Science Information Network at Columbia University, and the World Economic Forum. These tools and techniques impact the following stakeholders: management; employees; customers; stockholders; and creditors. The outcomes from the use of these tools include the integration of sustainable management into mainstream business management and reduction of the damage caused to the environment, while not decreasing shareholder value. Managers and employees also become aware of the environmental and social impact of their products and processes. Furthermore, management is provided with environmental indicators and statistics regarding doing business in a particular country.

In the external reporting category we presented topics with disciplinary roots in accounting, law, operations management, and environmental science. Key contributors include the International Accounting Standards Board, the International Financial Reporting Interpretations Committee, the Global Reporting Initiative, the World Resources Institute and the World Council on Sustainable Development. These tools and techniques impact shareholders, environmental groups, environmental protection agencies, government agencies, emissions trading programs, employees, management, insurers, and attorneys. The outcomes from the use of these tools include disclosure of financial responsibility for environmental remediation, reporting of emission credits as an intangible asset or liability, and the reduction of climate-changing greenhouse gases by firms.

By adopting these tools and techniques, the degree to which a firm supports sustainability increases. The first step for determining the appropriate sustainability tools for a firm is to become aware of the tools that are available; this is one of the objectives of this chapter. As firms continuously improve and observe trends in their industry, they will receive guidance on developing their understanding of the tools that are appropriate. Firms can receive assistance in tool selection through their involvement in industry associations. Internal and external auditors will provide expertise regarding the use of these tools and techniques. The selection and implementation of tools will be specific to the firm, industry, and country. For example, energy companies will need to select an emissions trading tool to trade their emission permits, while an insurance company will have less need for a tool of this kind.

The challenges in adopting these tools are partly a consequence of the expertise needed for successful implementation. Nongovernmental organizations (NGOs) can provide this expertise to firms. For example, the California Climate Action Registry provides a web-based tool for firms to calculate and report their greenhouse gas emissions. NGOs also provide documents (many of which are referenced in this chapter) that are helpful in training firms to use these tools. Another significant challenge is the interdisciplinary nature of many of these tools. For example, understanding of eco-efficiency indicators requires scientific, environmental, and financial expertise.

Climate tools will become more prominent in the foreseeable future. In particular, there are many exchanges for trading of CO_2 emissions, the most prominent being the Emissions Trading Scheme in the European Union. As more firms are required by regulation to account for and trade their emissions, the markets to trade these permits will become more prominent. Because of the current global focus on climate change, one key area of future research is climate-related tools and techniques.

Questions for reflection

Here are three questions for your further reflection on the issues broached in this chapter:

*   Which financial management tools to support sustainability apply to your industry or firm?
*   What voluntary or mandatory sustainability reporting exists in your industry?
*   What opportunities or requirements exist for your firm's participation in an emissions trading scheme?

Note

1 http://www.gsb.stanford.edu/PMP/pdfs/ClimateChange_2005PMI.pdf

References

Barth, M.E., McNichols, M.F., and Wilson, G.P. (1997) "Factors influencing firms' disclosures about environmental liabilities," *Review of Accounting Studies*, 2, 1, 35–65.

Ciba Specialty Chemicals Inc. (2006) *Eco-efficiency Indicators*. Online. Available HTTP: <http://www.cibasc.com/index/cmp-index/cmp-ehs/cmp-ehs-efficiency.htm> (accessed 3 July 2007).

DeSimone, L.D. and Popoff, F. (1997) *Eco-Efficiency: The business link to sustainability*, Cambridge and London: MIT Press.

Epstein, M.J. and Wisner, P.S. (2001) "Using a balanced scorecard to implement sustainability," *Environmental Quality Management*, 11, 2, 1–10.

Figge, F., Hahn, T., Schaltegger, S., and Wagner, M. (2002) "The sustainability balanced scorecard: Linking sustainability management to business strategy," *Business Strategy and the Environment*, 11, 5, 269–284.

Global Reporting Initiative (2006) *Sustainability Reporting Guidelines, Version 3*. Online. Available HTTP: <http://www.globalreporting.org/NR/rdonlyres/A1FB5501-B0DE-4B69-A900-27DD8A4C2839/0/G3_GuidelinesENG.pdf> (accessed 3 May 2007).

Idalina, D. and Reijnders, L. (2005) "Evaluating environmental and social performance of large Portuguese companies: A balanced scorecard approach," *Business Strategy and the Environment*, 14, 2, 73–91.

Idalina, D., Reijnders, L., and Antunes, P. (2002) "From environmental performance evaluation to eco-efficiency and sustainability balanced scorecards," *Environmental Quality Management*, 12, 2, 51–64.

Kaplan, R.S. and Bruns, W. (1987) *Accounting and Management: Field study perspectives*, Boston, MA: Harvard Business School Press.

Kaplan, R.S. and De Pinho, R.R. (2007) *Amanco: Developing the sustainability scorecard.* Online. Available HTTP: <http://doi.contentdirections.com/mr/hbsp.jsp?doi=10.1225/107038> Harvard Business School Case, # 9-107-038.

Kaplan, R.S. and Norton, D.P. (1992) "The balanced scorecard: Measures that drive performance," *Harvard Business Review*, 70, 1, 71–79.

Kaplan, R.S. and Norton, D.P. (1993) "Putting the balanced scorecard to work," *Harvard Business Review*, 71, 5, 134–142.

Kaplan, R.S. and Norton, D.P. (1996a) *The Balanced Scorecard*, Boston, MA: Harvard Business School Press.

Kaplan, R.S. and Norton, D.P. (1996b) "Linking the balanced scorecard to strategy," *California Management Review*, 39, 1, 53–77.

Kaplan, R.S. and Norton, D.P. (1996c) "Using the balanced scorecard as a strategic management system," *Harvard Business Review*, 74, 1, 75–85.

Liker, J. (2004) *The Toyota Way*, New York: McGraw Hill.

Lingane, A. and Olsen, S. (2004) "Guidelines for social return on investment," *California Management Review*, 46, 3, 116–135.

Rogers, C.G. (2005) *Financial Reporting of Environmental Liabilities and Risks after Sarbanes-Oxley*, Hoboken, NJ: Wiley.

Schaltegger, S. (1998) "Accounting for eco-efficiency," in B. Nath, L. Hens, P. Compton, and D. Devuyst (eds), *Environmental Management in Practice. Volume 1: Instruments for Environmental Management*, London: Routledge, pp. 272–287. Reprinted in B. Bartelmus and E.K. Seifert (eds) (2003) *Green Accounting*, Aldershot: Ashgate Publishing.

Schaltegger, S. and Sturm, A. (1989) *Ökologieinduzierte Entscheidungsprobleme des Managements: Ansatzpunkte zur Ausgestaltung von Instrumenten* [Ecology-induced management decision support: Starting points for instrument formation], Basel: WWZ.

Schmidheiny, S. (1992) *Changing Course: A global business perspective on development and the environment*, Cambridge, MA and London: The MIT Press.

Social Investment Forum (2006) *2005 Report on Socially Responsible Investing Trends in the United States: 10-year review.* Online. Available HTTP: <http://www.socialinvest.org/areas/research/trends/sri_trends_report_2005.pdf> (accessed 3 May 2007).

UNCTAD (United Nations Conference on Trade and Development) (2004) *A Manual for the Preparers and Users of Eco-Efficiency Indicators*, New York and Geneva: United Nations.

Waddock, S. (2004) *Corporate Disclosure of Social and Environmental Data: Mandatory vs. voluntary.* Online. Available HTTP: <http://www.bcccc.net/index.cfm?fuseaction=Page.viewPage&pageId=1172&nodeID=3&parentID=1170&grandparentID=885> (accessed 3 May 2007).

WBCSD (World Business Council on Sustainable Development) (1996) *Eco-Efficient Leadership for Improved Economic and Environmental Performance*, Geneva: WBCSD.

White, A.L. (2003) "Improving sustainability disclosure: The global reporting initiative guidelines," in S. Waage (ed.), *Ants, Galileo, & Gandhi: Designing the future of business through nature, genius and compassion*, Sheffield: Greenleaf Publishing.

Yale University (2006) *Environmental Measurement Project.* Online. Available HTTP: <http://www.yale.edu/esi/> (accessed 3 May 2007).

Zadek, C. and Raynard, P. (2004) *RR86 – The Future of Sustainability Assurance.* Online. Available HTTP: <http://www.accaglobal.com/publicinterest/activities/research/reports/sustainable_and_transparent/rr-086> (accessed 3 May 2007).

Part IV
Focusing systems

11 A development coalition for sustainability in healthcare

Svante Lifvergren, Tony Huzzard and Peter Docherty

Background

A systems premise regarding sustainability is that no single organization can be sustainable if those interdependent with it are not sustainable. Even modest achievements in sustainability cannot be realized without organizations working in concert with others in their system (see also Chapters 7 and 12 in this volume). This is the key point of departure for this chapter, which presents and analyzes an ongoing collaborative research project that embraces all the key actors in the healthcare system in the Lidköping area in the Västra Götaland region in Sweden. The main actors in the project are the primary care clinics, Lidköping Hospital, and the after-care departments in several local municipalities, together with a cross-disciplinary research team drawn from different universities (Ekman *et al.* 2007). The project reported here as a longitudinal case study was managed by a steering committee, with top management representation from each healthcare provider, union representatives, and working group representation from all levels.

In Sweden, as in many member countries in the European Union, most healthcare needs of all legally registered citizens are provided for by the state, at a moderate cost and at a reasonable resource level, with good accessibility to care and with good medical outcomes (OECD Health Data 2007). Care is mainly financed through individual and corporate salary-based taxes. Primary and hospital healthcare are organized at the regional level, while after-care services are organized at the municipal level. Most healthcare improvement efforts have previously taken place in individual care centres, clinics, and hospitals (Ekman Philips 2002).

In Sweden, as in many countries, life expectancy is increasing, and thus proportionately more people are developing multiple and complex diseases. New ways of organizing healthcare systems are required to provide high quality care in line with patient expectations, while cost containment is a pressing goal (Dent 2003; Harrison 2004). Specific targeted areas for improvement are patient safety, accessibility, increased patient focus, and improved efficiency and efficacy (Institute of Medicine 2001). Moreover, future health systems must not only balance stakeholder interests over the long term, they must also have a capacity for ongoing improvement, innovation, and development from within – what we refer to here as a *sustainable healthcare system*. But how can health systems move toward more sustainable practices?

Many change efforts in the healthcare sector are neither successful nor sustainable. Many projects fail because they do not start out from a patient perspective (Olsson *et al*. 2003). Moreover, the results of many efforts are not known or even measured. Where the efforts do bring about real improvements, it seems difficult to reproduce their results over time, and the care system concerned often relapses to the "old" ways of doing things – a state of affairs that has been termed "system decay" (Buchanan *et al*. 2006; see also Chapter 7 in this volume).

A sustainable work system is a system that regenerates human resources rather than consumes them (Docherty *et al*. 2002; see also Chapters 4, 8, and 15 in this volume). It is also a system that has high levels of employee and client participation and commitment, generated in turn by previous experiences of commitment and participation in the system's own evolution – the change management process that ushered in the move to sustainability. In this chapter, we illustrate how participation, involvement, and system-wide learning in the process of moving toward sustainability can legitimize a new system and thereby enhance its possibilities of endurance and ongoing renewal (see also Chapters 9 and 16).

The change process in this case started with new ideas on care practices generated by individuals on the front line and by the researchers. These ideas were subsequently developed through processes of dialogue in newly emergent relationships across traditional professional and organizational boundaries. After a period of time, such ideas became refined through experimentation and accepted across a broad coalition of stakeholders. Such a process has clear parallels with the 4I model of organizational learning (Crossan *et al*. 1999). Accordingly, we draw on this to show how new ideas on integrated care started out as moments of individual creativity and ended up being institutionalized across a region to form a permanent infrastructure for development that acts as a platform for system sustainability.

Toward sustainability – understanding systems learning

Lasting improvements have to evolve from within the system by continuous cooperation among all the care-providing organizations at the local level: primary care, hospitals, and after-care services – organizations that in Sweden are separate legal entities with separate cultures and practices (Cederquist and Hjortendal Hellman 2005). All stakeholders must be involved in the change process, entailing considerable effort in communication – vertically as well as horizontally – to achieve sustainable improvements. This implies a need for new forms of organizing work, cooperation, and interorganizational interaction and learning across the three kinds of care provision: the hospital, the primary care providers, and the local authorities (see also Chapter 9). In short, the diverse organizations and professions that comprise a healthcare system need to collaborate as a coalition to develop shared understandings of a new vision of care "around the patient." But how are such new health systems realized?

It is fruitful to analyze the evolution of a systems-level change process in terms of learning. For the various actors in Lidköping, the process was a leap into the unknown, a journey and a destination without precedent. Attaining sustainability entailed a process of creative thinking and second-order learning by individuals and the eventual management of the knowledge arising from this in the context of an entire healthcare system (Ekman Philips 2004), or a health development coalition as defined by Gustavsen *et al.* (1997: 14):

> In a "development coalition" there are a number of actors who develop joint platforms and frameworks but otherwise function on the basis of complementarity: management manages, union representatives represent, workers take care of the operational processes and researchers research. When they meet in joint arenas to create common platforms, they consider each other's points and arguments, but they are still there in the capacity of their ordinary role. When (they) agree on something, it is not because they have "taken over" each other's view, or, even, of necessity, developed a common view, it is because they have found it in their own best interest to support each other in a certain course of action.

Crossan *et al.* (1999), in the 4I model, see these four as distinct but interlinked activities that feed forward and backward from each other: 1) intuiting; 2) interpreting; 3) integrating; and 4) institutionalizing. This model has three important characteristics: first, it is multilevel, in that it connects individual, group, and organizational learning; second, it is dynamic, in that it specifies mechanisms that link the levels; and third, it identifies four distinct processes (Lawrence *et al.* 2005).

In the model, summarized below, individual learning does not necessarily imply organizational learning, but an organization learns when it is changed and changes through the experience of collective action. Although competence in organizations resides at the individual and group levels, it nevertheless requires support from the organization as a whole for competence to be integrated elsewhere in the organization. In this chapter, however, we modify the model in one key respect. At the highest level of aggregation, the model focuses on organizational learning; our interest, instead, is on learning at the interorganizational or systems level (see Table 11.1).

If results achieved are to be sustainable, the improvements emerging from various interactions eventually have to be institutionalized to become *the* way of providing care for the patients. This, in essence, is "the embedding of new ideas into the procedures and systems that structure organizational life" (Lawrence *et al.*, 2005: 183). We use the 4I framework for organizational learning to describe various challenges, obstacles, and balancing acts that presented themselves during a long-term effort to reach sustainable improvements in the patient pathways of elderly patients in the Lidköping area. First, we provide a brief background to the case.

Table 11.1 The 4I model of organizational learning (from Crossan *et al.* 1999)

Process	Level	Inputs and outcomes
Intuiting: the preconscious recognition of the pattern and/or possibilities inherent in a personal stream of experience. This is in essence an individual-level activity.	Individual (or small group)	Experiences/ideas, images, metaphors
Interpreting: the process of developing and feeding forward shared understanding among individuals. This occurs as individuals interact with others in small groups.	Individual (or small group) to group	Language, verbal explanation of ideas, conversation/dialogue/ understanding
Integrating: the process of developing and feeding forward shared understanding among individuals to enable coordinated action. Shared understanding develops within groups and is then fed forward to the system level.	Group to system	Shared understandings, clarity of implementation, move to action routines
Institutionalizing: the process of translating the new understandings to become part of the system's routines and/or standard operating procedures. This entails a process of feedback of new understandings and actions to individuals.	System to individual	Procedures for implementation, self-evaluation/ reflection

The case – the Lidköping health project

The case describes the initial phases of an ongoing development effort that took place in the Lidköping area from 2002 to 2006. The initiative started as a project in response to a directive from the head of the Västra Götaland regional healthcare board that care delivery should be closer to the patients, entailing fewer referrals and a higher standard of care provision. Its Lidköping Steering Committee consisted of the director of primary care, the director of Lidköping Hospital, and the chief executives of Lidköping City Council and other surrounding city councils. The Committee invited researchers to collaborate in the project, together creating a development coalition (Ekman Philips 2004; Ekman Philips *et al.* 2004; Ekman *et al.* 2007) consisting of politicians, patient groups, union representatives, the research team, and various front-line employees engaged in learning networks, each having a developmental responsibility. The concept of the "development coalition" is increasingly in use in other sectors in working life for supporting value creation (Ennals and Gustavsen 1999).

Case context

The aim of the project was to ensure that care delivery would be closer to the patients, by focusing the hospital's work on acute care, while the primary care providers and local authorities focused on routine care. The main project vision of the coalition was that this would result in better care from the patient's perspective. It would also entail improvements in the work organization and working environments of the councils and the regional health authority, through close working arrangements across traditional healthcare boundaries. The realization of such a vision clearly required new forms of working and interlevel cooperation – and this, in turn, required organizational change by the care providers and support services. The effort was initially conceived as a change project, but its character changed as it progressed to become an ongoing development coalition with a mission "until further notice," an organization with goals, plans, and budget currently extending through the year 2009.

Lidköping is situated in the eastern corner of Västra Götaland, one of the largest regions in Sweden, with an area of 24,000 square kms. The 1.5 million people who live in the region's 49 municipalities make up 17 percent of the Swedish population. The regional council is the political decision-making body responsible for healthcare and transport issues, and healthcare makes up 90 percent of the county's budget. The Lidköping Hospital serves a population of about 85,000 people. It is an acute care hospital with complete departments and staff on call. It has more than 160 beds and about 700 employees.

Patient pathways

The concept of the "patient pathway" formed the basis for closer cooperation and coordination between the different healthcare organizations. Information exchange and cooperation often work poorly across both organizational and professional boundaries. Typically, patients are referred from one care department to another without any connection between the departments or any consistency of treatment. This often leads to communication shortcomings, medical errors, and prolonged waiting times.

The idea of the patient pathway seeks to end the division of healthcare into separate functions so as to refocus from adding value to the provider toward a view where added value is seen from the perspective of the patient. Moreover, the concept seeks to satisfy the demands of healthcare personnel for a better working environment through participation, collaboration across boundaries, and more autonomy in the work process. Accordingly, this called for a multiple-perspective approach that focused the interaction between patients and staff and saw care activities integrated into a single patient process. The resulting patient pathways, a key output of the development coalition, are more than an emerging network between people, they are the formally decided key professional infrastructure for the flow of information about the patient and care to the patient within the healthcare system made up of the three main providers.

The improvement effort sought to establish the project groups as a number of learning networks comprising front line care staff, each with an assignment to map and develop new ways of organizing healthcare. Personnel development in Lidköping is strongly coupled to experiential learning through project tasks in a network. This case describes the activities of the Örjan project group (named after a model patient), which focused on quality improvements in the care of the elderly through assessing and improving quality in the patient pathway, using Total Quality Management (TQM) techniques. The elderly patient pathway project group named themselves the Örjan Network, and we use this term in presenting the case. "Elderly" patients (those aged 70 and older) were chosen for the first study, as they usually require inputs from all three major healthcare providers.

Network activities 2002–2006

From intuition to interpretation (2002)

The work started in 2002 with a dialogue conference, a method developed earlier by Shotter and Gustavsen (1999). All the stakeholders participated in this conference, which resulted in a basic analysis and listing of issues for action. One of the steering committee's first moves was to establish a patient pathway project with staff members at the different clinics of the Lidköping Hospital, together with nurses from the Lidköping local authority and two nurses and two doctors from the primary care providers. The project coordinator was a doctor at the hospital who was also responsible for quality management there. In its first year, the project saw the start of the collective, cross-professional, and cross-care-provider work groups, with their diverse intuitions and interpretations. Throughout the project, but especially in 2002, the researchers played an active role in both the steering committee and the projects, freely contributing with ideas and comments, i.e., intuiting and interpreting (Huzzard *et al.* 2007). When the groups were new, the intuitions of the healthcare personnel were often challenged in the dialogue conference and the project groups by representatives from other units or providers who had different attitudes, norms, experience, or practices. The researchers functioned as facilitators in these discussions.

The Steering Committee gave the patient pathway project group the assignment to describe and formulate proposals on how to improve those patient pathways linking the hospital, the primary care units, and the local authorities in the Lidköping area. The group first convened in 2002. The meeting revealed serious problems. Participants from the three organizations came from varying cultures with different knowledge of quality improvement and they did not share the same concept of the patient pathway. Even the name that was used to denominate the prime customer – the patient – differed from one organization to another. Consequently, the Örjan network initially had to invest considerable time in developing agreement on core principles and values for the improvement activities; presenting their conceptions and ideas (intuiting) and interpreting each other's ideas of a patient pathway. After a series of meetings, the participants were able to settle on a number of long-term principles, thereby building a common platform for further activities:

- A patient perspective in all activities.
- Broad-based care collaboration.
- Long-term process perspective.
- Improved communication.

From continuous interpretation to integration – developing a shared view and taking action (2003–2004)

The Örjan network expanded, so that by March, 2003, it consisted of 18 staff members. By 2005, the group had expanded to include nurses from all six surrounding local authorities. The network members had meetings every second month in order to plan activities, to discuss, and to reflect. No dedicated project time was allocated for the work, however, and the project was also hampered by a lack of external development funding. Accordingly, some of the doctors in the Örjan network did not attend all the meetings. However, based on the experiences from the first meetings, it became imperative for the members to create a shared picture of how the pathways were performing at the time. These activities had to take place in cooperation with front-line staff along the pathways. The Örjan network therefore decided on a process-oriented way of working. The method comprised four steps:

- Mapping the patient pathway.
- Analyzing and measuring weaknesses in order to identify "true" problems in the pathways.
- Designing and introducing improvements.
- Continuously evaluating implemented solutions.

Numerous multiprofessional groups were connected to the Örjan network. The different groups sought to map out their various pathways and the processes associated with them: tracking a fictive patient's journey from first contact with the healthcare authorities through the various care providers to a final return home in a state of wellness and recovery. A computer-based flow-chart model was used from which tentative pathways were drawn and sent to the front-line personnel for comment and correction. Twelve such models were established and integrated into a single, consolidated map. The composite and individual maps acted as useful tools for the animation of dialogue at individual workplaces on the various issues concerned. The outcome of such dialogues was then brought back into the regular meetings of the Örjan network for further reflection. Different strengths and shortcomings in the processes were thus identified. This process entailed collective learning in the subgroups, which was passed forward in a similar process in successive steps until it finally reached the project group as whole.

The next step involved measuring the perceived strengths and shortcomings in the patient pathways. Several problems could be identified. For instance, the case summaries containing medical information about the care provided during a hospital stay were poorly administered. In particular, it was often unclear whether the case summaries simply contained information or whether specific care instructions were also implicit. The summaries also lacked clarity, which led to difficulties for the primary care units in recognizing which doctor was responsible for the patient concerned. These inadequacies proved especially to be a problem for patients with multiple conditions, resulting in delays when trying to contact the correct doctor, and possibly leading to unnecessary admissions.

Another initiative of the group was to map the route of different documents along the pathway. The investigation revealed that more than 80 steps were involved in the process of planning care outside the hospital for one single patient. The expenses of the process were estimated to be in the range of €220–440 ($285–565). Such findings prompted the group to explore a single procedure across the three levels of care for care planning, thereby reducing the number of steps dramatically.

To get a better understanding of the patients' perspectives, focus groups were conducted with patients and their relatives. This initiative sought to find answers to what critical demands and needs the patients had concerning the care processes. A survey was then constructed from the answers and diffused throughout the different pathways to a large number of patients. Several improvement ideas were collected in this way. The responses revealed that more than 80 percent of the patients thought that care activities had been carried out satisfactorily.

Representatives of the Örjan network regularly reported to the steering committee about ongoing activities in the pathways. These meetings clearly influenced the attitudes of the members in the Committee. In the beginning of the project, the members anticipated rapid solutions to be suggested from the project group. For instance, there were expectations of the Project, with a capital "P," solving all the problems along a certain patient pathway and thus reaching closure and the disbanding of the project. Gradually, gaining more and more experience, the committee came to see their activities no longer as a temporary project, but as an on-going process embodied in the development coalition (cf. Chapters 6 and 7 in this volume). In the words of one member of the Committee: "The improvement activities in the patient pathways have to continue forever."

Ongoing integration of improvement activities (2004–2005)

Much effort was put into implementing and diffusing the different solutions from the process-oriented improvement activities, thereby integrating new ways of working in all three organizations. The steering committee played a decisive role in the diffusion of the new ways of working. The committee helped to anchor the project activities within the senior management teams of each organization to achieve the necessary legitimacy within the permanent organizations.

However, at the beginning of the project, the vertical communication with the line managers of the three organizations was ineffective. Several participants of the Örjan network were not allowed to attend the project meetings, mainly due to heavy workloads at their workplaces. The Örjan network members themselves therefore held meetings with the line managers from the various local areas as a way to provide information about the project activities, to generate involvement among middle managers and ensure that the issue of patient pathways was a permanent item on management's agenda. This led eventually to the members of the Örjan network and other groups connected to the activities being able to allot time to the project without objections being raised by middle management.

Another tactic for diffusing the work was engaging informal leaders or gatekeepers at each workplace. The Örjan network members made personal contact with the key actors in the pathway either personally, face-to-face, or via meetings.

The patient pathway project did meet obstacles and elements of resistance. Territorial thinking pervaded many of the workplaces across the three providers of healthcare and across different professional groups. Part of the problem here was that staff did not have the time or the capability to think from each other's perspectives (Boland and Tenkasi 1995). Assuming a patient's perspective in mapping out the care processes helped force the boundaries between the different organizational and professional territories. By systematically working with all stakeholders in the pathways, interpretation and integration of solutions and ideas slowly but continuously made their way through the three organizations. At the end of 2005, the network could present some key outcomes of its work:

- Elimination of waiting times for reception at the medical clinic (with the exception of heart ailments).
- Reduction in number of visits to the medical clinic by 15–18 percent.
- Initiation of process work in many other clinics and care units.
- Increase in staff awareness and learning regarding the patient pathways.

Institutionalization of improvement activities (2005–2006)

Following a dialogue conference, the members of the Steering Committee and the participants in the network identified several key factors critical to making permanent the infrastructure for sustainable improvements along the patient pathways. This entailed the creation of a permanent infrastructure for development, including both operational and strategic components. The Örjan Network was established as a permanent network to be a source of sustainable creativity and innovation across organizational and professional boundaries, as well as supplying inputs to senior management on broader strategy issues.

The Örjan network had argued from the beginning that one of their members should have a full-time development role. The steering committee had agreed to a halftime appointment from the beginning of 2004. This concession enabled the group to develop a new tempo in its activities. Later on, this was increased to a fulltime appointment and in 2005 it led to the creation of a formal development unit with a development manager, two newly recruited internal consultants, and a development budget, to support the project groups and facilitate the improvement activities.

On the strategic level, the establishment of shared goals among the three care providers was identified as the most important factor for institutionalizing sustainable improvement. The top managers in the Steering Committee decided to develop and implement a shared *balanced scorecard* (BSC) involving all three organizations (see also Chapter 10 in this volume). This formed a "cognitive learning mechanism" for the joint formulation and monitoring of the goals of the development coalition (see Chapter 9 in this volume; Docherty and Shani 2008.) The first version of the scorecard was designed by the Steering Committee in the spring of 2006. Four perspectives were used: the patient perspective; the process perspective; the co-worker perspective; and the financial perspective. The use of perspectives ensured that every aspect of the healthcare processes was taken into account when taking and implementing long-term decisions.

Thus the Committee could propose a shared vision for the healthcare chain. As one member of the Committee stated at a strategy meeting: "Together we create a first-class, seamless healthcare service providing care close to the patient" – a vision rather similar to the formulations in the initial central regional council directive. For every area in the BSC, long-term and short-term goals were proposed. For instance, the long-term goal for the patient's perspective was formulated as follows: "Our patients should experience excellent service without any organizational boundaries." Common to long- and short-term goals from all perspectives was the focus on enhanced collaboration and learning on all levels among the different care providers.

The first version of the scorecard was finalized in the summer of 2006. According to the members of the Committee, the previous collaboration in the group had developed shared values and a common understanding of the issues at large – integration had taken place. The scorecard process was only a way of putting these values on paper. Without the understanding previously generated in the project, the process would have been much more difficult. The members felt that they could really stand up for the content of the scorecard and that it focused on shared themes in the care process from a patient's perspective.

The process of mobilizing all the personnel behind the goals began in the autumn of 2006. The scorecard was presented to workers of all the organizations at three large meetings, which several hundred employees attended. The goals proposed were well received, although some workers, especially doctors, found some of the formulations a bit abstract and too far from the reality of their work.

Then 120 line managers from the three organizations attended a joint conference where the BSC was presented once again. During the conference, the managers were divided into cross-organizational groups in order to discuss the content of the scorecard. The managers attending the conference were content with the statements and only minor revisions had to be made to the document. A timetable for the implementation of the different critical success factors was set. The care developers subsequently engaged in continuously monitoring the implementation process and have reported to the Steering Committee once every quarter.

Although creative ideas for implementing sustainable solutions around the idea of integrated care originated with the intuition of individuals, such ideas only came to fruition through experiments in practice and discussions of the experience gained. In this instance, what was significant was not the teams within existing line management structures, but the newly formed boundary-crossing projects, such as Örjan network. But the networks established in the projects were not sufficient on their own as a means of arriving at the vision. The ideas for development and the lessons learned from their implementation required support, legitimacy, and resources from the wider healthcare system or development coalition before being made permanent as new forms of organizing that impacted on individuals at the workplace. It is here we can see a gradual transition through the 4I learning model as a prerequisite for achieving the institutionalization of a vision – an important step in attaining a sustainable health system. The process of managing the coalition toward a sustainable healthcare system is summarized in Table 11.2 below.

The developments during the first five years have been characterized by learning, which has been promoted and supported by learning mechanisms (see Chapter 9 in this volume). At the individual level, the focus has been on experiential learning through the conduct of studies and experiments in the framework of the development networks. Since 2005, this has been supported by a special budget for project work and the availability of supervisors in the development unit. The project groups and networks have functioned as a parallel learning organization (Bushe and Shani 1991). The development unit at the hospital has functioned as the central node in this organization, providing training in quality improvement methods for staff involved in development projects. The collection and analysis of data in the projects is a central part of the experiential learning planned when inviting staff to participate in a project. To date, more that 30 staff members have received training for "black belt" qualifications in Six Sigma methods, and more than 20 of these function as advisors and consultants to colleagues in the system. Learning between healthcare providers and between levels has also taken place in three dialogue conferences (Gustavsen 1992). Key linking roles have been played by the development unit and the action researchers.

Following the positive experience of the Örjan network, several other projects were launched to develop patient pathways for other patient groups, for psychiatry, rehabilitation, and information for healthcare planning for patients other than the elderly. Following the decision on common goals and the BSC, further patient pathway projects were started dealing with dementia, diabetes, and congestive heart failure. Having created a basic structure for the development coalition with a committed top management group, a highly professional and effective development unit, a management system, the joint balanced scorecard, and a general acceptance of the patient pathway perspective, the development coalition is moving on to the development of the micro-systems responsible for the treatment of specific ailments. The first such project was with the teams at the hospital and the different primary care centres dealing with Vitamin K-antagonist.

Table 11.2 The West Skaraborg Development Process, 2001–2006: A summary

Time	Activities: Lidköping Hospital	Activities: primary care	Activities: local authorities	Activities: steering committee	Learning Mechanisms	Barriers to Learning
January 2001 (Initiative from the Västra Götaland Region)	Medical clinic's own improvement initiative in 2001 (not described in the chapter).	Some improvement activities going on.	Very few improvement activities going on.	Interpreting the regional initiative.	Individual and experiential learning, evaluating and comparing initiative to own concepts and earlier experiences, dialogue conference, networks, project groups.	The level of improvement "maturity" differed significantly between the organizations.
Autumn 2001 Intuiting-interpreting	Networks created – ideas generated.			Difficulties translating the primary directive into a meaningful mission.	Interindividual experiential learning, trying to create shared views of the initiative in group, networks, project groups.	Difficulties in achieving sufficient participation from the doctors.
Spring 2002 Interpreting	Network meetings began.			Project-oriented, not process-oriented, approach.	Interindividual, but more situated learning – learning by participating in improvement activities and meetings, as above.	Values not shared. Lack of time to interpret ideas and values.
2003–2004 Interpreting-integrating	Continuous process-oriented work. In particular, network members from the local authorities were not always allowed to participate in meetings.			Received regular reports – vertical integration. Committee had its own learning process. Becoming more process-oriented. Trying to influence middle managers.	Interindividual experiential and situated learning, new mental models appear, at least in the project group. Dialogue conference, projects and networks.	Problems with different timetables at different organizational levels, difficulties engaging middle managers, difficulty finding assessment measures.

2004–2005 Integrating	Ongoing integration, most obviously in the hospital and in the primary care units. More problems in the local authorities. Steering Committee supporting integration. Much effort put into inspiring co-workers outside the networks to become involved. Regular meetings, awareness of the need for patience and support to involve middle managers and informal leaders. Territorial thinking/results-driven improvement efforts engaging front-line staff and focusing on the needs of the patient.		Organizational learning beginning to take place. Signs of changed self-concepts among members in project group/steering committee. Meeting arenas, projects and networks.	Not enough time to participate in improvement activities. Hard to maintain an even pace of change.
2005–2006 Institutionalization of improvement activities	All three organizations were already using balanced scorecards and had become accustomed to the nomenclature. Two internal consultants hired to support the network and facilitate all the improvement activities. Need for patience stressed, co-workers at all levels given time for dialogue, reflection and the possibility to influence long term direction and goals.	Members now had experience of learning together – easier to propose common goals.	Learning through exploitation from previous experiments on new practices. Dialogue conference. Joint goal setting and balanced scorecard. Networks and projects.	Lack of long-term direction in the efforts/ using the balanced scorecard as tool for long-term policy deployment. Not enough time to participate in improvement activities – the speed of change too low. Difficulties with policy deployment underestimated.

Discussion

Many lessons can be learned looking back on the first five years of improvement activities in a complex healthcare development process involving numerous stakeholders and three care providers. A sustainable system is one that continuously strives to handle changes and opportunities, delivering improvements that eventually becomes *the way* of doing things while also having the ability to update standardized working procedures and let in new ideas. The process of transition to sustainability, however, clearly involves many balancing acts.

Balancing the speed of change

Using the 4I model for understanding the process, it is obvious that change takes time. A typical comment here from a member of the Örjan Network at a focus group was that "if we'd gone more quickly, we would not have had any basis for making decisions. . . . I think unhurriedness is a critical success factor."

In this sense, the change process is best understood as a series of small steps, giving time for individual intuition followed by interpreting ideas together in different working groups, thereby gaining momentum to take joint action on improvement activities – integrating – while continuously learning (see also Chapters 2, 3, 7, 9, 12, and 16 in this volume). This would appear to suggest that there is a clear trade-off between the pace of change on the one hand and the quality of organizational learning on the other – if by quality we mean the degree of shared ownership and understanding of decisions and policies.

Balancing the different interests among key stakeholders and system components

Inviting all stakeholders to take part in the change process and giving them the opportunity to intuit, interpret, and integrate ideas and new concepts seems to make balancing different interests easier (cf. Chapters 9 and 12). Communication about activities with patients, politicians, managers, informal leaders, co-workers, front-line staff and directors therefore appears to be crucial. This presents the opportunity for questions to be asked – in both directions. A process-oriented way of working creates dialogue and broad participation (Ekman Philips *et al.* 2004).

Balancing the short term and the long term

Short-term, result-driven improvement activities foster motivation and involvement, but such efforts eventually have to be aligned with long-term, strategic goals in order to institutionalize the changes. This is a balance between short-term pressures to conform to rules and routines (a control logic) and a longer-term ambition to maintain a capacity to innovate and learn (an innovation logic). The requirement is for a patient focus through flexibility and relationship-building in the context of a process-based approach.

This was illustrated by the shift in the perception of the development work from being a discrete project to being an ongoing process. The concept of process suggests long-term, never-ending thinking about the challenges of change, and the acceptance of a new, ongoing way of working rather than a time-limited project frame. However, balancing in this setting also means retaining the ability to recognize and master the advantages of the project form when dealing with defined and focused improvement activities.

Balancing static and dynamic efficiency

Intuition and interpretation among co-workers and groups of co-workers encourages new ideas that sometimes lead to improvements. Obviously, health systems will require high levels of productivity, that is, producing a high volume of care with reduced resources; but this will need to be balanced by the need for sufficient levels of organizational slack to allow for individual and organizational development.

Learning, however, should not be only understood as a social-psychological process – it also has a political dimension (Huzzard 2004; Lawrence *et al.* 2005). In other words, it needs some element of energizing to make it happen, or to put it another way, there needs to be *power*. By power here we mean not so much domination or discipline but rather the productive aspect of power that allows us to achieve outcomes that we would not reach alone (Foucault 1977; Hardy 1996). This is partly a matter of discourse, particularly the talk of ongoing development arising from dialogic approaches to change. These had been established within the development coalition not least through the intervention of an action research team. But the learning activities across the coalition also had the key ingredient of employee participation to inform and inspire the development process (Ekman and Huzzard 2007). Accordingly, the outcome of the process – that is, a sustainable health system – was indebted to certain key features of the transition toward it, notably the ideas, involvement and enthusiasm of a wide range of front-line employees, both in the networks and at workplaces.

Balancing specialization and integration

There has long been a tradition of specialization in healthcare (Dent 2003). In order to fulfil the patient's expectations and needs, today's complex patient pathways require the integration of different competences while still developing quality within each speciality. In a sense, this can also be understood as balancing the individual needs of patients with a standardization of treatments on patient pathways.

Conclusion

The challenges facing the Swedish healthcare system are increasingly placing a premium on the capacity of health systems to generate new knowledge about how to manage and organize care practices and processes. Care organizations are thus increasingly required to develop a capacity to innovate (Ekman *et al.* 2007).

The content of change and development and the diverse range of boundary-crossing initiatives evident to date in this case imply that knowledge of potential solutions to the problems of integrated care is well diffused in the Swedish healthcare system. However, the problem, here and elsewhere, is that of translating such knowledge into practice or "doing" (Adler *et al.* 2003). This is a clear expression of what is referred to as the "knowing-doing gap" (Pfeffer and Sutton 2000), or, in the specific context of healthcare, "closing the quality chasm" (Institute of Medicine 2001). Yet each context is unique – a given blueprint or solution cannot be directly diffused from one context to another. Yet cases such as that of Lidköping can act as an inspiration to practitioners grappling with similar dilemmas elsewhere. In this sense, we can perhaps talk about the translation of ideas into action as a matter of developing process knowledge. This is a core principle of a sustainable health system.

Although there is a strong discourse around change evident in the Swedish health service, the notion of sustainability also concerns the balance between stability and change. It is necessary to acknowledge that the existing arrangements of managing healthcare are not all bad. There is a need to continue with what works well. However, sustainability also entails active monitoring to uncover the need to change. The future is not hemmed in or dependent on current organizational structures or personnel, and the needs of patients must always be the central concern. This means that the institutionalization seen as the outcome of the coalition or system learning process should not be a new "steady state." What should be institutionalized is a way of working that facilitates ongoing reflection and innovation in line with the evolution of patient needs, demands, and expectations. New intuitions from the healthcare front line and new external pressures will arise to challenge current, even new, practice. This is the true nature of *sustainable* improvement.

A further prerequisite is that of looking outward beyond the boundaries of one's home organization or profession. A sustainable, process-based system of integrated care must involve collaboration along care pathways, possibilities for collective reflection among personnel from diverse professions, and shared understandings around care processes. Fundamentally, the response to change in the health sector should not be seen as the setting up of discrete one-off projects for dealing with particular challenges. Rather, there is a need for a permanent infrastructure for development in which change is seen as natural, and solutions to the problems of change are seen as an opportunity for employees to channel their creative energies into innovative practices. This requires the establishment of learning mechanisms that allow for new relationships, knowledge exchange, and reflective practices across various healthcare communities (Ekman *et al.* 2007).

Healthcare innovation is often driven externally – by new patterns of treatment, emerging technologies, changing patient demands, and an often-volatile political policy context (Greenhalgh *et al.* 2005). Hospitals and other care providers need to be highly adaptive – receptive to change and able to build creative and appropriate responses. Internally-driven innovation also plays a key role in healthcare improvement – through the identification of risk, learning from mistakes, listening to patients, and opportunities to identify the scope for change. Continuous and sustainable innovation depends, above all, on cultures and work practices that value reflection and dialogue involving staff at all levels.

Finally, it appears that for a systems-wide learning process such as that in Lidköping to be triggered, an essential starting point is the conflict between the different institutionalized views that people hold (see also Chapter 12 in this volume). Only when people truly challenge their own way of perceiving reality can new intuitions emerge. Looking back on the five-year learning process of the coalition, foundations have been created for the management and administration of a sustainable healthcare system. The healthcare organizations plan to continue to develop the coalition by more closely focusing on different microsystems responsible for specific treatments (Batalden *et al.* 2002) and strengthening the cooperation among the four hospitals in the Skaraborg region of Västra Götaland.

Questions for reflection

Here are three questions for your further reflection on the issues broached in this chapter:

- How might we balance the need for routines in healthcare with practices for innovation and renewal?
- What new relationships are required for a system-wide change process in healthcare?
- What change efforts are typically framed in projects? How can we make permanent the practices and the energy that are found in project efforts?

References

Adler, P., Riley, P., Kwon, S.-W., Signer, J., Lee, B., and Satrasala, R. (2003) "Performance Improvement Capability: Keys to Accelerating Performance Improvement in Hospitals," *California Management Review*, 45, 2, 12–33.

Batalden P.B., Nelson E.C., Huber T.P., Mohr J.J., Godfrey, M.M., Headrick, M.A., and Wasson. J.H. (2002) "Microsystems in Healthcare: Part 1. Learning from High-Performing Front-Line Clinical Units," *Journal on Quality Improvement*, 28, 9, 472–493.

Boland, R.J. and Tenkasi, R.V. (1995) "Perspective Making and Perspective Taking in Communities of Knowing," *Organization Science*, 6, 4, 350–372.

Buchanan, D., Fitzgerald, L., and Ketley, D. (eds) (2006) *The Sustainability and Spread of Organizational Change: Modernizing Healthcare.* London: Routledge.

Bushe, G.R. and Shani, A.B. (Rami) (1991) *Parallel Learning Structures: Increasing Innovations in Bureaucracies*, Reading, MA: Addison-Wesley.

Cederquist, J. and Hjortendal Hellman, E. (2005) *Iakttagelser om Landsting* [Observations on county councils]. Stockholm: Rapport från KOMSAM, Swedish Ministry of Finance.

Crossan M.M., Lane, H.W., and White, R.E. (1999) "An Organizational Learning Framework: From Intuition to Institution," *Academy of Management Review*, 24, 3, 522–537.

Dent, M. (2003) *Remodelling Hospitals and Health Professions in Europe: Medicine, Nursing and the State*. Basingstoke: Palgrave.

Docherty, P., Forslin, J., and Shani, A.B. (Rami) (eds) (2002) *Creating Sustainable Work Systems: Emerging Perspectives and Practice*. London: Routledge.

Docherty, P. and Shani, A.B. (Rami) (2008) "Learning Mechanisms as Means and Ends in Collaborative Management Research," in A.B. (Rami) Shani, S.A. Mohrman, W.A. Pasmore, B.A. Stymne, and N. Adler (eds), *Handbook of Collaborative Management Research*, Thousand Oaks, CA: Sage Publishing, pp. 163–182.

Ekman, M. and Huzzard, T. (2007) "Developmental Magic? Two Takes on a Dialogue Conference," *The Journal of Organizational Change Management*, 20, 1: 8–25.

Ekman, M., Ahlberg, B. M., Huzzard, T., and Ek, E. (2007) *Innovationer i vårdens vardag: De små stegens väg* [Everyday innovations in healthcare]. Lund: Studentlitteratur.

Ekman Philips, M. (2004) "Action Research and Development Coalitions in Health Care," *Action Research*, 2, 4, 349–370.

Ekman Philips, M. (ed.) (2002) *Dialog over etablerade gränser: Om organisationsutveckling i sjukvården.* [Dialogue across established boundaries: On organizational development in healthcare]. Stockholm: National Institute for Working Life, Work Life in Transition series, no. 2002: 9.

Ekman Philips, M., Ahlberg, B.M., and Huzzard, T. (2004) "Planning from Without or Developing from Within? Collaboration across the Frontiers of Health Care," in W. Fricke and P. Totterdill (eds), *Regional Development Processes as the Context for Action Research*, Amsterdam: John Benjamin, pp. 103–126.

Ennals, R. and Gustavsen, B. (1999) *Work Organisation and Europe as a Development Coalition*. Amsterdam: John Benjamins.

Foucault, M. (1977) *Discipline and Punish: The Birth of the Prison*. New York: Random House.

Greenhalgh, T., Robert, G., Bate, P., Macfarlane, F., and Kyriakidou, O. (2005) *Diffusion of Innovations in Health Service Organisations*. Oxford: Blackwell.

Gustavsen, B. (1992) *Dialogue and Development*. Assen: van Gorcum.

Gustavsen, B., Colbjørnsen, T., and Pålshaugen, Ø. (1997) *Development Coalitions in Working Life*. Amsterdam: John Benjamins.

Hardy, C. (1996) 'Understanding Power: Bringing about Strategic Change', *British Journal of Management*, 7 (special issue): S3–S16.

Harrison, M.L. (2004) *Implementing Change in Health Systems: Market Reforms in the United Kingdom, Sweden and Netherlands*. London: Sage Publications.

Huzzard, T. (2004) "Communities of Domination? Reconceptualising Organizational Learning and Power," *Journal of Workplace Learning*, 16, 6, 350–361.

Huzzard, T., Ahlberg, B.M., and Ekman, M. (2007) "Constructing Inter-organizational Collaboration: The Action Researcher as a Boundary Subject," paper presented to the 5th Critical Management Studies Conference, Manchester Business School, July 11–13.

Institute of Medicine (2001) *Crossing the Quality Chasm – A New Health System for the 21st Century*. Washington, DC: National Academy Press.

Lawrence, T.B., Mauws, M.K., Dyck, B., and Kleysen, R.F. (2005) "The Politics of Organizational Learning: Integrating Power into the 4I Framework," *Academy of Management Review*, 30, 1, 180–191.

OECD Health Data (2007) *Statistics and Indicators for 30 Countries.* Paris: OECD.

Olsson, J., Kammerlind, P., Thor, J., and Elgh, M. (2003) "Surveying Improvement Activities in Health Care on a National Level – The Swedish Internal Collaborative Strategy and Its Challenges," *Quality Management in Healthcare*, 12, 4, 202–216.

Pfeffer, J. and Sutton, R.I. (2000) *The Knowing–Doing Gap.* Boston, MA: Harvard Business School Press.

Shotter, J. and Gustavsen, B. (1999) *The Role of "Dialogue Conferences" in the Development of "Learning Regions": Doing "from within" Our Lives Together What We Cannot Do Apart.* Stockholm: Centre for Advanced Studies in Leadership.

12 Three powers of feedback for sustainable multi-organizational learning

Hilary Bradbury

> *Because of feedback in living networks, systems are capable of self regulation and self organization. A community can learn from its mistakes, because the mistakes travel and come back along these feedback loops.*
>
> (Capra 2007: 13)

A sustainable work system may be defined as one that cooperates with nature's well-developed processes, allowing for feedback and self-regulation, such that activity may be sustained to meet present needs without reducing the capacity of future generations to meet their needs. This chapter proposes ways in which organizational leaders can collaborate across organizational boundaries to manage their work systems (including supply systems) more intelligently, toward such a sustainable future. The proposal is anchored in three action research cases. Enablers and obstacles are also identified. These ideas contribute to an emerging global conversation on learning processes for sustainability (Wals 2007). First I sketch the context of unsustainability to suggest design parameters for sustainable work systems.

We are so far from sustainability!

Our starting point is the realization that human activity no longer fits with nature. In contrast to other animals whose activity is finely attuned to natural systems, *homo economicus* takes nonrenewable resources and leaves growing piles of waste that nature cannot recycle. Having acted for so long as masters of nature, rather than part of nature, we now find ourselves having to redesign our socio-economic system. Because organizations have played such a critical role in producing our unsustainability, they play an equally critical role in efforts toward sustainable development (see also Chapter 3 in this volume). Nothing less than the systematic redesign of our entire socio-economic system is required. While this is the work of many generations, it is currently hindered by the epistemic and organizational-structural constraints that our assumptions impose on seeing and doing things differently (Bawden *et al.* 2007).

Work systems are embedded in a socio-economic community. Since the appearance of life on planet Earth, sustainable communities have emerged so that their ways of life are embedded with the rest of nature's well-developed processes. Cycles of interdependence – healthy relationships – are at the core of Earth's ability to sustain life. These relationships of interdependence allow for feedback and self regulation. For example, in a sustainable system, the output of one process (CO_2) becomes the input for another (chlorophyll production), leaving no accumulating waste. But as a result of an increase in population and heavier dependence on energy-intensive technologies, human impact on the planet can no longer be sustained over time. The waste products from human activity have grown too burdensome for natural ecological services to process, and thus we are witness to systematic increases in toxicity that make the ecosphere less hospitable to creatures like us with highly evolved nervous systems. Human lifespan has begun to recede in the industrialized nations – meaning that our children are no longer expected to live as long as their parents, due to toxic loads and health challenges such as diabetes. Nonhuman species loss is estimated to be at 1,000 times natural levels (Wilson 2002).

Sustainable business

Our sustainability crisis has come to be popularly referred to as "an inconvenient truth."[1] By at least one rigorous definition, articulated by The Natural Step and drawing on theories of thermodynamics and cellular evolution,[2] a sustainable business may be defined as one whose operations do not lead to systematically increasing:

1. Concentrations of substances extracted from the Earth's crust (e.g., fossil fuels).
2. Concentrations of substances produced by society (e.g., nonbiodegradables).
3. Degradation of nature by physical means (e.g., loss of productive green spaces).
4. Reduction in people's capacity to meet their needs (e.g., weakening leadership and community development).

Despite the radical stringency of these conditions ("we need move away from use of fossil fuels"!) numerous companies have begun to move in the direction suggested by these system conditions. For example:

IKEA, one of the first adopters of The Natural Step has developed child labour and forestry product certification practices that make them industry leaders of sustainability practices. Estimates of current profitability suggest that the company continues to be highly profitable in the home furnishings industry. **Interface**, the first adopter of The Natural Step in the United States, has developed an environmental quality management process that moves toward "zero waste" (or 100 percent profit as CEO Anderson says) with its carpet manufacturing (see Chapter 3 in this volume). **Wal-Mart** has also adopted rigorous sustainability goals and is also reporting financial benefits. In these instances and in many other similarly focused companies, what had seemed "inconvenient" was reframed as a business opportunity, or at least a necessity for doing good business over the long haul. Indeed, Hart and Milstein (1999) suggest that our response to sustainability will differentiate those businesses that innovate for sustainability from those that will die off as a result of unsustainable logics and activities.

Generally, business leaders respond to both "carrot" and "stick" rationales for embracing more sustainable practices. On the "stick" side we see an increase in regulations and stakeholder activism that encourage sustainable practices, reinforced by a growing scarcity of natural resources and growth in consumer pressures. "Carrots" include the recognition of a large LOHAS ("lifestyles of health and sustainability") demographic, willing to pay extra for "green" products and services. More generally, the positive relationship between stock price and sustainability practices is being recognized (Kiernan 2005).

Systems problems require systems solutions

The recent interest in all things sustainable may hide the fact that one company, no matter how big or how profitable, cannot be called sustainable unless all the companies it is networked with throughout the sourcing, manufacturing, and end use of its product are *also* sustainable (see also Chapters 7, 9, 11, and 13 in this volume). In other words, when we talk of sustainable business, the level of analysis is more properly that of the *entire system of business* than it is of a specific business or sustainable project within a business.

Let us make the abstract notion of "system" concrete by considering that the food on our plates, like so many goods in daily use, has travelled a great distance and passed through numerous hands, ports of entry, and agencies. "The typical item of food on an American's plate travels some fifteen hundred miles to get there," Michael Pollan writes in *The Omnivore's Dilemma*, "and is frequently better traveled and more worldly than its eater" (Pollan 2006). Even if the food is the product of sustainable practices, sometimes certified by NGOs, its transportation almost certainly was not. The food supply, like all supply chains, merely exemplifies how the components of our supply chains operate by different design logics, have different administrative jurisdictions, often do not communicate well, and at times are in direct competition with each other. The premise of this chapter is that no one organization can be sustainable if those interdependent with it are not also sustainable. Inherent in this premise is the assumption that a sustainable system resides at the intersection of environmental, social *and* financial vectors. A sustainable system is one that is managed with attention to the "triple bottom line" (Elkington 1997). Moreover as rates of interdependence are soaring in this globalizing age, the systems approach to sustainability can indeed seem daunting. Even modest achievements in sustainability cannot be realized beyond the silos of well meaning organizations without corporations' *willingness to work in concert with the rest of their supply and demand networks.*

The demands of coordinating a sustainable system in which all component organizations are "loosely coupled" (Weick 1976) are structurally challenging. Weick observes that loosely coupled systems often lack coordination and shared regulations, and although composed of highly connected networks, manifest very slow feedback times. The industrial era notion of "cracking the whip" generally will not work – forget for a moment if it's even ethical or not – to get to the organizational collaboration required.

Feedback powers

It is a truism by now that the whole (system) is more than the sum of its parts. However the "more" is not to be located outside the system, but in the interaction and relational space within the system itself. When we say that the whole is more than the parts it is not to suggest a magical epiphenomenon. It is instead to bring attention to exchanges and transformations that take place in the "spaces between" the parts. Moreover, when we consider those interactions we must concern ourselves with a feedback component.

Feedback may be thought of as a signal or information that loops back to control the system (http://en.wikipedia.org/wiki/System) within which it exists. This loop is called a feedback loop. In *cybernetics* and control theory, which are the basis for our understanding of feedback, we learn that some portion of an output signal of a system is passed (fed back) to the input. This in turn controls the dynamic behaviour of the system.

Biological systems contain many types of regulatory circuits, both reinforcing (more chickens results in more eggs) and balancing (more wild prey results in more predators). A system can include both types of feedback, which means it is oscillating. Such a system is the *stock market*, because both reinforcing (bull) and balancing (bear) feedback mechanisms are present.

Gregory Bateson's work on system components aimed at clearly drawing the distinction between energy and matter, on the one hand, and *information*, on the other. Unlike energy or matter, information is a nonsubstantial phenomenon that cannot be located in space or time. Hence, Bateson maintained that cybernetic systems best exemplify mental processes. That is, given the unique status of information and communication as nonsubstantial phenomena that nevertheless govern and control cybernetic systems, he insisted that cybernetic models and metaphors are most appropriately applied to the mental realm of cognitive systems, i.e., mind systems – both artificial and natural (Bateson 1979).

Grappling specifically with feedback of information in human systems, Kurt Lewin was the first to adapt the language of cybernetics to the work of organizational development and as such was the instigator of the action research orientation to knowledge development (Reason and Bradbury 2001). Argyris and Schön's notion of learning, also within the paradigm of action research and later adopted by Senge and allied with other learning tools such as dialogue and visioning (Senge 1990), suggested that our ability to learn is equivalent to our ability to invite feedback so that we improve our ability to generate desired results over time. The distinction between single- and double-loop learning and feedback is important. The former is found in *financial audits* (http://en.wikipedia.org/wiki/Financial_audit), *performance appraisal* (http://en.wikipedia.org/wiki/Performance_appraisal), *shareholder* (http://en.wikipedia.org/wiki/Shareholder)

meetings, stakeholder engagement, and customer *surveys* (http://en.wikipedia.org/wiki/Survey). This type of feedback helps recipients meet predetermined goals such as market expectations or explicit customer needs. Double-loop learning, in contrast, is made possible when feedback is used to reflect upon the very values that inform goal setting in the first place. As a consequence, such learning enables increased adaptivity to the environment.

Current scholarly norms seek to avoid subjectivity. When making the epistemological shift to systems thinking – itself a radical break with reductionist science – if one also embraces considerations of consciousness or purpose, it may seem too far beyond convention. Nonetheless, to reduce our conversation about systems to material, quantifiable forms of feedback is also to miss too much (see also Chapter 15 in this volume). Contemporary organizational scholarship, such as that by William Torbert (see especially Torbert and Associates 2005), offers a particularly important bridge from reductionist to systems thinking – because it also embraces the power of the early reductionist paradigm. A similar move to embrace a more encompassing perspective on systems, and with it an effort to work with sometimes irreconcilable paradigms, is offered by Hamalainen and Saarinen. They suggest that the search for objectivity in system dynamics needs also to be balanced with attention to the subjective, the relational, and the intuitive. They write, "People thrive on meaning. As a result, the most forceful forms of system intelligence intervention are likely to be those that touch basic human aspirations" (2007: 196).

When we think of feedback as it relates to sustainability, we can therefore think of the ways in which elements in a work system – materials and energy – can inform each other. Concretely, this means creating a space in which intelligent flows of information can be used to inform the whole system. Practically, this means bringing together decision makers who operate in a shared, if fragmented, system so that they are enabled to operate more intelligently together.

Fragmentation is inimical to sustainability; the more fragmented a system, the less intelligently it can operate. However, merely assembling representation of a work system to coordinate – itself a very difficult task – is not enough to make the system more sustainable. At the core of any system are the system's people and the intelligence they bring. People, uniquely among the parts of a system, participate both in system operations and system development, using qualities of double-loop learning. What is going on internally for any individuals involved includes issues of meaning making and self-identity, which can help or hinder how individuals relate to a sustainability agenda. The quality of people's engagement may therefore help explain the success or failure of each of the types of feedback described below.

Three powers of feedback

In the following section, I present three important types of feedback for consideration, and suggest that all three are required if we are to learn our way out of the high levels of unsustainability we face. As suggested by the foregoing, feedback loops that redirect information and intelligence through an ecology of learners become the core mechanism for moving their shared system toward sustainability.

Feedback among social learning actors in collaborative learning

Transforming systems of work, community institutions, and practices requires collaboration across traditional boundaries – of community actors, disciplines, and sectors – as well as ongoing learning from multiple ways of knowing and knowledge generation (see also Chapters 9 and 11 in this volume). In these efforts the emergence of intelligent action is seen to require interweaving of three types of spaces (Senge *et al.* 2007):

1. *Relational space* fosters relationships and collaboration among diverse organizations, and among the consultants and researchers working with them.
2. *Conceptual space* emerges from collective reflection that enables people from different organizations to "see themselves in one another."
3. *Action space* leverages engagement by individual organizations through cross-institutional links that instigate and sustain transformative changes that otherwise would die out.

The "Social Learning Loop" as defined in Figure 12.1 (from Senge and Scharmer 2001) brings attention to reweaving different kinds of knowledge. In this figure, social learning is represented as a stock-flow diagram of a knowledge-creating system. The actors in this social learning loop are practitioners (i.e., they are situated in business and are rewarded for creating and applying practical know-how), researchers (i.e., they are situated in academia and are rewarded for creating

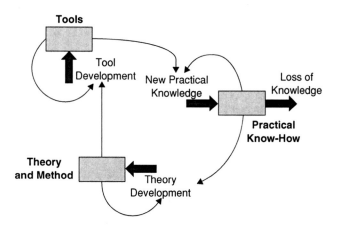

Figure 12.1 A stock-flow diagram of the knowledge creating system (from Senge and Scharmer 2001)

and advancing theory and method) and boundary spanners (i.e., civil society activists, or more generally consultants, who are rewarded for creating and developing tools and solutions). Actors can simultaneously reside in more than one community of practice. In the context of action research – where knowledge is created in a context of action – the ideal social learning system requires an unbroken loop of people operating both inside a particular community and comfortable moving across communities. In reality, different communities of practice that are part of this loop often have gaps in communication as well as gaps in understanding and mutual regard. These gaps sometimes slow down and occasionally threaten to break the loop entirely.

We may conclude then that what is powerful for sustainable change among multi-organizational systems is the emergence of feedback loops among social actors from business, academia, and civil society aimed at developing actionable knowledge. This process may also be referred to as action research (Reason and Bradbury 2001). These efforts – illustrated in the following examples – help create and recreate loops of social learning. The prerequisite for this is to open communicative space that attracts and retains representation from academia, business, and civil society. In effect, those involved are called upon to integrate theory and practice, action and reflection, empirical analysis and normative vision, critique and affirmation, explanation and action, vision and current reality.

Feedback from experience to continuous learning

The cycle of experiential learning comprises four phases. In integrating the work of Dewey, Jung, and Piaget, David Kolb (1984) suggests that there are two ways a person can take in experience – by abstract conceptualization (thinking) or by concrete experience (feeling). In addition, there are two ways a person can "process" their experience – by reflective observation or by active experimentation. When we use both concrete and abstract modes, and both reflect and act on that experience, we expand our potential to completely engage in a learning process. A productive learning experience allows us to cycle through four phases – experience, reflection, conceptualization, and experimentation – however, it is common that learners skip certain phases and focus primarily on the phase with which they have greatest facility.

An individual's tendency to skip phases of learning is related to that person's preferred learning style. To generalize, based on the findings of many thousands of studies completed using the Kolb learning style inventory (Kolb 2005), the typical business entrepreneur operates in a more "feeling" or intuitive way through concrete experience and is more likely to experiment (or jump in) with their learning; in turn, this mode of active learning is often rewarded in their community of practice. In contrast, a scholar typically processes reality through abstract conceptualization and is most likely to reflect and observe. The scholar may have theories at the ready and can become quite facile in describing experience through conceptual frameworks. This is what is valued in their community of practice. It's important to understand that different professional bodies show a *marked* tendency to prefer a certain phase of the learning style, for example, a typical engineer easily turns concepts into methods. Moreover, these tendencies are the outgrowth of both professional socialization and the need to respond to stimuli, such as rewards, in their environment. The tendencies, however, can and do shift through life and may become more flexible.

We may conclude, then, that what is powerful for sustainable change among multi-organizational systems is developing feedback loops for the individual participants that allow them to see the advantages and limitations of their particular learning style and to increase their ability to learn from experience. In a social learning situation, feedback loops between technical-rational ways of knowing, and more whole thinking and intuitive ways, can be developed among diverse players with diverse learning styles. In turn, new stocks of knowledge emerge and offer feedback to social learning.

Feedback between dialogue and experimentation: The genesis of a "lifeworld"

A collaborative learning community is not a place for debates on the merits of change, but a place for people who are already convinced that there are important issues to be dealt with.

Both vision and action are important: while a sustainable effort must avoid devolving into mere tactics, it must also avoid ivory tower theory that is not actionable (Bradbury 2008). Reflective and analytical efforts, when aimed at reestablishing lifeworlds are critical for moving toward sustainability in a collaborative learning endeavour.

The concept of lifeworld (Habermas 1984) is helpful for understanding how the human cultural nexus of everyday life is maintained through social relationships and brought to action through conversation, which Habermas calls "communicative action." However, a lifeworld can come, over time, to be experienced as a dictate rather than a choice. In turn, power structures serve to make what was initially a choice developed in conversation appear instead as a reified and unchangeable reality (Berger and Luckman 1966). An example might be how our conversations about partnership and coordination at work can become externalized as company policy, which can then lock employees into stringent patterns of relating that can become, ironically, quite unrewarding and maladaptive. As this example shows, institutional structures can take on a life of their own, and the lifeworld comes to support – rather than generate – institutional structures, norms, and behaviours. As institutional structures move increasingly toward functionalist rationalization (Habermas 1984), the possibility of changing people's lifeworlds – which undergird institutions – grows more difficult with the passing of generations. Both Giddens (1984) and Bourdieu (1977) point out how individuals come to deeply embrace, at a precognitive, somatic level, the taken-for-granted norms of the institutions into which they are born.

Nonetheless, however difficult change is, it is not impossible. Despite the tenacity of institutional structures, impediments to a more sustainable society are not necessarily enduring. Indeed, we have seen significant institutional change occur in just a few generations, such as employee empowerment, concern for diversity, consideration of ethics, and a broader circle of stakeholders, not to mention the larger social movements such as the rise of gender equality and other developments that allow for the liberation of human potential from dominator logics (Eisler 2007).

In all cases, the lifeworld offers the opportunity for regeneration, through which new ideas spread in conversations and get enacted in the behaviours of the participants. As much as the lifeworld acts as the root of institutional structures, it can also re-root and re-generate these structures. A learning collaborative therefore privileges practitioner action and know-how. By implication, it is built around organizations grappling with the practical issues of work system sustainability.

We may conclude, then, that what is powerful for sustainable change among multi-organizational systems is emerging feedback loops that link dialogue and experimentation, avoiding the pressures to be either merely tactical, or limited to good intentions. The regeneration of the lifeworld cannot overcome habituated power structures. However, it can reawaken participants to the possibility of new ways of imagining and acting within their system. It does this first by allowing them to see how their actions are producing a system they likely do not wish to produce.

Illustrations of a collaborative learning approach to sustainable work systems

The perfect collaborative-learning approach to systems change would be formulated around the insights on feedback noted above. It would necessarily be different from how most change efforts have been approached in the past. This reflects the reality that while individual organizations must confront complex, systemic problems that their stakeholders require them to engage, organizations individually are incapable of making systemic change.

A collaborative learning approach offers a place for decision makers in a system to think together and solve their own problems in a way that will likely prove more efficient than what those who stand outside the system (such as regulators) can effect.

The following three illustrations are offered as examples of work developed around the ideas proposed. While far from perfect, they suggest how more sustainable systems can emerge as ideas meet practice and practice, in turn, shapes ideas. Following a short introduction to each, concrete outcomes are described.

All the cases are loosely connected to the Society for Organizational Learning Network (also called SoL, see "www.solonline.org") that was formed in the 1990s to bring together people engaged in the work of organizational learning in the organizational world.

The meta aim of the efforts described is to build a learning community committed to action, capable of collaboration, and using and building the three types of knowledge represented in Figure 12.1, namely know-how for theory, tools, and action.

The Sustainability Consortium of the SoL Network

The Sustainability Consortium was founded in 1998. The Sustainability Consortium is a voluntary association of about a dozen member organizations, including university-based researchers who share an interest in learning with and from each other regarding practical sustainability challenges. Most members of the Sustainability Consortium are large corporations including Ford, Nike, BP, Harley-Davidson, and Unilever, but there are others such as Plug Power (a small fuel-cell company) and the World Bank. As an inter-organizational learning alliance of organizational leaders, the Sustainability Consortium has applied principles of organizational learning and dialogue (cf. Senge *et al.* 1994) to develop and institute new business practices that incorporate concern for broader social and environmental issues.

Numerous projects were undertaken as a result of the Consortium, details of which are shared elsewhere (Senge *et al.* 2007). Three project descriptions (Cool Fuel, Women Leading Sustainability, and Materials Pooling) may suffice here to suggest the diversity of outcomes and also the movement from smaller to larger numbers of participants over time. *Cool Fuel* began in 2000 as a collaboration between an energy company and a carpet manufacturing company. The project encouraged use of oil from a single company and established the amount used in manufacturing. In turn, the tracking allowed for offsetting the carbon associated with that use and contributed to the green reputation of that company. The carbon reduction effort was then certified by a third party NGO. *Women Leading Sustainability* is a dialogue group founded in 2000 by and for women in the consortium. It meets by teleconference every six weeks and hosts semiannual face-to-face meetings. The first international meeting in April 2006 was capped at 80 participants, 40 of whom came from the developing world and in turn comprised scholars, practitioners, and members of NGOs. The *Materials Pooling* project began in 2002 and involves companies working together on eliminating toxins from their value chain by addressing their market needs to the chemical suppliers. This continues to evolve in regular meetings, teleconferences and in person. Emphasis is limited to removal of a few key primary toxins from the shared materials streams. Consideration is given to the input of schools and NGOs.

Weatherhead Institute for Sustainable Enterprise (WISE)

Started in Cleveland in 2000, WISE developed for seven years as a partnership between the Case Weatherhead Organizational Development program and the Entrepreneurs for Sustainability Network, a Cleveland-based NGO. A cohort of 30 executive management students worked in teams within an academic context so that five projects with local businesses were completed each year by each cohort. The projects engaged regional business leaders who were interested in issues of sustainability but struggling in various ways. Projects included mostly for-profit midsized companies, but the range comprised not-for-profits and large companies. The partnership is partly responsible for a vibrant network of 300 businesspeople who meet each month at events hosted by the Entrepreneurs for Sustainability Network to discuss and further their sustainability projects in business.

Two projects suggest the diversity of outcomes, Garick Corporation and The Intergenerational School. *Garick Corporation* was founded as a startup providing soil supplements for Ohio's booming gardening industry. Upon learning about principles of sustainable development as articulated by The Natural Step, the CEO re-conceptualized his business as a way of "turning waste into food." In action research mode, students connected this company with suppliers and customers to discuss the potential for working together to turn food waste from an industrial food supplier into compost that could be sold through major retail chains. His company has since grown 300 percent and supplies national retail outlets. *The Intergenerational School* is a startup charter school serving Cleveland children. It was sited at a nursing home and surrounded by gardens. The nursing home came to be seen as a resource, offering mentors with time enough to help kids with reading and homework. In turn, the elders enjoyed offering this contribution. The gardens became an opportunity for teaching organic kitchen garden practices. Since the start of the project, state mandated reading scores have assessed the reading ability of these underprivileged children at slightly above average.

Sustainable Enterprise Executive Roundtable (SEER)

SEER is a project of the USC Center for Sustainable Cities. SEER enables collaborative learning among Southern California business leaders so that more sustainable practices may result, benefiting the environment and the bottom line, through the implementation of sustainability-oriented projects. The economic lifeblood of the Southern California region is the Alameda Corridor, which begins at the Port of Los Angeles and is the main distribution channel for meeting around 45 percent of US consumer demand for imported goods. The corridor, built along the Los Angeles River, is a hub of economic assets for commerce.

SEER started in December 2006 when 24 business leaders were attracted to an initial meeting. The participants discussed possible synergies with regard to the movement of products, materials, and supplies to their place of use. It was agreed that collaboration would focus on making the system more sustainable and improving efficiencies, savings, innovations, environmental outcomes, and stakeholder satisfaction. The founding corporate cohort included: Port of Los Angeles, Disney, Toyota, Mattel, CDM, YTI/NYK (Ocean Carriers), Volvo, and Waste Management.

SEER is designed to meet both regional sustainability needs and individual participants' business needs. The companies involved have agreed to meet quarterly to engage in at least one concrete project, examples of which include:

1. Creating strategies for optimizing the journey of a standard transport container unit and simplifying/greening supply chains.
2. Developing new approaches to product packaging, using lifecycle analysis to compare alternative redesign scenarios.

Five innovations in practice

Generally speaking, the projects described emerged within a background of what has elsewhere been described as "relational space" deemed necessary for the type of trust required for innovative collaborations (Senge *et al.* 2007; see also Chapters 9 and 11 in this volume). The following suggests innovations in practice that allow for this new way of dealing with complex problems to take root and endure.

1. The work starts with a *celebration of practitioner know-how*. This happens for pragmatic reasons. Although originally convened at universities (MIT, Case, and USC respectively) there was never a sense that participants would willingly move from a scholarly stock of knowledge or that contribution to traditional scholarship was primary for practitioners. First privileging practitioners' know-how allowed the practitioner-actors to engage with the consortium as their own, to make it work for themselves, while scholarly knowledge was recognized as being present but not foreground. As the work continues, all forms of learning may exist more harmoniously.
2. Individuals learn. Some have a better capacity for integrating the types of feedback outlined. Additionally, the culture of some organizations can help or hinder that. As we consider what is at play in all these forms of feedback, we see our attempt to move toward a more holistic mode of inquiry that leads to a practice of not blocking emotions and movement. In this way, all manner of concrete active engagement can be included – such as field trips and role play – which allows participants access to an important element that creates learning over time.
3. Academia does not support the development of actionable knowledge. Scholarly practitioners (or action researchers) who create value in collaborative learning efforts are called upon to unify oppositional approaches that include the integration of theory and practice, action and reflection, empirical analysis and normative vision, critique and affirmation, explanation and action, vision and current reality. In a culture, especially academic culture, that more readily replaces "and" with "or," this will always be a challenge. Moreover, this type of work is not easily practised, because it requires multiple competencies. Practitioners must be part scientist, part matchmaker, and part entrepreneur, not to mention the broad skill set required – interpersonal skills, meeting design, artistic representation, project management. As the will to practical results will likely never fade, however, the question is simply whether conventional social science can keep open a place for dialogue with this holistic, dialogical orientation to science. A richer understanding

of quality, along with a richer practice that leads to research of consequence in which actionability is considered central, can be accomplished.

4. Business participants are overly busy. Because participation is voluntary, practitioners involved are motivated to engage in the work of the learning collaboratives. However, even strong internal motivation can't easily overcome the challenge of time scarcity. Scheduling meetings and talking times is difficult. Some ways through this problem that allow for success are to break into smaller working groups and allow for meetings that are easier to manage. But over all, beyond some personal learning and reflection time, it really is difficult to build capacity for companies with regard to sustainability when operating in this mode. Time pressures become more manageable to the degree that practitioners become engaged in sustainability projects that are sufficiently close to their real business issues that they align with their job responsibilities, including people whose jobs become redefined to work on these projects. Then, their participation is not just voluntary. But such projects often represent considerable prior effort based on beliefs of participants that such mission-critical issues do exist and that they need to become internal champions within their organizations for them. It is around such determined efforts to bring such projects into being that the consortium organizes itself.

5. Practitioners' normal mode of getting help is to hire consultants. The illustrations, on the other hand, suggest how people meet and organize their own collaboration. It is helpful therefore to be aware that the very design of this way of working does not strike practitioners as familiar. It may also seem, and often is, exhausting. We have found it best to reiterate a core notion of this type of action research, namely that "we are in this together!" Doing so reminds all of us that there are no products or services to be simply trotted out and "sold." Participants actually convene to cocreate something new, combining already available knowledge and resources, to meet the challenge they together decide to embrace.

Reflections

The illustrations describe processes that are designed and facilitated so that relational, conceptual, and action spaces can emerge. Each illustration exemplifies how business professionals, scholar-practitioners, and members of NGOs can work together to create a system in which intelligence is amplified through the social learning loop. In turn, projects with measurable benefit are developed with the input of each participant.

Generally speaking, the more the participants involved have been socialized within a particular type of space (e.g., business people are used to a transactional space in which there is a press to action, academically situated people are used to a conceptual space in which the press is toward analysis), the more emphasis needs to be placed on the development of additional experiences that stimulate the appreciation of what other spaces can provide. This leads, ideally, to a harmonious balance among relational, conceptual, and action spaces. A further complexity, however, is that relational space is undervalued in the momentum of our Western, technical-rational institutions. The norms of patriarchy have made "caring work" nonvaluable, at least from an economic perspective. Despite the structural and epistemic constraints, however, we find nonetheless that participants do grasp the importance of integrating the spaces.

A particularly important constraint to overcome is that people come to collaborative learning already deeply talented with only one learning style. They are also often quite oblivious of the fact that it is but one of a number of learning styles. Because of habituation among those with similar styles in their community of practice, too rarely do participants initially appreciate what is offered by the complementary styles of others from different communities of practice. Even among those commonly thought sophisticated, the experience of someone with a very different learning style is experienced as a "problem," rather than an opportunity for leveraging diversity. Hence, attention is required to designing a learning process that touches on all learning styles and in which dialogue and experimentation can occur in an integrated way. In all the cases, significant experimentation was undertaken alongside significant reflection, as a core practice of action research. Measurable benefit arose for those involved. The ways in which reflection and experimentation come alive are different in each context. In the second case example, those involved in projects enjoyed regular class time in which reflective analysis was assumed as an element. In the other cases, reflection is built into regular, if infrequent, meetings using guided dialogue as a way to move toward next cycles of coordinated action. In between meetings, considerable effort is given to maintaining momentum through regular telephone calls and teleconferences.

All these cases therefore show how feedback mechanisms provide for intelligent self-regulation of a shared system. Because the experiments are geared toward more sustainable outcomes, as informed by the criteria of The Natural Step and other sustainability parameters, the action that is coordinated is seen to increase sustainability in the system.

Stepping away from these cases to look at the larger economic-cultural system in which they operate, we can see that many of our existing businesses and institutions, developed with industrial era logic and practices, have contributed to a growing crisis of unsustainability. In the face of the quiet crisis of our time (Brown 2006), transformative learning and collaboration are needed. The cases therefore suggest that collaborative learning may be an important element in mitigating the looming ecological crisis (see also Chapters 9 and 11 in this volume).

The cases and the theory of change they help develop highlight an emphasis on a humanistic approach to technical change. This comes in contrast to the typical way of approaching sustainability, which has privileged the already dominant technical-rational logic that gives technical advances a higher priority than related human-behavioural change. The three feedback powers offered above have proven useful across the different contexts illustrated. The goal is to create sustainable work systems that are truly sustainable in the sense that they allow for intelligent action to emerge in a way that moves us beyond the industrial era silos. This remains the work of many generations if we are to survive as a species. Are we going to have that long to accomplish this work?

Questions for reflection

Here are three questions for your further reflection on the issues broached in this chapter:

- Define a sustainable work system. Can sustainability of any one of the three core elements – environmental, social, and financial resources – be left out and still have the system meet present needs without reducing the capacity of future generations to meet their needs?
- How is organizational learning relevant to sustainability?
- What is the special role of action researchers (or scholar-practitioners) in enabling collaborative learning among business practitioners?

Notes

1 In reference to the Al Gore film of the same name.
2 Bradbury 2008.

References

Bateson, G. (1979) *Mind and Nature: A necessary unity.* New York: Bantam Books.
Bawden, R. Guijt, I., and Woodhill, J. (2007) "The critical role of civil society in fostering learning for a sustainable world," in A. Wals (ed.), *Social Learning Towards a Sustainable World*, Wageningen, Netherlands: Wageningen Academic Publishers, 133–148.
Beck, U. (1994) "The reinvention of politics: towards a theory of reflexive modernization," in U. Beck, A. Giddens, and S. Lash (eds), *Reflexive Modernization: Politics, tradition and aesthetics in the modern social order*, Stanford, CA: Stanford University Press, 1–55.
Berger, P.L. and Luckmann. T. (1966) *The Social Construction of Reality: A treatise on the sociology of knowledge.* Garden City, NY: Anchor Books.
Bourdieu, P. (1977) *Outline of a Theory of Practice.* Cambridge: Cambridge University Press.
Bradbury, H. (2008) "Quality, consequence and 'actionability': What action researchers offer from the tradition of pragmatism," in A.B. Shani, S.A. Mohrman, W.A. Passmore, B. Stymne and N. Adler (eds), *Handbook of Collaborative Management Research*, Thousand Oaks, CA: Sage Publications.
Brown, L. (2006) *Plan B.2.0. Rescuing a Planet under Stress and a Civilization in Trouble*, New York and London: W.W. Norton.
Capra, F. (2007) "Foreword," in A. Wals (ed.), *Social Learning towards a Sustainable World*, Wageningen, Netherlands: Wageningen Academic Publishers, 13–15.
Eisler, R. (2007) *Real Wealth of Nations: Creating a caring economics.* San Francisco: Berrett-Koehler.

Elkington, J. (1997) *Cannibals with Forks: Triple bottom line of 21st century business.* Oxford: Capstone Publishing

Giddens, A. (1984) *The Constitution of Society: Introduction of the theory of structuration.* Berkeley, CA: University of California Press.

Habermas, J. (1984) *The Theory of Communicative Action.* Boston, MA: Beacon Press.

Hamalainen, R. and Saarinen, E. (2007) "Systems intelligence: A key competence for organizational life," *Reflections,* 7, 4, 191–201.

Hart, S.L. and Milstein, M.B. (1999) "Global sustainability and the creative destruction of industries," *Sloan Management Review,* 41, 1, 23–33.

Kiernan, M.J. (2005) "Eco-value, sustainability, and shareholder value: driving environmental performance to the bottom line." *Environmental Quality Management,* 10, 4, 1–12.

Kolb, D. (1984) *Experiential Learning: Experience as the source of learning and development.* Upper Saddle River, NJ: Prentice Hall.

—— (2005) *The Kolb Learning Style Inventory.* Boston, MA: Hay Group, Inc.

Pollan, M. (2006) *The Omnivore's Dilemma.* New York: The Penguin Press.

Reason, P. and Bradbury, H. (eds) (2001, 2008) *The Handbook of Action Research.* London: Sage Publications.

Senge, P. (1990) *The Fifth Discipline.* New York: Doubleday Press.

Senge, P. and Scharmer, O. (2001) "Community action research: Learning as a community of practitioners, consultants, and researchers," in P. Reason and H. Bradbury (eds), *The Handbook of Action Research,* London: Sage Publications, 238–249.

Senge, P., Kleiner, A., Roberts, C., Ross, R., and Smith, B. (1994) *The Fifth Discipline Fieldbook,* New York: Currency Doubleday Press.

Senge, P., Lichtenstein, B., Kaeufer, K., Bradbury, H., and Carroll, J. (2007) "Collaborating for systemic change: Conceptual, relational and action domains for meeting the sustainability challenge," *Sloan Management Review,* 48, 2, 44–53.

Torbert, W.R. and Associates (2005) *Action Inquiry.* San Francisco: Berrett-Koehler.

Wals, A. (ed.) (2007) *Social Learning Towards a Sustainable World.* Wageningen, Netherlands: Wageningen Academic Publishers.

Weick, K. (1976) "Educational organizations as loosely coupled systems," *Administrative Science Quarterly,* 21, 1–9.

Wilson, E.O. (2002) *The Future of Life.* New York: Knopf.

13 Labelling and sustainability

The case of specialty coffee

Mikael Román

Introduction

Coffee is the world's second largest trade commodity and, as such, has a profound impact on the lives of nearly half a billion people involved in the industry. At the same time, the link between the coffee market and development is not without problems. The global coffee industry has in the last decade seen major structural changes, involving over-production and new entrants, leading to falling commodity prices and, ultimately, dire social consequences for local producers in the developing world. The word "crisis" is presently permeating the coffee industry, and the challenge is how to revitalize the market.

More generally, the coffee crisis illustrates the particular sustainability challenges facing developing countries, where weak internal institutional structures and high dependency on external economic markets affect the social and environmental conditions of both societies and individuals. Ultimately, it also constitutes a practical illustration regarding the most efficient means to stimulate sustainable development in these regions. Are large-scale planned interventions required, or shall we rely on pure market incentives?

The present article takes the current coffee crisis as a starting point for a discussion on the specific challenges facing developing countries in their quest for sustainability. More specifically, it discusses to what extent the creation of sustainability labels, with the ambition to boost the global coffee market and simultaneously create sustainable working conditions, has had the intended effect. What is the driving rationale behind these efforts? What are the opportunities and challenges for substantive sustainability outcomes related to an approach of this kind?

Conceptual framing

The upcoming discussion will evolve around a few core concepts.

The first is *sustainability*, which here is synonymous with sustainable development, or "development that meets the needs of the present without compromising the ability of future generations to meet their own needs" (World Commission on Environment and Development 1987: 43). According to this notion, sustainable development resides on three "interdependent and mutually reinforcing pillars" (economic development, social development, and environmental protection) that should be dealt with interactively (see also Chapter 1 in this volume). Nowhere is this interconnectedness more apparent than in developing countries (see also Chapter 14). Hence, this interpretation of sustainable development will be critical for our understanding of the coffee industry. Moreover, to understand fully the various drivers behind the creation of sustainability labels we shall distinguish between sustainability at the industry level and firm level.

A second critical term is *labelling*, which is understood as a type of voluntary standard, or code of conduct, created to ensure that social and environmental values are reflected in the production or traits of certain items. Technically, labels may differ in degree of formality, and some are only provided by certifying bodies. Still, while any interest group potentially can define such standards, they complement government laws and regulations and represent an evolution of the regulatory framework.

Another critical concept is the notion of *supply-chains*, which specifies the activities by which raw materials and components are transformed into a finished product for the end consumer. More concretely, the supply-chain allows us to describe and analyze the interaction between individual firms in their respective value-chains (Nagurney 2006). This is particularly relevant for the coffee sector, where, according to some estimates, coffee beans change hands up to 150 times before they reach the supermarket shelf (Fairtrade Foundation 2002: 4). It is right here, in this intricate web of intermediary institutions, that sustainable development converts into a local, regional, and global concern (Ponte 2004: 2).

This brings us, finally, to the principal theoretical assumption of this article, namely *the potential use of environmental and social regulations as a source of competitive advantage for individual firms*. Most fundamentally, individual firms gain competitive advantage through strategic positioning (i.e., by performing activities differently or by performing different activities than rivals), combined with a strategy for dealing with regulation (Porter 1998: 40). Contrary to general belief, companies may under certain circumstances favour more stringent regulations, because regulations: 1) increase predictability and allow for long-term planning; 2) create production, distribution, or financing cost differentials; 3) generate demand for existing products; 4) define new market segments; and 5) control sources of inputs (Kahn 1988). This argument holds true also for environmental and social regulations (Reinhardt 2000). Following the same logic, individual corporations may under certain conditions alter the competitive landscape to their own benefit by seeking more stringent regulations that mandate certain unique sustainability practices in either the production process or the product. Thus, once improved environmental and social sustainability is regarded as a *means* to gain economic competitive advantage, rather than an *end* in itself, we could potentially see a "trading-up" in regulatory stringency, driven by individual competitive concerns in the private sector. This distinction between means and ends is critical since it suggests that there are, in fact, several drivers for improved environmental and social sustainability performance. Put differently, the latter could thereby come out as a positive side-effect of competitive strategies among firms.

Methodology

This chapter has evolved through a series of semistructured interviews with various actors in the coffee sector, mainly in Brazil and Costa Rica, in the years 2003 to 2005. Also, the author had the opportunity to attend meetings at the International Coffee Organization (ICO) in London as an observer. This primary information has been complemented with various secondary sources, such as reports and newspaper articles.

The coffee industry case

The coffee market and its recent crisis

Coffee is, as already indicated, an enormous industry, with exports worldwide totalling US$ 8.7 billion in the year 2000, affecting the lives of up to half a billion people directly or indirectly involved in the industry. At the same time, the coffee market illustrates the traditional North–South dilemma insofar as the production resides in developing countries while the markets are found in the industrialized world. Adding to this complexity, coffee is one of the few international commodities that are still produced mainly by small-scale farmers (around 70 percent of total production). These 25 million people are the principal focus of this discussion (Fairtrade Foundation 2002: 4; Sorby 2002a: 1; and May *et al.* 2004: 10).

The coffee industry is presently undergoing a radical and, for many, painful overhaul. This development started with the breakdown of the International Coffee Agreement (ICA) in 1989, which until then had determined supply levels through fixed export quotas for producing countries, in order to keep the price of coffee relatively high and stable. Once the Agreement collapsed, however, the industry soon converted into a free-market system, and coffee prices have since then been determined on futures markets in London and New York (Gresser and Tickell 2002: 17; Kohler 2007: 6).

In the aftermath of the collapse of the ICA followed the so-called "coffee paradox," in which commodity prices continued to fall and retail markets grew rapidly, while at the same time consumers paid continuously higher prices for more diversified products (Daviron *et al.* 2005). The principal benefactors from this development are intermediary actors like traders, roasters, and retailers, who earn higher profits (Kohler 2007: 3). For millions of producers and the environment they live in, the consequences are dire. This overall trend raises some serious concerns about the coffee industry and its role in regard to sustainable development. Let us therefore analyze the current situation from the perspective of each of the three pillars (economic, environmental, and social).

Economic sustainability

Economic sustainability refers fundamentally to the efficient use of resources (usually expressed in monetary terms) and implies the maintenance of capital, or keeping capital intact (Goodland 2002). In effect, market-based economic instruments are also increasingly applied to promoted sustainable practices.

At the same time, ideal-type market conditions are rare in real life, particularly in regard to natural resource management, where market failures in practice abound. Even more problematic, efforts to overcome these problems through regulatory measures are often difficult since they inevitably entail step-wise adjustments and occasionally even generate perverse effects. The coffee industry is a case in point on both incidences.

There are essentially two factors explaining the oversupply following the termination of the ICA, i.e., changes in land-use policies and technology development, both incited by the deregulation. In the years between 1990 and 2000, Vietnam, which had until then been a marginal coffee producer, suddenly increased its production from 1.5 million to 15 million bags, to become the world's second-largest coffee producer. This meteoric rise resulted from the Vietnamese government's decision to open up the country's agricultural economy and, by combining proper investments with World Bank loans, to promote coffee production through different subsidies and the provision of irrigated land (Fairtrade Foundation 2002: 7f.). Still, the principal reason for falling world prices was the rapid production growth in Brazil, the world's largest coffee producer, where the deregulation soon generated new technology investments and management strategies that all contributed to increased yields (Gresser and Tickell 2002: 18). This had direct impacts on the global market. What took Vietnam ten years to achieve was still less than a single year's increase in Brazil (going from 33 million bags in 2001/2002 to 47.5 million in 2002/2003) (Roberts 2002).

This supply increase resulted in a continuous fall in commodity prices until, in 2000 and 2001, they reached their lowest levels in 30 years. The situation was further aggravated by considerable price fluctuations that also impacted producers. Those who suffered the most, however, were not the large producers (Brazil, Vietnam, and Indonesia) but the poor countries, mainly in Africa and Central America (Burundi, Uganda, Guatemala, and Nicaragua), which were the most dependent on coffee for their export earnings. Burundi had in 2001 more than 80 percent of its export revenues from coffee but represented only a marginal share of the world market. Once coffee prices plummeted below production cost, entire societies were effectively paralyzed (Varangis *et al.* 2003: 3). The social consequences were severe. By 2002, nearly 540,000 people had lost their jobs in Latin America alone, with losses in foreign exchange receipts amounting to US$713 million (Bounds and Mulligan 2002). Moreover, the effects were not equally distributed among the developing countries.

At the industry level, there was an increasing market concentration after the fall of the ICA, with traders and roasters taking a growing share of the revenues. As for trading, around 45 percent of the market is presently controlled by three companies (Neumann, Volcafé, and Ecom), while, at the roaster level, Philip Morris, Nestlé, Procter and Gamble, Sara Lee, and Tchibo account for 69 percent of the market (Kohler 2007: 8). In this process, the producing countries' share of the final profit has dropped substantially (May *et al.* 2004: 8). This suggests that producer countries are unable to seize the aggregate value coming from the manufacturing and packaging of coffee. Several sources of data confirm this pattern. In 2000/2001, for example, a staggering 94 percent of all coffee exported from developing countries crossed the border in its green bean state. The bulk of the remaining 6 percent had been processed in Brazil, India, and Colombia (Gresser and Tickell 2002: 33).

The pattern of oversupply persists. The year 2006/2007 produced 122 million bags to satisfy a total world consumption of 116 million bags (International Coffee Organization 2007: 3f.). The resulting competition has generated a progressively more diversified consumer market in which profits increasingly remain at the roaster and retailer end of the supply-chain (*ibid.*).

Social sustainability

The impact of the coffee crisis on social sustainability is obvious, yet not sufficiently elaborated. More broadly, social sustainability concerns the development and maintenance of social capital, or the investments and services that create the basic framework for society (competence, well-being, and trust). A critical component thereof is to lower transaction costs to facilitate cooperation, and, accordingly, social sustainability presupposes shared rules and norms and a transparent and fully operating judicial system, along with full and equal access to information for all citizens. The qualitative endgame of these efforts is to meet minimal needs regarding economic living standards, health, and sanitation (Goodland 2002).

There are many social sustainability problems in the coffee industry. At the heart lies a structural problem, with coffee being one of the few internationally traded commodities that is still mainly produced by peasant households (Gresser and Tickell 2002: 6f.). In fact, around 70 percent of all coffee is grown on small-scale farms, even though farm size and coffee growing areas differ considerably between producer nations (May *et al.* 2004: 10). This has various implications. First, it creates significant problems for other economic sectors (education, housing, food, medical services), as coffee farmers almost exclusively depend on coffee as a primary source of hard currency (Ponte 2004: 6). Second, the scattered nature of production prevents workers and farmers from engaging in collective bargaining strategies (i.e., unions and producer associations), leaving hired labour as an even poorer segment of the supply chain and individual farmers effectively unable to negotiate a fair price on their production (May *et al.* 2004: 10; Ponte 2004: 6). This situation, in turn, is further aggravated by the physical and cultural distance between producers and consumers, which makes farmers dependent on middlemen, and the further diversification of the end market, with its new requirements on export licenses, minimum volume, and quality criteria (Ponte 2004: 3). Third, more technologically advanced farming systems have also created new health and safety risks for coffee workers and their communities. Finally, this overall trend further exacerbates traditional gender distinctions that place women at a social and economic disadvantage (*ibid.*: 6).

Consequently, poor coffee farmers are currently struggling to survive, often without any alternative. Phasing out a coffee plantation takes up to five years and requires both investment capital and an alternative crop. Most often, neither is available. The failure of international aid donors and national governments to promote rural development, along with protectionist policies preventing developing country farmers from benefiting from other commodities, are all serious obstacles.

Environmental sustainability

Recent developments in the coffee industry have also had considerable impact on environmental sustainability. There are various criteria defining the latter term. One refers to the output side of the equation and states that harvest rates of renewable resource inputs must be kept within regenerative capacities of the natural system that generates them (Goodland 2002). Another criterion is to avoid loss of biodiversity. The coffee industry faces serious challenges on both accounts, with new production technologies and techniques affecting both the quality of coffee as well as the environment in which it grows.

Environmentally speaking, coffee is a delicate matter with more than 80 percent of the 11.8 million hectares devoted to coffee production globally situated in areas of former or current rainforest. Traditionally, coffee is grown in close relation with the surrounding ecosystems, but this pattern is changing as new production technologies and irrigation schemes enable large-scale plantations in the open sun. This shift from "diverse shade" systems to "monoculture shade" systems has considerable environmental effects. Latin America, for example, has seen a 50 percent reduction in avian biodiversity under sun growing conditions. Similarly, the reduced forestation associated with sun and monoculture production is frequently causing soil erosion and has also contributed to a 30 to 50 percent reduction of carbon sequestration (Ponte 2004: 4f.).

In addition, new technology has generated a double decline in coffee quality, involving a gradual move from Arabica beans to the lower-quality Robusta, and a deterioration in quality of the Robusta itself (Gresser and Tickell 2002: 29). (See box on p. 208). Incidentally, the effects of the latter can be lessened by additional technology that masks the bitterness of the cheaper and lower-quality coffees (*ibid.*: 28). The result is a self-reinforcing vicious cycle with considerable environmental values at stake.

Summary

The various sustainability issues affecting the coffee industry could conveniently be summarized as market failures, of which the principal are:

Arabica and Robusta

There are two main varieties of coffee. The *Coffea Arabica* bean grows in the tropical highlands and is produced mainly for its quality and superior flavour. Currently it holds about 2/3 of the market with Colombia as the largest producing country. The *Coffea Robusta* bean is a high-yielding variety with good resistance to pests and diseases, which, due to its more acid taste, is widely used for soluble coffee and stronger roasts. The production of *Robusta* has traditionally taken place in Africa and Brazil, but more recently Vietnam has made considerable inroads on this market.

- a mismatch between supply and demand;
- market instability;
- inequitable market power;
- information asymmetry;
- limited access to finance and capital;
- under-provision and under-conservation of social and environmental public goods;
- the introduction of inappropriate technologies and techniques.

Suggested solutions to remedy the situation

There are numerous suggestions for how to solve the current coffee crisis. Apart from a reintroduction of quotas, which few see as a viable option, they all seek to increase competitiveness within the existing market system. Briefly, the various initiatives fall under four broad categories (Varangis *et al.* 2003: 24–34).

- *Product differentiation*, which implies promoting sales for individual producers or producer groups such as cooperatives, and forcing inferior competitors out of the market. This can be achieved either by improving quality along the production line, or by promoting new value-added products.
- *Supply chain management*, in which producers work directly with retailers to develop private labels and bypass cumbersome trading channels, reduce the dependence on middlemen, and increase local manufacturing so as to capture the added value of the final product.
- *Promotional strategies* to increase coffee sales through, for example, internet auctions, "Cup of Excellence" competitions, and different forms of agro-tourism that complement the actual production of coffee. Still more important are the efforts to enter new and hitherto unexplored markets (such as Eastern Europe and China) and to increase domestic promotion and consumption in producer countries.

- *Price risk and volatility management* can be achieved through traditional economic instruments such as futures contracts, linking price insurance to a loan agreement, inventory and management techniques, and models for weather and environmental risk analysis.

In the present chapter we focus primarily on product differentiation through labelling.

Specialty coffee and labelling

The link between product differentiation and sustainability has gained increasing attention in recent years. Briefly, the assumption is that market segmentation based on quality and sustainability criteria not only may generate a price premium for the producer but also provide improved sustainability outcomes as a secondary effect, all depending on the criteria used for the label.

Specialty coffee is currently the fastest growing segment in the coffee industry, and even though it still only accounts for 2 percent of consumption, it offers attractive benefits for about 0.75 million farm households as well as other actors along the entire supply chain (Giovannucci and Koekoek 2003: 16). The principal markets are found in Europe, where sales of organic products in general are increasing by 23 percent per year (Sorby 2002a: 5). On the retail side, distribution channels for sustainable coffees have also expanded greatly in recent years, with supermarkets and high-volume multiple store chains joining the specialty retailers in this business (Giovannucci and Koekoek 2003: 18).

Different certified sustainability labels

There are presently five different certified sustainability labels (shade-grown, bird-friendly, organic, FairTrade and sustainable coffee) that differ with regards to at least three dimensions: 1) the focus and scope of the labelling (single or multiple criteria); 2) the source of verification (first-party or third-party); and 3) the principal instigator of the labelling scheme (public, private or other interest group) (Commission for Environmental Cooperation & TerraChoice Environmental Services 2004: 9). To illustrate the differences we shall discuss three labels in more detail.

Shade-grown coffee

The shade-grown coffee label specifies that the coffee in question has grown under the shade of trees. This label emerged on the initiative of environmental interest groups. Its aim is to reduce the effects of large-scale production that, on the one hand, makes it possible to raise output up to three times, but only through a parallel introduction of pesticides and chemical nutrients, which, on the other hand, reduce biodiversity, affect soil quality, and provoke negative health effects among workers – apart from affecting the quality and taste of the beans. Hence, a leading argument among the proponents of this single-criterion scheme is that it has multiple positive effects (Sorby 2002b: 3). Leading certifying organizations are the Smithsonian Migratory Bird Center and the Rainforest Alliance.

Organic coffee

A second biodiversity-enhancing standard is the "organically grown" coffee label. Its guiding principle is that no chemical pesticides or fertilizers are allowed. Instead, the farming system is based on crop rotation, natural pest control, minimal irrigation, and strict control of runoff erosion. Most organic coffee standards have therefore evolved from already existent organic organizations, and both auditing and certification thereby follow established organic principles in importing countries. The organic labels distinguish themselves from the shade-grown standard by emphasizing health rather than environmental concerns (Commission for Environmental Cooperation & TerraChoice Environmental Services 2004: 11; and Sorby 2002b: 5). The organic label is the most sought-after of all coffee standards.

FairTrade

The FairTrade label takes a somewhat different approach than the previous labels by focusing on the farmers' socio-economic situation. Its main ambition is to nurture a partnership between consumers and socially responsible importers that cuts out the middlemen. In effect, it constitutes an attempt to combine market incentives and moral values. As such, it is built upon seven principles: 1) fair wages; 2) cooperative workplaces; 3) consumer education; 4) environmental sustainability; 5) financial and technical support; 6) respect for cultural identity; and 7) public accountability. In adhering to these objectives, FairTrade coffee also guarantees the social and environmental conditions stated in the International Labour Organization conventions on working conditions. As a logical consequence, FairTrade certification is also free for the farmer, while importers and roasters pay a license fee to work with FairTrade products, which covers the costs of certification. After organic coffee, FairTrade is the best-known and most sought-after certification (Fairtrade Foundation 2002: 20; Kohler 2007: 20; Sorby 2002b: 5; Commission for Environmental Cooperation & TerraChoice Environmental Services 2004: 13).

Other sustainable coffee labels

In addition to the certified labelling efforts mentioned above, there are also other labelling initiatives that could have a positive impact on the coffee market.

Specialty brands

One type of initiative is specialty branding, by which a country or region builds a name around origin (appellation) rather than sustainability. The strategy has been quite successful, as in the case of Jamaica and its Blue Mountain brand. Once quality becomes the driving force behind production and competitive strategy in the coffee sector, it can be expected to enhance sustainability in the broader sense (Gresser and Tickell 2002: 42).

Company programs

Perhaps the most interesting labelling efforts, however, are the wide array of company programs that are currently emerging at the corporate level. These private sustainability initiatives must all be taken seriously since they potentially include large volumes of coffee. The initiatives themselves, however, differ considerably from one another. Some focus on social accounting and environmental management policies and assessments, like the agreement Neumann Kaffee Gruppe signed with The Rainforest Alliance to integrate sustainability into its procurement (Giovannucci and Koekoek 2003: 56). Other initiatives, pushed by Nestlé, are more specific and train farmers in more sustainable practices and improved management capacity. Instead of paying farmers a premium price for their coffee, the companies work with them to lift quality, for which they can charge a higher price (*ibid.*: 57). It is still unclear, though, to what extent these corporate efforts produce concrete results. One problem so far has been the lack of transparency. This, however, is possibly changing, as schemes like Starbucks CAFE initiative and Utz Kapeh allow for more scrutiny (*ibid.*: 58).

This development towards more elaborate sustainability standards is also evolving at the industry level. In December 2006, for example, 37 stakeholders of coffee production (including trade and industry, civil society organizations, public organizations and individuals) founded the Common Code for the Coffee Community Association (4C Association), an independent, open, nonprofit membership association based on multi-stakeholder participation. Unlike the FairTrade certification system, which guarantees price premiums to growers following specific guidelines aiming at a high-end niche market, 4C targets the mainstream green coffee industry. It is explicitly market-driven and makes no attempt to set coffee prices. Instead, it outlines more than 30 social, environmental, and economic principles for all actors in the coffee supply chain (farmers, plantation owners, coffee product manufacturers, exporters, and traders) that, if adhered to, will ensure sustainability in the coffee industry. A critical component is to optimize transparency and traceability along the entire supply chain. This is claimed to increase the awareness of individual responsibilities in the production, processing, and trading of coffee (Singer 2005; *Business World* 2007).

Several 4C projects have already been initiated in some of the major coffee-producing countries, such as Colombia, Brazil, and, perhaps most importantly, Vietnam. Many of the larger coffee companies, like Nescafé, play an active role in this process (*Financial Times Information* 2006; *BusinessWorld* 2007).

Labelling as a source of competitive advantage

So, what are the driving concerns behind the current labelling schemes?

A first issue concerns economy of scale and production costs. In the expanding coffee industry, small-scale farmers cannot compete with large producers and the lower production costs following from scale advantages. However, the organic production standard alters this competitive situation by effectively removing all large-scale advantages. Under these new conditions, the big producer is likely to opt out. Put differently, the organic standard has shifted production costs to the benefit of the small producer, and has also segmented a new market where the small producer will be able to compete more effectively.

A similar pattern is seen among roasters, where there is an emerging plethora of different sustainability standards. In this "battle over labels," apparently aiming at end consumers, the ultimate objective is to segment the market and thus gain a higher premium. An analogous strategic move towards end consumers is McDonald's stated ambition to serve certified sustainable coffee in its restaurants throughout Europe. In this case, though, the driving concern is public image, and it reflects thereby the ambition of outlets and other commercial institutions to differentiate themselves by serving certified sustainable products. What matters here is size. Once companies like McDonalds and Wal-Mart make similar commitments, the market for sustainable coffee may well grow rapidly in a short time (*Gourmet Retailer* 2007).

Finally, the competitive logic is also reflected at the industry level through the different "codes of conduct" initiated by large corporate players, which effectively operate as regulatory frameworks for the entire industry. The competitive rationale is obvious and the 4C initiative is probably the best example of such an effort. Explicitly intended to benefit producers, the 4C initiative is set up as a benchmarking process with the ambition to reduce, or even prevent, a growing number of different standards. The question, though, is whose interest is then being served. Clearly, the ones less interested in a scattered market with multiple standards are, precisely, the dominating players who profit under the current system. Consequently, they preempt other initiatives and define the rules that serve them. This is a shared interest, which provides incentives for collaboration. Importantly, though, these initiatives are not necessarily less demanding. Quite the contrary, by imposing tougher standards along the entire supply-chain, large industry actors can effectively kill off minor competitors that cannot meet the new demands. Interestingly, some producing countries are now also endorsing these schemes. More recently, Brazil announced for example that 100 percent of its coffee production would meet the 4C qualification within three years (Batista 2007). It is no surprise that African producers have been more hesitant about the 4C scheme, because it will be comparatively more difficult for them to take on the necessary investment costs and hence will make them less competitive (Singer 2005). Again, we see how competitive strategies occasionally raise the sustainability bar.

Obstacles and pitfalls from certification

So, will these developments ultimately benefit the social conditions of small-scale farmers? Again, evidence suggests otherwise. In fact, there are a number of problems related to certification that also illustrate some of the broader problems related to sustainability in a developing-country context.

The first and most obvious problem is *the limited scope of sustainable certification*. In fact, total sales of sustainable coffee still only constitute 2 percent of the global market (Giovannucci and Koekoek 2003: 16), of which the more socially oriented FairTrade label accounts for a miniscule 0.24 percent (Ponte 2004: 11). The development of specialty coffees has, in other words, been important to a considerable number of farmers, but it does not provide the systemic solution needed to solve the coffee crisis (Gresser and Tickell 2002: 3).

This emphasizes, in turn, the *unclear relationship between quality, sales, and industry structure*. While taste is the most important determinant of coffee purchase, demand for high-quality products, it is argued, will lead to sustainable practices (Sorby 2002a: 6). Quality, however, is more than anything else a function of industry structure, and commodity markets, like the coffee industry, do not necessarily reward superior quality, even though they hold minimum quality requirements. Hence, to improve sustainability in the coffee sector it is equally important to consider the process of production and trading relationships (Giovannucci and Koekoek 2003: 16).

Another critical aspect of sustainable certification is *current and future price premiums*. These have always been the principal incentive for sustainable coffee production. In effect, organic green bean premiums show a considerable variance and FairTrade coffee is roughly 50–150 percent more expensive than comparable coffees at the retail level. One factor explaining these differences is the relatively higher production expenditure following from licensing and transaction costs (Ponte 2004: 12). However, the high premiums are also the result of information asymmetries and a lack of competition and have allowed retailers to gain relatively higher revenues. This situation of high premiums, however, is likely to change as the sustainability market expands (Giovannucci and Koekoek 2003: 20). With the disappearance of price premiums the main incentive for sustainable coffee production will also disappear.

A fourth concern is that sustainable certification *creates oversupply and stalls innovation*. This critique is mainly directed at the FairTrade scheme, which, according to some economists, removes all incentives for diversification and innovation. By offering farmers guaranteed sales at a high and fixed price, FairTrade in practice incentivizes farmers to stay in coffee production, when they might have been better off seeking alternatives. The result is long-term oversupply (Gresser and Tickell 2002: 42). Moreover, because the FairTrade pricing system is effectively detached from coffee quality it reduces the need for producers to innovate and thereby increases their vulnerability in the long run (Ponte 2004: 12).

Another critical issue concerns the *costs of certification*. More generally, a problem for all certification schemes is that quality improvement and implementation of sustainability standards are costly, and, in absence of any premium, these costs will be shifted to producers who are already undergoing a crisis. In other words, what was from the outset a competitive advantage for the small producer in regard to production costs will turn into a liability once the costs for certification and assessments enter the equation. Again, certification becomes an instrument for cost shifting but in this case it will hit small-scale farmers who have no financial backup (Kohler 2007: 18).

A final issue raising serious questions regarding certification as a means to promote sustainable performance in the coffee sector is the *plethora of labels and standards*. The problem is present at several levels. To the consumer, certification schemes are ideally a source of information; but once such schemes become marketing tools, they could confuse consumers and potentially undermine the credibility of the whole effort (Kohler 2007: 16). To producers and businesses, the proliferation of standards and labels has instead increased the complexity and costs of seeking certification (ISEAL Alliance 2003: 4).

Final reflections and current trends

The question of whether voluntary regulations in the form of sustainability labelling improve environmental and socio-economic performance in the coffee sector has no clear-cut answer. On the one hand, anecdotal evidence indicates that living conditions have, indeed, improved for thousands of individuals. At the same time, certification does not solve the more profound, systemic problems in the coffee industry.

So, in what ways will competitive concerns influence future sustainability in the coffee sector? Some current trends are instructive. Clearly, there is a growing "label-fatigue," and there are increasing demands for an overarching "super seal" for sustainable coffee. The reasons for this stance, however, vary between the actors. Labelling organizations, for example, are concerned about the complexity and costs of certification (ISEAL Alliance 2003: 4), while retailers seek to avoid a further segmentation of the market (Giovannucci and Koekoek 2003: 19). Similarly, consumer organizations want coherent and comprehensive labelling schemes that are understandable to all consumers (*ibid.*: 55), while the main objective of the large producers is to mainstream the market (Commission for Environmental Cooperation & TerraChoice Environmental Services 2004: 16).

Ironically, this implies that competition itself at some point may erode the incentive for a regulatory "trading up." Once sustainability becomes the standard operating procedure defined by the dominating actors, the motivations for further improvement, some fear, will be gone. As one observer put it: "The general impression [that] everybody is becoming fair represents [in itself] a threat for the fair trade movement" (Kohler 2007: 51).

Discussion

The present chapter has taken the current coffee crisis as a starting point for a discussion about the specific challenges facing developing countries in their quest for sustainability. More specifically, it has discussed to what extent market mechanisms in the form of voluntary certification improve sustainability in the coffee industry. This interplay between sustainability performance, public and private competitive concerns, and regulations is one of the more influential contemporary policy issues and is likely to remain so over the coming years.

Questions for reflection

Here are three questions for your further reflection on the issues broached in this chapter:

- What are the main problems in the coffee market and how do they affect sustainability and competition?
- What are the principal opportunities and pitfalls with the current proliferation of voluntary sustainability standards in the coffee industry?
- What are the principal differences between developing and industrialized countries with regard to sustainability?

References

Batista, Fabiana (2007) "Coffee producers earn more through exports." *Gazeta Mercantil Online* (São Paulo). Online. Available HTTP: <http://www.gazetamercantil.com.br> (accessed via LexisNexis 7 April 2007).

Bounds, A. and Mulligan, M. (2002) "Crisis call to coffee growers: development agencies are warning that changes in market structure are permanent," *Financial Times.* Online. Available HTTP: <http://www.ft.com> (accessed via LexisNexis 6 June 2007).

BusinessWorld (2007) "Nescafé adopts code of conduct for sustainable coffee farming." Online. Available via LexisNexis (accessed 14 April 2007).

Commission for Environmental Cooperation & TerraChoice Environmental Services (2004) *Environmental and Other Labelling of Coffee: The Role of Mutual Recognition, Supporting Cooperative Action.* Winnipeg, MB: IISD. Online. Available HTTP: <http://www.iisd.org/pdf/2004/sci_coffee_labelling.pdf> (accessed 8 April 2007).

Daviron, B., Ponte, S., and Technical Centre for Agricultural and Rural Cooperation (Ede, Netherlands) (2005) *The Coffee Paradox: Global Markets, Commodity Trade, and the Elusive Promise of Development.* London: Zed.

Fairtrade Foundation (2002) *Spilling the Beans on the Coffee Trade.* London: Fairtrade Foundation. Online. Available HTTP: <http://www.fairtrade.org.uk/downloads/pdf/spilling.pdf> (accessed 5 May 2003).

Financial Times Information (2006) "Agriculture Vietnam seeks to join common code for coffee community. Vietnam News Briefs." Online. Available via LexisNexis (accessed 14 April 2007).

Giovannucci, D. and Koekoek, F.J. (2003) *The State of Sustainable Coffee: A Study of Twelve Major Markets,* London: ICO & IIED. Online. Available HTTP: <http://www.iisd.org/pdf/2003/trade_state_sustainable_coffee.pdf> (accessed 6 April 2007).

Goodland, R. (2002) "Sustainability: human, social, economic and environmental," in T. Munn and P. Timmerman (eds), *Encyclopedia of Global Environmental Changes,* Chichester: John Wiley and Sons.

Gourmet Retailer (2007) "McDonald's U.K. to serve all rainforest alliance certified coffee," 8 January. Online. Available HTTP: <http://www.gourmetretailer.com/

gourmetretailer/esearch/article_display.jsp?vnu_content_id=1003528901> (accessed via LexisNexis 7 April 2007).

Gresser C. and Tickell, S. (2002) *Mugged: Poverty in your Coffee Cup.* London: Oxfam Publishing. Online. Available HTTP: <http://www.oxfamamerica.org/newsandpublications/ publications/resear.ch_reports/mugged/mugged_coffee_report.pdf> (accessed 23 May 2003).

International Coffee Organization (2007) *Letter from the Executive Director – February 2007.* London: International Coffee Organization. Online. Available HTTP: <http://www. ico.org/documents/cmr0207e.pdf> (accessed 3 April 2007).

ISEAL Alliance (2003) *An Opportunity to Define International Standard-setting Procedures,* Kaslo, BC: ISEAL Alliance.

Kahn, A.E. (1988) *The Economics of Regulation: Principles and Institutions.* Cambridge, MA: MIT Press.

Kohler, P. (2007) *The Economics of Fair Trade Coffee: For Whose Benefit?: An Investigation into the Limits of Fair Trade as a Development Tool and the Risk of Cleanwashing.* Geneva: Graduate Institute of International Studies. Online. Available HTTP: <http://hei.unige.ch/sections/ec/pdfs/Working_papers/HEIWP06-2007.pdf> (accessed 8 April 2007).

May, P.H., Mascarenhas, G.C.C., and Potts, J. (2004) *Sustainable Coffee Trade: The Role of Coffee Contracts.* London: IISD. Online. Available HTTP: <http://www.iisd.org/ pdf/2004/sci_coffee_contracts.pdf> (accessed 8 April 2007).

Nagurney, A. (2006) *Supply Chain Network Economics: Dynamics of Prices, Flows and Profits.* Cheltenham, UK and Northampton, MA: Edward Elgar.

Ponte, S. (2004) *Standards and Sustainability in the Coffee Sector: A Global Value Chain Approach.* Winnipeg, MB: IISD. Online. Available HTTP: <http://www.iisd.org/pdf/ 2004/sci_coffee_standards.pdf> (accessed 8 April 2007).

Porter, M.E. (1998) *On Competition.* Boston, MA: Harvard Business School Press.

Reinhardt, F.L. (2000) *Down to Earth: Applying Business Principles to Environmental Management.* Boston, MA: Harvard Business School Press.

Roberts, A. (2002) "Bumper Brazilian crop prompts fears of glut," *Financial Times.* Online. Available HTTP: <http://www.ft.com> (accessed via LexisNexis 6 June 2007).

Singer, B. (2005) "Kenyan growers say 4c coffee code too costly for EA farmers," *Africa News,* 23 November. Online. Available via LexisNexis (accessed 7 April 2007).

Sorby, K. (2002a) *Coffee Market Trends,* (Background paper to World Bank Agricultural Technology Note 30, "Toward more sustainable coffee"), Washington D.C.: World Bank.

Sorby, K. (2002b) *What Is Sustainable Coffee?* (Background paper to World Bank Agricultural Technology Note 30, "Toward more sustainable coffee"), Washington, DC: World Bank.

Varangis, P., Siegel, P., Giovannucci, D., and Lewin, B. (2003) *Dealing with the Coffee Crisis in Central America: Impacts and Strategies.* Washington, DC: World Bank.

World Commission on Environment and Development (1987) *Our Common Future.* Oxford: Oxford University Press.

14 An initial exploration of sustainable work systems in China

An issue of imbalance between economic and social reform

Sharon Moore and Julie Jie Wen

Introduction

China is increasingly viewed as a dominant and essential participant in the global economic future. What social and business models is it building on? In particular, what are the impacts of reform and privatization on its work systems? The inherent conflict between traditional values and the requirements of contemporary capitalism is placing enormous pressures on China. What is disturbing is China's commitment to the development of its national economy even at the expense of environmental and social sustainability.

To date, sustainability, and especially sustainable work systems, are relatively new concepts in China. They are not even reflected yet in Chinese research literature, to say nothing of practice. On the contrary, there are frequent indications of lack of sustainability. This is evident in industrial disputes and daily examples of companies putting people and the environment at risk. In this research, we define "sustainable work systems" as those pertaining to the process of achieving personal and institutional goals within societal constraints. Sustainable work systems are based on "triple-bottom-line" management, i.e., management with special focus on ecological, economic, and social outcomes. This means the development of a more mutual and interdependent, systemic approach toward the management of sustainability (see also Chapters 12 and 13 in this volume). Our sustainability vision is for the adoption of a stakeholder perspective, with corporate accountability to stakeholders and respect for future generations, and wealth defined as increased and shared community value. This involves developing a new social and ecological contract, which involves the renewal of people and their environment. Our perspective has a focus on the connection between economic reforms and social sustainability, especially work–life balance, and our discussion is concerned with issues such as gender equality, family care provision, and career development as key areas on the social sustainability agenda. By examining current practice in China, we aim to provide some insights into how China's work systems may be improved.

Our research aims to discuss the impacts of reforms on work systems and to document problems originating from lack of awareness of the need for sustainability approaches. The chapter begins with a historical analysis of economic and social reform in China from 1978, to explore the hypothesis that globalization and work intensification together with the speed and direction of China's reforms have made the lives of Chinese people more prosperous and much more challenging and complex. Afterwards, this chapter identifies opinions from business leaders in a range of industries in China by drawing on surveys, interviews and focus group data collected in Guangzhou in 2003–2005. This section analyzes the experience, attitudes, and aspirations of middle to senior executives in contemporary China, including a focus on work and life issues. The data suggests that although economic reform has delivered economic growth, this has not been accompanied by a similar development in terms of sustainable social systems at work and in organizations. This is the major issue of our research, and one that requires further conceptualization and empirical analysis.

Overview of Chinese reform

During the past 30 years, China has been undergoing a process of transition from a centrally planned economy to a market-oriented economy. In 1978, the Third Plenary Session of the 11th National Congress of the Chinese Communist Party launched economic reform and an "Open Door" policy for China. It was announced that the Party would shift its focus from the ideological struggle to economic development. This would involve deregulating the state sector of the economy, restructuring state-owned enterprises and banks, dealing with bad debts, and radically reducing the regulations applying to the private sector. The first move was the decollectivization of agriculture; other reforms progressed gradually throughout the first half of the 1980s to encompass much of Chinese industry.

Thus, China's economic structure has recently undergone a significant change, with the private sector increasingly displacing the state-owned and collective sectors, and the manufacturing and service sectors expanding at the expense of agriculture (Mina and Perkins 1997). Recent economic reforms are even more systematic and fundamental. Instead of partial liberalization, the Government has adopted a package of policy changes in areas that require urgent attention. These include, for example, the reform of property rights, the roles of the state-owned enterprises (SOEs), factor markets, prices, goods distribution, social security, foreign trade, and government functions (Chen *et al.* 2006).

Nevertheless, the economy still faces serious interrelated challenges. First, Chinese policy is still locked on economic expansion without addressing the imbalances in the fundamental economic structure. It was the dream of the former president Jiang Zeming that, despite problems in the society, "efforts will be made to quadruple the GDP of the year 2000 by 2020 by optimizing structure and improving economic returns" (Jiang 2002). Second, the reform of the banking system is in jeopardy; there are problems especially when it comes to dealing with nonperforming loans. These could seriously increase the Government's fiscal burden and undermine growth prospects. Banks have been "transfusing blood" to SOEs with the government's approval. With over 25 percent of loans non-performing, the banks run a severe risk of not being able to meet their responsibility for funding and resourcing state-owned assets (Holz 2002). In addition, governmental attention will be needed in order to reduce the burden on peasants and to improve rural productivity (China Modernisation Research Centre 2007).

At the same time as this economic reform was taking place, social changes have been emerging. Traditional values and social structures are facing challenges as a result of globalization, increasing materialism, and changes in employment patterns. Following the privatization of the SOEs, redundant labour has been laid off, creating overwhelming demand for social welfare benefits in the absence of sufficient private insurance (Dong and Putterman 2003). As a result of economic restructuring, there are obvious funding shortfalls, where funds would previously have been allocated for social security and retirement benefit liabilities. This may well undermine longer-term social sustainability and the future security of the Chinese people (Appleton *et al.* 2002). Increasing disparity between the East Coastal area and Inland China, between urban and rural areas, between men and women, and between different industries and professions, has aggravated relative poverty in some social groups (Wen and Moore 2007; Chen *et al.* 2006). Researchers and policy makers, both within China and abroad, have expressed concerns about the lack of work–life balance, increasing stress and insecurity, sacrifice of equality and equity associated with privatization and reforms now seen in China (Liu, Chen, and Neysmith 2006; Moore and Wen 2006).

The study

Research was conducted with managers undertaking Master of Business Administration (MBA) studies in a joint venture between the Sydney Graduate School of Management and Kingold Education Centre, in Guangzhou, southern China. The aim of the study was to better understand the impacts of economic and social changes on work systems and social sustainability in China, mainly in terms of work–life balance and quality of working life, as well as career management issues in the contemporary China.

The business executives in the sample could be seen to represent a new element in China's burgeoning economy. They were well informed about the reform and its impact on industry, organization and society. They were open and informative, and extremely committed to their work and professional development. In fact, the MBA they were studying required them to complete one core unit per month over 12 months, with attendance at lectures over two weekends from Friday evening to Sunday evening, an essay due the following weekend and an exam on the fourth weekend of each month. Many commuted to the teaching venue from outlying regions and cities. Their study commitment was on top of full-time leadership and management roles in many of China's leading-edge businesses.

They were asked questions related to social sustainability issues, such as the impact of economic reform on their industry, their organization, and society, and how their life and career have been affected by the social changes resulting from privation and major economic restructuring. Information was collected about their position and role, what was important to them about their work, and their aspirations and concerns, both personally and professionally, in a rapidly changing environment. The following section presents an analysis of the study.

The empirical results

This study involves data collected from 322 respondents by using a single data collection instrument and questions during 2003 and 2005. Seventy-five subjects were surveyed in June, 2003; 84 in October, 2003; 86 in 2004, and 77 in June, 2005. Among the subjects, 226 were males and 96 were females. Interviews and focus groups were also conducted as part of the research. Participation was voluntary, with over a 90 percent response rate. (See Appendix 1 for details of the survey questions.) The majority of the business executives in the sample were married or partnered. Their ages ranged from mid-twenties to late forties, with most falling in the 30–35-year category. Most of those who were married had one child. More than half worked for large international companies, mainly European or North American, with the remainder employed in state-owned enterprises undergoing major economic reform and partial privatization.

Demographic observations

The following demographic data are for descriptive and analytical purposes. The survey data was collected in order to obtain an overall picture and identify any career and human management trends in the situation facing middle to senior managers in the sample population of MBA students. The focus was on the employment relationship experienced by the MBA students, and how it contributed to the social sustainability of their organizations and of society in general.

Although the average age of the business executives in the sample was around 35, a significant number did not give their age. During more detailed discussions, the researchers were given many examples of ageism in recruitment

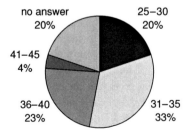

Figure 14.1 Age distribution in years

and promotion, resulting in respondents' fear of indicating their age. This reflects an increasingly competitive environment, in which managers, who traditionally were respected and revered for age and experience, are put into the position of competing for fewer positions in an increasingly globally competitive labour market. The result of competitive pressures is the reverse of the traditional Chinese attitude; the selection criteria in recruitment are now favouring younger managers from the private sector.

The skewed nature of the gender distribution (two-thirds male) in the surveys reflects the focus toward the prevalence of male managers in China, as elsewhere. In general terms, the equity agenda in China is rapidly growing less important with the progress of privatization. For example, the current proportion of male to female MBA students is in dramatic contrast to the decreasing numbers of female business executives' entry into MBA programs in China (Cai 2004). In the UWS–Kingold MBA program, the proportion of women business executives in the program has fallen from approximately 50 percent in intake one in 2001 to less than 20 percent in intake seven in 2005. This indicates a general worsening of management opportunities for talented women in business across many industries in China. It also reflects a move away from social sustainability and equity. Sustainable and sustaining corporations, which are committed to their employees, stakeholders, and communities, could be expected to have more diverse managerial staff in terms of age and gender.

Changes in industry sector

Changes in economic development and the introduction of new industries also pose challenges for social sustainability in China. Significant shifts in industries and their ownership patterns can be observed in this brief period. The relative proportion of managers from SOEs dropped markedly from 2003 to 2005 in our sample, as did that from joint ventures, while the proportion from solely foreign-owned and multinational companies rose sharply. This indicates the declining economic power of the state sector, and the shift from joint ventures to solely foreign-owned ventures as foreign direct investment (FDI) adjusts its entry criteria in China.

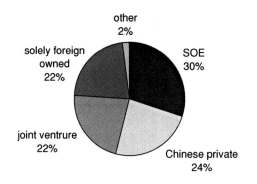

Figure 14.2 Industry ownership

Traditionally, SOEs and the public sector have supported equity and HRM programs much more actively than the private sector, reflecting a global pattern. For this reason, the burgeoning Chinese private sector dominated by multinational companies appears to be less active in supporting employees and business executives. This could also be interpreted as a weakness in the capitalist system. While sometimes it is thought that privatization is good as such, this indicates how a government-regulated system also may have good sides in terms of more equality-focused policies. For example, the emerging glass ceiling for female business executives in China is a result of economic changes toward privatization and growing dominance of multinational companies, with a corresponding lack of support for equal opportunity in employment (Liu *et al.* 2006; Wen and Moore 2007).

The sample reflects significant changes in industrial production in China. For example, the proportion of business executives from manufacturing industries among the students fell from 32 percent in the survey conducted in 2003 to 20 percent in the survey of June, 2005, with an average of 25 percent across all three surveys. Contrasting trends occurred in the finance, IT, and services/sales industries, where significant increases in the proportion of executives in the sample occurred in this very short period.

Career moves

A decrease in average length of employment with the same organization was also apparent, and was supported by numerous examples from the respondents. The researchers were told that the average time spent in an organization has decreased markedly, with younger business executives being more likely to move more frequently. Women and older respondents were less likely to change jobs.

This reflects the decrease in participation in MBA programs of business executives from SOEs in the sample. Traditionally, SOEs have been long-term employers with significant budgets for training and career development (Wen and Moore 2007). With the privatization of SOEs and more managers working in the private sector, employment length in any one organization seems to be on the

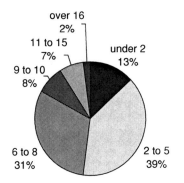

Figure 14.3 Years with the current organization

decrease. According to Justine Lau (2003), the average staff turnover rate in China is 11.7 percent per year, while the global average is estimated at between 3 percent and 7 percent. Frequent job change is a sign of choices for managers, but may also mean lower job security and lower engagement with the organization.

Increased career pressures

When asked whether reform has made business executives' situation more difficult, most respondents indicated that reform has improved their career opportunities. This reflects the general improvement in economic life and opportunities across China, particularly in the cities of southern China.

A surprisingly high "Yes" response (53 percent) to the question of whether increasing demands on employees, such as being asked to work longer hours and take on new and more demanding roles, have made respondents' life generally more difficult, reflected the common feeling of rising pressure.

However, decreasing community and family support for child rearing and continued commercialization of education have led to over 40 percent of respondents believing that life for women in business is becoming more difficult. This reflects the reality that women are still responsible for the great majority of unpaid work, including family support for children, and elder care, and also indicates men's reluctance to share the caring and domestic duties.

Lack of career advancement and promotional opportunities

Respondents were asked about such issues as how the type, size, and ownership model of their business contributed to satisfaction and increased work performance; what were the major threats to success and career development; and whether women and men were treated equally in employment. The respondents in this research were often very successful, particularly in international business, because of their skill levels and personal qualities. They felt that they were very well-regarded by senior management. However, they also reported that it was very difficult for Chinese-born business executives to get beyond middle level and operational management roles. Few respondents were members of top executive teams in the enterprises they worked in, particularly in international businesses. This seemed to be a serious concern warranting further attention, particularly as respondents were outperforming many of their superiors with overseas backgrounds (Wen and Moore 2007). The lack of opportunity to work internationally is considered a serious career limitation, and few of the respondents had worked overseas. However, the role and contribution of multinational companies are significant in China in terms of human resource management, the focus on global business, and the fact that working for a multinational corporation enables Chinese managers to experience international best practices, as well as set benchmarks for Chinese performance. Those respondents working for multinationals were experiencing the most positive work environment, albeit one that was increasingly stressful and competitive.

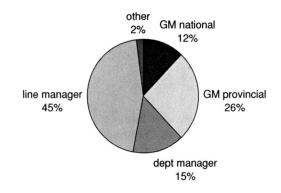

Figure 14.4 Roles and positions in businesses

Mentoring in the sense of professional and organizational development opportunities and assistance was minimal. Formal mentoring processes as such did not exist; what was available was informal and inconsistent. Few examples of formal and consistent ongoing professional development and executive leadership training were evident.

Although most of the respondents were optimistic about their career opportunities, there are warning signs for their professional advancement. For example, female business executives were mainly working in four management areas, sales and marketing, HR, finance, and administration, while men were clustered in IT, operations, and other specialist areas. Our research findings are supported by those of Cai (2004). This means limited opportunities for Chinese business executives to join top executive teams and obtain leadership roles unless they gain more generalist experience in finance, general management, and strategic leadership.

The dominant proportion of line business executives in the sample (45 percent) reflects two factors. First, a shift from systemic company support (paying for tuition and time allowance) to a more individually focused position (functional and line business executives are paying for their own studies to advance their careers to more strategic and general management roles). Second, the management market is more competitive and there is growing pressure to strive for better qualifications in order to adapt to more demanding jobs and short-term roles.

Economic reform and employment contracts

Respondents agreed that quality of working life was not a topic discussed in China, despite companies' talk of empowerment. Human resource management and industrial management are minimal, while command-and-control-style management remains firmly in place. For example, salary packages or employment contracts are designed to include performance-based payment and high bonuses that are difficult to achieve, so business executives are under enormous pressure. Only one business executive surveyed in 2003 was not subject to a contract mainly based on performance-based payment. This indicates an enormous change in a very short period. On the one hand, this represents a more flexible employment approach. However, it is not supported by commitment to workers' rights and entitlements. Many multinational companies will not allow employees to be members of trade unions, while the state-controlled trade union movement is more political than industrial in its role and activities. The international media and union movement are acutely aware of the repressive situation for Chinese labour, including its executive class, but are largely powerless to influence its development.

At the individual firm level, many business executives, especially some women, accepted a low rate of pay, as well as less flexible working arrangements. Few of the respondents enjoyed the flexibility of working virtually or flexibly in terms of core hours, job sharing, or family leave. The lack of effective human resource management and industrial relations management is further compounding the difficulties faced by business executives, most of whom are also parents and care-givers. The lack of human resource and industrial relations policy and practices is a serious challenge for Chinese business. The agenda of equity in working life is largely ignored, and unfair practices remain the norm. It is extremely unfortunate that work–life balance issues continue to be of little or no interest to Chinese companies, whether public, private, or foreign-owned. Thus, the lack of commitment to the social system is a serious challenge to social sustainability in China.

The widening gap for women in China today

The authors' ongoing research proposes that although the economic and social status of women continues to rise in China, the gap between career opportunities available to men and women shows little sign of narrowing (Wen and Moore 2007). In a society where men are traditionally regarded as superior, economic reforms actually undercut women's status by withdrawing state assistance and increasing gender-based inequality. Women are increasingly having to shoulder more responsibility for family duties, including child care and elder care, in the face of the withdrawal of social care provision. The changing policy context toward a mixed economy and neoliberalism further reinforces this trend (Moore and Wen 2004, 2006).

While gaining a foothold in the new economy and international business, women are also experiencing some negative impacts of China's next "great leap forward." The one-child policy, for example (also known as the "little emperor policy"), may result in a sense of loss for some executive women. For other working women, it may offer economic liberation/opportunity. Similar impacts are evident in changes in consumption patterns and increased wealth and materialism. Increasingly, women are being encouraged to leave paid employment for roles in the home, reminiscent of the post-World-War-II retreat to the home in some Western economies (Wen and Moore 2007).

The privatization of social care formerly provided by the state has caused a radical shift in thinking about care and caring. The ideology of care is now incorporating private care models for both children and old people, resulting in new challenges in terms of who pays and who are the care-givers. Quality education and training for care-givers are on the policy agenda, alongside a strong continuing commitment to family-based care provision. In this way, China has adopted Western care models in less than a decade in many parts of the country. Care-givers are being imported from rural and less industrialized areas to support the careers of working professionals and meet the needs of industrialization.

Work–life balance

With increasing intensification of work, and the 24/7 phenomenon (24 hours a day, 7 days a week), most of the respondents said they had little or no work–life balance. Business executives reported that challenges for balancing their professional and personal life were enormous. There were also clear emerging areas of concern in relation to parenting and elder care responsibilities. This finding may also reflect the traditional Chinese value of commitment and hard work, coupled with the business demand for 110 percent commitment, especially by private and family firms. As stated earlier, work–life balance is not deemed worthy of comment or analysis in China because of the overwhelming commitment to economic success.

Questions relating to responsibility for child and elder care resulted in answers from respondents that indicate declining public support for children and parents, and the need for our respondents to pay for private support. This indicates the general retreat from an equity agenda and less public commitment to social sustainability, including work–life balance issues. Economic reforms have brought dramatic changes to work units, including the demand for greater efficiency and a stronger profit orientation, usually resulting in shedding non-profitable occupational welfare roles (Liu *et al.* 2006). There is no work unit or government support for childcare except in some SOEs. Some parents get some support from their children's grandparents. This solution has limited applicability, as many of the business executives live far away from their parents and family community, in many cases in a different city or province. Adults still see themselves responsible for their parents, with many contributing financially.

Conclusion

The Chinese economy is facing many critical crossroads, especially the rapid transformation from a traditional agricultural society to a modern industrial society. Great changes have been seen in the relationship between rural and urban areas, between different regions, and between industries. Such changes are regarded as double-edged. On the one hand, they provide development opportunities for the Chinese economy; on the other hand, they impose many challenges to employment, population, resources, and environmental conditions in China. At present, the GDP per capita in China has reached US$1,200, which is treated as a "golden stage" for national economic development according to international practice (Research Group of State Council of China 2006). However, it is also an era of conflicts. The economy can only be developed smoothly if appropriate control is maintained at the macro level. Otherwise, it would take more time to reactivate the economy if it experienced a serious slump.

The Chinese management respondents interviewed face great challenges to work–life balance. They are affected on a very personal level by the intensification of work in global business environments, and are embracing these challenges with enthusiasm and some anxiety. Their lives are very different from those experienced by their parents, who raised their families during the Cultural Revolution, and their grandparents who grew up in pre-Revolutionary China. The speed at which change – both societal and personal – is occurring is breathtaking, and the path for business is very challenging.

In relation to economic and class differences, the women managers included in the research represent the emergence of a new executive class of Chinese women. In addition, Chinese society is rapidly constructing a set of economic and social relationships almost identical to the business and family experiences of Western business over the past quarter-century, a significant finding worth elaboration and more research, and one which offers further room for meaningful cross-learning.

Employment policy needs to include social as well as economic development. Health care, the education industry, and child and elder care are all key elements and are benchmarks of a civil society. International best practices derive from many leading examples of both corporations and small-to-medium-sized enterprises (SMEs) that have become "employers of choice" directly as a result of commitment to family and community issues. Productive diversity – valuing the contributions of all employees – means that all business employees are encouraged to contribute their experience and skills and are given appropriate support and recognition. However, this is a Western construct, and one which remains undeveloped as a concept in many Chinese organizations.

The research indicates that there are several factors to be recognized at a policy level in China today. There is a clear role for centralized planning in terms of coupling industrial development with social development, particularly at regional and local government levels. Families are being forced out of paid work by industrialization, and there is a huge army of potential care workers for the service sector. What is critical is that increasing mobility and migration patterns do not result in poor-quality informal care arrangements in the grey zone of an unregulated private care system. The current policy shift to a more "balanced scorecard" approach to planning that involves resourcing rural and less-developed regions is a welcome initiative. This would assist the development of a more equitable and sustainable balance between industrial production and social reproduction, including quality elder care and child care, among many other issues in the social sustainability context.

Most recent Chinese policy statements on sustainable business development highlight key areas for improvement, including the employment relationship, equal pay, equitable contracts, work conditions, and maternity leave (Research Group of State Council of China 2006). China is an economy in transition between plan and market. While the market mechanism now has been introduced throughout most of the economy, the complex task of establishing the necessary institutional framework to underpin and facilitate the operations of a market-based system is still in progress. However, it is clear that China's transition to a market economy is advancing strongly, and that this process is irreversible (EAU 2002).

The latest version of the *China Modernisation Report* (China Modernisation Research Centre 2007), compiled by experts and scholars from the Chinese Academy of Science, the Ministry of Science and Technology, and China's top universities, ranked China 100th on a list of 118 developed and developing nations in terms of sustainability. The consequent lack of social sustainability is implied rather than highlighted in this report, and yet it is a clear social and economic challenge. The critical period would be from 2010 to 2030, as industrialization and urbanization near completion (China Modernisation Research Centre 2007). It is urgent for China to address these challenges.

This chapter has been exploratory. It is an initial attempt to link economic reform strategy with actual business developments. Thus it aims to assess the impact of economic reform and related social changes at both macro and micro levels. However, what is evident is the lack of attention to a sustainable work system approach, particularly in terms of social sustainability. Meanwhile the authors remain cautiously optimistic. While sustainable work systems are yet to be realized in contemporary China, there are beginning signs that the government is aware of a need to change the practice from rhetoric to reality, particularly focussing on the need for local and regional government reform implementation.

Questions for reflection

Here are three questions for your further reflection on the issues broached in this chapter:

- How can improving sustainable work systems be incorporated into the process of reform, especially in the context of increasing corporatization, decentralization, and privatization?
- In this new era for China, will the opportunities and conditions of working life for women be any different (a) from those in the past and (b) from those in Western experience? How might any of the following elements contribute to change: feminist leadership; social legislation; strong media models; intellectual leadership; work-based child care; a return to publicly provided social infrastructure?
- How are the work systems of workers different from those of the respondents in this research, i.e. of managers?

References

Appleton, S., Knight, J., Song, L., and Xia, Q. (2002) "Labor retrenchment in China, determinants and consequences," *China Economic Review*, 13, 2–3, 252–275.

Cai, Zhiming (2004) "Analysis of Chinese women in joint ventures," http://theory.people.com.cn/GB/index.html (accessed 16 May 2006).

Chen, G., Gu, C., and Wu, F. (2006) "Urban poverty in the transitional economy: a case of Nanjing, China," *Habitat International*, 30, 2006, 1–26.

China Modernisation Research Centre (2007) *China Modernisation Report: China Environmental Modernisation Study*, China Academy of Science, Beijing: Beijing University Publishing House.

Dong, X.Y. and Putterman, L. (2003) "Soft budget constraints, social burdens, and labor redundancy in China's state industry," *Journal of Comparative Economics*, 31(1): 110–133.

EAU (Economic Analytical Unit) (2002) *China Embraces the World Market*, Canberra: Department of Foreign Affairs and Trade.

Holz, C. (2002) "Long live China's state-owned enterprises: deflating the myth of poor financial performance," *Journal of Asian Economics*, 13, 4, 493–529.

Jiang, Zeming (2002) "Building a Well-off Society in a All-Round Way and Create a New Situation in Building Socialism with Chinese Characteristics," 16th Party Congress of CCP, Beijing: Beijing Publishing House.

Lau, J. (2003) "China's growth puts staff in a spin," *Financial Times*, October 30, http://news.ft.com/home/asia (accessed on 18 June 2005).

Liu, M., Chen, X., and Neysmith, S. (2006) *Women and Social Work in China*, Beijing: Beijing Publishing House.

Moore, S. and Wen, J. (2004) "Economic reform and business management in China today," *International Journal of Applied Management*, 5, 2, 66–84.

Moore, S. and Wen, J. (2006) "Reform of state owned enterprises and challenges in China," *Journal of Technology Management in China*, 1, 3, 279–291.

Mina, G. and Perkins, F. (1997) *China's Transitional Economy – Between Plan and Market*, Canberra: Department of Foreign Affairs and Trade.

Research Group of State Council of China (2006) *China Sustainable Development Strategy Report*, Beijing: China Science Press.

Wen, J. and Moore, S. (2007) "Economic reform, urban women and 'hidden poverty' in China," in C. Tistell (ed.), *Poverty, Poverty Alleviation and Social Disadvantage: Analysis, Case Studies and Policy*, New Delhi: Serials Publications, pp. 738–749.

Appendix 1: survey questionnaire, China

1. Your Age: Your Gender: (   ) M or (   ) F
    Marital status: (   ) Married; (   ) Single; (   ) Divorced
    Number of Children: _____
    If married, is your spouse in paid work? (   ) Yes or (   ) No

2. What is your salary per year? $_____; What is your position? _____

3. What proportion of your salary is performance based?

4. How long have you been with the current organization? _____ years

5. What are the challenges to your career (please rank 1 to 5 in order of importance)?
    (   ) Globalization & economic restructuring; (   ) Mergers and acquisitions

( ) Economic cycle; ( ) Organizational restructuring
( ) Ageist attitudes; ( ) Sexist attitudes
( ) Cultural barriers; ( ) Family roles and care duties
( ) Health; ( ) Other (please describe)

6. Are women and men treated equally in your organization in terms of:
    a. Senior appointment at executive and board level: ( ) Yes ( ) No
    b. Job security: ( ) Yes ( ) No
    c. Promotional opportunities: ( ) Yes ( ) No
    d. Remuneration: ( ) Yes ( ) No
    e. International postings: ( ) Yes ( ) No
    f. Interstate postings: ( ) Yes ( ) No
    g. Other opportunities (please describe): ( ) Yes ( ) No

7. What kind of business are you in (please tick one)?
    a. Manufacturing   b. Services
    c. IT   d. Finance / insurance
    e. Other (please describe)

    What is the size of your business (no. of employees):

8. Ownership of business:
    a. Public   b. Private
    c. Family-owned business d. Foreign-owned company
    e. Other (please describe)

9. Is your company involved in international business?   ( ) Yes   ( ) No
    If no, do you think international business a source of competitive advantage and potential growth strategy?   ( ) Yes   ( ) No

    If yes, please answer the following questions:

10. What percentage of the business is international?

11. Describe the business approach, partnership arrangement, management, and leadership issues

12. What are your business's growth strategies? New markets? Future directions?

13. Is triple-bottom-line planning part of your international business strategy (are you trying to integrate the people side of the business with the economic and environmental strategy)?

    If yes, how is sustainability addressed?

14. Are you hoping to work internationally in your current organization in the next three years?

    If yes, what country or region do you plan to work in, and why?

15. What additional preparation and resources do you need for global management role?

16. Please describe the top three concerns and challenges in your career. What are their sources? What strategies would you recommend to deal with them?

    Sharon Moore and Julie Wen thank you for your assistance. If you want a copy of the research findings, please leave your email address.

Part V

Future of sustainable work systems

15 Sustained by work

Individual and social sustainability in work organizations

Mari Kira and Frans M. van Eijnatten

Introduction

The classical description defines sustainability as the satisfaction of our current needs in a way that does not endanger the satisfaction of the needs of future generations (World Commission on Environment and Development 1987). Such definition talks about the utilization of various resources in a way that does not destroy or impoverish them or endanger the process through which they become regenerated. Even though resources are utilized to satisfy current needs, they also are left intact for future utilization. When applied to working life, the concept of sustainability means that a work organization operates in a way that does not deplete the various resources involved – the human and social resources along with the economic and ecological resources. Indeed, we would like to set an even stricter criterion for organizational sustainability. A sustainable work organization not only preserves the resources it utilizes, but actually supports their growth and development. This is because an organization, in addition to utilizing the various resources, is also formed by them. In order to develop itself, an organization has to promote the development of its resources (see also Chapters 2 to 6 in this volume).

This chapter focuses on work-organizational sustainability in regard to human and social resources. Our aim is to explore how employees individually and collectively can be sustained by work or, in other words, how human and social resources may be developed and integrated at work. Our underlying proposition is that the development and integration of various human and social resources supports individuals and organizations to find ways to function when facing challenges. And precisely this ability to function is, in our approach, the key to human and social sustainability.

The chapter is organized as follows. First, we will provide further definition of what we mean by human and social sustainability in work organizations. We will define some concepts (such as functional capacity and the complexity of resources) that have a central role in sustainability in individuals, groups, and organizations. We will also identify those human and social resources that need to be sustained in work organizations. We discuss sustainability separately in people and in organizations, and we also pay special attention to the way that sustainability deals with both the tangible and intangible aspects of people and organizations. Finally, we will discuss organizational development and design, to recognize some paths through which sustainability can be promoted.

Sustainability: complexity of resources and functional capacity

We define a sustainable work organization as an organization that is continuously changing and developing in order to be able to function in the changing situations it faces. A sustainable organization is able to adapt to its environment, and also is able to be creative, critical, and proactive (see also Chapters 3, 9, and 11 in this volume). Both adapting and shaping new possibilities for existence are keys to sustainability (e.g., Hart and Milstein 1999). Therefore, at the work-organizational level, we define sustainability as *a sustained functional capacity* or an ability to at times adapt, and at times proactively create new opportunities. As long as an organization is able to function in some form or manner, there is a chance that it can sustain itself in the face of emerging challenges.

Throughout this book, sustainability is defined as a multilevel and multiactor phenomenon aiming at the simultaneous development of various organizational stakeholders. Therefore, in order to reach not only longevity but sustainability, a sustainable organization sustains its functional capacity by promoting the sustainability of its human and social resources, and also its economic and ecological resources. In line with work-organizational sustainability, we define the sustainability of human and social resources as deriving from an ability to function when facing different life and work events. Employees and groups need to be able to create new work opportunities, to adapt to emerging events, and to find ways to change their situations. Individuals, groups, and whole organizations stand a chance to influence their destinies in a positive manner when they are able to function. Therefore, we define human and social sustainability in working life as the ability of employees, groups, and organizations to keep on functioning in any situation faced.

An ecosystem is sustainable when it is able to adapt to environmental changes, which is made possible by its biodiversity. Sustaining an ecosystem requires, therefore, securing its biodiversity (see, e.g., Holling and Gunderson 2002). But what are the resources to be sustained in organizations and in employees that make it possible for them to be sustainable and able to function? Biodiversity has to do with the richness of diverse biological resources, and also with the integration of these resources into a resilient ecosystem. By analogy, we suggest that *the complexity of resources* is the foundation for the functional capacity and consequent sustainability both in organizations and employees. The concept of complexity is used in various ways in various scientific fields, but many of the definitions of complexity share the same basic idea: complexity stands for *the uniqueness of system elements and their integration into a coherent whole* (e.g., Heylighen 1999). Complexity is thus different from complicatedness: complexity refers to valuable distinct resources that have found an optimal integration among themselves. We propose that both an employee's and an organization's ability to function in a sustainable manner are founded on the complexity of their resources – on the uniqueness of distinct resources and their harmonious integration into a whole person or a whole organization.

Sustainable employees and sustainability-conducive work experiences

When it comes to individual employees, the complexity of resources means a coherent integration of distinct personal and professional resources. The various skills, pieces of knowledge, mental models, beliefs, and other diverse resources of a sustainable employee have grown unique and valuable, and are integrated into a well-functioning whole, into a person and a self. A sustainable employee is thus a highly complex being with rich, integrated resources.

Such complexity shows both in an individual's thoughts and actions. For instance, instead of holding a simplistic, one-dimensional view of reality, a complex self is able to consider even contradictory ideas and perceive the world as a many-dimensional, yet integrated place. Such complex comprehension of the world provides an individual with a rich repertoire of alternative ways to mentally respond to events faced. A complex self is also able to take action in various situations due to such complex comprehension of the world and the possession of various skills and competencies (cf. Antonovsky 1987). The complexity of individual resources thus promotes both mental and action-related functioning. Furthermore, Csikszentmihalyi (1990) states that complex persons are also able to combine successfully their individuality and social integration. Csikszentmihalyi (*ibid.*: 41) formulates this in the following way:

> Differentiation implies a movement towards uniqueness, toward separating oneself from others. Integration refers to [. . .] a union with other people, with ideas and entities beyond self. A complex self is one that succeeds in combining these opposite tendencies.

In sum, a sustainable individual has valuable and integrated personal resources that help in comprehending and managing life's situations, and that allow the individual to function both alone and as a part of a social community. However, we would like to emphasize that employees' functional capacity also depends on motivation. It is not enough for individuals to have various unique and integrated skills or to be unique persons able to integrate with others, if they do not *want to* use these skills and engage in interactions with others. Only when individuals find work meaningful do they experience the demands they encounter as being worth an investment of energy, commitment, and engagement, and exert an effort to carry out their work (Antonovsky 1987). It is clear that a sense of meaningfulness is an additional, vital element in securing individuals' ability to function.

An organization wanting to support the functional capacity and sustainability of its employees needs, therefore, to look for ways:

1)   to promote employees' mental models and comprehension of work to grow more complex;
2)   to enable employees to take actions and learn to manage in various work situations;
3)   to support employees' sense of meaningfulness at work.

But how, in practice, can this be done?

Employees' more complex mental models and more complex comprehension of work can be supported by work experiences that carry a wealth of information and transmit a full picture of the complexities of work (Antonovsky 1987). Work should, therefore, be "transparent." In transparent work, employees are able to see the material and information flows, causes and effects, stakeholders and priorities in their work. An organization should therefore devise ways to provide its employees with information about work processes and outcomes, as well as about the demands emerging from the various stakeholders, such as customers or environmental regulations. Also the way individual jobs have been designed plays a role in rendering work transparent and informative. Each job has to consist of a coherent set of tasks forming an understandable whole (e.g., Thorsrud and Emery 1969). Fragmented tasks and jobs only transmit fragmented pictures of workplace events, while coherent and whole work can render visible the complexities of work.

Employees' functional capacity is further promoted by work experiences that allow employees to devise specific sophisticated work actions that integrate into a comprehensive work performance. Sustainable work thus also promotes the growing complexity of employees' work activities. A fundamental factor in contributing to employees' ability to take actions and manage work situations relates to the availability of tangible, intangible, social, and personal resources (Antonovsky 1987). The resources available for and usable to employees should be in balance with the demands set by the situation (Karasek and Theorell 1990): both overload and "underload" reduce the action potential of employees. A continuous overload on resources decreases employees' belief that they can manage in the situation. In each working situation, there needs to be a balance, for example, between time required to carry out a task and time available for it, between the extent of the task and the level of staffing. But also underload may hamper employees' preparedness to take actions. Employees with monotonous jobs start over time to feel that they will not be able to manage disruptions of even the most basic kind; they lose their ability to take actions (see Chapter 5 in this volume).

The experience of meaningfulness at work necessitates room for personal choices. Being externally directed tends to reduce personal engagement in the activity and make it meaningless. Work experiences that promote employees' functional capacity therefore support employees' complex and personal engagement at work: they can participate both in various work events and also in shaping their work – e.g., its priorities, boundaries, and methods (see Chapter 4 in this volume). A sense of meaningfulness requires also that employees can perceive the whole work process and their connections to it as meaningful. Such sense of meaningfulness derives from employees' personal values, but also from the way society in general evaluates their work and work organization (see, e.g., Antonovsky 1987).

The functional capacity of employees is, therefore, founded on complex mental models of work, on sophisticated and integrated (complex) ways to act and manage in work situations, and on a complex engagement and sense of meaningfulness at work. To promote such functional capacity of its employees, a sustainable organization advances its employees' knowledge of what their work is all about and how it contributes to a product or service to a customer. This promotes the development of more complex mental models of work and sense of meaningfulness. Developing and maintaining the ability to take actions in the face of sudden overload or underload situations at work necessitate that work be usually characterized by a balance between work demands and available organizational resources. A sustainable organization thus actively seeks to balance various resources and demands at work. Being appreciated as an equal partner at work and being appreciated for the work one is doing also promote employees' engagement at work and their motivation to keep on functioning. That is why a sustainable organization establishes ways of showing appreciation for each and every employee and also creates jobs where employees can directly make a difference to their collaborators and customers.

Social sustainability in organizations

The complexity of resources at the work-organizational level means first that employees are able to grow more complex through their work experiences: this is the human aspect of social complexity discussed above. In addition, the complexity of social resources depends on the integration among the sustainable, complex employees. The whole organization gains potential for sustainable functioning when its complex employees integrate into coherent work groups, teams, and networks. Integrated and interacting employees cocreate and share mental models, social structures, and operation practices that enable them to operate collectively. In an analogy to the individual-level motivation, the organizational ability to function depends strongly on the shared will to keep on functioning. At the organizational level, a shared sense of meaningfulness originating from shared values and sense of purpose is needed to allow an organization to remain functional as whole (see also Chapters 2 and 3 in this volume).

A sustainable organization thus builds on the integration of its unique members, and from this integration something further emerges – group-level and organizational-level phenomena that can be shared by, but go beyond, individual members. However, in an optimally complex organization, the integration of distinct individuals is not too tight, but flexible. There still remains room for diverse, even contradictory, ideas that can be constructively debated. That is why in a sustainable organization, the shared mental models, structures, and practices end up being not one-dimensional, but complex: they all are characterized by wholeness growing from the flexible integration among different points of view. As the explicit aim in a sustainable organization is to allow the integration of various points of view, shared mental models and operation methods integrate both a deep and broad understanding of various interconnected issues of the work situations. For instance, business, social, and ecological outcomes will be equally emphasized in a complex, sustainable organization.

Therefore, an important aspect of the functional capacity and, therefore, sustainability of an organization is the integration among its employees. An organization does not grow more complex and sustainable if its employees develop individually without any development in their integration. This simply results in an organization with many "star players" but little collective power as a team. Similarly, better integration in an organization without any development in the individuals does not lead to sustainability either, but instead creates a peculiar system of good collaboration between people who have very little new to say to each other. Organizational sustainability requires, first, that its members grow more complex in their thoughts and actions and find their work meaningful and worth the effort. Second, these members have to be able to learn jointly and become better integrated into groups, departments, and an organization with shared, complex mental models and action patterns. To promote this kind of sustainability, an organization has to be approached as a network of interacting individuals and groups whose development hangs together (see also Chapters 7, 8, and 11).

To illustrate the challenges in such integration, we turn to an empirical example from Kira and Frieling (2007). They studied manufacturing workplaces in which employees have many opportunities to learn and develop during their daily work. Work takes place in autonomous shift groups; each shift group has the responsibility to operate a manufacturing machine during a shift. A group decides how tasks are divided among the group members, solves any emerging problems, and devises new work methods. A complex comprehension of the work is supported by information flows within the groups and by jobs designed to cover all tasks to be performed on a machine. This latter factor also contributes to the employees' ability to take actions and manage their work; they learn all the distinct work actions that integrate to comprehensive performance on the machine. The group-level autonomy makes the group members proud of what they do, and they experience their work as meaningful. Kira and Frieling (*ibid.*) document how, at the individual and group level, learning and complexity development take place.

However, there are several machines of similar type and several shift groups working on these machines: these machines and groups form an integrated whole, a production system. The employees from various machines and shift groups have very few opportunities to communicate with each other and share shift-group-specific new ideas. There are few, if any, forums for the employees to convene and learn together. Even promising ideas from specific shift groups go unshared. The collective complexity development that might originate from an organizationally supported interaction among the production system's employees and groups does not take place. This is frustrating for the increasingly complex individuals, and the organization as a whole misses many opportunities to develop more complex mental models of work and operating practices.

The need for integration has clear implications for the power relations in an organization. In the example above, the employees are not able to develop together because the organizations in question harbour a tacit mental model according to which organizational renewal is the task of the managers rather than the employees. Consequently, meetings for idea exchange are not arranged with employees, and ideas from particular shift groups or individuals cannot become seeds for organizational transformation. It is therefore important for employees and managers to also perceive employees as sources for complexity development. This probably is one of the greatest challenges for work-organizational sustainability. In order to reach true social sustainability – the complexity development at both individual and collective levels – an organization has to establish its operations on a basis of power equality instead of top-down authority. This is because solutions for individual and collective complexity development are created in action. They cannot be stipulated by managerial decisions, only fostered by managerial choices that give room for interaction and employee influence.

The complexity of interior and exterior resources

The chapter thus far has discussed individual, social, and organizational sustainability growing from the complexity of resources and from the consequent functional capacity. This section and the following one focus on two specific and intriguing aspects of sustainability shared by all these aggregation levels, yet only implicitly addressed above. First, we draw attention to the fact that sustainability is not only a structural or "exterior" matter, but also engages the "interior" domains of people and organizations. Second, we will discuss the dynamics involved in creating sustainability and emphasize how reaching toward sustainability means both conscious efforts and patience for an organic change. It also means both creating something new and letting go of the old.

From the discussion above, it is clear that functional capacity at both employee and organizational levels depends not only on the tangible or exterior aspects; also many intangible or interior aspects play a role in sustainability (see also Wilber 1996). We have, for instance, discussed how the functional capacity of employees is secured only when they are able to develop a more complex comprehension of their work situation and when they are able to experience work activities as meaningful. Both of these refer to interior, rather than exterior development. We, nevertheless, also emphasized that employees' sustainable functional capacity refers to an ability to take action in various situations; this refers to exterior, expressive development. Also, at the organizational level, we have characterized sustainable functional capacity as depending equally on the complexity of shared mental models and the presence of viable action alternatives.

If we return to the workplace-learning study discussed above (Kira and Frieling 2007), development in the workplaces studied has had a rather one-sided focus on the exterior aspects of the organization. The aim of these workplaces has been to increase flexibility, competence, and competitiveness, and they have made a structural decision to establish autonomous shift groups as learning and working environments for employees. However, this exterior change has also caused interior changes. Individual employees and shift groups have not only learned new professional actions. Kira and Frieling (*ibid.*) point out how the employees have also started to consider improved methods for the production processes as a whole. The professional actions are now more complex, and the comprehension of the whole system and the sense of purpose in relation to its improvement have become more complex as well. The employees would like to share their insights on work and ways of working with others. However, management has not been prepared for this interior development. Traditional top-down approaches to organizational development remain, leaving employees little opportunity to change the system they are part of and thus express their interior development. Collective learning is not taking place as the employees have few opportunities to share their ideas, interpret them with others, and integrate them into the collective ways to comprehend, manage, and find meaning at work (see also Crossan *et al.* 1999; Chapter 11 in this volume). Therefore, the research indicates how individual and collective functioning abilities are not truly promoted when only exterior aspects are paid attention to.

The development and design of complex individual and social resources

The development toward the complexity of human, social, and organizational resources can take place in two interrelated ways: through organic, spontaneous development processes or through planned design efforts (see, e.g., Trullen and Bartunek 2007). When it comes to spontaneous development, in any given workplace people learn and create new ways to work and collaborate every day. Complexity development at the employee level is a consequence of such unpredictable processes of workplace learning. This complexity development is *an emergent process* in the sense that it cannot be preplanned or controlled (see, e.g., Fitzgerald 2002; van Eijnatten 2004; van Eijnatten and van Galen 2005). At the organizational level, new complexity – a new integration among complex individuals – is similarly forged in daily interaction, in the exchange and elaboration of ideas and ways of working. Both managers and employees are contributors to these emergent collective processes.

However, this type of emergent development may be precarious for two reasons. It can take place in a haphazard fashion and not be benefited from; just as was the case in the workplace-learning study of Kira and Frieling. Emergent development may end up being partial development: individuals or distinct resources may develop, but systemic development is not achieved. The complexity of resources does not grow. That is also why this kind of organic, emergent development has to be founded on a shared goal. We suggest the enhancement of complexity in human and social resources as a general developmental goal. Both individual and collective workplace learning should aim at the development of distinct resources and at the integration of these resources into a coherent, functioning whole.

In addition to the danger of partial, haphazard development, there is also another risk. When left to develop on its own, the integration formed among organizational elements can turn to rigidity (cf. Holling and Gunderson 2002). In a rigid organization, unique resources and established integration patterns among them are not questioned or altered even in the face of an environmental change or opportunity. The organization thus becomes unresponsive to the environment and loses its creativity. In this situation, an organization needs to regain its viability by letting go of the existing answers and by making room for change. This is the stage for planned, goal-oriented development with an aim to assess the existing complexity, find the areas of stagnation, devise a way to break up the old complexity, and till the earth for new complexity to grow. Unpredictable and organic development needs, at times, to be accompanied by orderly, planned development.

For instance, van Aken (2007) outlines such planned development from the perspective of design science. The aim can be to create a new organizational design – a model of distinct resources and their integration – that can put the organization back on the track of sustainable functioning. However, van Aken also emphasizes that one cannot make a new work-organizational design, implement it, and expect it to work. Instead, work-organizational design is not simply a model, but a process of participative actions. Design, as a process, starts with formal recognition of a problem and explicitly stated development goals. After that, a task force may develop a "first design" – a general, yet well-grounded, model of the new organizational complexity (the new resources and their interaction). But the first design is not the final design. The members of the organization need to appropriate it, mould it, and contextualize it. Further still, when a new solution has been thus found, the members of the organization need to engage in emergent learning processes through which the new type of complexity is brought to life. The organization returns to the emergent and organic phase of development.

Managing a work organization in a sustainable manner thus means mastering two types of situations wisely: carefully honing the emergence of complexity in individuals and the work groups they form, and being sensitive about the need for letting go when the existing approaches for comprehending, acting, and attaching meaning to work become outdated. A sustainable organization is thus not a stable structure. During its life, it strives to maintain its functional capacity by reaching higher levels of resource complexity. But it also changes and relinquishes structures and solutions once found. Moreover, it may also – partly or wholly – cease to exist. What is important is that the growth in the complexity of resources has also been supported in the parts of an organization (e.g., in employees) during its existence. In this sense, the heritage of a sustainable work organization is conducive to future sustainable functioning of those who have been its members (see Chapter 8 in this volume).

Conclusion

Sustainability has much to do with the interconnected nature of the world. First, the need for sustainability grows from this interconnectedness. As human, social, economic, and ecological resources influence one another across space and time, it is not possible to develop only some of them while disregarding the others. In the long term, these resources can only maintain their functioning abilities together. To reach not only relative longevity but also sustainability, an organization has to promote the sustainable development of all resources engaged in its operations. Second, the interconnected nature of the world provides pathways toward sustainability. Development in one resource can give rise to wider development processes. In this chapter, we have focused on how the development of human complexity can offer seeds for social and organizational complexity: learning and development among employees provides a foundation for collective workplace learning. Similarly, we have discussed how providing opportunities for interconnected exterior (action-related) and interior (comprehension- and meaningfulness-related) complexity development is needed to secure employees' and organizations' ability to function. Moreover, the cyclically connected emergence and disappearance of complexity have been recognized as characteristic of dynamic functional capacity in the changing world.

The movement toward social sustainability in organizations takes place on two different levels – in the ways work tasks and activities are shaped and in the ways the whole organizational system is understood, analyzed, and developed. When it comes to sustainable work, we have especially emphasized participation and interaction as paths toward sustainability. Alone and together, employees have to be able to access work events and information that makes the work situation comprehensible. They have to be able to take action to manage their work situation and to maintain the functional capacity of the organization as a whole. Only through social integration and self-directed participation in work events does the sense of meaningfulness grow. When it comes to socially sustainable organizations, we have argued for integration between employees and power equality, which allow employees to shape their organizations. We have also discussed the importance of proactive dynamics in an organization: in order to remain sustainable, an organization has to allow its complexity to fluctuate.

Table 15.1 summarizes the main messages from this chapter. We recognize the three basic design elements promoting individual and work-organizational sustainability. Each element can be translated into concrete design goals and tasks that an organization can pursue when striving to promote human and social sustainability, and also organizational sustainability.

The first design element emphasizes the creation of interactive organizations with power equality. Both employees and managers shape an organization and, in order to promote individual and collective complexity development, the opportunities of both groups to influence their work and the organization as whole should be promoted. In practise, actors who should be involved in dialogue with an aim of joint learning have to be recognized in dynamic fashion (e.g., "Should

Table 15.1 Summary: some design elements and tasks to promote human and social sustainability in organizations

Design element	Meaning of the design element	Design tasks for managers and employees	Some tools for design
Interactive organization with power equality (e.g., Heckscher 1994)	• Both employees and managers are understood to shape an organization with their thoughts and actions. • Collective learning is supported to take place in free, equal, dynamic interaction.	• Continuous redesign of collaborative connections based on emerging work-related needs. • Identifying collaboration needs and arranging opportunities for collaboration to take place. • Engagement in collective learning: sharing one's learning, learning from others.	• Dialogue (e.g., Bohm 1996) • Post-bureaucratic power approaches
Organization with sensitivity to interior and exterior aspects (e.g., Wilber 1996)	• People have innate need for action, and also for comprehending and experiencing meaningfulness (Antonovsky 1987). • Individual and collective mental models shape reality at least as much as structural choices or external actions (see Fitzgerald 2002).	• The aim of work design: Not only manageable, but also comprehensible and meaningful work. • Identifying shared mental models: Do they allow us to develop? • Continuous reflection on and development of individual and shared mental models of work and work organization.	• Dialogue • Reflection
Dynamic learning and development processes toward higher levels of complexity	• Sustainability as a functional capacity is founded on the complexity of system resources. • By definition, complexity grows only when parts and a whole develop at the same time. • Complexity emerges from learning in individuals and collectives. • Complexity dynamics: emergent development and intentional dismantling of outdated solutions.	• Space and time are reserved for comprehending (making sense of) work, and finding ways to design it to be manageable and meaningful. • Space and time is reserved for sharing and interpreting learning. • Planned design is initiated by managers or employees at the first sign of stagnation.	• Dialogue • Reflection • Collective and individual workplace learning (e.g., Kira and Frieling 2007) • Design approaches (e.g., van Aken 2007)

our group meet with the neighbouring group to develop a new work method?"). Both employees and managers need to be aware of their integration and their impact on organizational complexity development: they need to share the outcomes of their own learning and engage in learning with others. In practice, this design element can be realized in an organization with such tools as dialogue (e.g., Bohm 1996) and post-bureaucratic power approaches (see, e.g., Heckscher 1994) acknowledging that the power to change the organization originates from many sources in an organization, not only from its hierarchical top.

The second design element calls attention to addressing both interior and exterior aspects in work and work-organizational development. For instance, complexity-promoting work design has to recognize that human and social functional capacity depend on complex comprehension and an innate sense of meaningfulness at work, as well as on expressive ability to take action. In all work and organizational development, it should be remembered how individual and collective mental models shape reality in equal measure with structural choices and external actions. Therefore, in addition to structural and procedural solutions, organizational development should address – through reflective, dialogical processes – such issues as shared mental models of work and its priorities, or the experienced meaningfulness of current work and organizational purpose and design.

The final design element emphasizes the continuous processes of learning and unlearning that create higher levels of complexity and also release complexity that has turned to rigidity. Complexity is perceived as a resource – the richness of unique resources and their dynamic interaction – at individual and collective levels. By definition, it is acknowledged that individuals with few personal development opportunities and with few opportunities for interaction cannot form a complex, functioning organization. Equally, in a loose organization with little ambition to be complex and functioning, individuals find fewer opportunities to grow and develop. This element of organizational sustainability also emphasizes how an organization actually is a verb rather than noun, a process rather than state. Striving toward higher levels of complexity means continuous *organizing* that aims at providing employees and groups new ways to develop and flourish in their work (see also Chapters 2 and 4 in this volume). Space and time are reserved for making sense of and comprehending work and making it manageable and meaningful. As things change in and around an organization, this has to be done continuously in collaboration between employees and their closest managers. Similarly, space and time are reserved for sharing and interpreting learning – thus turning it into individual and collective complexity development. In addition to such daily activities of organizing, both managers and employees are alert to stagnation. They sound the alarm for more formal design processes to start when resources and interactions created earlier are no longer responsive to challenges and opportunities faced. Tools such as dialogue, reflection, collective and individual workplace learning, and design approaches are used to achieve dynamic emergence and disappearance of complexity.

Questions for reflection

Here are three questions for your further reflection on the issues broached in this chapter:

• In traditional sociotechnical systems the semi-autonomous work group or self-managing team is the ultimate goal of structural change. What exactly is designed and aimed for as an ultimate goal in a sustainable work organization?

• In this chapter we discuss complexity and complicatedness. What is the difference between the two concepts? Can you think of concrete examples in a work organization?

• Sustainable work organizations can be seen as a next phase in the development of working life. What do you think of the following statement: In a sustainable work organization, managers should no longer strive for workers' productivity? Explain your reasoning in terms of either/or and both/and logic.

References

Aken, J.E. van (2007) "Design science and organization development interventions: aligning business and humanistic values," *Journal of Applied Behavioral Science*, 43, 1, 67–88.

Antonovsky, A. (1987) *Unraveling the Mystery of Health: How people manage stress and stay well*, San Francisco: Jossey-Bass Publishers.

Bohm, D. (1996) *On Dialogue*, London: Routledge.

Crossan, M.M., Lane, H.W., and White, R.E. (1999) "An organizational learning framework: from intuition to institution," *Academy of Management Review*, 24, 3, 522–37.

Csikszentmihalyi, M. (1990) *Flow: the Psychology of Optimal Experience*, New York: Harper Perennial.

Eijnatten. F.M. van (2004) "Chaordic systems thinking: some suggestions for a complexity framework to inform a learning organisation," *The Learning Organization*, 11, 6, 430–449.

Eijnatten. F.M. van and Galen, M.C. van (2005) "Provoking chaordic change in a Dutch manufacturing firm" in K.A. Richardson (ed.), *Managing Organisational Complexity. Volume I: Philosophy, Theory, and Application*, Greenwich, CT: Information Age Publishing, pp. 521–56.

Fitzgerald, L.A. (2002) "Chaos, the lens that transcends," *Journal of Organizational Change Management*, 15, 4, 339–58.

Hart, S.L. and Milstein, M.B. (1999) "Global sustainability and the creative destruction of industries," *Sloan Management Review*, 41, 23–33.

Heckscher, C. (1994) "Defining the post-bureaucratic type," in C. Heckscher and A. Donnellon (eds.), *The Post-Bureaucratic Organization: New perspectives on organizational change*, Thousand Oaks, CA: Sage, pp. 14–62.

Heylighen, F. (1999) "The growth of structural and functional complexity during evolution," in F. Heylighen, J. Bollen, and A. Riegler (eds), *The Evolution of Complexity: The violet book of "Einstein meets Magritte"*, Dordrecht: Kluwer Academic Publishers, pp. 17–44. Online. Available HTTP: <http://pespmc1.vub.ac.be/Papers/ComplexityGrowth.html>.

Holling, C.S. and Gunderson, L.H. (2002) "Resilience and adaptive cycles," in L.H. Gunderson and C.S. Holling (eds), *Panarchy: Understanding Transformations in Human and Natural Systems*, Washington, DC: Island Press, pp. 25–62.

Karasek, R. and Theorell, T. (1990) *Healthy Work: Stress, productivity, and the reconstruction of working life*, New York: Basic Books.

Kira, M. and Frieling, E. (2007) "Bureaucratic boundaries for collective learning in industrial work," *Journal of Workplace Learning*, 19, 5, 296–310.

Thorsrud, E. and Emery, F.E. (1969) *Medinflytande och Engagemang i Arbetet: Norska försök med självstyrande grupper* [Participation and commitment at work: Norwegian experiments with self-regulating groups], Stockholm: Utvecklingsrådet för samarbetsfrågor.

Trullen, J. and Bartunek, J.M. (2007) "What a design approach offers to organization development," *Journal of Applied Behavioral Science*, 43, 1, 23–40.

Wilber, K. (1996) *A Brief History of Everything*, Dublin: Gill & Macmillan.

World Commission on Environment and Development (1987) *Our Common Future* (General Assembly Documents, A/42/427), New York: United Nations, Brundtland Commission.

16 Toward a sustainable work systems design and change methodology

Michael W. Stebbins and
A.B. (Rami) Shani

Introduction

There is a growing literature on Sustainable Work Systems (SWS) and reflective design theory (see, for example, Stebbins and Shani 2002; Stebbins *et al*. 2006b; Stebbins *et al*. 2006a), but in this school of thought, theory seems to lead practice. Our point of departure is that within the field of organization studies we can find comprehensive organization theory, comprehensive organization design theory, and comprehensive planned change orientations. Within the emerging field of SWS, the contributions have been mainly conceptual, with a limited number of applied design projects treating some, but not all, aspects of the theory (Docherty *et al*. 2002; Boud *et al*. 2006; and Chapter 15 in this volume). Significant applied research on sustainability and reflective design, the principles that guide change projects, and the dynamics of change projects is barely under way. This is unique, as prior design theories and change approaches have evolved mainly from practice. One important development is to directly consider business design and organization design together as part of a comprehensive change management program (Nadler and Slywotsky 2005). We will explain distinctions among these concepts early in the chapter. The aim of the chapter is to integrate and discuss organization design and organization change methodologies that seek to promote sustainability.

Our view is that SWS design builds upon and transcends prior organizational design approaches. *Design* is thought to be a blend of theory (organization science), knowledge embedded in the particular industry/sector and work situation, and the contributions of those who participate in the design process (Mackenzie 1986). SWS design involves a proactive, purposeful, and holistic effort to design the organization as an integrated system, including all of its internal processes, for the purpose of achieving sustainability for the individuals, the organization, and the society. Moreover, design is treated as a complex task that will align people, resources, work, and the environment (see, for example, Galbraith 2000). In mature organizations, design projects are conducted to unravel what has often been an unplanned evolution of the enterprise. We will argue that in today's environment, the list of participants in redesign projects should include a cross-section of employees in the organization, key suppliers, union representatives, and customers. However, if this is done, there is potentially a wide separation between a science-based solution that a manager might hope to use and one that will meet the needs of different constituents and work well in practice.

SWS design has strong roots in collaborative research and action research theories. Collaborative research is an effort by two or more parties, at least one of whom is a member of an organization or a system under study and at least one of whom is an external researcher, to work together in learning about how management and employee actions, management methods, and organizational arrangements affect outcomes. There is considerable trial and error involved as people deliberate with others in the pursuit of change. Collaborative research relies on methods that are *scientifically based* with the intent of *improving performance* of the system and *adding to the broader body of knowledge* in the field of management (Shani *et al.* 2008). Collaborative research includes the whole family of approaches to inquiry that are participative, grounded in experience, and action-oriented (i.e., action research, appreciative inquiry, action science). In keeping with collaborative research theory, SWS design provides flexibility to deal with emergent goals and technology changes that occur in real time. In this chapter we focus on action research and introduce some of the literature.

We begin our exploration of SWS design with an overview of leading design approaches in use today. We then take up the topic of strategy, as it is an important component of concurrent design thinking (Nadler and Slywotsky 2005) and SWS design. The discussion integrates theory on the context for design, business design, organization design, and the integration of design efforts through a sound planned-change process. We then cover SWS change process principles and briefly consider connections with the academic fields of architectural design and product design. Next, we summarize self-design, action research, and sociotechnical systems contributions to the problem of managing the change process. The IDEO case provides a bridge to our discussion of a sequence for making design decisions within the SWS design process, which we call "eclectic SWS design." We conclude with a discussion of research issues and challenges faced in pursuing SWS design.

A design perspective

Organization design has evolved over the past six decades as a field of academic study and as an applied organization development technology. In the 1970s and 1980s, Jay Galbraith, Henry Mintzberg, and others wrote excellent reference books on the subject, but the early trend for authors was to ignore each other's writings and to establish separate frameworks and processes (Stebbins and Shani 1995). In time, three leading approaches emerged: the information processing model (for example, Galbraith 1977, 2000; Nadler and Tushman 1997), sociotechnical systems (for example, Pasmore 1988; Taylor and Felten 1993), and self-design (for example, Weick 1977; Mohrman and Cummings 1989). All three approaches have *guiding macro models* of the dimensions involved in organization design. They also have *design principles* that establish fundamental values and guide change programs, they have well-developed design sequences or processes, and they have track records of successful application within a wide variety of organizations (Stebbins *et al.* 1995). An in-depth analysis of the three approaches is beyond the scope of this chapter, but brief summaries of the macro organization theory aspects are provided below.

The sociotechnical systems school

Eric Trist of the Tavistock Institute coined the term "sociotechnical" to describe the interrelatedness of the social and technological subsystems of organizations. The principle of joint optimization is the backbone of this theory. An organization will function best if the social and technological systems are designed to fit the demands of each other and the environment (see also Chapters 4, 5, 6, and 15 in this volume). Sociotechnical systems (STS) theory is recognized worldwide, with somewhat different principles and processes followed in different countries. STS design theory rests on pioneering work by Lewin (1951), Trist (1981), Emery (1959), and many others. Strong STS efforts in Britain, Norway, Sweden, the United States, and eventually Holland have been documented in the STS literature (see, for example, Pasmore *et al.* 1982; Taylor and Felten 1993; Eijnatten *et al.* 2008). STS is a flexible theory and relies on a contingency approach, instead of insisting that there is one best way to organize. While the approach is often associated with redesign of manufacturing operations, the theory has recently embraced strategic considerations and has been extended to services, knowledge work, and high technology settings (see, for example, Stebbins and Shani 1995; Chapters 4 and 6 in this volume).

Information processing theory

Galbraith states that organization design is a decision-making process involving strategic choices. It also involves finding coherence or fit among strategy, task, structure, information technology, and processes to assimilate and reward people (Galbraith 1977). The approach takes into account the uncertainty of the organization's task, since uncertainty determines the amount of information that is processed during task execution. Galbraith's macro model is the most recognized design theory in the United States and is the basis for conceptual models used by leading management consulting firms (for example, McKinsey and Company). Information processing theory has been extended in recent years to include elaboration of the redesign change process (Nadler and Tushman 1997) and designing organizations to compete globally (Galbraith 2000).

Self-design

Self-design is an outgrowth of sociotechnical systems and information processing theory, and it essentially assumes that the organization has a well-conceived mission and organizational strategy to deal with environment and competitive issues. Further, the theory explains how organizations can alter strategies, structures, and organizational processes on a dynamic basis. The problem is to conduct work process mapping so that the right teams can be created, to determine the deliberations that must take place within and across teams, and then to create the appropriate management structures, integration processes, and performance management processes to sustain the total organization. Self-design is a high involvement approach, relying on a continuing cycle of review by different stakeholders. This approach has also been widely used in industrial, services, and high technology settings (see, for example, Mohrman and Cummings 1989; Mohrman *et al.* 1995; Chapters 4, 5, and 9 in this volume).

Strategy and organization design

In most modern theories of organization design, strategy is either considered a critical component of design or something that must be worked out before the redesign project begins. This notion has rather old origins in managerial consultation theory and practice. In earlier times (1930–1960), consultants worked in both strategy and organization practice areas (Nadler and Slywotzky 2005). Consulting pioneers such as Marvin Bower of McKinsey and Company viewed strategic planning and organizing as indistinguishable (Greiner and Poulfelt 2005). However, with increasing global competition the management consulting model shifted to interpreting environmental trends, developing strategy based mostly on economic considerations, and then creating designs to deal with the new realities. During the 1970–2000 era, there was an explosion of research and writing on strategy as distinct from organization design. Economists and engineers created breakthroughs in strategy by identifying sources of competitive advantage (Porter 1986) and creating advanced models that focused on value creation and strategic business design choices. In contrast, organization design theory evolved from the behavioural sciences and the breakthroughs were based on systems theory (Leavitt 1964), macro models such as the "star model" that involved fit among strategy, structure, and management processes (Galbraith 1977), and change management theory in general and its emphasis on managing transitions (see, for example, Beckhard and Harris 1987).

According to some observers (Nadler and Slywotzky 2005), the time is now right to bring the sometimes conflicting approaches to strategy and design into one change-management-based framework. This model (see Figure 16.1) has been labelled *concurrent design*. It begins with a proactive approach to understanding the environment followed by an integrated, iterative approach to business design and organization design. *Business design* includes selection of customers, creation of value for the customers, profit-taking and profit control, and finally, decisions about which activities to perform in the value chain. *Organization design* is essentially as defined in the introduction to this chapter. Concurrent design with strong dialogue among those managing the business design, organization design, and change management processes holds promise for resolving some heated issues in theory and practice, such as the merits of top-down strategic design

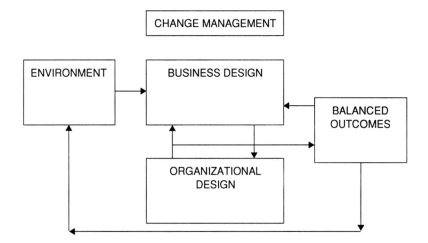

Figure 16.1 Concurrent design consulting model[1]

versus bottom-up design around core work processes. Change management is the key to integration of both strategic and organizational capabilities. More will be said about the dynamics inherent in this model later in this chapter when we discuss the problem of involving multiple stakeholders during redesign projects.

SWS design as concurrent design

Currently, SWS design theory lacks a coherent visual model of what is involved in business and organization design. Accordingly, we propose that the concurrent design consulting model (Figure 16.1) is a sound framework for explaining the dimensions involved in design, and is useful in framing emerging SWS values, concepts, and principles. For example, SWS design theory evolves to a considerable degree from the idea of achieving sustainability for individuals, the organization, and society. Most notably, this follows the principle that there should be equal attention in redesign on improving working conditions and competitive performance (Docherty *et al.* 2002). The effective organization thus seeks balanced outcomes (Figure 16.1) by achieving goals related to market share, productivity, financial performance, and employee development and satisfaction. The core concept of sustainable work systems is that resources deployed are regenerated by the system. Considering human resources, the resources to be fostered include skills, knowledge, innovation, employability, constructive industrial relations, and also the broader institutional/societal requirements such as educational institutions and training systems (see also Chapters 5, 7, and 8 in this volume).

Sustainable work systems theory stems from work by both European and American scholars. Certain common values have emerged, and the values relate to the context for initiating change, the change management process, and the desired outcomes. SWS is very different from prior design approaches in that it explicitly considers the global competitive context, the country context, the institutional context, and other environmental influences on design activities. For example, in coordinated market economies such as Germany, training systems, internal labour markets, forms of participation by workers, and labour relations are organized differently than in deregulated market economies such as those in America and Great Britain. In Germany and in many other Northern European countries, worker training is organized by industry, providing skills that are portable across companies. The skills are monitored by unions and by co-determination arrangements such as works councils or plant-level labour union groups. This creates a situation of interdependence that has both individual and societal benefits (Hancke 2002).

Other SWS values stress innovation and high quality of work life. High quality of work life includes attention to the intellectual, emotional, and physical needs of every individual. The eye is on the entire context as well as the target – enjoyable jobs and "good work." During the SWS change management process, it is not enough to design innovative work processes, as attention must include healthy work teams and worker well-being and enjoyment (Kira 2002). The firm's strategy and business model drive much of what occurs in the way of organization design, but there are both top-down and bottom-up forces that support creation of enriched jobs and increased employee capacity to cope with work changes.

Connections to the field of architectural design

While designing organizations is not the same as designing buildings, there are some common issues in both contexts (Weick 2004). In each case, a skeleton form is created early, with the idea that users can ultimately finish the design work. There is a need to under-specify early in the process. It is felt that the designers should not try to pin down all the details of structure and processes. (A similar argument is made in Chapter 7 in this volume.) Instead, self-organizing activities will flesh out the skeleton. The skeleton reflects the original dream, and the new forms created during the redesign process show a history and evolution of models. The entire redesign process infuses a capability to self-organize. This type of thinking is found in the fields of architecture and construction, and also in literature about innovation that occurs during new product development (see, for example, Gehry 2004; Kelley and Littman 2005).

The change management perspective

We have said little so far about change management perspectives and principles and the discussions that must take place during redesign. Figure 16.2 is a visual depiction of what takes place during concurrent design, with emphasis on learning. During all phases of the redesign process, diverse stakeholders participate in deliberations about the vision and goals for redesign, diverse participants take part in the conduct of the study through self-design groups, and the learnings

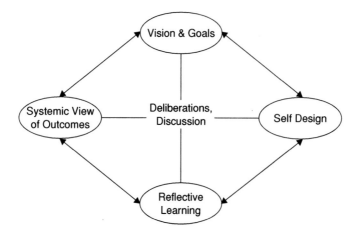

Figure 16.2 Reflective design requirements

from design experimentation are integrated into the deliberations and attendant outcomes. Reflection is a crucial part of the redesign process (see Chapters 2, 3, and 4 in this volume). We have argued that SWS design and reflective design are one and the same (Stebbins *et al.* 2006a). SWS design is a reflective methodology of intervention – a type of enlightened, self-critical design approach that accepts differences in science and practice. By definition, reflective design means to mirror or direct back the redesign work. We propose the following principles for the change management program:

- Alternative theoretical design models and processes must be discussed with participants at the beginning of the change program. Participants should have the opportunity to investigate and choose among redesign approaches that might fit the unique situation.
- During the program, participants self-apply theory, methods, and practices. In keeping with self-design values, participants take ownership of the change process through high involvement at all stages. In a spirit of inquiry, all parties (including any internal and external consultants or researchers) consider both theory and practice and discuss ways to link them during the program.
- Participants are encouraged to identify and explore meanings and implications of possible dilemmas – for example, that team-based designs can produce frustrations and stress.
- There is emphasis on the iterative nature of design activities. Deliberations among stakeholders occur throughout the program to ensure that redesign produces the desired outcomes, including enjoyable jobs.
- New work and organization designs are subject to continuous modification and improvement. Transitions require evaluation checkpoints, and designs must be modified to reflect feedback and new information. The change process

requires a tolerance for ambiguity and a willingness to consider multiple designs.

- Unintended side effects are explored. It is recognized that good design work can have unintended consequences, and all parties are aware that even the best processes can produce work intensity.

On the matter of vision, goals, and design criteria

The SWS perspective advocates high stakeholder participation in development of the overall vision, goals, and criteria for the change management program. However, this principle is controversial and is seldom observed in the literature on redesign programs (see, for example, Nadler and Tushman 1997). In most redesign programs taking place in industry, vision for the overall change management program is developed by the top management team, consistent with the results of strategic planning. But there is evidence that additional stakeholders may be successfully involved in crafting change management goals and design criteria in programs that follow the SWS design approach (see Stebbins *et al.* 2006b, and the example provided below). Design criteria are statements that describe, in ideal terms, those functions that the new design should perform. Design criteria usually have an action verb; they state that the design should facilitate, promote, encourage, provide for, or motivate (Nadler and Tushman 1997). Design criteria reflect the values of the different stakeholders and are written in response to competitive conditions, the vision, the tasks to be executed, the collective sense of current problems and perceived causes of problems, and other constraints. Without high stakeholder involvement in development of design criteria, change management programs run the risk of ignoring employee needs and sustainability values in favour of strictly economic concerns (see, for example, Stebbins *et al.* 2006a). Design criteria drive the entire decision-making process and provide links to strategy, technology integration, and the development process that occurs in design cycles.

Since design criteria provide the fundamental values and assumptions behind redesign work, they can be used to assess whether the change program is on track. However, with greater stakeholder involvement, it is sometimes difficult to achieve consensus on design criteria. Conflict is often rampant as perspectives clash. This is particularly evident when work force reduction is a goal. Yet this discussion sets the stage for dialogue throughout the redesign process. It is worthwhile to spend time on both criteria language and criteria ranking, so that guidelines exist to help with the inevitable trade-offs that occur during the redesign process. For example, in a major redesign project at Kaiser Permanente (Nadler and Tushman 1997), the design team generated 13 criteria, including:

- The design alternatives should drive the organization toward a customer focus.
- The designs should enhance partnerships with patients, members, suppliers, purchasers, communities, and labour unions.
- Maximize capacity for organizational learning.

- Reduce the hierarchy to ensure that those serving the customer have information, resources, and freedom to act.
- Support individual and team accountability for results.

In the Kaiser example, managers alone initially developed the list of criteria. The list did not directly include reference to meaningful work for employees or other dimensions of quality of work life. Employee and customer perspectives emerged in later stages of the redesign project and became part of the guiding change philosophy; they were missing at the outset. In contrast, SWS theory calls for high involvement at all stages, including the front-end work. Limited experience with SWS design to date suggests that a ranking of criteria helps the participants stay on track. A sense of priority is crucial when alternative designs are created and compared, and when impact analyses are conducted regarding potential affects on various stakeholders (see, for example, Nadler and Tushman 1997).

Collaborative design during experimentation

There is considerable agreement among SWS authors that the design process must consider individual and team capacity to cope with changing work. One of the most compelling aspects of SWS redesign is the emphasis on personal support, learning, and individual capacity to deal with workplace issues (see also Chapters 2, 3, 5, 8, and 9 in this volume). During redesign, individual experimentation takes place within the context of group work and intergroup relationships. Change cannot occur without social support mechanisms. The Kaiser Permanente case in Chapter 9 shows that successful redesign work requires the active involvement of those who must live with the changes. Accordingly, SWS can be characterized as collaborative design.

In our view, *collaborative design* means that greater attention is given to the different stakeholders, and that there is genuine participation of stakeholders at various stages of the change process. The design team that usually leads the effort is composed of both organizational members and outside experts. The designers are alert to workplace implications of design changes, and individuals are supported as they attempt to change work processes and job content.

As noted in Figure 16.2, SWS design processes provide time for learning and development of competence in work. This includes deliberations within the normal project stages as well as time for spontaneous and unplanned learning and reflection. The focus is on learning that takes place among people through deliberation and discussion. The process of change centres on the knowledge and experience of those who are closest to the work at hand (see, for example, the case in Chapters 4, 5, 8, and 9 in this volume). Learning, coping capacity, and other individual capabilities support people as they experiment with new work processes, roles, and relationships. Successful transformation depends upon effort put forth, individual capabilities, and sound facilitation of the overall change management process.

Change and development process

So far in this chapter, we have not explicitly acknowledged foundations for SWS design process theory, and we have not recommended a specific step-wise sequence for redesign and the change management process. Accordingly, we will now deal with foundations, provide a contemporary case that illustrates SWS design thinking, and then propose our eclectic change process.

Three developments in the field of organizational change have had enormous impact on contemporary design thinking in general, with strong guidance for managing change programs: action research, sociotechnical systems, and self-design theories. At a basic level, most design processes follow an action research sequence. Planning, diagnostic, and experimental activities seem to be included in most change management programs. Fundamental concepts advanced by Lewin, Shepard, Beckhard, and other action research pioneers (see Reason and Bradbury 2001/2008; Shani *et al.* 2008) are evident in contemporary redesign case examples. A similar history exists with sociotechnical systems theory where, acknowledged or unacknowledged, recommended redesign processes show STS principles (see, for example, Ostroff 1999). Recently, STS change processes have been invented to extend the reach of redesign to include issues such as knowledge transfer and work-based learning (Raelin 2000). Self-design provides a highly developed redesign process that is particularly suited to knowledge work settings (Weick 1977; Mohrman and Cummings 1989; Mohrman *et al.* 1995; Weick 2001).

Action research

Kurt Lewin introduced the general notion of action research in 1946 as an innovative process for changing behaviour. His attempts to resolve social problems using data collection and feedback approaches were pioneering and are the foundation for design theory and practice (Susman and Evered 1978; Stebbins *et al.* 1982). Lewin, John Collier, and William Whyte observed that research needed to be closely linked to action if organizational members were to use it to manage change. Action research is thus viewed as an emergent inquiry process, embedded in a partnership between researchers and organizational members, for the purpose of solving organizational problems and simultaneously generating scientific knowledge (Shani and Pasmore 1985). Furthermore, action research seeks to improve the organization's ability to understand and help itself (Friedlander and Brown 1974). Action research projects also identify issues related to survival and growth of the organization as a system and therefore address sustainability.

Sociotechnical systems design

Sociotechnical systems interventions build upon the original work conducted in the 1950s by Eric Trist and his associates at the Tavistock Institute in London. Tavistock became dedicated to action research, with equal emphasis on the advancement of knowledge, the resolution of practical organizational problems, and democratizing the workplace. STS design process theory rests on the pioneering work by Lewin, Trist, Bion, Rice, Emery, and many others (see Eijnatten *et al.* 2008). The early emphasis on people and their reaction to work, particularly individual outcomes related to job satisfaction and mental health, is noteworthy. In the 1970s, Davis and Cherns (1975) identified development of human capacities, growth and use of knowledge with others in the workplace, and the balance between life at work and life at home as criteria affecting individual outcomes. Most contributors to STS theory offer values-based design principles that can be used to guide the redesign process and outcomes. Accordingly, we can conclude that SWS design theory concerning desired changes and the change process itself has strong action research and STS roots.

Self-design

Self-design is an outgrowth of STS theory and practice. First proposed by Karl Weick (1977), self-design was applied as an academic exercise involving NASA's Apollo 3. For Weick, self-design suggests new values: improvisation and looking for opportunities, inventing solutions that fit local situations, dialogue and argument, the pursuit of contradictions, and performance assessment systems beyond accounting. In sum, organizations must value things that they used to disparage. This type of thinking is explicitly found in SWS design principles (see Chapters 3, 6, and 9 in this volume).

Weick's path-breaking thoughts on self-design have been recognized and enhanced by Mohrman and Cummings (1989). The ideas of design as an ongoing process and design as a recipe are pursued with vigour. In this instance, a recipe is not a blueprint, but rather a set of contributions that require varying amounts of improvisation. Emphasis is on the processes that are responsible for creating new designs rather than the designs themselves. SWS design adopts this call for action learning and iterative processes (see Figure 16.2) that involve multiple stakeholders; accordingly, the organization is prepared for continuous adjustment and significant redesign.

Self-design begins with a mutual learning phase involving all stakeholders. The participants work together to create a guiding conceptual model for change. Special emphasis is placed on the identification of skills and training required for the successful implementation of the program.

As we will see in the section below on eclectic change process, SWS design is similar to self-design at the startup phase but it is enhanced to include evaluation of multiple redesign models and local choice and development of the process to be used during the change program. In self-design theory, the design team conducts diagnostic activities to investigate institutional, work, and organization issues. This is expanded under SWS thinking to include home-grown creation of diagnostic tools and involvement of diverse stakeholders in the diagnosis. Identification of design criteria follows the diagnostic work and this again involves dialogue among relevant stakeholders as an SWS enhancement.

The benefits of self-design and SWS design can be seen in the following case example.

Lessons from the field: the IDEO case

While the SWS journey has just begun and the identification of design principles is therefore problematic, certain patterns are emerging in "model" firms. Not surprisingly, many of these firms are in high technology settings, with external environments ranging from fiercely competitive and time-paced, to insulated and relaxed. IDEO Product Development of Palo Alto, California, is an example of the latter environment. IDEO was founded by a Stanford University engineering professor and is now the largest firm in the United States with a mission of helping client companies develop new products and become more innovative. IDEO employs over 500 engineers, industrial designers, human factors specialists, and social scientists, who work on projects that average ten to twelve months in duration. In the manufacturing realm, IDEO contributions range from rough sketches of products to complete new products. Recently, IDEO has moved into the services sector to tackle difficult health care delivery and customer contact issues. Employees work out of offices in diverse locations including San Francisco, Boston, London, and Tokyo. The firm has won numerous awards for design work, and has been acclaimed "the world's most celebrated design firm" (Sutton and Kelley 1997).

The founders of IDEO wish to create an environment that supports good relationships and creativity. Accordingly, the physical layout is purposely centred on small buildings with open facilities design. There is no visible administration – buildings all have a reception desk for visitors, and the rest of the space is devoted to the engineers and laboratories where prototypes are created. The small building and limited number of employees eliminate the need for extensive security; employees know each other and know who should and should not be present. The psychological climate at IDEO incorporates many features associated with ideal conditions for knowledge workers. In general, unspoken norms take the place of policies and rules. There is little or no structure; management encourages employees to take the initiative and use their knowledge and skills. For example, employees design their own workplaces, consistent with the idea of periodic movement to new projects and work locations in the building. Office designs are open, featuring distinct partitions such as a DC-3 wing suspended from the ceiling. Most work locations also offer space to work alone in peace and quiet on a given day if the open environment begins to intrude.

Given IDEO's reputation and their commitment to learning, tours and interviews are an ongoing part of employee life. Most employees participate in showing visitors work in progress. Employees say that a common topic of interviews is "how to maintain energy and creativity as the small firm grows." The secret is apparently in employee involvement in selection of clients and projects, and allowing employees to gravitate to projects or client companies that fit their interests. Clients participate in an estimated 20 percent of brainstorming sessions, and clients work side by side with the staff for one or two weeks at a time to observe, learn, and try out IDEO work practices. In some cases, clients are colocated at IDEO for up to a year when long-term alliances are desired. In Palo Alto, employees from each building meet once a week for an hour, sitting on the floor in a large circle to share information on team activities, discuss new technologies, demonstrate new products, and give very brief updates on progress and setbacks on products for 15–40 clients. They also take time out once a week for an organized bike ride through the hills of Palo Alto.

Much of the work is team-based. IDEO employees are trained in facilitation techniques and all brainstorming sessions in design teams are facilitator-led. Team members also host special sessions to demonstrate new work practices and technologies to others in the building. An example is the frequent practice of running involvement workshops to teach other staff to observe users, brainstorm new designs, and build working models. IDEO employees are experts at teaching rapid prototyping, and are frequent contributors to Silicon Valley engineering and business school programs.

Interviews indicate that IDEO employees remain with the company because of the unique working environment. As relatively young people with advanced degrees in engineering and related fields, they are well-paid, but could do better elsewhere. Compensation is not on a merit or performance increase basis, but rather increases with time and market conditions. Management believes that typical merit schemes create a competitive environment, and are "not nurturing." When employees leave, it is often for a sabbatical or to gain advanced education.

At IDEO, the founders wished to preserve freedoms that they enjoyed as inventors and entrepreneurs when the company was small. With growth, they were careful to create simple forms of structure supported in part by the limitations on the size of offices and laboratories. A small-company atmosphere was maintained by growing new units in separate office buildings. Moreover, employees influenced strategy by creating their own projects and having a say in outside projects that IDEO might select. In some ways, projects take the place of formal structures and managerial processes. Employees participate in all aspects of the business, including training others in IDEO work practices. Consistent with SWS thinking, employees have a sense of security and personal support. Turnover is very low despite attractive outside opportunities in the Silicon Valley area. High quality of work life and solid financial performance and other indicators suggest that IDEO is a sustainable work system.

The IDEO organization design and change process

The upper management team at IDEO considered the fit among strategy, structure, and organizational processes during the evolution of the company as a leading force in the product design field. The strategy is to be the world's most recognized product design consultancy, known for product and service innovation. According to the founder, Tom Kelley (Thomke and Nimgade 2000), the CEO's task is to "build the stage rather than perform on it." The key in a product design organization is to be a set designer: "We have had the belief that a creative office is like a well-designed stage or movie set that contributes to overall performance" (Kelley and Litman 2005). Part of the redesign process involves constant modification of the design and layout of offices. Allowing employees to shape the character of their workspace helps reinforce a company persona that is fun, welcoming, and stimulating. Employees create collaborative spaces for "neighbourhood" or community teams. Set designers create project spaces, making room for projects to live and breathe for weeks or months. Set designers balance private and collaborative space, giving people room to collaborate but also providing sanctuary for intensely individual work (Kelley and Littman 2005). In designing the organization, IDEO has adopted processes used in other innovative organizations such as George Lucas's Industrial Light and Magic (ILM). ILM has a flexible approach to workspace and huge fluctuations in workload at different stages in film development. IDEO and ILM have exchanged knowledge and staff to understand how project processes and space can be altered during major projects to make spaces creative and stimulating. They have learned to remap eclectic office environments to suit the changing needs of project teams (Kelley and Littman 2005).

Office designs and work processes reflect the unique needs of the country context, business setting, customers, and employees. Each office location around the world is operated independently and seeks business locally, but communications are strong across locations and talent is shared. The overall redesign process is incremental: gaining agreement on promising areas for growth, replicating the simple structure with each formal move to new facilities and country offices, allowing design of personal and team spaces to mesh with project demands, and building a positive work climate in all office and laboratory units. Emphasis is on lean structures and managerial processes that support individuals and teams as they develop innovative solutions for customers.

An integrated eclectic SWS design and change perspective

In the spirit of the IDEO case and action research, sociotechnical systems, and self-design theories, we have recommended a change process called Eclectic SWS Design (Stebbins and Shani 1995). As depicted in Figure 16.3, SWS design has some familiar program phases, but with minimal constraints. That is, the phases or steps are merely guidelines and exist to support invention, experimentation, reflection, assessment, and adjustments. Step 1 draws guidelines for scoping the overall change management program from Nadler and Tushman (1997). Researchers and managers who will guide the program need to conduct a preliminary analysis covering the elements in the concurrent design model (Figure 16.1), in order to understand the organization and its environment. If business design is to proceed in tandem with organization design, then change program goals will be complex and the design teams will be interrelated. Based on the preliminary assessment, responsibilities are sorted out and the initial program steering group is formed. Step 2 has been covered earlier. It should be noted that a call for education about alternative design models and change processes is unique to SWS thinking, and it is vital that participants understand the chosen approach in depth. We have argued that information processing, STS, self-design, and SWS design models are all viable alternatives, and it is only crucial that participants self-select the best model for the situation. Step 3 is familiar to those in the organization development field, as it addresses concerns of different stakeholders and results in managerial and employee support for the change effort (see, for example, Jick 1993). Step 4 calls for creation of learning mechanisms, moving beyond the steering group to creation of a network of redesign teams along with supportive processes. Design team efforts must mesh with efforts of the other teams in the overall change management program as well as with work conducted by existing teams in the current organization. The topic of learning mechanisms, step 5, has been covered in Chapter 10, and is briefly described later in this section. These mechanisms help build support for design experimentation, step 6. The remaining steps cover reflection on experimentation and predictions of impacts on various stakeholders, transitions required in moving from prototypes to widespread operations changes, and continuing reflection on outcomes.

The SWS eclectic change process is tailored to each country and company situation. In keeping with self-design learnings and SWS theory and practice, design activities can recycle to earlier phases as different stakeholders join the design process. As noted earlier, it is a tactical issue whether to bring stakeholders together from the outset or whether to include them at later phases. Regardless, the articulation of needs, vision, goals, and design criteria must reflect diversity of the work system. When agreement on design criteria has been established, design teams can proceed to consider different strategic and operational matters. Checkpoints are established to allow reflection/assessment before new designs are extended to other work groups. Design is not at all superficial, but instead allows maximum freedom for individuals and work groups to reconfigure core work processes. The "magic" of SWS redesign is regeneration of resources – learning and enhanced capabilities through active experimentation, assessment, and work adjustments.

One of the compelling issues in SWS design is how to orchestrate the change process so that role overload and stress do not result, and so that employees have

Steps

1. Preliminary project planning.
2. Reviewing alternative design models and change processes.
3. Motivating the change effort and involving stakeholders.
4. Establishing design criteria.
5. Creating organizational learning mechanisms.
6. Building personal and social support for work design experimentation.
7. Comprehensive impact analysis.
8. Extending prototypes and work processes to other work units.
9. Documenting SWS outcomes and providing feedback.

Figure 16.3 Eclectic planned SWS design change process

support for local experimentation. Learning mechanisms may be the answer. In Chapters 6 and 9 in this volume it was noted that learning mechanisms are planned proactive features that enable and encourage organizational learning (Popper and Lipshitz 1998; Shani and Docherty 2003). The literature on learning mechanisms identifies three types: cognitive; structural; and procedural (Shani and Docherty 2003). The cognitive mechanisms are the bearers of language, concepts, symbols, theories, frameworks, and values for thinking, reasoning, and understanding developed in creating new organizational capabilities. These mechanisms are most usefully employed in the first three steps of eclectic SWS design. In contrast, structural learning mechanisms are organizational, physical, technical, and work system infrastructures that encourage practice-based learning (*ibid.*). These mechanisms support discourse and the sense making entailed as individuals and groups learn from experience and are deployed in steps 1 and 4 of eclectic design. The procedural mechanisms concern the rules, routines, methods, and tools that can be institutionalized in the organization to promote and support learning (Popper and Lipshitz 1998). These mechanisms are most applicable in the final three steps of the eclectic design process.

For example, a structural learning mechanism such as a parallel learning design configuration (see Bushe and Shani 1991; Shani and Docherty 2003, 2008; and the discussion in Chapter 9 of this volume) can coordinate design activities and gauge training needs at different phases of the change management program. Training activities would emphasize simulation and other experiential methods that increase employee capacity to cope with change. We suggest the following:

- Simulation activities that increase the individual's capacity to create order and meaning in a seemingly disordered situation.
- Brainstorming sessions, with emphasis on forces that promote manageability and meaning in work.
- Relationship-building conferences and exercises that promote goodwill and problem-solving by different stakeholders in the transformation process.
- Person-centred training interventions that focus on (1) managing the personal work environment: time management, task variation, overload avoidance; (2) lifestyle management: maintaining a balance, taking time off from work; and (3) response-directed options such as relaxation, meditation, physical outlets, and emotional outlets.

As shown in Figures 16.2 and 16.3, as the design work unfolds, the steering group must provide opportunities for comprehensive *impact analysis* (see Nadler and Tushman 1997, for an in-depth discussion about what is involved). This analysis tracks outcomes for different stakeholders and players in the larger context. It also increases the probability that new designs can be extended to other groups and locations within the organization. The IDEO case provides help here, in that it shows that a skeletal strategic design can be replicated if sufficient freedom is provided workgroups to self-design activities within the new work unit.

Directions for future research

From university and science perspectives, action research, collaborative research, sociotechnical system, SWS design, and self-design are preferred over traditional management consulting change processes (Cummings and Worley 2006). Regarding research on change, it is recognized that organizations and communities are often complex entities and cannot be solely studied using traditional reductionist methods. Field experiments, ethnography, and case studies appear often in social science journals, and the situation is much improved over the 1950s climate when resistance to these methods was so strong (Pasmore 2001). SWS design theory continues the collaborative research and action research-based traditions even though the price of high-involvement design can be delays, competing perspectives, and chaos. The thinking is that involvement and dialogue with a purpose will raise human needs above the technical and economic pressures that consume organizations in post-industrial society.

SWS design is solidly grounded in collaborative research, action research, and self-design concepts, and the approach has the ability to anticipate and deal with many obstacles. But it is not foolproof. We believe that companies and managers will be drawn to SWS design because it focuses on development of human resources and capabilities at all levels. We also predict that it will be welcome in high technology and professional services settings and where employers seek to be recognized as "employers of choice." Here, employers are motivated to create positive working conditions and environments as they must compete and retain scarce human resources. In keeping with STS and the foundations of work life quality, companies will strive to create enriched and manageable jobs and healthy work teams. SWS design theory supports both knowledge creation and knowledge transfer, and fosters a philosophy of continuous learning. It is obvious that these conditions do not exist in much of post-industrial society, but they are consistent with what many organizations hope to accomplish in both "old economy" and knowledge-work settings. Research is needed to discover the extent to which SWS has appeal to all parties within different economic sectors, industries, and employee groups.

As SWS scholars begin to study atypical organizations such as IDEO, they will likely focus on problems associated with these organizations as reported in the literature. Regarding new product development (NPD), work process dynamics are often difficult to study. In such settings, companies are preoccupied with time to market and with expediting development processes. Participants may not have time to engage in collaborative research or action research projects that explore new product development processes. Moreover, front-end development work is always uncertain. It involves activities such as investigating alternative technologies and evaluating the market potential for an initial product concept. Tracking such activities requires new research methods. These difficulties have many implications for the SWS design process.

Since the context is so difficult with knowledge work, the SWS redesign process must be adjusted. The SWS process calls for major time commitments and training in SWS concepts and tools, and this poses a conflict. At the same time, we feel that the promise of improved NPD processes, increased individual capabilities, and inter-project learning will make the time spent worthwhile.

In production and services settings, an investment in SWS redesign is less controversial. There is already a huge body of empirical evidence that action research, information processing redesign, STS, and self-design produce improvements in workflow and jobs. We expect that SWS will continue this tradition. SWS builds on these modern approaches, and the redesign process itself is a vehicle for uncovering and resolving problems along the way. In ideal form, SWS requires dedication of support resources (training, budgets for experimentation, creation of measurement systems, ergonomic analysis, and the like). Given history, the worry is that SWS will fail in the context of competitive work systems, and in full implementation of concepts that produce qualitatively better conditions for employees (see Chapter 1 in this volume) and the community. Full implementation of SWS design involves "emancipatory research," which seeks to improve outcomes, the self-understanding of participants, and critique of the larger social and work setting (Kemmis 2001).

Pasmore argues that most organizations are firmly caught in the grasp of technological determinism and scientific positivism. Therefore, any approach that promises to push human needs to the forefront will be welcomed by those conducting emancipatory and collaborative management research. SWS is one way to challenge the dominant development paradigm. The challenge of SWS redesign is to build a comprehensive theory that includes a sound eclectic design and change process. This chapter has articulated some of the design process requirements and change process. We have offered an eclectic change process that should be useful to those hoping to try SWS design. We have also explored some foundation approaches and concepts that will undoubtedly play out in future SWS thinking in ways that mesh with the rapidly changing post-industrial context.

Questions for reflection

Here are three questions for your further reflection on the issues broached in this chapter:

- What are the challenges faced by the manager who is interested in pursuing a sustainable work systems change project?
- How does the sustainable work systems approach build on self-design concepts, principles, and processes?
- In what ways is the eclectic sustainable work systems design process different from past design approaches?

Note

1 Modified from Nadler and Slywotzky (2005), p. 91.

References

Beckhard, R. and Harris, R. (1987) *Organizational Transitions: Managing Complex Change*, Reading, MA: Addison-Wesley.

Boud, D., Cressey, P., and Docherty, P. (2006) *Productive Reflection at Work*, London: Routledge.

Bushe, G.R. and Shani, A.B. (Rami) (1991) *Parallel Learning Structures: Increasing Innovation in Bureaucracies*, Boston, MA: Addison-Wesley.

Cummings, T. and Worley, C. (2006) *Organization Development and Change*, South-Western Publishing.

Davis, L. and Cherns, A.B. (1975) *The Quality of Working Life*, New York: Free Press.

Docherty, P., Forslin, J., and Shani, A.B. (Rami) (2002) *Creating Sustainable Work Systems: Emerging Perspectives and Practices*, London: Routledge.

Eijnatten, F., Shani, A.B. (Rami), and Leary, M. (2008) "Socio-Technical Systems: Designing and Managing Sustainable Organizations," in T. Cummings (ed.), *Handbook of Organization Development*, Thousand Oaks, CA: Sage, pp. 277–309.

Emery, F. (1959) *Characteristics of Socio-Technical Systems*, Tavistock, document 527.

Friedlander, F. and Brown, L.D. (1974) "Organization Development," *Annual Review of Psychology*, 25, 313–341.

Galbraith, J.R. (1977) *Organization Design*, Reading, MA: Addison-Wesley.

Galbraith, J.R. (2000) *Designing the Global Corporation*, San Francisco: Jossey-Bass.

Gehry, F.O. (2004) "Reflections on Designing and Architectural Practice," in R. Boland, Jr. and F. Collopy (eds), *Managing as Designing*, Stanford, CA: Stanford University Press, pp. 19–35.

Greiner, L. and Poulfelt, F. (2005) *The Contemporary Consultant: Insights From World Experts*, Mason, OH: Thomson South-Western.

Hancke, B. (2002) "Institutional Contexts," in P. Docherty, J. Forslin, and A.B. Shani (eds), *Creating Sustainable Work Systems: Emerging Perspectives and Practices*, London: Routledge, pp. 76–86.

Jick, T.D. (1993) *Managing Change: Cases and Concepts*, Burr Ridge, IL: Irwin.

Kelley, T. and Littman, J. (2005) *The Ten Faces of Innovation*, New York: Doubleday.

Kemmis, S. (2001) "Exploring the Relevance of Critical Theory for Action Research: Emancipatory Action Research in the Footsteps of Jurgen Habermas," in Reason and Bradbury, pp. 91–102.

Kira, M. (2002) "Moving from Consuming to Regenerative Work," in Docherty *et al.*, pp. 76–86.

Leavitt, H. (1964) *Managerial Psychology: An Introduction to Individuals, Pairs, and Groups in Organizations*, Chicago: University of Chicago Press.

Lewin, K. (1951) *Field Theory in Social Science: Selected Theoretical Papers*, New York: Harper and Row.

Mackenzie, K.D. (1986) *Organization Design: The Organizational Audit and Analysis Technology*, New York: Ablex.

Mohrman, S.A. and Cummings, T.G. (1989) *Self-Designing Organizations: Learning How to Create High Performance*, Reading, MA: Addison-Wesley.

Mohrman, S.A., Cohen, S.G., and Mohrman, Jr., A.M. (1995) *Designing Team-Based Organizations: New Forms for Knowledge Work*, San Francisco: Jossey-Bass.

Nadler, D.A. and Slywotzky, A.J. (2005) "Strategy and Organization Consulting," in Greiner and Poulfelt, pp. 75–95.

Nadler, D.A. and Tushman, M.L. (1997) *Competing by Design: The Power of Organizational Architecture*, New York: Oxford University Press.

Ostroff, F. (1999) *The Horizontal Organization*, Oxford: Oxford University Press.

Pasmore, W.A. (1988) *Designing Effective Organizations: The Sociotechnical Systems Perspective*, New York: Wiley.

Pasmore, W.A. (2001) "Action Research in the Workplace: The Socio-Technical Perspective," in Reason and Bradbury, pp. 38–47.

Pasmore, W.A., Francis, C., and Shani, A.B. (Rami) (1982) "Sociotechnical Systems: A North American Reflection on Empirical Studies of the Seventies," *Human Relations*, 35, 12, 1179–1204.

Popper, M. and Lipshitz, R. (1998) "Organizational Learning Mechanisms: A Cultural and Structural Approach to Organizational Learning," *Journal of Applied Behavioral Science*, 34, 161–178.

Porter, M.E. (1986) *Competitive Advantage*, New York: Free Press.

Raelin, J.A. (2000) *Work-Based Learning: The New Frontier of Management Development*, Upper Saddle, NJ: Prentice-Hall.

Reason, P. and Bradbury, H. (2001, 2008) *Handbook of Action Research. Participative Inquiry and Practice*, London: Sage.

Shani, A.B. (Rami) and Docherty, P. (2003) *Learning by Design*, London: Blackwell.

Shani, A.B. (Rami) and Docherty, P. (2008) "Learning by Design: A Fundamental foundation for Organization Development Change Programs," in T. Cummings (ed.), *Handbook of Organization Development and Change*, Thousand Oaks, CA: Sage, pp. 499–518.

Shani, A.B. (Rami) and Pasmore, W.A. (1985) "Organization Inquiry: Towards a New Model of the Action Research Process," in D. Warrick (ed.), *Contemporary Organization Development*, Glenview, IL.: Scott, Foresman and Company, pp. 438–448.

Shani, A.B. (Rami), Mohrman, S., Pasmore, W.A., Stymne, B., and Adler, N., (eds) (2008) *Handbook of Collaborative Management Research*, Thousand Oaks, CA: Sage.

Stebbins, M.W. and Shani, A.B. (Rami) (1995) "Organization Design and the Knowledge Worker," *Leadership and Organization Development Journal*, 16, 1, 23–30.

Stebbins, M.W. and Shani, A.B. (Rami) (2002) "Eclectic Design for Change," in Docherty *et al.*, pp. 201–212.

Stebbins, M.W., Freed, T., Shani, A.B., and Doerr, K.H. (2006a) "The Limits of Reflexive Design in a Secrecy-Based Organization," in Boud *et al.*, pp. 80–92.

Stebbins, M.W., Hawley, J., and Rose, A. (1982) "Long-Term Action Research: The Most Effective Way to Improve Complex Health Care Organizations," in N. Margulies and J. Adams (eds), *Organizational Development in Health Care Organizations*, Boston, MA: Addison-Wesley, pp. 105–136.

Stebbins, M.W., Sena, J.A., and Shani, A.B. (Rami) (1995) "Information Technology and Organization Design," *Journal of Information Technology*, 10, 101–113.

Stebbins, M.W., Shani, A.B. (Rami), and Docherty, P. (2006b) "Reflection During a Crisis Turnaround: Management Use of Learning Mechanisms," in Boud *et al.*, pp. 106–119.

Slywotski, A.J. (1996) *Value Migration*, Boston, MA: Harvard Business School.

Susman, G.I. and Evered, R.D. (1978) "An Assessment of the Scientific Merits of Action Research," *Administrative Science Quarterly*, 23, 583–603.

Sutton, R.I. and Kelley, T.A. (1997) "Creativity Doesn't Require Isolation. Why Product Designers Bring Visitors 'Backstage,'" *California Management Review*, 40, 1, 75–91.

Taylor, J.C. and Felten, D.F. (1993) *Performance by Design: Sociotechnical Systems in North America*, Englewood Cliffs, NJ: Prentice Hall.

Thomke, S. and Nimgade, A. (2000) *IDEO Product Development*, Harvard Business School Case 9-600-143, Boston, MA: Harvard Business School Publishing, pp. 1–21.

Trist, E. (1981) *The Evolution of Sociotechnical Systems*, London: Tavistock.

Weick, K.E. (1977) "Organization Design: Organizations as Self-Designing Systems," *Organizational Dynamics*, 6, 30–46.

Weick, K.E. (2004) "Rethinking Organizational Design," in R. Boland, Jr. and F. Collopy (eds), *Managing as Designing*, Stanford, CA: Stanford University Press, pp. 36–53.

17 Sustainable work systems

Past, present and future of social sustainability

Peter Docherty, Mari Kira, and A.B. (Rami) Shani

Sustainable work systems: basic point of departure

Chapter 1 presented the principal objectives, motives, and theory-based framing of this book. Here we will briefly restate our definition of sustainable work systems before analyzing and summarizing the lessons we draw from the cases in the book. In Chapter 1, we defined work as an intentional value-creating process, characterized by situation-specific goals, rules, resources, and contextual conditions. We argued that sustainability at work entails concurrent development in the economic, ecological, human, and social resources engaged in work processes. At the most basic level, a sustainable work system is one that is able to function in its environment and achieve economic or operational goals. However, on top of that, the functional capacity of a sustainable work system builds on and promotes the development of the human, social, ecological, and economic resources engaged in its operations.

An important factor necessitating such concurrent and mutually supportive development is the network of interdependencies across the ecological, economic, and social spheres of sustainability. Attaining and maintaining sustainability is a difficult and continuous endeavour, demanding due consideration of many interdependent goals, interests, processes, and conditions within these several spheres. These efforts are made by people at work in organizations and systems in the field of social sustainability. The maintenance of ecological and economic sustainability may be seen as dependent on the existence of well-developed social sustainability. If social sustainability is only an assumption taken for granted and is left out of an organization's vision, strategy, and plans, then ecological and economic sustainability will be at risk.

We also defined sustainability in work systems as the dynamic state of becoming, being, and staying sustainable, while we used the term *sustainable development* to refer to the purposeful efforts of people to support this dynamic condition of sustainability.

Although the notion of sustainable systems is borrowed from ecology, this book focuses mainly on the other types of resources – human, social, and economic. What is common to the ecological sustainability models and our approach is the awareness that many resources are finite or unique (and thus irreplaceable), and it is important to develop toward forms of production that can be competitive without depleting resources – i.e., without depleting the capital base, in all its forms, upon which a system depends. Even though industrial society has an infamous record of creating wealth through the ruthless exploitation of resources, we are convinced that technological and social innovations can and must be used for promoting sustainability. What can make the difference are the goals, values, and ambitions underlying the business and work activities. One of the lessons demonstrated repeatedly through the chapters in this volume is that sustainability in a work system is, first and foremost, a *value* choice; a conscious choice to promote the concurrent development of various resources in the work system. Sustainability, therefore, makes visible the multiple responsibilities of people at work and work systems as a whole. In Chapter 3, a member of Interface Inc. describes the company's ongoing work toward sustainability:

> Each time we have a decision to make around here, we have to consider three questions: is it good for the environment, is it good for people and will it make us money? We are constantly juggling these three questions.

This value base has concrete implications for all the aspects of work systems: how work is designed and organized, how people are treated and allowed to develop, how economic resources are invested, how changes are carried out in the system, and how the system connects to its stakeholders. The message from all the chapters in this book is that sustainability, as a theoretical and a practical concept, makes it possible for employees and managers alike to combine their need for a meaningful life with positive outcomes from their work: for their business and for its environment.

Sustainability – a multidisciplinary, multiperspective issue

We will now elaborate our generic definition of sustainable work systems in the light of the experiences presented in the cases in Chapters 2 to 14. We examine the perspectives that have been adopted when striving after sustainability, the disciplinary bases of these perspectives, and the key analytic concepts that the authors used in their discussions and when framing the complex issues of work system sustainability in these cases. The cases demonstrate concretely the multidisciplinary nature of sustainable work systems. Either instinctively or consciously the researchers in these cases have relied on multiple disciplinary bases as they approach the issues of sustainability in various contexts. It seems that work system sustainability cannot be captured by simply using a single disciplinary base or a certain perspective. Table17.1 presents a summary of six perspectives resulting from our analysis of the cases.

The individual at work

Several of the chapters explore sustainable work systems from the perspective of the individual. For instance, Weichel *et al.* (Chapter 5) discuss sustainable ageing at work, while Brödner (Chapter 4) explores the possibilities for the growth

Table 17.1 Main concepts of sustainability and sustainable development

Sustainability perspective	Disciplinary base	Key analytic concepts
Individuals at work	Psychology, education, organizational behaviour, work science, ergonomics	Work (routine/non-routine, craft, knowledge-based, professional), work design, work organization, human resources management (HRM), work ability, workplace learning, personnel development, participation, discretion, diversity
Social collectives at work	Social psychology, sociology, management and organizational science	(Self-managed) teams, team design, team dynamics, communities of practice, collective learning, power, leadership dynamics, emergent organizing
Resources at work	Psychology, sociology, engineering, economics, management science, philosophy	Value-base, competences, intellectual and social capital, discretion, organizational capabilities, product life cycles, technological resources, time, equality and complexity of resources, economic resources
Change and learning processes at work	(Educational) psychology, organizational change and development, organization science, complexity theory	*(Resonant) leadership:* tipping points, dialogue, joint sense making, networks, coalitions *Management:* cognitive learning mechanisms, visions, value base, balanced scorecards, development models, tools, strategies *Learning mechanisms:* structural, parallel, procedural, bench learning, second-order (double-loop) learning, organizational learning, organizational institutionalization
Systems at work	Systems theory, network theory, institutional theory, stakeholder theory, political economics, political science	Development coalitions, "home and away" networks, supply and value chains, community and societal regulation, coordination, externalized/internalized costs, community/societal/ecological embeddedness

of human resources in knowledge-intensive work. The chapters focus on work design and work-organizational factors, as well as human resources management practices that impact the sustainability of human resources. The individual-based perspective is, as may be expected, anchored predominantly in the behavioural and social science domains (see Table 17.1). The key analytic concepts recognize different types of work situations (e.g., routine and non-routine work, professional and craft work, knowledge-based work). It seems clear that sustaining human and social resources is a context-specific process in which the special features of the work situation have to be taken into account.

There are no universal job characteristics for sustainable work, but rather principles that can guide efforts to promote individual-level sustainability in different settings. A key principle seems to be continuous learning and development at work; the researchers discuss, for example, employees' work ability and workplace learning. Practical HRM and personnel development tools can be used to promote work ability, workplace learning, and employee development. Two other key principles relate to employee participation opportunities and discretion, and diversity. The first, participation and discretion, concerns the sustainability requirement that employees be involved in shaping their own work situation. The second, diversity, concerns taking into account employees' individual attributes in sustaining their resources.

Groups and communities of workers

The social collective perspective is also present in many chapters, perhaps not in as a central role as the individual-level perspective, but as a supporting theme in understanding how individual- and organizational-level sustainability are bridged (see Table 17.2). However, Boyatzis (Chapter 7) focuses explicitly in his chapter on sustainable teams. The social collective perspective is anchored predominantly in the domains of sociology, social psychology, and management and organizational science. The key analytic concepts recognize the importance of teams and communities of practice as environments for individual growth and development, and as platforms for wider system sustainability. The chapters also elaborate on collective development and learning; collective sustainability originates from individuals being able to learn together and create new, shared solutions for sustainable work. The chapters also draw attention to issues of power and leadership dynamics, and repeat the message of participation as a key issue in creating sustainable work systems. For instance, Cox (Chapter 2) emphasizes that solutions for ecological, economic, and human sustainability can be found through daily actions in workplaces: appreciating emergent solutions and organizing promotes sustainability.

Resources in work systems

The book as a whole approaches sustainability from the resources perspective, focusing on the development and growth of various resources engaged in work systems. Different resources are the focus in different chapters. Some pay attention to human resources sustainability (e.g., Chapters 4, 5, and 15). With a relational view, the concept of resources becomes social resources that reside in the relations among individuals, social groups, and institutional actors (e.g., Chapters 8, 9, 11, and 12). Other authors focus on products and technology as pathways to work system sustainability (e.g., Chapters 6 and 8). Using these cases, the book discusses the need to sustain different resources and also recognizes that various resources can be used to promote work system sustainability as whole. Resources can thus be seen to have complementary roles and meanings in sustainable work systems: on the one hand, they need to be sustained, and on the other hand, a given resource can be applied to promote sustainability in other resources (cf. the reasoning on complementarities of Pettigrew *et al.*, 2003). Many chapters also emphasize the importance of intangible resources in achieving sustainable economical outcomes. As noted, first and foremost, sustainable work systems are value-based systems, and, for instance, employee discretion and participation are seen as key resources for sustainability in employees and in whole work systems. Time is also an important resource for sustainability: sustainable work systems are not static and permanent systems, but they change and transform through time – and time, of course, is needed for the creation of sustainability solutions. The foundations of the resource-based perspective can be found in the fields of psychology, sociology, engineering, economics, management science, and even philosophy.

Change and learning processes at work

Many chapters in the book recognize sustainability as a dynamic, learning-oriented state. There are no ready solutions for sustaining the various resources engaged in work system operations – solutions can only be sought continuously (Bradbury, Chapter 12). This is emphasized in the change and learning perspective on work. In the field of change and learning, we can distinguish the use of *leadership* and *management* as related key analytic concepts in various chapters. On the one hand, sustainability, as a dynamic process, requires leadership activities that can involve people in networks and coalitions and engage them in joint sense-making and dialogue to create conditions such that new sustainability solutions can emerge (Boyatzis, Chapter 7). On the other hand, in day-to-day operations, practical management practices and structures are needed, including strategies and visions, management systems such as balanced scorecards, development models, and discussion forums. Stebbins and Valenzuela, for example (Chapter 9), emphasize that managers can consciously seek to create learning situations and learning opportunities toward sustainability by designing various learning mechanisms in an organization. The change and learning perspective is founded in the fields of educational psychology, organization change and development, organization science, and complexity theory.

Systems at work

Finally, the chapters from 9 to 14 focus on the intraorganizational and inter-organizational levels of work systems. These chapters help us to understand the impacts of various factors on work system sustainability or the sustainability of resources involved in these systems: communication between companies or organizational units (e.g., Stebbins and Valenzuela, Chapter 9; Cerf and Savage, Chapter 10; Lifvergren *et al.*, Chapter 11; Bradbury, Chapter 12) and broader national, societal, and business sector conditions (e.g., Román, Chapter 13; Moore and Wen, Chapter 14). These chapters illustrate the importance of creating coalitions and networks in which the complex issues relating to work system sustainability can be discussed and resolved. The systems at work perspective is anchored predominantly in systems theory, network theory, institutional theory, stakeholder theory, and political economics and political science.

Multidisciplinary illustrations

The cases and empirical illustrations presented in Chapters 2 to 14 come from the United States, northern Europe, China, and South America. They illustrate that sustainability can be thought of, designed, and managed in many ways. However, all cases share a multidisciplinary nature. The authors in this volume rely on different disciplinary bases and key analytic concepts, yet they have been able to create coherent scientific and practical argumentation in their chapters. Table 17.2 summarizes the main messages from each chapter and presents our assessment of the degree to which they utilize the different sustainability perspectives recognized in Table 17.1. Each example focuses on specific aspects of sustainability while referring to others. In each case, utilizing the different disciplinary perspectives reveals some unique insights into the holistic nature and complexity of sustainability.

Individuals and groups

In Table 17.2, we can clearly recognize two groups of chapters. Chapters 2 to 8 focus on the individual and/or social-collectives perspectives of sustainability, while only secondarily referring to the wider systems perspective. These chapters address individual- or group/team-level sustainability in work systems. They provide illustrations of how resources, changes, and learning processes at individual and collective levels can promote the sustainability of a work system or its individual members. The chapters illustrate how work system values and identity development can promote sustainability (Cox, Chapter 2; Amodeo, Chapter 3) and they discuss how individual factors, such as ageing (Weichel *et al.*, Chapter 5), or the type of work, such as its degree of knowledge intensity (Brödner, Chapter 4), impact human sustainability at work and work system sustainability as a whole. These chapters show how ergonomic work design and organizational practices

Table 17.2 A comparative synopsis of the illustrations. Weight in illustration: L = low, M = medium, H = high

Illustration	Essence of the case	Individuals at work	Social collectives at work	Resources at work	Change & learning processes	Systems at work
2. Visions	Top entrepreneurial managers prioritize visions and partnership to embed values in their organizations.	H	M	H	M	L
3. Identity	An extended, holistic, and multifunctional program changes a company identity from traditional to green.	H	L	M	H	L
4. Knowledge work	Work redesign gives software engineers more discretion to control contradictory work demands.	H	M	H	M	L
5. Ageing	Work, team, and technical redesign enable worker capabilities to maintain manufacturing performance.	H	L	M	M	L
6. Technological support	Coordinated sociotechnical development enables personnel, product, and business development.	M	M	H	M	L
7. Sustainable teams	Utilization of intentional change and complexity theories leads to sustainable teams.	M	H	M	H	L
8. Heritage	Ability to focus change and develop (manage tipping points) heightens personnel employability in crises.	H	L	M	M	L
9. Learning mechanisms	Planned and systematic use of learning mechanisms facilitates the development of sustainable work groups.	M	L	H	M	H
10. Financial management	Available systems, methods, and tools allow managers to make good decisions on sustainability.	L	L	H	M	M
11. Development coalitions	A development coalition enables the development of system sustainability by integrating the value chain.	L	M	M	H	H
12. Feedback	A collaborative network between companies and researchers develops feedback processes for shared tasks.	L	M	M	H	H
13. Labelling	Is labelling a strategy for boosting global markets and creating sustainable working conditions?	M	L	L	L	H
14. Work-life balance	Managers' low perceived level of work-life balance indicates an imbalance in economic and social policies in China.	L	L	M	M	H

entailing participation and power sharing are central in attaining sustainability. They also demonstrate how changes in the work system or its units (such as teams) can have both positive and negative consequences for human and collective sustainability. Wilhelmson and Döös (Chapter 8) indicate how sustainability may fluctuate in a work system, and how even seemingly negative developments may pave the way for new sustainable solutions and strengthen employees' sustainability. Boyatzis (Chapter 7) illustrates how creating a sustainable team is a process of pleasant and unpleasant discoveries as the team tries to achieve its Ideal Self and be the best it can. Sustainable development is not a smooth path, but surmounting difficulties may occasion learning that can sustain people and work systems.

Work systems

There is a clear work systems perspective in the last six cases, Chapters 9 to 14. These chapters discuss intraorganizational and interorganizational coalitions and networks as forums for discussing and solving the value, attitudinal, and operational problems that undermine sustainability in work systems (Chapters 9, 11, and 12), and they also point out how broader market and societal norms, structures, and practices can threaten sustainability (Chapters 13 and 14). Sustainability is clearly not an easy issue. Business has shown that previous successes can be a severe hindrance to further innovation. It would be a serious mistake to assume that it is possible to attain sustainability and then relax. It is clear that sustainability is a dynamic state: each coalition and network must continually reevaluate its earlier advances to create more appropriate solutions that are conducive to sustainability in new situations. Also in Chapters 9 to 14, the systems at work perspective is often connected with either the resources at work perspective or with the change and learning processes perspective. For instance, Stebbins and Valenzuela (Chapter 9) discuss organizational learning mechanisms through which human, social, and economic resources may grow. Lifvergren *et al.* (Chapter 11) and Bradbury (Chapter 12), in their turn, connect collaborative coalitions or networks to the promotion of change and learning for sustainability. In summary, chapters 9 to 12 discuss collaborative networks and systems as forums for sustainable resource development through change and learning efforts. Chapters 13 and 14 focus on how national and business sector cultures and regulations impact the sustainability of work systems and work system members.

The development of sustainability change processes

In Chapter 1, we reserved the term *sustainable development* for those actions that seek to reach and maintain a state of sustainability. Several of the cases in the book present models of sustainable development: they outline the phases through which an organization progressed toward the dynamic state of human, social, economic, and ecological resource regeneration. As such, the sustainable development perspective is viewed as a system-wide planned effort, usually initiated by senior management, for the purpose of improving the sustainable balance of the dynamic state of a system's human, social, economic, and ecological resources. Table 17.3 captures the essence of the planned change approach utilized in seven of our cases. The rows in Table 17.3 represent the phases in the planned change effort. Even though we have grouped together some of the phases, it can be seen that the authors actually identify rather similar phases for sustainable development.

First stage – awareness, recognition, and insight

The first phase is about awareness, recognition, or insight. A key actor or several key actors in a work system realize that there is an urgent need for more sustainable operations. These key actors in most cases are at the top level of the system, but in the case studies that were reported by Lifvergren *et al.* (Chapter 11) and Bradbury (Chapter 12) we can see that employees seem to have been a driving force by realizing the need for sustainability and starting to work toward it. The case studies by Cox (Chapter 2), Amodeo (Chapter 3), Stebbins and Valenzuela (Chapter 9), and Stebbins and Shani (Chapter 16) illustrate clearly that strong leverage for sustainability can be generated by the personal insight and commitment of a CEO, other executives, and company owners. Based on the findings of Boyatzis (Chapter 7), we can see that this phase is founded on a perceived dissonance between what one wants to be and what one is. Lifvergren *et al.* (Chapter 11) and Bradbury (Chapter 12) also demonstrate how a strong impetus for change can be provided by encounters between different ways of looking at the world. In these two chapters, people from different backgrounds who are connected by a shared work-related interest started their journey toward sustainability by understanding that the world is more complex than their individual ways of thinking about it. In sum, these chapters indicate how a realization that there are alternative ways to be, think, and act in the world can open the door to the search for sustainability (cf. Bjerlöv's (1999) process concepts of differentiation and decentration in dialogues between people with different backgrounds). Encountering alternative ways to be, think, and act makes it clear that the regeneration of resources in a work system demands that one consider alternatives to one's usual approaches.

Several chapters also recognize that the sudden and intense recognition of an existing problem can initiate a sustainability journey. For instance, Stebbins and Valenzuela (Chapter 9) describe how an acute financial and competitive crisis in a company formed the starting point for a search for more sustainable ways to work. In Chapter 3, a CEO came to see his company as "a plunderer of the Earth" and started to work toward ecological sustainability based on this insight.

Where many of the chapters present rather dramatic problem- or dissonance-based insights into the need for sustainability, Cox (Chapter 2) demonstrates how sustainability can also build on the existing personal value base of work system actors. Often, sustainability and sustainable development are perceived as requiring a considerable change in mental models and ways of thinking. However, we are convinced that more and more people are acquiring or already have acquired

Table 17.3 The phases of sustainable development

SUSTAINABLE DEVELOPMENT PHASE	Chapter 2 Creating a sustainability vision	Chapter 3 Creating a sustainability identity	Chapter 7 Creating sustainable teams	Chapter 9 Learning & sustainable work design	Chapter 11 Development coalition for sustainability	Chapter 12 Feedback & sustainability networks	Chapter 16 Sustainability design/change methodology
Becoming aware, recognizing, gaining insight	Sense of personal purpose Sense of business purpose	Awakening to the importance of sustainability	Discovering ideal self Contrasting ideal self to real self	Experienced urgent need for a change	Confronting radically different institutional perspectives Presenting new ideas, insights, & intuitions	Becoming aware of one's learning style	Realization of the need for change
Mobilizing, building commitment, and setting direction	Sustainability vision	Cocooning: from scepticism to understanding	Establishing a learning agenda	Design of learning mechanisms	Interpretation of ideas Organizing broad stakeholder involvement	Creating relational, conceptual, and action spaces	Preliminary project planning and reviewing alternative design models Motivating the change effort and involving stakeholders Establishing design criteria
Design, experimentation, and implementation of specific change mechanisms and processes	Collaboration with a broad range of stakeholders Engaging in transformative interactions	Metamorphosis: from understanding to belief Emergence: from belief to commitment	Experimentation and practice with new behaviours	Experimenting with new approaches Educating others	Experimentation and dialogue leading to integration of ideas in a common understanding	Experimentation and dialogue Collaborative learning among actors from different backgrounds	Creating learning mechanisms Building personal and social support for work design experimentation Comprehensive impact analysis
Establishing a state of sustainability and an ongoing development process	Emergent, ongoing organizing	Engagement and commitment	Trusting and resonant relationships	Diffusing lessons and practices system-wide	Institutionalizing: decisions on development structures and processes generating engagement & trust	Learning community for collaboration, building know-how for theory, tools, and action	Extending prototype and work processes to other work units Reviewing mechanisms for continuous improvements

such mental models. Anita Roddick (of The Body Shop) and Jeffrey Hollender (of Seventh Generation), presented in Chapter 2, were pathfinders for sustainability, and the examples they and executives like them are showing, together with examples from NGOs and the popular and political debate on sustainability, are helping to spread the values and mental models of sustainability. We are approaching the situation where a realized need is no longer the threshold for sustainability; the threshold is now the inability to move toward theoretical and practical approaches to promote sustainability.

Second stage – mobilization, commitment building, and direction setting

The chapters in this volume provide us with ideas about how sustainable development in work systems can go beyond ideas, values, and mental models. The second common phase we identify deals with mobilization, commitment building, and direction setting. Work system actors need to build a plan for how they want to change toward sustainability. A vision or an understanding of what sustainability in a particular work system can be is formed (Chapters 2, 3, and 16). Interpretations of alternative ways of thinking (Chapter 11) allow comprehension of the complex situation in which sustainability is sought. A learning agenda is devised to bring the ideal state and the existing state of affairs closer together (Chapter 7). And a stage is built for actions toward sustainability. Stebbins and Valenzuela (Chapter 9) refer to creating learning mechanisms in a work system to promote sustainability, while Bradbury (Chapter 12) refers to the need for shared spaces – relational, conceptual, and action spaces – in which sustainability can be sought.

Third stage – design, experimentation, and implementation

The second phase sets the stage for a third phase: designing, testing, and implementing specific change mechanisms. We recognize that collaboration, exchange, and learning among a wide set of stakeholders are pivotal factors for actually moving toward sustainability. As new, more sustainable ways to function have to be found, it seems that the key is collaboration and social exchange that allow different voices and priorities to be heard. This convinces us of the idea that sustainability is truly a collaborative effort. Creating a work system where various resources – human, social, economic, and ecological – are able to regenerate and flourish means considering many dissonant ideas and priorities. Perhaps there are people who are able to fit all these ideas and priorities into their individual mental models, but these cases seem to indicate that stakeholders need to come together to ensure that the different ideas really are considered in a work system's decision making. As stakeholders present and represent their personal or work-related priorities, while at the same time respecting those of the others, solutions for sustainability can be found. Sustainability is truly something for a generation of peers who respect one another and believe in the power of collaboration instead of the power of hierarchy. The second clear feature of this activity phase is experimentation. New solutions that may be more conducive to sustainability and the balancing of different priorities and needs have to be tested through experimentation (see, e.g., Chapters 7, 9, 11, and 12).

Fourth stage – dynamic sustainability, ongoing development

Sustainable development leads eventually to the dynamic state of sustainability in which the various resources engaged in work system operations are regenerated and encouraged to grow. The long path of awareness, mobilization, and experimentation toward sustainability leads to a phase in which a work system is able to operate in a dynamic manner and to always search for sustainable ways to operate. There is a shared commitment to sustainability that underlies all operations (e.g., Chapters 3 and 11). The participants in a sustainable work system are also committed to the learning community formed by various stakeholders, which collaborates continuously to find solutions for sustainability. There is trust among actors and willingness to keep on respecting various priorities, needs, and ideas. Chapters 2, 11, 12, and 16 indicate that the state of sustainability is very dynamic in the sense that, while the framework of stakeholder collaboration for the search of sustainability solutions may be relatively fixed, the solutions themselves live and change. Bradbury (Chapter 12) states that a learning community has been created for the building of know-how for theory, tools, and action. Cox (Chapter 2) shows how the search for sustainability is an ongoing process of emergent organizing in a work system. New solutions need to be found, and the work system as whole trusts in its ability to find these solutions. Instead of top-down managerial decisions, solutions that emerge in various parts of the work systems are embraced. Lifvergren *et al.* (Chapter 11) speak of the creation of a management meso-level organization providing the basis for broad sustainability development at the microsystem level, i.e., in individual wards and clinics (cf. Nelson *et al.* 2002).

As we have seen, several chapters in this volume describe sustainable development in a work system as a complex system-wide planned change process. We delineated four distinct phases that such processes have in common: Awareness, recognition, and insight; mobilization, commitment building, and direction setting; designing, experimentation, and implementation-specific change mechanisms; and the outcome state of dynamic sustainability, an ongoing process. The total process is a long-term endeavour. It entails the formation of new coalitions and stakeholder communities, with an underlying aim of creating conditions in which solutions for sustainability can emerge. For instance, as reported in Mona Amodeo's (Chapter 3) account, Interface's journey toward sustainability started in 1994 and the company is aiming to reach "the summit of the Mount Sustainability" by 2020.

Sustainability is clearly not reached overnight. It may mean adopting new values, attitudes, and mental models or reshaping existing ones. It means translating these models to plans and actions, and it means engaging various stakeholders and collaborating with them, changing and establishing new relationships.

Boyatzis (Chapter 7) writes about *tipping points* between various phases of the sustainability journey. Tipping points are situations where a work system and its members have progressed such that a small, incremental change can push them over to a new developmental phase. From this perspective, one cannot hurry sustainability. A next phase can only be reached when a previous one has been lived through and learned through. This is an important message from our book – because sustainability requires contextual solutions to emerge, each work system has to travel its own sustainable development path and find its own tipping points as it progresses toward sustainability. However, inspiration and knowledge are never wasted. We hope that the case illustrations in this book can help different types of work systems to recognize where they are in terms of sustainable development, and what they need in order to move forward toward the dynamic state of sustainability.

The future – directions for research

In this chapter, we have attempted to capture some of our learning from this project. Due to the emergent nature of the field, its scope, context, mechanisms, and dynamics, it is impossible to provide a comprehensive path for research and practice. In this section of the chapter, our objective is to identify a few areas that we view as critical for both research and practice.

As can be seen from the different disciplinary perspectives on sustainability and the cases described and examined in this book, sustainability is an emerging complex phenomenon and a field of study that is in need of much research and discussion.

The multiple nature of research issues regarding sustainable work systems

The complexity of sustainable work systems, coupled with the emergent nature of the theoretical knowledge, calls for a holistic, interdisciplinary, and multi-level perspective. The cases in this book provide evidence of the need for this approach. As pointed out in Chapter 1, sustainability is an intergenerational, multiscale, and multiple-domain phenomenon. Nevertheless, we must develop methods that will allow us to conduct the complex research projects required.

Disciplines tend to develop theories and knowledge-based ways of thinking that are isolated from those of other disciplines. Many disciplines advocate specific levels of analysis and tend to develop distinct approaches to inquiry that not always are complementary. Our cases show that when continuous dialogue between researchers from different disciplines takes place over time, as the research projects get formulated, carried out, and analyzed, a true interdisciplinary perspective can emerge. Achieving an interdisciplinary perspective requires a major commitment by all the parties involved, and a willingness to work through some very difficult disagreements that may be both theoretical and methodological in nature.

Other key areas for further research concerning the design of work and work organization are:

- the creation of collaborative organizations with a greater level of power equality between management and co-workers, based on dialogue and collective learning;
- work design that promotes a richer comprehension of the complexity of work systems and an innate sense of meaningfulness at work;
- the development of resources, primarily the development of human complexity, through learning, leading to shared mental models and an experience of meaningfulness that is shared between management and co-workers.

The need for extended studies of sustainability

The level of analysis of the studies reported in this book can be viewed as the level of sustainable structures or processes. Much has been learned from such studies about the features of sustainability, its dynamics, and possible drivers and inhibitors in particular settings at particular points or periods. These indicate that there can be marked fluctuations in sustainability over time, and we need more research regarding the factors in the systems studied and their contexts that give rise to these fluctuations: what are the key contextual conditions, the critical tipping points in the development processes? How are learning and development promoted or hindered by limited or extensive design, or by maintaining different paces in the change process (Boud 2006)?

The rise of contextualism as a scientific theory and method provides a possible new approach to the study of change and sustainability (Pettigrew *et al.* 2001). Based on the results from the cases reported in this book, we advocate that future research on sustainability should explore the contexts, content, and processes of sustainability together with their interconnections over time. Pursuing this kind of research will require key analytical decisions about how many levels of analysis to include in the treatment of the context – for example, individual, group, organization, network, and/or region. In addition, decisions are required as to which processes or mechanisms should be included or excluded from the study – for example, change, learning, and/or adaptation. The complexity of such an approach is evident, not least because the concept of sustainability will have different implications for different levels, processes, and mechanisms. The combination of the chosen levels of context, the processes, and the interaction field brought into an analysis is likely to generate new insights into the phenomenon of sustainability.

There are, however, practical difficulties in arranging longitudinal studies. Generally, they are dependent on the willingness of the organization participating in the study to make a significant contribution to the costs of the research partner, either as a contract researcher or consultant. Such was the case in several of the cases reported here. Few government research financing agencies are prepared to finance longitudinal case studies.

The need for collaborative research

Actionable knowledge is viewed as knowledge that can simultaneously serve the needs of science and of living systems, e.g., work units, organizations, networks, or societies (Argyris 2003). Meeting the needs of both is not only critical (and achievable) but generates a more meaningful insight into the phenomenon that is being studied (Reason and Bradbury 2001). The issues of sustainability are of such critical social, economic, and ecological importance that the development of actionable knowledge must be on the research agenda, and actors in workplaces and organizations must increasingly be brought in to participate in the research process.

The focus on sustainability lends itself to the exploration and utilization of different alternative *participative inquiry approaches*. These include varieties of collaborative research forms such as participative inquiry, action research, action science, intervention research, clinical field research, developmental action inquiry, and appreciative inquiry (Stebbins and Shani, Chapter 16). Such research points toward the possibility that the scientific process chosen is likely to enable the further development of the system under investigation and thus enhance its sustainable nature. Mohrman and Shani (2008) point out that the quality of such collaborative research is dependent on the alignment of the researcher-practitioner partners' purposes in the study, the institutional and resource context of collaboration, the mechanisms that enable learning in the collaborative relationships, and the convergence of the languages of practice and theory. Pasmore *et al.* (2008) maintain that collaborative research must be characterized by high levels of rigour regarding standards of scientific proof; of reflection regarding the partners' joint creation of new insights and theories; and of relevance regarding significant value generated to the participating organization(s).

Difficulties may well arise in such studies around issues of transparency (the making public of information regarded as commercially or socially sensitive), of necessary resources (not least regarding practitioner participation or the duration of the study), and of what issues are addressed and how (sustainability studies tend to challenge the status quo and question current assumptions and ways of doing things). Stebbins and Shani (Chapter 16) accept that some contexts may not be available for such study. Nevertheless, much more research is needed in order to explore the relevance of different participative research forms as well as the possible causal relationship between the research forms and the facilitation of system sustainability.

The nature of partnership in sustainable work systems

Our research indicates that sustainable work systems seem to be based on true partnership and joint efforts between organizational members. Partnership and participation are both an end and a means in the context of sustainability. Our cases dealing with the design of work and work organization indicate that partnership is an important feature of sustainable work. In addition, such jobs and organizations can be achieved by means of joint commitment and the collaborative efforts of management and organizational members. Joint effort demands that a productive dialogue based on mutual respect and understanding be established. However, our theoretical knowledge of true partnership, its key features, and its dynamics in the context of creating sustainable work systems is limited.

Partnership and participation today take various forms in different labour markets and different sectors. Different applications exist for direct and representative participation. Different systems exist for representative participation, focusing on local levels (shop stewards) or central levels (committee members). Management and unions in companies have on occasion agreed on the division of human resource development tasks among themselves (Shani and Docherty 2003). Another form of partnership is between different organizations along a value or a supply chain (e.g., the health care provision chain in Chapter 11). Inquiry into the developmental nature of partnerships and sustainability processes and outcomes is clearly of importance at this stage of theory development.

The need for sustainability change processes

Sustainable development, as we have seen in this book, requires a comprehensive guiding framework for action. Several of the cases identified phases through which firms progressed toward a dynamic state of human, social, economic, and ecological resource regeneration. Table 17.3 captures the essence of the planned change orientations that were taken by seven of the cases in the book. We have advanced a four-phase planned change approach for system transformation. Notwithstanding these initial steps, this interdisciplinary, emerging field, as indicated by the scientific literature on sustainable development, seems to be lacking a clear template for action.

The literature in the field of organization development and change has advanced a small number of comprehensive, system-wide, planned change approaches, such as sociotechnical system planned change and organization culture transformation. An empirical investigation that examines alternative approaches to sustainable development and their potential merit is likely to shed some light on the possible approaches, their phases, key activities, key processes, and respective outcomes.

Learning, learning mechanisms, and sustainability

Sustainability provides a moral and intellectual focus for social as well as cognitive development. We must "learn our way out" of our present situation toward a more sustainable world. This requires encouraging people to reflect on how and why certain decisions are being taken, and to make a practice of becoming aware of the available real alternatives. The cases in the book dealing with the design of work and work organization indicate that processes of learning and development are important for individual and collective sustainability.

Despite initiatives for change, organizations manifest a remarkable stability. Interventions from internal or external experts, new policies, joint agreements, and government reforms often appear to have little effect on the reality of shop or office floors. The wind of change soon blows by, and "business as usual" is resumed, often after a considerable waste of resources. Repeated change projects with no clear benefit demoralize – and are, in fact, a basic cause of such negative phenomena as burnout (Barklöf 2000). Research on the decay or reversal of change processes is needed.

From a mechanistic viewpoint, change means moving from one steady state to another, based on single-loop learning. Theories of organizational learning have been concerned with the (lack of) capacity for double-loop learning. A goal for a sustainable organization is not simply double-loop learning but the ability to learn to learn, coupled with a capacity for innovation.

The processes of learning and development in organizations, including experiential learning, tacit knowledge, communities of practice, learning mechanisms, creativity, and development, have all been acknowledged as of great importance but are still enigmatic and require much further research. Similarly, the design, appropriateness, efficiency, and efficacy of diverse learning processes and their combinations need further study, as do the design and use of more sophisticated methods such as parallel learning structures and bench-learning structures (Shani and Docherty 2003, 2008; Docherty and Shani 2008; Karlöf *et al.* 2000).

Integrating the issues of economic, social, and ecological sustainability

There is a pressing need for the political and social involvement of all sectors of society ("social responsibility") to ensure that knowledge in the areas of social, ecological, and economic sustainability may develop at comparable rates, and that the issues integrating them are allotted due attention and resources. There is a real risk that knowledge regarding the social dimension will fall behind and consequently that economic and ecological sustainability will remain to be achieved. At the beginning of this chapter, we argued that economic and ecological sustainability are highly dependent on people's creativity and efforts and thus on socially sustainable work systems.

Methods and tools in management science

At the organizational level, the integration of the different dimensions of sustainability is a key issue for management – the development of theoretical frameworks, methods, and tools for planning, monitoring, and evaluating the use and development of the organization's tangible and intangible resources. This is now a key area in management science (Bounfour 2003; Roy 2003; Skoog 2003; Cerf and Savage, Chapter 10 in this volume). One of the most important areas in this context is the development of the sustainability Balanced Scorecard (BSC) method. As Cerf and Savage point out, there is a wide range of sophisticated methods and tools at management's disposal to enable planning and decision making on sustainability issues, but what we have little information about is the extent to which such methods and tools are in fact utilized, when, in what contexts, and by whom, with what results? Which tools and methods have proved their worth? What difficulties have been met in their application and how are they being handled? Experiences from the private sector are often shared in "best practice" circles, but experiences from the public sector are more generally available only in their efforts to spread good practice. The healthcare sector has been making serious efforts in this field in several countries, for example in the United Kingdom, the Netherlands, and Sweden (Käll 2005).

Learning, creativity, and innovation

In the context of sustainability, the balanced scorecard method aims to ensure that management makes active, conscious decisions in all key areas of business – decisions that very often involve balancing conflicting important and legitimate goals and interests. One such task is that of balancing static and dynamic efficiency, production and development. Development is mainly dealt with in the sustainability literature in terms of individual and collective learning, and sometimes in terms of intellectual and social capital. In addition we wish to mention here organizational competences, or rather, organizational business capabilities and dynamic capabilities, concepts that emerge from the strategy literature (Helfat 2003). Teece *et al.* (1997) define dynamic capabilities as those that enable managers to build, integrate, and reconfigure internal and external competences to address rapidly changing environments. These are the basis for their companies' sustained competitive advantage, their companies' capacity to adjust, change, and develop. (The development of dynamic capabilities was broached in Chapters 6, 11, and 12.) A key issue is to identify the competences and skills necessary to develop and maintain sustainability. In our definition, organizational capabilities are the skills involved in making use of an organization's resources; are bundles of competences and routines; are embedded in an organization, its technologies, its social structures and processes; give coherence to the organization; comprise both tacit and explicit knowledge; and are firm-specific and developed over time. Together, they enable a firm to develop a distinctive competence. A specific issue is the learning process for embedding new knowledge in organizations. This concerns the transfer of knowledge from individuals to groups to organizations (Lifvergren *et al.* Chapter 11), and the transformations between tacit and explicit knowledge (Nonaka and Reinmoeller, 2002).

Growth and renewal are now emerging as an alternative to the 1990s model of being "lean and mean." But organizations, especially if they are large and well-established, are often unlikely to challenge or reexamine their assumptions about themselves or their environments (Dougherty and Hardy 1996; Tushman and O'Reilly 1996). This results in new potential business initiatives being limited to those based on former core competences or current strategy. Managing innovation is regarded as difficult; innovation is an elusive term that has mainly been used in relation to changes in products, services, and production processes. But the term may well be expanded to cover innovations in management, encompassing the ability to innovate, to strategize, and to renew the organization. Managing the innovation process entails refocusing from serial development to providing institutional conditions for innovation, for example by providing generous organizational slack and by combining concepts and ideas from such fields as organizational creativity and motivation, initiative taking, stress management, and organizational culture and values (cf. Richtnér 2004). An important area for research is the development of sustainability-oriented innovations. But measuring progress and success in innovation is difficult and constitutes a further dimension in such research (Fitzgibbon 2000).

Development coalitions, networks, and systems

There is, however, considerable experience of collaborative effort between practitioners and researchers, between companies, NGOs, and regional and government agencies and authorities in pursuit of mutual learning, development, and innovation. Such networks and coalitions have often been very successful in regional development (Fricke and Totterdill 2004; Gustavsen *et al.* 1998; Walshok and Stymne 2008), in university-driven networks (Senge *et al.* 2006; Bradbury, Chapter 12 in this volume) and in networks to foster technical innovation (Docherty 1988). However, we need further research regarding the factors that determine the development and success of such networks and their life cycles.

Important contextual factors facilitating the creation of sustainable work systems

The cases in Chapters 13 and 14 discussed how societal measures can support the development of social sustainability. Chapter 13 focused on the extent to which market mechanisms in the form of voluntary certification may improve sustainability in the coffee industry. This interplay between sustainability performance, public and private competitive concerns, and regulation is one of the more significant contemporary policy issues and is likely to remain so over the coming years. Chapter 14 focused on the imbalance emerging in Chinese society as a very strong political policy on economic development exists at the same time as there are no social reforms strengthening social sustainability in working life or outside of it.

Most of the cases presented in the book come from countries in which there are well-developed labour markets and social legislation and policies in such areas as health and safety, the work environment, social equality in the workplace, and industrial relations. There are even policy discussions on such issues as corporate social responsibility and ethics in the workplace. The Netherlands, for example, has already conducted a research programme on the reporting of corporate social responsibility (Cramer and Loeber 2007). There is a need for research on how such formal measures can influence the development of social sustainability and sustainable work systems.

A concluding thought

Frederick Winslow Taylor, the father of Scientific Management, ended life rather embittered and, as he saw himself, misunderstood and opposed by his contemporaries. Like many of today's organization development consultants, he complained about the narrowness and conservatism of his time.

> Scientific management does not exist and cannot exist until there has been a complete mental revolution on the part of the workmen working under it, as to their duties toward themselves and toward their employers, and a complete mental revolution in the outlook for the employers, toward their duties, toward themselves, and toward their work men.
>
> Frederick Taylor (1911) *The Principles of Scientific Management.*

Taylor was indignant about wasteful management. However, he did, at least posthumously, manage to change the mental setup of the whole industrialized world. Maybe the mental revolution that Taylor demanded was the *rationality of modernism* and a final break with the conceptions and value system of the agricultural past. Now, nearly a century later, we feel that realizing sustainable work systems may well demand another mental revolution. Taylor's challenge was to lead people from one state of mind to another. The challenge is now probably of a different kind: not to move from one state to another, but rather to establish a dynamic flexibility – because sustainability is a process, not a state.

Questions for reflection

Here are three questions for your further reflection on the issues broached in this chapter:

• What are some of the distinctive features of projects to develop sustainable work systems and social sustainability that make them especially challenging?
• Attaining and maintaining social sustainability is a long process. What do you see as important stages in this process?
• There are many challenges that remain. What issue do you regard as the most important and how would you suggest tackling it?

References

Argyris, C. (2003) "Actionable Knowledge," in H. Tsoukas and C. Knudsen (eds), *The Oxford Handbook of Organization Theory: Meta-theoretical perspectives*, Oxford: Oxford University Press, pp. 423–452.

Barklöf, K. (2000) *Magra organisationer* [Lean organizations], Stockholm: Swedish Council for Work Life Research.

Bjerlöv. M. (1999) *Om lärande i verksamhetsanknutna samtal* [Learning in work-based discourse]. Stockholm: National Institute for Working Life, Work and Health scientific series: 1999: 1.

Boud, D. (2006) "Creating Space for Reflection at Work," in D. Boud, P. Cressey, and P. Docherty (eds), *Productive Reflection at Work: Learning for changing organizations*, London: Routledge, pp. 158–169.

Bounfour, A. (2003) *The Management of Intangibles: The organization's most valuable assets*, London: Routledge Advances in Management and Business Studies Series.

Cramer, J. and Loeber, A. (2007) "Learning about Corporate Social Responsibility from a Sustainable Development Perspective: A Dutch experiment," in A.E.J. Wals (ed.), *Social Learning towards a Sustainable World: Principles, perspectives and praxis*, Wageningen, Netherlands: Wageningen Academic Publishing, pp. 265–277.

Docherty, P. (1988) *Expertsystem i Storbritannien* [Expert systems in the United Kingdom], Stockholm: Teldok rapport 37.

Docherty, P. and Shani, A.B. (Rami) (2008) "Learning Mechanisms as Means and Ends in Collaborative Management Research," in A.B. Shani, S.A. Mohrman, W.A. Pasmore, B.A. Stymne, and N. Adler (eds), *Handbook of Collaborative Management Research*, Thousand Oaks, CA: Sage, pp. 163–182.

Dougherty, D. and Hardy, C. (1996) "Sustained Product Innovation in Large, Mature Organizations: Overcoming innovation-to-organization problems," *Academy of Management Journal*, 39, 5, 1120–1153.

Fitzgibbon, M. (2000) "Of Shadow and Substance: The dilemma of measuring innovation," *Journal of the Irish Academy of Management*, 21, 2, 1–13.

Fricke, W. and Totterdill, P. (2004) *Action Research in Workplace Innovation and Regional Development*, Amsterdam: John Benjamins Publishing.

Gustavsen, B., Colbjønsen, T. and Pålhaugen, Ø. (1998) *Development Coalitions in Working Life: The "Enterprise Development 2000" program in Norway*, Amsterdam: John Benjamins Publishing.

Helfat, C.E. (ed.) (2003) *The SMS Blackwell Handbook of Organizational Capabilities: Emergence, development and change*, Malden, MA: Blackwell Publishing, Strategic Management Society Book Series.

Karlöf, B., Lundgren, K., and Edenfeldt Froment, M. (2000) *Bench Learning: Förebilder som hävstånd för utveckling* [Reference examples as levers for development], Stockholm: Ekerlids Förlag.

Käll, A. (2005) *Översättningar av en managementmodell* [Translating a management model. A study of the introduction of the Balanced Scorecard in a county health authority], Linköping: The Swedish Research School of Management and Information Technology, Linköping University, Studies in Science and Technology Thesis no. 1209.

Mohrman, S.A. and Shani, A.B. Rami (2008) "The Multiple Voices of Collaboration: A critical reflection," in A.B. Shani, S.A. Mohrman, W.A. Pasmore, B.A. Stymne, and N. Adler (eds) *Handbook of Collaborative Management Research*, Thousand Oaks, CA: Sage, pp. 531–538.

Nelson, E.C., Batalden, P.B., Huber, T.P., Mohr J.J., Godfrey, M.M., Headrick, M.A., Wasson, J.H. (2002) "Microsystems in Health Care: Part 1. Learning from high-performing front-line clinical units," *Journal on Quality Improvement*, 28, 9; 472–493.

Nonaka, I. and Reinmoeller, P. (2002) "Knowledge Creation and Utilization: Promoting dynamic systems of creative routines," in C.E. Lucier, M.A. Hitt, and M.R. Amit (eds), *Creating Value: Winners in the New Business Environment*, Oxford: Blackwell Publishers and the Strategic Management Society, pp. 104–128.

Pasmore, W.A., Woodman, R.W., and Simmons, A.L. (2008) "Towards a More Rigorous, Reflective and Relevant Science of Collaborative Management Research," in A.B. Shani,

S.A. Mohrman, W.A. Pasmore, B.A. Stymne, and N. Adler (eds), *Handbook of Collaborative Management Research*, Thousand Oaks, CA: Sage, pp. 567–582.

Pettigrew, A.M., Whittington, R., Melin, L., Sánchez-Runde, C., Bosch, F.A.J. van den, Ruigrok, W., and Numagami, T. (eds) (2003) *Innovative Forms of Organizing: International perspectives*, London: Sage.

Pettigrew, A.M., Woodman, R.W. and Cameron, K.S., (2001) "Studying organizational change and development: Challenges for future research," *Academy of Management Journal*, 44, 4, 697–713.

Reason, P. and Bradbury, H., (eds) (2001) *Handbook of Action Research*, London: Sage.

Richtnér, A. (2004) *Balancing Knowledge Creation: Organizational slack and knowledge creation in product development*, Stockholm: Stockholm School of Economics, published Econ.D. thesis.

Roy, S. (2003) "Navigating in the Knowledge Era: Metaphors and stories in the construction of Skandia's Navigator," Stockholm: Stockholm University Business School, Ph.D. thesis.

Senge, P., Laur, J., Schley, S. and Smith, B. (2006) *Learning for Sustainability*, Cambridge, MA: Society for Organizational Learning.

Shani, A.B. (Rami) and Docherty, P. (2008) "Learning by Design: Key mechanisms in organizational development," in T.G. Cummings (ed.), *Handbook of Organization Development*, Thousand Oaks, CA: Sage, pp. 499–518.

Shani, A.B. and Docherty, P. (2003) *Learning by Design: Building sustainable organizations*, Oxford: Blackwell Publishing.

Skoog, M. (2003) "Intangibles and the Transformation of Management Control Systems," Stockholm: Stockholm University Business School, Ph.D. thesis.

Teece, D.J., Pisano, G., and Shuen, A. (1997) "Dynamic Capabilities and Strategic Management," *Strategic Management Journal*, 18, 7, 509–533.

Tushman, M.L. and O'Reilly, C.A.I. (1996) "Ambidextrous Organizations: Managing evolutionary and revolutionary change," *California Management Review*, 38, 4, Summer, 8–30.

Walshok, M.L. and Stymne, B. (2008) "Collaboration in the Innovative Region," in A.B. Shani, S.A. Mohrman, W.A. Pasmore, B. Stymne, and N. Adler (eds), *Handbook of Collaborative Management Research*, Thousand Oaks, CA: Sage, pp. 293–214.

Index

CPSIA information can be obtained at www.ICGtesting.com
Printed in the USA
LVOW121016160312

273396LV00002B/3/P